NEO-KANTIANISM IN CONTEMPORARY PHILOSOPHY

NEO-KANTIANISM
in Contemporary Philosophy

edited by **RUDOLF A. MAKKREEL** *and* **SEBASTIAN LUFT**

INDIANA UNIVERSITY PRESS
Bloomington and Indianapolis

Publication of this book is made possible in part with the assistance of a Challenge Grant from the National Endowment for the Humanities, a federal agency that supports research, education, and public programming in the humanities.

Indiana University Press
601 North Morton Street
Bloomington, IN 47404-3797 USA

www.iupress.indiana.edu

Telephone orders	800-842-6796
Fax orders	812-855-7931
Orders by e-mail	iuporder@indiana.edu

© 2010 by Indiana University Press

(∞) The paper used in this publication meets the minimum requirements of the American National Standard for Information Sciences—Permanence of Paper for Printed Library Materials, ANSI Z39.48-1992.

Manufactured in the United States of America

LIBRARY OF CONGRESS CATALOGING-IN-PUBLICATION DATA

Neo-kantianism in contemporary philosophy / edited by Rudolf A. Makkreel and Sebastian Luft.
  p. cm. — (Studies in continental thought)
 Includes bibliographical references and index.
 ISBN 978-0-253-35389-4 (cloth : alk. paper) — ISBN 978-0-253-22144-5 (pbk. : alk. paper)
 1. Kant, Immanuel, 1724–1804. 2. Philosophy, Modern.
I. Makkreel, Rudolf A., date II. Luft, Sebastian.
 B2798.N45 2009
 193—dc22
                          2009020411

1 2 3 4 5 15 14 13 12 11 10

Contents

ACKNOWLEDGMENTS   vii

INTRODUCTION / *Rudolf A. Makkreel and Sebastian Luft*   1

PART 1. **Phenomenology, Hermeneutics, and Neo-Kantianism**

1. Neo-Kantianism and Phenomenology: The Problem of Intuition / *Helmut Holzhey*   25

2. The Hermeneutics of Perception in Cassirer, Heidegger, and Husserl / *Rudolf Bernet*   41

3. Reconstruction and Reduction: Natorp and Husserl on Method and the Question of Subjectivity / *Sebastian Luft*   59

4. The Neo-Kantian Heritage in Gadamer / *Jean Grondin*   92

PART 2. **The Nature of Transcendental Philosophy**

5. Interpreting Kant Correctly: On the Kant of the Neo-Kantians / *Manfred Kühn*   113

6. The Highest Principle and the Principle of Origin in Hermann Cohen's Theoretical Philosophy / *Jürgen Stolzenberg*   132

7. Transcendental Logic and Minimal Empiricism: Lask and McDowell on the Unboundedness of the Conceptual / *Steven G. Crowell*   150

PART 3. The Neo-Kantians and the Sciences

8. Ernst Cassirer and Thomas Kuhn: The Neo-Kantian Tradition in the History and Philosophy of Science / *Michael Friedman*   177

9. To Reach for Metaphysics: Émile Boutroux's Philosophy of Science / *Fabien Capeillères*   192

PART 4. History, Culture, and Value

10. Wilhelm Dilthey and the Neo-Kantians: On the Conceptual Distinctions between *Geisteswissenschaften* and *Kulturwissenschaften* / *Rudolf A. Makkreel*   253

11. The Multiplicity of Virtues and the Problem of Unity in Hermann Cohen's Ethics and Philosophy of Religion / *Reiner Wiehl*   272

12. Is Cassirer a Neo-Kantian Methodologically Speaking? / *Massimo Ferrari*   293

LIST OF CONTRIBUTORS   315

INDEX   319

Acknowledgments

The editors would like to thank the following persons for their invaluable help since this volume was conceived in 2004: Our sincere thanks to John Sallis as the series editor of Studies in Continental Thought, for agreeing to publish this volume in the series; to Dee Mortensen at Indiana University Press, for shepherding this volume through the editorial process from beginning to end; to Laura MacLeod, also at Indiana University Press, for her help with the details of the contract and other issues related to the production process; to Stephen H. Watson at the University of Notre Dame, for his circumspect and helpful report on the original manuscript proposal—we have sought to incorporate his recommendations wherever possible; to Benjamin Keough and Amanda Renee Baker, assistants to Rudolf Makkreel, and to David McPherson and Celeste Harvey, research assistants to Sebastian Luft, for their editorial work on the essays—especially those which were translated into English. We also thank the translators of the essays by Rudolf Bernet (Paul Crowe), Jürgen Stolzenberg (Colin J. Hahn), Reiner Wiehl (Michael J. Ystad), and Massimo Ferrari (Frances Bottenberg), for their work of rendering these texts into English. Finally, we thank David L. Dusenbury at the University of Wales, for his meticulous copyediting of the manuscript.

NEO-KANTIANISM IN CONTEMPORARY PHILOSOPHY

Introduction

Rudolf A. Makkreel and Sebastian Luft

Who Were the Neo-Kantians?

The present volume is the first of its kind to be published in English, and it is published in the hopes that it will secure Neo-Kantianism a significant place in contemporary philosophical discussions. Since Neo-Kantianism manifestly does not have such a place at present, it is perhaps best to open with the question: Who were the Neo-Kantians?

While one will often encounter the names of Neo-Kantians in accounts of the development of thinkers such as Edmund Husserl, Henri Bergson, and Martin Heidegger, few philosophers today have any real sense of who they were and what they stood for. And indeed, to characterize Neo-Kantianism across its different schools, movements, and sub-currents in continental Europe can be daunting. Yet it ought to be attempted. A simple description might read as follows:

> *Neo-Kantianism was the most dominant philosophical movement in Europe between approximately 1870 and 1920, and had the express intention of reawakening the spirit of Kant's philosophy after the so-called collapse of German Idealism following Hegel's death.*

While this description is correct as far as it goes, it certainly does not convey much; nor does it do justice to the profundity, diversity, and reach of this philosophical tendency. How then should we proceed toward a fuller definition?

Neo-Kantianism's connection to the name *Kant* itself, while certainly important, is potentially misleading. Indeed, the name "Neo-Kantianism" did not become standard until late in the nineteenth century; alternative names included "Neo-Fichteanism," "Neo-Criticism," or simply "Criticism." Hence, Kant was not always taken to be the focal point of the movement. But since Neo-Kantianism can be said to be importantly and indubitably connected to the philosophy of Kant, the next question to arise is: Which tenets, methods or concerns can count as truly Kantian? Each Neo-Kantian school claimed to deliver the *real* Kant—both as it *wanted* to understand him, and in the way it treated the "letter" of his writings (which Neo-Kantians helped to promote, together with Wilhelm Dilthey, by publishing critical editions of his works). So, it is impossible to give any single philosophical answer to the question of who the Neo-Kantians were, and what they stood for as philosophers.

But what if the question is asked on a more strictly historical basis? Even the question of who should be *considered* a Neo-Kantian receives different answers—and this situation is not new. Some philosophers such as the "realist" Alois Riehl insisted that they belonged to Neo-Kantianism, but this was contested by Neo-Kantians who were more sympathetic to Kant's idealism. Others saw their projects as "critical" in the Kantian sense, but nevertheless rejected the Neo-Kantian label. Such was the case with Dilthey, who spoke in 1867 of the need to return to Kant, but "not by silently passing over Hegel, Schelling, and Fichte."[1] As with any movement, then, questions of politics and personal alliance enter into the process of defining boundaries and identifying members; and this is perhaps especially acute with Neo-Kantianism, which happened to be incredibly successful in academia. So, it is also impossible to give any single historical answer to the question of who the Neo-Kantians were.

A relatively new approach to defining Neo-Kantianism rests upon sociological analyses of the societies and universities in which it flourished. This approach is represented by Klaus-Christian Köhnke's excellent work,[2] which situates the study of German Neo-Kantianism within a Kuhnian method of writing the history of science. (A similarly comprehensive work on French Neo-Kantianism is lacking.) In this light, Neo-Kantianism in Germany could be viewed as a typical phenomenon of the Bismarckian era or of the last manifestations of the German *Kaiserreich*. Indeed, at the end of the First World War, Neo-Kantianism itself seems to have come to an end in Germany: The end of a political era thus coincided with that of a philosophical era. As superficial as this approach might appear, it is not completely inappropriate. For instance, it has been claimed that the German defeat in 1918 also heralded the end of a type of society, with its particular values and sense of culture, which the Neo-Kantians tried to defend *philosophically* but which quickly became obsolete. (The fact that some Neo-Kantians, such as Paul Natorp, wrote "war literature" promoting the "genius of the German war" certainly did not help their reputation in the aftermath of the First

World War.) With necessary caution, then, such an approach may prove at least provisionally helpful for a rough definition and historical classification of Neo-Kantianism.

Yet another way of approaching the Neo-Kantians would simply be to call attention to their power-centers in Germany and France respectively, and to catalogue the prominent figures: The most concentrated school in Germany was the Marburg School, centered in the small university town of the same name. Its foremost representatives—not counting early and rather idiosyncratic proponents such as Otto Liebmann and Friedrich Albert Lange—were Hermann Cohen, Paul Natorp, and Ernst Cassirer. (Though Cassirer spent most of his academic life outside of Marburg, he is rightly regarded as a Marburg Neo-Kantian.) The other dominant school in Germany was split between Heidelberg and Freiburg universities, both of which were in the state of Baden in southern Germany. This was referred to as the Southwest or Baden School of Neo-Kantianism, or sometimes also as the "value-theoretical" (*werttheoretische*) school, due to its philosophical interest in the status of values. Its main representatives were Wilhelm Windelband, Heinrich Rickert, and Emil Lask. Other German-speaking Neo-Kantians could be mentioned here, though they did not represent a particular school and will not be considered in what follows—these include Alois Riehl, Richard Hönigswald, Eduard Zeller, Hans Vaihinger, and Bruno Bauch. In France the most important representatives, who generally lived in Paris, were Émile Boutroux and Léon Brunschvicg; their predecessors included Félix Ravaisson and Jules Lachelier.

This will have to suffice as a very brief, initial orientation to Neo-Kantianism, as well as an indication of some of the difficulties that are involved in discussing it. To turn to the present, then, we should also ask: And where is Neo-Kantianism now? Although they constituted a strong philosophical force in continental Europe from the last third of the nineteenth century through the first third of the twentieth century, the Neo-Kantians are largely neglected today. This book aims to show why such a development is lamentable. To this end the essays presented here, all of which are written by recognized and highly regarded scholars in Europe and North America, will reintroduce philosophers to this fascinating and provocative constellation of thinkers—and most importantly, to their thought.

It is our particular hope that these essays will stimulate interest in Neo-Kantianism in North America. Now that philosophers are moving beyond the decades-old distinction between "continental" and "analytic" philosophy, and are looking back on the history of twentieth-century philosophy; now that philosophers, at the outset of the twenty-first century, are increasingly committed to assessing the historical roots of their own terms, themes, and issues[3]: It is surely time for a renewed encounter with Neo-Kantianism, a movement which—through its own commitment to a progressive and creative reclaiming of its past—shaped twentieth-century philosophy and should continue to be felt in the twenty-first century. Signs of revitalization have been evident for some time now in continental Europe, and to a lesser degree in Britain—so renewed attention in North America will be timely.

Many aspects of Neo-Kantian thought promise to resonate in contemporary philosophical discussion,[4] and some of these will be indicated later in the introduction. We will turn now, however, to a brief review of Neo-Kantianism as it provided the basic context within which early twentieth-century philosophy developed.

Neo-Kantianism and the Transition into Twentieth-Century Thought

In a letter to the Marburg Neo-Kantian, Ernst Cassirer, Edmund Husserl writes:

> In my own development, originally hostile toward Kant, . . . I first started out from Descartes and from there moved to the pre-Kantian philosophy of the eighteenth century, certainly also influenced by important impulses from Brentano, Lotze, and Bolzano. However, when I, driven by the basic problems in theory of science most proximate to me as a mathematician to ever new problems in a necessary consequence, made a breakthrough to the method of eidetic analysis of consciousness . . . ; when, with the phenomenological reduction, the realm of the fundamental sources of all cognition opened up before me, at that point I had to acknowledge that this science developing before my eyes, although in an entirely different method, encompassed the total Kantian problematic (a problematic which only now received a deeper and clearer sense), and that it confirmed Kant's main results in rigorous scientific grounding. . . . Naturally, I could not become a Neo-Kantian according to the Marburg form and method; however, I could appreciate the great achievement of this school for the preservation and furthering of Kantian thoughts. After having learned to see Kant from my own perspective, I can now also—and especially in the most recent years—receive rich instructions from Kant and the true Kantians.[5]

This statement is paradigmatic for the relationship of Husserl and the phenomenological movement to Neo-Kantianism, but it is also indicative of the attitude of the entire philosophical scene in continental Europe, between roughly 1870 and 1930, toward the Neo-Kantians.[6] Indeed, the Neo-Kantian movement[7] provided the *backdrop* in these years for most philosophers as they attempted to delineate their own positions. This goes for all philosophical tendencies of the time—for phenomenologists (such as Scheler and Heidegger) no less than for the life-philosophers who preceded them (such as Dilthey and Bergson); for members of an emerging Vienna Circle (such as Schlick and Carnap)[8] as well as for members of an emerging Frankfurt School (such as Horkheimer and Adorno). The Neo-Kantians were also, and for this reason, the prime *target* in other philosophers' attempts to launch their own systems or styles of thought.

But it is doubtful that such advances simply *overcame* the Neo-Kantians, which alone would justify contemporary philosophers and historians of philosophy in viewing the Neo-Kantians as they are widely viewed at present— namely, as irrelevant or of secondary historical significance. For instance, in the standard account of post-Kantian philosophy—which is mirrored in university curricula in the United States and Britain—one usually looks at the German Idealists, then at non-academic (and quite alienated) philosophers of the nineteenth century, such as Schopenhauer, Kierkegaard, and Nietzsche. Then popular tendencies in the twentieth century are taken up: Generally this means phenomenology and later trends such as existentialism, hermeneutics, and deconstruction; or Wittgenstein's work and ensuing developments in Anglophone philosophy. The Neo-Kantians are altogether missing from such accounts of the transition from the nineteenth to the twentieth centuries. But the fact that they are forgotten in this way may result more from efforts to minimize their influence and importance, than from a true *Auseinandersetzung* with their intellectual achievements.[9]

For instance, one usually sees Heidegger's harsh criticisms of the Neo-Kantians—of Rickert, Windelband, Natorp, and Lask in his Marburg lecture-courses, and of Cassirer at Davos in 1929—as attempts to develop his own fundamental ontology. Apart from the fact that in such criticisms Heidegger is almost deliberately unfair in presenting Neo-Kantian philosophers, scholarship today rather ignores that his discussions of them were primarily attacks on then-prevalent theories in epistemology, value theory, logic, and theory of science to which Heidegger hoped to make original contributions—rather than entirely overcome them, as one tends to read him in the light of his later *Kehre*.

And earlier, when Dilthey formulated his ground-breaking ideas regarding the status of the human sciences (*Geisteswissenschaften*) beginning in 1875, he set the stage for the Neo-Kantian distinction between the natural and cultural sciences and their respective methods, which Southwest Neo-Kantians (particularly Windelband and Rickert) used as a starting point for their reflections on the methods of the sciences. (The views of Dilthey and the Neo-Kantians on these issues are commonly forgotten today, or are poorly described.) Similarly, Dilthey's focus on life and "lived experience" (*Erlebnis*) was itself a critique of transcendental (Kantian) conceptions of subjectivity, as is indicated by his famous statement that in the veins of Kant's cognizing subject there "flows no real blood"[10]—an assertion which anticipates Natorp's focus on concrete life in his late philosophical systematics.

Such dynamics are also at work in phenomenology. Husserl's transcendental turn in *Ideas I* (1913) was widely perceived as a growing sympathy for the Neo-Kantian transcendental method and its idealism. Any self-assertion on the side of phenomenology—a movement which was just beginning to emerge at the time—was mostly by way of critique of the established theories of the Neo-Kantians. Yet for Husserl (as the cited letter to Cassirer shows), an initial opposition to the Neo-Kantians was rendered null and void after his transcendental turn, his own "method" notwithstanding. Similarly, the Vienna Circle's commitment to the logical analysis of language was intended to correct a Neo-Kantian emphasis on epistemological questions concerning the status of the cognizing (transcendental) subject—but the founders of the Vienna Circle nevertheless drew heavily on Neo-Kantians, especially Lask and Cassirer. And finally, Neo-Kantian (particularly Marburg) political and social theories were closely studied in the Frankfurt School, especially in the years prior to 1933—the Frankfurt School's left-leaning tendencies emerged in direct opposition to what they perceived to be bourgeois positions proposed by Neo-Kantians.

In each of these instances, Neo-Kantians provided the implicit frame of reference for what was to come. Neo-Kantianism provided the main themes and issues that philosophers grappled with—and these are far from obsolete today. But one result of this Neo-Kantian dominance in all areas of philosophical inquiry, was that dissenters leveled scathing criticisms at the movement—and it is to these that we will now turn.

Why the Neo-Kantians Have Been Neglected

In general, the term "Neo-Kantianism" has tended to function as a polemical one: It subsumed a range of philosophers under the rubric of research devoted, in a broad way, to Kant's critical philosophy. Neo-Kantianism allegedly promoted a problematic interpretation of Kant, which could receive any number of loaded descriptions: Neo-Kantians were identified with "idealist" or "transcendental philosophy," and commonly criticized as "subjectivist" or "epistemological." But only very rarely did the name "Neo-Kantian" itself, or the sense of such descriptions and critiques, become sufficiently clear to be philosophical, rather than polemical. Furthermore, diversity within the movement was frequently unrecognized or denied. (As previously mentioned with regard to the interpretation of Kant, there was considerable disagreement between the Marburg and Southwest Neo-Kantians.) And indeed, the term "Neo-Kantian" could often simply be used to identify a position as "outdated." It is not difficult to see how such characterizations of "Neo-Kantianism" would fail to do justice to the Neo-Kantians, who were nevertheless respected as thinkers of the highest quality.

But the Neo-Kantians also received forceful and more rigorous critiques—precisely because their theories were considered to be threatening or appealing, but regardless based on ground-breaking research. Thus, around the turn of the twentieth century, Neo-Kantianism was widely regarded as one of the most imposing philosophical movements to have ever existed in Germany: All this raises the question, then, of *why* the Neo-Kantians have fallen into oblivion.

No historian of philosophy would dispute a considerable dominance of Neo-Kantianism over a number of decades; rather, it is as individual thinkers of real originality that the Neo-Kantians have been largely forgotten. This forgetfulness began to set in at the end of the First World War, as previously mentioned, and rapidly increased after the Second World War, in part due to entirely unphilosophical motives. These motives are in the first instance historically contingent, but they are by no means trivial or negligible. Indeed, they form part of the most terrible episode in the twentieth century: Some of the more prominent Neo-Kantians—including Cohen, Hönigswald, and Cassirer—were of Jewish descent and suffered from anti-Semitism even prior to 1933. Those who lived in Germany into the 1930s were not able to remain there safely after Hitler's rise to power, but it had been difficult for Jews to obtain academic posts in Germany even prior to Hitler.

The National Socialist treatment of Jews in academia and beyond is widely known, as they were systematically driven from all areas of cultural and social life in Germany.[11] But already during the cultural crisis that came in the wake of the First World War, Neo-Kantianism was coming to be perceived as an outmoded, academic philosophy of the *Kaiserreich*—and Neo-Kantianism was mainly an academic phenomenon. Help in such turbulent times seemed less and less likely to come from a university lecture hall. Moreover, the Neo-Kantian strongholds had been weakened or seemingly dissolved by the late 1920s, due simply to the passing away of its founders and a lack of "fresh blood." By the time Neo-Kantian protégés began to emigrate, their geographical distribution worked against collaboration and new locations often hindered the reception of their work. Cassirer enjoyed considerable success in the United States, but died there shortly before the Second World War ended. Unfortunately, he was mostly seen as a classical historian of ideas, rather than the creative philosopher of the *Philosophy of Symbolic Forms*, and the works he wrote in exile are introductory versions of his main works composed for a new audience, rather than original work.

In Germany—and Europe in general—the interwar years had also seen the rise of new, vocal critics of Neo-Kantianism within the universities. The prominence of phenomenology and a fashionable "existence-philosophy," as well as the personal appeal that Heidegger and Scheler (for instance) had for the new generation, meant that none of the leading Neo-Kantians at Marburg, Heidelberg or Freiburg had heirs with comparable success.[12] And indeed, the most promising philosophers who trained under Neo-Kantians were seen as forsaking their original orientation: This was the case with Heidegger, who had studied under Rickert; and this was also the case with Gadamer, who had studied under Hönigswald and Natorp.[13]

Philosophical motives, however, might also account for the neglect of the Neo-Kantians—motives which are immediately related to the cultural and intellectual crisis in Europe at the time: Issues that were seen as decisive for Neo-Kantian philosophy—questions of system-building and systematics, of ultimate foundations (the now-infamous problem of *Letztbegründung*),[14] and of value theory (whereby "objective values" could be determined)—had seemingly had their day and could, it was felt, be safely neglected. Phenomenology's call to the "things themselves,"[15] to "concrete" philosophical issues concerning the subject immersed in a "life-world," to freedom from the specialization of the sciences and the confinements of a philosophical system; all this seemed much more appealing than conceiving of philosophy as a transcendental "reconstruction" of reality, or as ancillary to the positive sciences, or as an aid to building a "worldview" (*Weltanschauung*).

Neo-Kantianism, for the most part, came to be seen as reducible to such concerns, while the problems which occupied phenomenologists—whether constitutive, existential or "ontological"—appeared to be more urgent and significant in the interwar years. There was a widely felt "crisis" of the sciences and of Western culture as such. It was thought that a remedy could only come from a wholly *new* style of philosophy. But attempts at such a philosophy could only proceed by *covering up*—and not eliminating—the Neo-Kantian elements in them. For instance, Husserl's late attempt to connect the "abstract" sciences to the "concrete" life-world was a Neo-Kantian trope that can be found much earlier in Cohen's work; and when he used the word "crisis" as *Leitbegriff* in his last work, Husserl was merely alluding to a catch-phrase Neo-Kantians had used during and after the First World War.

But in sum: The ascendancy of phenomenology, existentialism, and hermeneutics after the Second World War was certainly due in part to their connection with the *Zeitgeist*; and this involved at least their *claim* to renew philosophy by breaking with its dominant, nineteenth-century paradigms. And these paradigms were most forcefully represented by the Neo-Kantian movement. So it seemed as if philosophers were justified in passing over—and then forgetting—this movement which had reached its climax in the last years of the previous century, and then necessarily declined.

But there is now increasing discontent with the rhetoric of a radical break in twentieth-century philosophy, and there is also a growing recognition that the Neo-Kantians have been prematurely silenced. A philosophical discussion which conceivably could (and should) have continued uninterrupted through the twentieth century and into our own, was effectively broken off. It is certainly clear that decisive nineteenth and twentieth-century philosophers cannot be appropriated or even adequately interpreted without recourse to the contexts in which they developed their philosophies—and we have seen the significance of Neo-Kantianism in this regard. And it is no different with philosophical terminology, methodology, and concerns: Central topics which have been mentioned here—the appeal to the concept of "life," the return to the "things themselves," a phenomenologically motivated turn to the objects of the life-world instead of abstract reflections on subjectivity, questioning the concrete subject rather than conceiving subject*ivity* merely in terms of formal *a priori* structures—all of these can only be understood as variously but essentially related to Neo-Kantian positions and concerns.

A reassessment of the Neo-Kantians is necessary, then, in terms of the history of philosophy and the interpretation of philosophers who remain decisive for us. But it is also necessary in terms of furthering and evaluating contemporary philosophy. To give but one example: As is perhaps most apparent in the philosophy of mind (notably Strawson, Sellars, McDowell), some scholars assert that many of the points being raised in ongoing discussions parallel (or indeed revive) Neo-Kantian arguments and retrace developments in Neo-Kantianism. Surely then, a conscious and sustained engagement with Neo-Kantian sources could only sharpen such developments in contemporary philosophy.

It should be clear from the preceding paragraphs that any account of modern or contemporary philosophy which disregards Neo-Kantianism— that is, which *perpetuates* the generalized neglect of Neo-Kantianism—is decidedly lacking. Such an account will necessarily miss, not least importantly, the systematic contributions that Neo-Kantian thinkers made to modern Western philosophy. And it is these that we will now highlight.

The Systematic Import of Neo-Kantianism

Beyond the historical considerations in previous sections, we will here indicate how the Neo-Kantians have *systematically* contributed to a variety of issues that are of abiding value for philosophy. Because of this, Neo-Kantianism remains not only a viable but indeed an indispensable resource in ongoing discussions of genuine philosophical problems. What exactly are these contributions, and where could they be of particular relevance today? In what follows, we will enumerate but a few striking instances where the contributions of Neo-Kantian "criticism" could come to fruition in contemporary scholarship. All of these contributions are addressed in a more focused way in the essays in this volume.

Subjectivity

For two decades now there has been a revival of the topic of subjectivity, not only in continental attempts to resituate the question in Kant, early German Romanticism, and German Idealism (notably by Dieter Henrich and Manfred Frank), but also in analytic philosophy (by John Searle and Thomas Nagel, for instance). The main insight here is that one cannot disregard the original nature of subjectivity; here, strictly "objectivistic" or "naturalistic" accounts of the world are inadequate. This trend indicates a particularly significant self-criticism in analytic philosophy, which is beginning to realize that it has tended to accept reductionistic accounts of subjectivity. Such reflections on the singular nature of subjectivity and its structures, which make experience possible, used to be called "transcendental."

The question concerning the role and status of subjectivity was at the forefront for most Neo-Kantians. Indeed, under a new vocabulary—such as Nagel's insistence on the necessary question of what it is *like* to be a subject and to have subjective (mental) episodes—traditional Neo-Kantian questions and arguments can readily be connected up with contemporary efforts. For instance, Cohen's influential interpretation of Kant's theory of experience (in which he takes Kant's concept of experience as solely that of the philosopher of science), as well as Natorp's philosophical psychology (which was developed as a critical response to Cohen's Kant-interpretation), provide a sophisticated and paradigmatic example of the type of arguments that can be generated for and against such an account of subjectivity. Furthermore, the question of subjectivity also raises and forces us to address the threat of psychologism (with the skepticism and relativism that attend it), and it is this that constitutes a Neo-Kantian alliance with Husserl's work, especially in the *Logical Investigations.* Neo-Kantian and phenomenological standpoints are not incompatible in this regard, but are in many respects complementary. Lastly, Heidegger's framing of the human subject in terms of *Dasein's* finite being-in-the-world is a deliberate antithesis to Cassirer's emphasis on the infinity of the symbolic universe, of which the human subject can be part as participating in culture, whereby one can free oneself of the shackles of finitude.[16]

The Nature of Transcendental Philosophy and Philosophical Systematics

Deeply informed by and critical of the legacy of German Idealism, Neo-Kantian thought is at all times decidedly a reflection upon the role of philosophy within an overarching systematics or a "system" of culture. Their guiding assumption here is that philosophy must be framed in systematic terms which relate the transcendental problem and the concrete human subject. Neo-Kantian systematics therefore always includes some meta-philosophical reflection on the role of philosophers in the cultural life-worlds they inhabit. This is not to say that a clear consensus was ever reached—as is evident in Cassirer's reflections on the question of whether philosophy itself constitutes a "symbolic form." However, at the very least, Neo-Kantians commonly acknowledged such systematic questions as necessary ones, and their reflections on these issues are highly original. The evasion of systematic issues would, for them, amount to a refusal to question the philosopher's responsibility as a scientist, a citizen, and a participant in culture. In other words, systematics involves reflection on the relation of theory and praxis, which lends itself directly to ethical or political or even (as in Natorp) pedagogical considerations. Echoes of these reflections can be discerned in Husserl's efforts to build a "system of phenomenology," and his concurrent talk of philosophers as "functionaries of mankind,"[17] as well as in Heidegger's resolute dismissal of a theory-praxis dichotomy.

It is especially in this systematic respect that the Neo-Kantians, notably Cohen and Rickert, reached a level of reflection which compares to the best in German Idealism. And though system-building seems to have fallen into disrepute, especially when connected to the question of an absolute foundation, the Neo-Kantians display a most impressive manner of doing philosophy; a Nietzschean attitude that would simply dismiss systematics is not convincing here. The Neo-Kantian systems developed by Rickert, Cohen, Natorp, and Cassirer display a speculative power which remains in touch with the life-world and the sciences—and contemporary philosophy appears to be ready to consider again the sorts of questions that inspired their systematic reflections.

Theory and Philosophy of Science

Connected with the last point, and though the situation in the positive sciences was vastly different a century ago, one problem that motivated the whole Neo-Kantian enterprise was the need to bridge the ever-increasing gap between the positive sciences and philosophy, thereby battling a positivistic worldview in which philosophy would ultimately become obsolete. Undoubtedly, this is still a topic of concern for contemporary philosophy. Moreover, contemporary philosophy of science is built on the foundations laid in the late nineteenth and early twentieth centuries when the Neo-Kantians were, along with Dilthey, among the first to seize on these issues after the putative collapse of German Idealism. Indeed, hardly any philosophical school has paid so much attention to the positive sciences—their results, methods, and underlying presuppositions—and has attempted to present a philosophical counter-balance to them.

The Neo-Kantians regarded the results of the exact sciences not as threats, but as challenges that required intensive thought and scrutiny both from within the sciences' own "logics of scientific discovery," as well as from without, in philosophical reflection as to their meaning for society and culture. Such penetrating reflection, in conjunction with (and yet critical of) the positive sciences and their newest results, resulted in seminal works in the theory and philosophy of science, such as Cohen's *Principle of Infinitesimal Method,* and Cassirer's *Substance and Function, Einstein's Theory of Relativity,* and *Determinism and Indeterminism in Modern Physics.* Such Neo-Kantian works provided an important stimulus for other contemporaneous efforts—notably, Husserl's reconstruction of the "crisis" of modern science, starting with Galileo; Carnap's and Weyl's works on the philosophical foundations of physics; and later, if less directly, some of Kuhn's and Feyerabend's ideas. And surely the Neo-Kantian approach to the sciences—one of critical and historical, highly reflective and respectful engagement—is as admirable now as it was when they were writing.

Kant Scholarship and the Critical History of Ideas

Philological and exegetical efforts on the part of Neo-Kantians were among the first to lay the groundwork for solid philological Kant scholarship and most Kant-interpretations to come. But they furthermore, and systematically, identified the main lines of inquiry which could be pursued in the attempt to go beyond Kant while remaining true to the spirit of his critical philosophy. The Neo-Kantians are, therefore, responsible in significant ways for the state of Kant scholarship today—something which may sound strange even to some Kant scholars.

Given the erudition and systematic interest of most Neo-Kantians, their scholarship self-consciously went beyond the letter of Kant's texts. But more broadly, it was one of their paramount intentions to read the history of philosophy in a similar way—one which combined historical and systematic analysis. Neo-Kantian history of philosophy was carried out in the definite conviction that this type of research was neither limited to nor immersed in the past: It was, rather, a way into understanding the present. The history of philosophy did, of course, determine how one should understand the past—and this precluded a Hegelian sense of "sublating" all prior philosophical attempts according to some naïve teleology. Rather, their historical research was carried out in order to understand the present situation of the sciences—and ultimately also of culture and society—by reconstructing the genesis of modern issues and problems: For the Neo-Kantians, then, it is the present as a *problem* that should initiate historical research, and not at all the present as a synthesis or resolution of the past. Their *history of philosophy* was therefore impossible without a *philosophy of history*.

It is for this reason that magisterial Neo-Kantian interpretations of philosophical figures and epochs—Windelband's history of philosophy, Natorp's influential and controversial Plato-interpretation, Cassirer's works on Renaissance philosophy and the "problem of knowledge" in modernity—constitute real *philosophical* achievements, and are improperly regarded as mere historical compendia. And this is also why Neo-Kantian historical interpretations provoked no less significant philosophical counter-interpretations: In this category belong Heidegger's *Kantbuch*, Mahnke's phenomenological interpretation of Leibniz, and Husserl's original appropriation of Descartes in the *Cartesian Meditations*.[18] Gadamer's critical concept of *Begriffsgeschichte* (history of concepts) is also indebted to Neo-Kantian history of philosophy, since it is pitted against their concept of *Problemgeschichte* (history of problems). And even now, any problem-oriented history of philosophy owes its theoretical foundations to Neo-Kantian philosophical historiography.

Philosophy of Culture, Value, and Ethics

One of the lasting Neo-Kantian contributions to modern philosophy is the idea of a philosophy of culture. Although it culminated in Cassirer's *Philosophy of Symbolic Forms*, this idea was already evident in Cohen's works on ethics and religion and in Natorp's socio-political philosophy. The idea of culture was also prominent in the works of the Southwest School, especially in Windelband and Rickert, who developed Kant's moral philosophy into a doctrine of values. This is where important connections to the work of Hermann Lotze and Wilhelm Dilthey can be made. All these attempts were intended as systematic contributions to cultural and moral philosophy, and have had effects not only within philosophy but also for cultural anthropology, for ethical reflections in phenomenology (with Husserl and especially Scheler), and for scientific disciplines such as linguistics, modern philology, history, ethnology, etc.

Given the systematic ideals of Neo-Kantianism, transcendental philosophy as a philosophy of culture sought to elaborate a philosophical system that would clarify and uphold cultural and moral achievements no less than scientific ones. Neo-Kantianism's work in cultural domains forcefully refutes the idea that it subjugated philosophy to science, demoting it the status of a "handmaiden of the sciences": To the contrary, Natorp could write that "philosophy is nothing but the consciousness of the centrally founded unity—of the unsevered, never to be severed unity—of cultural life."[19] One can mock the totalizing, architectonic attempts this inspired, but the ideal of unity acts as a powerful stimulus to thought, even if it remains unattainable. Similar attempts have been undertaken again in the latter half of the twentieth century, for instance, in Niklas Luhmann's system theory and Jürgen Habermas' discourse ethics.

It is our hope that the preceding sections have served to situate Neo-Kantianism systematically as well as historically. We have highlighted its influence on and intersections with other philosophical tendencies in the nineteenth and twentieth centuries—and this should suffice to correct the impression that life-philosophy, phenomenology, logical positivism, the Frankfurt School or hermeneutics could have emerged without reference to Neo-Kantian ideas. The near-total *neglect* that Neo-Kantianism has suffered, then, by no means reflects a clear *overcoming* of their influence in the twentieth century.

The essays in this volume will further demonstrate the historical significance of Neo-Kantianism. They will also address systematic issues and topics that deserve to be reconsidered—topics which were much-discussed by Neo-Kantians and representatives of the other movements we have named, and which can make substantial contributions to problems still being discussed in contemporary philosophy.

Organization of the Essays

The essays in this volume are arranged into four parts: The first relates Neo-Kantianism to its context, the second examines how it redefines the meaning of transcendental philosophy, and the third and fourth consider its relation to the natural and human sciences respectively.

Phenomenology, Hermeneutics, and Neo-Kantianism

The essays in part 1 are placed at the outset because phenomenology and hermeneutics are arguably the most influential movements in the first half of the twentieth century to have developed in close proximity to Neo-Kantianism. We have already indicated Husserl's relation to the Neo-Kantians. While hermeneutics has its own lineage stemming from Schleiermacher and Dilthey to Heidegger and Gadamer, it eventually intersects with Kantian reflections on symbolism and meaning, as brought to fruition in Cassirer. Phenomenology and hermeneutics (together with *Lebensphilosophie*) were the first to deal critically with Neo-Kantianism, thereby establishing *themselves* as movements. The chapters compiled here will offer comparisons between Neo-Kantianism and these schools of philosophy which developed under its influence and by way of critique of its theories.

Helmut Holzhey's piece, "Neo-Kantianism and Phenomenology: The Problem of Intuition," offers an excellent introductory comparison of phenomenology and Neo-Kantianism, especially with regard to questions relating to the nature and primacy of intuition. Holzhey, an eminent Neo-Kantian scholar, demonstrates how essential aspects of the "transcendental method" developed in the Marburg School, particularly by Natorp, as well as Husserl's and Heidegger's conceptions of phenomenology and its method, were clarified by way of intricate reflections on the notion of intuition.

Rudolf Bernet's piece, "The Hermeneutics of Perception in Cassirer, Heidegger, and Husserl," compares another crucial problem—namely perception—in phenomenological and Neo-Kantian accounts. Specifically, Bernet identifies and develops a "hermeneutic mode of perception" in Cassirer, and proceeds to relate this to Husserlian phenomenology and Heideggerian "hermeneutics of facticity." The essay concludes with a critical account of the Davos debates in 1929, and a reflection on the very possibility of a "hermeneutic philosophy."

Sebastian Luft's essay, "Reconstruction and Reduction: Natorp and Husserl on Method and the Question of Subjectivity," focuses specifically on Husserl's and Natorp's methods and their ensuing theories of subjectivity. This essay follows Holzhey's examination of these philosophers, especially in regard to Natorp's influence on Husserl, which was greater than is usually acknowledged. Indeed, Natorp anticipates problems and issues which Husserl's approach later addressed, and for which Husserl arguably offered more convincing arguments, but which would not have been possible without Natorp.

Jean Grondin's contribution on "The Neo-Kantian Heritage in Gadamer," highlights a Neo-Kantian influence which is generally overlooked, but which Gadamer hinted at in his autobiographical writings. Grondin opens questions which Gadamer himself may have sought to avoid: While paying personal tribute to his Neo-Kantian teachers, Gadamer is generally (and markedly) silent with regard to their philosophical influence on his hermeneutics. This influence is especially notable in Gadamer's understanding of the history of philosophy as a "history of concepts" (*Begriffsgeschichte*), though he aims for this to supplant the "history of problems" (*Problemgeschichte*) of Neo-Kantianism. Grondin's account is supported by highly interesting excerpts from the (as yet) unpublished correspondence between Gadamer and Heidegger.

The Nature of Transcendental Philosophy

Part 2 moves into a systematic discussion of what transcendental philosophy aims to accomplish, by taking up several Neo-Kantian theoretical concepts. This was one of the domains in which the Neo-Kantians made their most impressive systematic contributions. Certain of their theoretical accomplishments here pertain both to Neo-Kantian advances over Kant, as well as to their concomitant interpretations of Kant—interpretations which shaped Kant into the figure he has become for twentieth-century philosophy.

Manfred Kühn's provocative essay, "Interpreting Kant Correctly: On the Kant of the Neo-Kantians," is belied by the simplicity of its title. Opening sections review Neo-Kantian interpretations of Kant by linking them up with their interpretations of Plato: A "transcendentalized Platonism" was, Kühn argues, at the heart of the Marburg and Southwest Schools' interpretations of Kant. In later sections Kühn relates this Platonism to Hermann Lotze and a crisis of "value" in the wake of Nietzsche, before taking up Heidegger's critique of the Marburg Kant-interpretation. The essay closes with a discussion of the possibilities and dangers involved in "reconstructing" Plato or Kant in the manner that Neo-Kantians self-consciously attempted.

Jürgen Stolzenberg's "The Highest Principle and the Principle of Origin in Hermann Cohen's Theoretical Philosophy" addresses the status of fundamental concepts in Cohen's works on *Kant's Theory of Experience* and the *Logic of Pure Cognition*. Both of these texts carried forward Cohen's appropriation of Kant in striking ways and forcefully shaped the Marburg School. Cohen's concept of "ground-laying" (*Grundlegung*) is of decisive importance for his theoretical philosophy, and by clarifying its relation to the "highest principle" of his transcendental method, Stolzenberg hopes to resolve a debate in contemporary Cohen-research. He also sheds light on the core concern of Neo-Kantian systematics—namely, with the form or "moment" of lawfulness as the "origin" of philosophy.

In his insightful piece, "Transcendental Logic and Minimal Empiricism: Lask and McDowell on the Unboundedness of the Conceptual," Steven G. Crowell compares Emil Lask's influential Kant-interpretation with that of John McDowell, a significant voice in recent Anglo-American philosophy. After laying out parallels between transcendental logic in Lask and McDowell, Crowell progressively demonstrates how the latter's conception of the "unboundedness of the conceptual" falls short of Lask's idea of the "limitlessness of truth." McDowell's desire for a minimal empiricism cannot be realized, Crowell suggests, so long as he lacks a concept of what Lask calls "immediate living in truth." It is the latter concept—in which Crowell remarks a definite anticipation of Heidegger—that relates perceptual experience to judgment in such a way that Lask can develop a truly *transcendental* logic. Whereas Stolzenberg's piece focuses on a seminal Marburg School reading of transcendental philosophy, Crowell's essay accomplishes the same for the Southwest School of Neo-Kantianism.

The Neo-Kantians and the Sciences

As has been mentioned, one of the most important Neo-Kantian contributions around the turn of the twentieth century pertained to the natural sciences and to interpreting their significance for philosophy. The Neo-Kantians arguably drafted the first serious philosophy of science in the sense that we know it today. Accordingly, the essays in part 3 assess these contributions and highlight an area of research in which Neo-Kantianism is receiving new levels of attention.

In his essay, "Ernst Cassirer and Thomas Kuhn: The Neo-Kantian Tradition in the History and Philosophy of Science," Michael Friedman reviews Neo-Kantian contributions to the philosophy of science as they related to the revolutionary results of scientific research in the late nineteenth and early twentieth centuries. Intimately connected to these contributions, were Neo-Kantian works in the history of science: Kuhn himself acknowledged that the "ultimate sources" of his historiography lay in Neo-Kantian philosophy. While mainly dealing with Cassirer's works, Friedman's essay explores Marburg Neo-Kantianism in terms of its vital (but contentious) interpretation of Kant, but no less as an ongoing (and thus historicized) Kantian project. As such, Friedman is concerned throughout with the relevance of a Marburg-style "genetic conception of knowledge" to contemporary, post-Kuhnian difficulties in the history and philosophy of science.

Fabien Capeillères' piece, "To Reach for Metaphysics: Émile Boutroux's Philosophy of Science," is a methodical account of French Neo-Kantianism that focuses on the pivotal figure Émile Boutroux. In opening sections, Capeillères closely observes the dispute between "spiritualist" philosophers and their positivistic critics in France, from the 1840s to the 1870s. These sections provide the necessary context for understanding the "philosophy of nature" that Boutroux drafted while studying under the early Neo-Kantian, Jules Lachelier. In later sections, Capeillères explicates Boutroux's "metaphysics of science" as it was formulated in his dissertation of 1874 and refined over the following decades. Socio-historical and interpretive throughout, the "constellation-analysis" carried out in this essay clearly demonstrates Boutroux's significance in a philosophical trajectory that relates him to Maine de Biran and Félix Ravaisson no less than to Bergson and Poincaré. Since this is the only essay in the volume that is devoted to French Neo-Kantianism—a movement which was informed by its German counterpart, but also distinct from it in interesting ways—the editors deemed it appropriate to include a text of this magnitude.

Part 4 concentrates on systematic Neo-Kantian contributions to philosophy beyond the natural sciences, thereby indicating the full scope of the movement. While the essays in part 3 foreground Neo-Kantians' work in the philosophy of science, these essays correct the misperception that their concern was exclusively with the "developing fact" of mathematical-natural science. Massimo Ferrari cites a representative comment by Natorp, to the effect that transcendental philosophy must commence with and extend to "facts of science, of custom, of art, of religion"—that is, to "the entire creative work of culture."

Rudolf A. Makkreel's essay addresses the dispute between Wilhelm Dilthey and the Neo-Kantians with respect to the distinction between *Geisteswissenschaften* (human sciences) and *Kulturwissenschaften* (cultural sciences). One of the main issues that set Dilthey in opposition to Baden Neo-Kantians was the status of psychology: Dilthey attempted to re-conceive psychology as a descriptive human science intent on *understanding* the meaning-structures of lived experience, while the Neo-Kantians wanted to maintain it as a law-based natural science. Windelband proposed a nomothetic-idiographic distinction to replace Dilthey's explanation-understanding distinction; Dilthey responded by showing that the human sciences are not simply idiographic. Rickert accepted this critique, in part, and insisted that historical particulars must be understood in relation to complexes of absolute values. In the second half of the essay, Makkreel transitions from the Dilthey-Baden School controversy to concentrate on hermeneutics as it figures in Dilthey and the Marburg Neo-Kantian, Cassirer.

In the following essay, "The Multiplicity of Virtues and the Problem of Unity in Hermann Cohen's Ethics and Philosophy of Religion," Reiner Wiehl addresses a domain not mentioned heretofore in the volume—namely, ethics and its relation to religion. This relation was of special concern for Cohen in his final years. As Wiehl's valuable essay shows, the questions which arise here—and which are intimately related to Cohen's theoretical philosophy—were decisive for Cohen's attempts at unifying his systematic philosophy. Wiehl shows how Cohen's ethical intentions are already present in his early works, but only come to full fruition in his last unifying vision, which Cohen interprets as a worldview that withstands philosophical scrutiny precisely due to its differences from Christianity. In the latter part of the essay, Wiehl lays out Cohen's system of ethical and religious virtues which places the individual human in relation to the idea of God. This nexus of relations becomes manifest in Cohen's philosophical system, the *Ethics of Pure Willing,* and then in his last work, *Religion of Reason from the Sources of Judaism,* which was posthumously edited by his pupils Martin Buber and Franz

Rosenzweig. Cohen's philosophy of religion has been influential for other philosophers in the Jewish tradition, such as Rosenzweig and Emmanuel Levinas, and remains of interest, given a renewed prominence of Jewish philosophy of religion in recent years.

Massimo Ferrari, a Cassirer specialist, devotes the last essay in the volume to the question, "Is Cassirer a Neo-Kantian Methodologically Speaking?" Ferrari gives a detailed overview over Cassirer's mature philosophy as a philosophy of culture, thereby addressing the important question of whether Cassirer's late "anthropological turn" entails a departure from his "Marburg roots," while at the same time highlighting Cassirer's importance for contemporary philosophy of culture and its view of the human subject. The reason this article is placed at the end of the collection is because Cassirer is arguably the most influential and widely read Neo-Kantian today, whose philosophy of science and of culture offers various possibilities to be connected to contemporary thought. Cassirer, however, is often interpreted as having moved out of the Neo-Kantian camp. Showing convincingly that this is not the case, Ferrari's essay offers a signal, concluding argument for the continued relevance of Neo-Kantianism for philosophy today.

NOTES

1. Wilhelm Dilthey, *Gesammelte Schriften*, 26 vols. (Göttingen: Vandenhoeck & Ruprecht, 1914–2006), vol. 5, 13.

2. Cf. note 6, below.

3. Attempts in this direction are already being undertaken in other areas, especially in analytic philosophy—for instance, Dummett and Brandom have explored Frege's role in the genesis of Anglo-American thought. In phenomenology, increased attention is being paid to Brentano and his school for the development of phenomenology—especially the early "realist" phenomenology—as well as to previously less recognized figures such as Bergson. While such scholarship gives us important pointers for reassessing twentieth-century philosophy, it has almost entirely bracketed the Neo-Kantian import.

4. For instance, the Kant scholar Manfred Baum points out that the discussion of Kant in the Anglo-Saxon literature concerning "transcendental arguments" (following Strawson's interpretation) "is but a repetition (*Neuauflage*) of the 'transcendental method' of Neo-Kantianism." Cf. Manfred Baum, *Deduktion und Beweis in Kants Transzendentalphilosophie* (Königsstein: Hein, 1986), 17–18.

5. Letter of 3 April 1925, *Husserliana-Dokumente* III: *Briefweschel*, vol. V (The Hague: Kluwer, 1950ff.), 4.

6. As mentioned, though the term "Neo-Kantianism" has prevailed in most historical accounts, there were other, competing titles such as "Neo-Fichteanism," "Neo-Criticism," or simply "Criticism," especially outside of Germany. For a number of reasons, one could argue that "Criticism" is a much better term to describe

this movement, but for the sake of identification the common term "Neo-Kantianism" shall be used throughout.

7. For a historical account of the Neo-Kantian movement, cf. Helmut Holzhey's article "Neukantianismus" in the *Historisches Wörterbuch der Philosophie* (Darmstadt: Wissenschaftliche Buchgesellschaft, 1984), vol. 6, 747–754; as well as the extensive historical narrative in Klaus-Christian Köhnke, *The Rise of Neo-Kantianism: German Academic Philosophy Between Idealism and Positivism*, trans. R. J. Hollingdale (Cambridge: Cambridge University Press, 1991). Köhnke's book, a translation from the German, is the only account of the history of Neo-Kantianism in Germany which is available in English; its account ends, however, roughly in 1900. Since the present volume aims not at a *history* of Neo-Kantianism—in itself a clear desideratum in English-language scholarship—but instead at a presentation of its *philosophical* import for twentieth-century and contemporary philosophy, we shall confine ourselves at present to merely pointing out such historical accounts.

8. This connection has recently been reconstructed by Michael Friedman in *A Parting of the Ways: Carnap, Cassirer, and Heidegger* (Chicago and La Salle: Open Court, 2000), which focuses mainly on the 1929 dispute at Davos between Heidegger and Cassirer, an occasion which Carnap attended.

9. See, for instance, Richard Rorty's mischaracterization of Neo-Kantianism in his influential work, *Philosophy and the Mirror of Nature* (Princeton: Princeton University Press, 1980), esp. 133–136.

10. Wilhelm Dilthey, *Introduction to the Human Sciences*, in *Selected Works*, ed. Rudolf A. Makkreel and Frithjof Rodi (Princeton: Princeton University Press, 1989), vol. 1, 50; cf. vol. 1, 500–501.

11. One prominent young member of the Southwest School of Neo-Kantianism, the "Aryan" Bruno Bauch, was responsible for anti-Semitic attacks on Cassirer already in the 1920s. Bauch turned to Nazism and became a highly regarded member of the academic establishment under Hitler, thereby renouncing ties with his academic teachers and their liberal ideas. Cf. Ulrich Sieg, "Deutsche Kulturgeschichte und Jüdischer Geist," *Leo Beck Institut Bulletin* 88 (1991): 59–71; also Ulrich Sieg, *Aufstieg und Niedergang des Marburger Neukantianismus* (Würzburg: Königshausen & Neumann, 1994), 399–402.

12. They had no comparable success as lecturers—but this is not to imply that Neo-Kantians had no salient successes in Germany in these years. For instance, Cassirer was the first Jewish scholar to assume the rectorship of a German university. He held this position in Hamburg from 1929 to 1931.

13. It should be noted that a small number of philosophers, for instance Wolfgang Cramer and Hans Wagner, considered themselves to be heirs to Neo-Kantianism after the Second World War; they were sometimes referred to as "Neo-Neo-Kantians." These philosophers attained neither the academic success nor the philosophical stature of eminent Neo-Kantians in the nineteenth century. As Köhnke shows in his *Rise of Neo-Kantianism* (cf. note 7, above), some of the movement's earlier success derived from Neo-Kantians being highly positioned in the university system; surely some of the hostility displayed by their critics was due to this as well.

14. This critique of modern philosophy as "obsessed" with the project of epistemic

"foundationalism" is repeated almost verbatim in Richard Rorty's *Philosophy and the Mirror of Nature* (cf. note 9, above). In Rorty's sweeping account, modern philosophy is chastised for its obsession with epistemology—and the wrongheaded, epistemological project he excoriates culminates, on his account, with the Neo-Kantians.

15. It is interesting to note that the phenomenological call "to the things themselves" was a clarion call of the early, "realist" phenomenologists in favor of a turn to the *object* and *not,* as one usually assumes, as a turn to the world-constituting subject. In other words, it was meant as a turn *away* from the immanence of the subject to the "objective" constitution of the world. Only later, and mainly through Heidegger's interpretation of this motto in § 7 of *Being and Time,* did it take on the negative sense of moving away from speculation and toward a description which is unencumbered by theory. Cf. chapter 1 in the present volume, where Helmut Holzhey expounds this issue in some detail.

16. See the Davos debate between Heidegger and Cassirer in Martin Heidegger, *Kant and the Problem of Metaphysics,* 5th ed., trans. Richard Taft (Bloomington: Indiana University Press, 1997), 193–207, here 202, 205–206.

17. For Husserl's efforts concerning a "system of phenomenology," cf. *Husserliana* XXXV (the lecture-course of 1922–1923, "Einleitung in die Philosophie"), and his drafts for such a system from the 1930s in *Husserliana* XV, xxvi–xl. Regarding Husserl's famous phrase identifying philosophers as "functionaries of mankind," see his *Crisis of European Sciences and Transcendental Phenomenology* (*Husserliana* VI, 15). (*Husserliana* will be cited hereafter as "Hua.")

18. Husserl's "flirting" with the Neo-Kantians in the 1920s deserves a renewed look, especially after the recent publication of Husserl's 1922 London lectures. Attention should also be given to his 1922–1923 lecture-course, "Einleitung in die Philosophie" (Hua. XXXV), and the 1927 lecture, "Natur und Geist" (Hua. XXXII); his long-known lecture-course, "First Philosophy," of 1923–1924 (published in 1954 as Hua. VII and VIII) will have to be reconsidered in this regard.

19. Paul Natorp, "Bruno Bauchs 'Immanuel Kant' und die Fortbildung des Systems des Kritischen Idealismus," *Kant Studien* 22 (1918): 426–459, here 426.

PART 1

Phenomenology, Hermeneutics, and Neo-Kantianism

Neo-Kantianism and Phenomenology: The Problem of Intuition

Helmut Holzhey

If one attempts to explicate the proximity and distance between Neo-Kantianism and phenomenology with respect to the concept and function of intuition in both philosophical schools, then it makes sense to take their respective relation to Kant's doctrine of intuition as a point of departure. In broad strokes, one might characterize the two schools as having destroyed the equilibrium between intuition and thinking that Kant had asserted. In phenomenology, this occurs through the strong emphasis on intuition; the opposite is the case in Neo-Kantianism, which attempts to dissolve the moment of intuition in cognition into a moment of determinateness of thought. Yet immediately one has to be more precise. Kant's famous passage reads as follows: "Thoughts without content are empty, intuitions without concepts are blind. It is thus just as necessary to make the mind's concepts sensible (i.e., to add an object to them in intuition) as it is to make its intuitions understandable (i.e., to bring them under concepts)" (KrV A 51/B 75).

What characterizes an intuition vis-à-vis a concept? An intuition refers to objects *immediately;* it is an *individual,* not a general representation; this is due to the fact that objects are *given* to us in sensible intuition. This epistemological recognition that the intuitive and the conceptual moments of objective cognition are equally important has to be distinguished from the rejection of intuition as a philosophical method. Intuition receives a positive interpretation in Kant, where it is, as a moment of cognition, an explicit *theme* of philosophical cognition. But intuition is rejected as the *method* of philosophical cognition: "*Philosophical* cognition is *rational cognition from concepts*" (KrV A 713/B 741), and not cognition from intuition. From a methodological standpoint, however, intuition is relevant for *mathematics,* which is a "*concern of reason* through construction of the concepts" (KrV A 724/B 752): "For the construction of a concept . . . a *non-empirical* intuition is required, which consequently, as intuition, is an *individual* object, but which must nevertheless, as the construction of a concept (of a general representation), express in the representation universal validity for all possible intuitions that belong under the same concept" (KrV A 713/B 741). With reference to these Kantian passages, one can already give a more precise specification when confronting these two post-Kantian schools: Whereas in Neo-Kantianism, as far as I can tell, intuition is always and only thematized as a moment of the *cognition of objects,* phenomenology, especially Husserl's, operates methodologically—in a manner yet to be clarified—with "intuition." Here, phenomenology is especially interested in solving the problem that Kant described for mathematics—i.e., how an individual intuition can claim general validity for philosophical cognition (key terms: categorial intuition, *Wesensschau*).

Intuition as the Path to the "Things Themselves"

I shall begin with a presentation and discussion of the phenomenological path to the "things themselves." What, in general, was it that led Husserl to his "principle of all principles," according to which "*every originarily giving intuition is a legitimizing source of cognition,* that *everything originarily* (so to speak in its 'personal' actuality) *offered* to us in *'intuition' is to be accepted simply as what it is presented as being,* but also *only within the limits in which it is presented here*" (Husserl 1976, 51)? In the introduction to the second volume of the *Logical Investigations* (1901) he phrased his program with the well-known motto: "we must go back to the 'things themselves'" (Husserl 2001, 168/1992, 10). It is clear from the context that this proposition emphasizes a central methodological moment of epistemological-critical work in pure logic. What is at stake is the meaning of logical concepts: Critical of a "mere symbolic understanding of words," which is characteristic of *reflection,* Husserl demands *intuitions* in which "what the word-meanings . . . truly stand for" (Husserl 2001, 168/1992, 10) become evident. Hence, the motto "to the things themselves" was intended to tear phenomenological researchers away from sheer quibbling about words and merely conceptual thoughts; indeed, it proposed to distance phenomenologists from all theoretical constructions. In intuition, Husserl asserted, "the originally *empty* meaning-intention is now fulfilled" (Husserl 2001, 192/1992, 44), that is, the *meant* is brought to *givenness.* That intuition which "fulfills" a meaning-intention (significative intention) leads directly, or more directly, to the thing itself and thereby to "cognition." The increase in intuitive fulfillment implies increased cognition, and the goal of absolute cognition is reached with the "*adequate self-presentation of the object of cognition*" (Husserl 2001, 192/1992, 597–598; cf. Tugendhat 1967, 54–55): "But to judge rationally or scientifically about things signifies to conform *to the things themselves* or to go from words and opinions back to the things themselves, to consult them in their self-givenness and to set aside all prejudices alien to them" (Husserl 1983, 35/1976, 41). Here not only constructs stemming from the (natural) sciences are submitted to critique; so also are philosophical-theoretical constructs—namely, the psychologistic grounding of logic, the representational theory of cognition, naturalistic explanations of emotive life, etc. In Husserl's own words: "*The impulse to research must proceed not from philosophies but from things and from the problems connected to them,*" if philosophy is to be established as the "science of true beginnings, or origins, of *rhizómata pantôn* . . . a science concerned with what is radical" (Husserl 1981, 196/1987, 61).[1] On the way to these roots one has to be radical, that is, one has to break through to the "lowest field of work of absolutely clearly given things." I emphasize: The "things" qua origins themselves provide a field of work; thus, they do not consist of simple ideas, impressions or data, and neither of axioms or of one or several basic principles, as Husserl later clarifies in the *Cartesian Meditations*; and, they must be given absolutely clearly. Thus the contours of an alternative to an empiricistic or positivistic approach come into relief in Husserl's explicit rejection of the identification of the phenomenological "things" with empirical "matters of fact," since one would become "blind with respect to ideas, which are indeed absolutely given in such great degree to immediate intuition" (Husserl 1981, 196/1987, 61). These things become accessible through intuition, more precisely, through originarily giving intuition, which is to guarantee that philosophy can attain the status of a philosophy beginning with ultimate clarity. Husserl mobilizes intuition in order to cash in his commitment to a philosophy that "goes back to ultimate origins."

The younger phenomenologists who collaborated with Husserl were in agreement with him in the demand for radical presuppositionlessness, in the wish to distance themselves from the eternal battle of philosophical positions, and in the rejection of philosophizing for the purpose of a worldview. Yet they came to disagree deeply in their interpretation of the "things themselves" to which one was committed. Under the broad title of "phenomena," in the Göttingen Circle the "things" quickly became objects whose essence had to be investigated. In view of this "essential phenomenology"— which Husserl disapprovingly called "picture book phenomenology"—the analysis of subjective modes of givenness receded into the background (cf. Spiegelberg 1971/I, 170). Already in the *Logical Investigations* Husserl had completely rejected such a turn to the object. If it was his intention here to fight the empirical-psychological grounding of logical objects, he carried out this critique precisely by going back to intentional consciousness. Instead of arguing for a phenomenological realism, it was his intention to go back to a realm before these relations, to a context in which the opposition between subject and object could arise in the first place (cf. Gadamer 1972, 162). In a later clarification he emphasized the necessary two-sidedness in the philosophical investigation of logic and rebuffed the allegation that in the "subjectively directed consideration of logical objects" he had fallen back into psychologism (Husserl 1974, 159ff.). "'The things themselves' . . . only appear originarily in the subjective processes or achievements of intuitive self-givenness" (Held 2003, 13). Husserl's approach to a transcendental philosophy of subjectivity gave the circle of his earlier pupils, who had grown increasingly estranged from him, even more incentive to embrace the objectivistic interpretation of the motto "to the things themselves!" in the sense of a "theory-free intuition of essences of reality in all of its dimensions," which oftentimes resulted in phenomenology's being discredited as practicing an "amethodological intuitionism" (Landgrebe 1949, 74).

The Phenomenological Method

There was already a tension in *Husserl's* understanding of phenomenology as philosophical foundational science vis-à-vis the views of his contemporaries, for whom "phenomenology is at best a title for specializations, for quite useful detail work in the sphere of introspection" (Husserl 1981, 197/1987, 37). (This minimalist estimation has to this day hardly changed outside the circle of philosophical experts.) For Moritz Lazarus, for instance, phenomenology was a subdiscipline of psychology; namely, as descriptive psychology, an "explicating description of appearances in psychic life in contradistinction to a dissecting explanation" (Lazarus 1878, 346). Husserl adopted the term "phenomenology" from psychology and with it a psychologically developed methodology in order to ground, with his novel interpretation of this discipline, a specifically *philosophical* fundamental science; a science that was to be critical of psychology and yet to be developed from it. According to his program, this science should, on the one hand, *ground* empirical psychology and should hence be conceived as an *a priori* science. On the other hand, it should be the basis of a critique of cognition, albeit "in an entirely different manner" than empirical psychology. What is to be attained in a phenomenology of cognition is an "insight into the essence of the modes of cognition which come into play in their utterance and in the ideal possibility of applying such propositions, together with all such conferments of sense and objective validities as are essentially constituted therein" (Husserl 2001, 165/1992, 6). This goal of *essential insight* separates descriptive phenomenology of inner experience from empirical psychology. The desired essential insight is not only insight with respect to modes of cognition in their act character, but with respect to "conferments of sense and objective validities essentially constituted therein." One has to distinguish between the act (*noesis*) and that which is meant therein (*noema*) (cf. Husserl 1983, 210ff./1976, 200ff.), between sense and validity. But they have to be related back to each other correlatively while at the same time being distinguished from one another. The critique of psychologism immediately opens up an encompassing new task of research—an investigation of the *a priori* correlations between subjective experiencing and the ideal matters of fact.

The intention of positing phenomenology as the basis for a critique of cognition is also the driving motive for the further development of the concept of "phenomenology." The following definition from *Ideas I* sketches the region as well as the specific method of phenomenology: "[P]henomenology is . . . a *purely descriptive* discipline, exploring the field of transcendentally pure consciousness by *pure intuition*" (Husserl 1983, 136/1976, 127). In delineating this region it is clear that, according to Husserl, phenomenology is a philosophy of consciousness. "Consciousness" is thereby not conceived as the psychic state of being conscious (in contradistinction to being unconscious or pre-conscious or the like), but instead the intentional "experience" (*Erlebnis*) (of perceiving, of willing, of judging, and so on) or the sum total of such "experiences." Consciousness is always consciousness of something (cf. Husserl 1983, 67ff./1976, 70ff.). Phenomenology is the science of intentional consciousness—the science of the pure essence of intentional consciousness, and especially the science of transcendental consciousness in which "transcendent" being manifests itself (Husserl 1983, 170, cf. 209/1976, 159, cf. 198). In studying this transcendental consciousness, phenomenology investigates the "primal source" (*Urquelle*) from which the problem of the "objectively valid cognition of transcendent being" (Husserl 1983, 239/1976, 228) can be solved.

While phenomenologists are able to access essences through the so-called "eidetic reduction," with the "transcendental-phenomenological reduction" they transfer reality, which exists as a matter of course in our "natural attitude," into pure givennesses for consciousness, i.e., into "phenomena" (cf. Husserl 1983, 51ff./1976, 56ff.). Methodologically they proceed, as Husserl says, "purely descriptively," and in so doing make use of "pure intuition." While in contemporary, everyday speech a proposition can be said to be "intuitive" when it rests on an idea or insight and is not yet secured (theoretically or empirically), for Husserl, "intuition" (*Intuition*) has a strictly methodological character and is used interchangeably with the German *Anschauung*. For phenomenologically speaking, this approach is not put to use for the re-presentation (*Vergegenwärtigung*) of something real or factual that transcends consciousness; rather, it is intended to give conscious experiences the kind of embodiment that can exhibit their essence. For the former—bringing the experiences to givenness—the "phenomenological attitude" is required; while the latter—the intuition of their essence—comes about with the transformation of an individual intuition of an object into essential intuition (ideation) (cf. Husserl 1983, 8/1976, 13). In this sense, phenomenology is "a *descriptive* essential doctrine of transcendentally pure mental processes as viewed in the phenomenological attitude" (Husserl 1983, 167/1976, 156).

As has been pointed out repeatedly in scholarly literature, Husserl's concept of intuition with the immediacy attributed to it does *not* stand in opposition to thinking, or more precisely, to the synthetic achievements of thinking, as is familiar from Aristotle and Kant; rather it stands in opposition to "mere opining, which is far removed from the things" (Tugendhat 1967, 50). Elisabeth Ströker specifies, with regard to the frequent contamination of "intuition" and "perception," "that even the objects of intuition, if we mean by them objects of sensual perception, require for their complete cognition an intuitive fulfillment as well" (Ströker 1992, 42). The intuition understood as the element of the phenomenological method (precisely as "intuitive fulfillment"), means with respect to the sensual perception of an object that "the implications contained in this perception, which refer to other aspects of the object," can be fulfilled (Ströker 1992, 42). Phenomenological intuition is, hence, neither sensual nor intellectual intuition; instead it is to be understood, according to Ströker, in Husserl's entire oeuvre "never otherwise than from the *function* of intuition for *cognition,* namely, in its function of fulfilling empty intentions" (Ströker 1992, 43). To avoid any misunderstanding of this passage from Ströker, I should like to emphasize that she refers to the function of intuition with respect to *phenomenological-philosophical* cognition and that the terminology of intention and fulfillment, derived from the *Logical Investigations,* must be understood in a very broad sense. The "principle of all principles" is phrased in a universal manner: Every theory is to derive its truth from originary-intuitive givennesses and "every statement which does no more than confer expression on such data by simple explication and by means of significations precisely conforming to them is . . . an *absolute beginning*" (Husserl 1983, 44/1976, 51). Husserl goes so far as to even include mediate authentication in phenomenology, conceived as a "phenomenology of reason." Accordingly, everything meant and uttered in rational speech must be capable of being led back to "originary evidence" or, in the classical case of deduction, to "mediate evidence" (cf. Husserl 1983, 339/1976, 329).

Heidegger's Critical Reinterpretation of the Phenomenological Method

In 1927 Heidegger places his work for the last time, at least according to the letter, under the phenomenological maxim "to the things themselves"

(Heidegger 1996, 24/1993, 27–28). To him, the "phenomenological treatment" consists in "direct indication (*Aufweisung*) and direct demonstration (*Ausweisung*)" (Heidegger 1996, 30/1993, 35). *In nuce,* this characterization of phenomenology already contains a fundamental critique of the manner in which Husserl employs intuition methodologically. To *indicate* something means to let something become visible, which at first was not (in this way) visible or graspable. Something becomes demonstrated *directly* when it comes to appearance *from itself* and not merely *as itself.* This indicates a first difference from Husserl. A second difference becomes apparent in Heidegger's reflection on the *logos* of phenomenology. While Husserl relies on the originarily giving intuition and considers the problem of its linguistic articulation secondary, Heidegger is from the very start attentive to the problem of the linguistic mediation of the "phenomena" and seeks to solve this problem by determining the *logos* itself as a "making manifest in the sense of letting something be seen by indicating it (*im Sinne des aufweisenden Sehenlassens*)" (Heidegger 1996, 29/1993, 32).

In this passage the differences from Husserl remain hidden, since Heidegger's more precise definition of phenomenological indicating, too, has primarily a prohibitive character. In general, in the phenomenological school one is interested in those things that are traditionally not approached in a direct indication—the meaning of expressions, the essence of truth, the relation between logical laws, aesthetic judgments, and so on. But what is indicated here? Both Husserl's as well as Heidegger's phenomenology were put to the test where signs of a discrepancy between the scientific conception of a phenomenon and its factual "experiencing" became apparent, for example in the medical treatment of psychosomatic ailments or in symbolic interpretation of dreams in psychoanalysis. This discrepancy is obviously significant for the phenomena of human life. In natural science, subjective experiencing or understanding is suspended in the interest of an exact fixation of facts and their causal explanation. The phenomenological approach precisely intends to "save" this subjective experiencing by replacing theoretical construction, which blocks the view to the "things themselves," with direct indication. In each case phenomenology had to go back behind these constructs—behind psychological constructs to save psychic phenomena, behind epistemological constructs to save the phenomena of cognition, and behind natural-scientific constructs to save the objects and forms of quotidian life.

Upon closer inspection, these are relative postulates. The demand for a direct indication in an absolute sense, as Husserl intended, already collapses in view of the linguistic character of indication. As the phenomenologist attempts to indicate, for instance, the perspectival nature of perception, this indication, too, is already placed within a horizon of meaning. To the phenomenological method belongs not only a "reduction"—and already the reduction is oriented, in Husserl, to the problem of the rational cognition of reality—but also a "construction," that is, a projection of meaning only in the horizon of which something can be indicated (cf. Heidegger 1988, 18, 20ff./1989, 24, 28ff.; cf. also Heidegger 1996, 141, 213, 298/1989, 151, 231, 324). Heidegger already presented this critique in his early lectures. Under the title *Phenomenology of Intuition and Expression* (*Phänomenologie der Anschauung und des Ausdrucks*), in the summer of 1920 he very deliberately developed, as the subtitle says, a "theory of philosophical concept formation," which attempts to develop from the "phenomenological basic attitude (*Grundhaltung*)" a conception of phenomenological philosophy more radical than Husserl had achieved with his rather traditional orientation to classical philosophical systematics. In his lecture-course *Basic Problems of Phenomenology* (*Grundprobleme der Phänomenologie*), in the winter semester of 1919/1920, Heidegger applies this critique directly to *intuition:* "It is a merit of contemporary phenomenology to emphasize the principal meaning of *intuition,* the originary return to the phenomena themselves. Nevertheless, this concept of *intuition,* though grasped genuinely on the way back to its origin, is not originary enough. There is the danger of equivocating phenomenological 'intuition' with the intuition of objects." That this is the case becomes clear in Husserl's constant "exemplification by way of sensual perception." There is the threat of equivocating phenomenological intuition with the grasping of "relations of order" (*Ordnungsbeziehungen*) (Heidegger 1992, 237).[2] But *life*—here Heidegger still uses Dilthey's term—is no object; instead life exists "always concretely in situations": "Lived experiences are no things, they are nothing individuated, but expressive formations of tendencies stemming from concrete life situations." Phenomenology, as "science of experiences," unfolds on the basis of "originarily giving intuition of the nexus of experiences," which explicates itself in "pure *understanding*" (Heidegger 1992, 233). Understanding, not intuition, forms the "first step of phenomenological research" (Heidegger 1992, 233).[3] If, however, "all sight (*Sicht*) is primarily based on understanding," as Heidegger concludes in *Being and Time* of 1927, then "we have taken away from pure intuition the ontological priority of objective presence. . . . Even the phenomenological 'intuition of essences' (*Wesensschau*) is based on existential understanding" (Heidegger 1996, 138/1989, 147).

The Critique of Intuition in Marburg Neo-Kantianism

Concerning the distinction between philosophy and psychology and between the transcendental standpoint and psychologism, Paul Natorp—in his lecture of 1912, "Kant and the Marburg School" (*Kant und die Marburger*

Schule)—retrospectively asserts that, "for us not all that much remained to be learned from Husserl's splendid expositions (in the first volume of the *Logical Investigations*), which we could only welcome gladly" (Natorp 1912a, 198). Neo-Kantians and phenomenologists were in agreement in their fundamental principle, namely, in rejecting a psychological grounding of philosophical thought. In their concrete work concerning the "things," however, differences also clearly came to the fore. In his 1901 review of the above-mentioned first volume of the *Logical Investigations*, Natorp already worries whether Husserl would truly be able to overcome psychologism if he admitted, besides an investigation into the logical conditions of a theory, also an investigation of its "noetic" conditions; whether Husserl, in other words, converted an object theory completely into a logic. "I believe," Natorp writes, "that a purely theoretical logic has absolutely nothing to say about the psychological experience of evidence. Such a logic only claims that relations of correspondence obtain within thought contents, conditioned by these or other determined basic relations of content" (Natorp 1973a, 5). Of course, Natorp admitted, an *insight* into these "atemporally" obtaining relations was necessary. But none of the temporal characteristics of the experience of this insight enter into its content. The debate between Natorp and Husserl, hence, concerns the "dispute over the demarcation (*Grenzstreit*) between logic and psychology" (Natorp 1973a, 7–8). This becomes even more plain in a comment in Natorp's *Allgemeine Psychologie nach kritischer Methode* (*General Psychology According to Critical Method*) of 1912. Here, Natorp expresses his surprise over the fact that what followed in the second volume of the *Logical Investigations* "as a continuation of logical investigations—instead of a mere objective grounding, as initially demanded and promised in the first volume—was a 'phenomenological' grounding of cognition which, at least according to our terminology, would have to be called psychological, not logical" (Natorp 1912b, 280). Now nothing could be further from Natorp's intentions than "to exclude psychology as such from philosophy, to confine it exclusively to empirical research"; it was only that drafting a philosophical psychology should not be the first, ground-laying but instead the last, ultimate task of a philosophical systematics (Natorp 1912b, 198).

Already early on Natorp recognized the necessity of adding a subjective grounding of cognition to its objective counterpart (Natorp 1981/1887), the topic of which he conceived as a "critical psychology" divorced from epistemology. Thus, he distanced himself from Husserl in two respects. For one, he deemed Husserl's distinction between description and theory inappropriate; both are "objectifications," whereby the problem arises as to how subjectivity could be described without objectifying it. Moreover, Natorp criticized Husserl's notion of eidetic intuition by claiming that the immediately intuited essences are abstractions "and thereby *objectifications* on a different level," and that the subjectivity Husserl aimed at could become accessible, instead of in description, only in a "reconstruction" in infinite approximation; namely, in a *procedural* "creative intuiting" (*Erschauen*) or "creative thinking" (*Erdenken*), which fulfills the meaning of the concept of origin (Natorp 1912b, 280–290).[4]

As is known, the centerpiece of the *objective* grounding of cognition, as Hermann Cohen and Paul Natorp developed it in the last quarter of the nineteenth century in Marburg, is the *transcendental method*. It is closely related to the definition of epistemology (*Erkenntnistheorie*), also understood as logic of cognition (*Erkenntnislogik*), which was conceived as a foundational philosophical discipline with respect to an investigation of the conditions of the validity of *scientific* cognition. (This is so, even if the transcendental method would later be revised and reformulated in view of the philosophical system, especially concerning the transcendental-philosophical grounding of ethics.) Philosophical investigation proceeds, accordingly, in two steps. In a *first* step it presupposes the factual validity of scientific cognition. This presupposition implies that the philosophical analysis of cognition is not grounded on sense data or "sensations" as the allegedly "pure" given. The type of cognition taken as a point of departure is not of interest insofar as it is a psychical or social event, but only as a proposition with the claim to truth. Philosophical investigation begins with the logical reality of scientific cognition. And, in a *second* step, the investigation attempts to prove and logically justify the conditions of the validity of this presupposed scientific cognition. For Cohen, the potential of the transcendental method is put to the test first and foremost in the question concerning the conditions of cognition's *relation to reality*. Cohen grounds the relation to reality exclusively on a categorial determination—more precisely, on the "thought-medium" of "reality" (*realitas, Sachheit*)—and he rejects any reliance on something given to intuition. In this sense, he is interested in establishing an *idealistic* "doctrinal constitution" (*Lehrverfassung*) of philosophy (Cohen 2005b, 594) on the basis of a pure *logic* of cognition. He thereby reaffirms his commitment to the "spirit of genuine philosophy, which for all times presents the worldview (*Weltanschauung*) of Idealism" (Cohen 2005b, xii).

In his book *Das Prinzip der Infinitesimal-Methode und seine Geschichte* (*The Principle of the Infinitesimal Method and its History*) of 1883 (cf. Cohen 2005c), Cohen still claims that "one may well be permitted to consider the distinction between intuition and thinking as antiquated" if one can disregard the fact that intuition—as the "relation of consciousness to something given"—brings this something, i.e., the reality-moment of cognition, to cognition more solidly than does a categorial thought determination (Cohen 2005c, § 25).[5] In his later work, the relation to something *given* increasingly becomes the stumbling block for an idealistic epistemology. Cohen's primary critique, thus, is directed toward Kant's notion of sensation and his idea of something "given to intuition." Yet by eliminating sensation as the empirical moment of intuition, it seems that, in a second critical step, Kant's *pure* intuition also becomes superfluous and, consequently, the entire distinction between intuition and thinking is rendered incomprehensible. Cohen criticizes Kant for clinging to the dualism of intuition and thought, (1) by confirming the prejudice that something must be given to thought in order for it to become cognition, (2) by only defining his thoughts about synthesis fragmentarily, and (3) by not doing justice to the radical "originariness" (*Ursprünglichkeit*) of thinking (Cohen 2005b, 27–28). If one reflects on the "logic" of Cohen's "doctrine of the generation of content through thinking," it seems, on the one hand, consistent that both the thematized cognition as well as the transcendental method, which is the guiding clue for this thematization, are conceived without any relation to intuition. On the other hand, it is obvious that in so doing, Cohen cannot evade the "shadow" of a sensible-material moment (Cohen 2005c/II, 66). As Richard Kroner has shown, the expression "pure cognition" already proves that in Cohen's ("our")[6] thought the antithesis between "transcendental rationalism" and "transcendental empiricism" remains irreconcilably virulent (Kroner 1924/25, 95).[7]

Further Developments

Paul Natorp was the only philosopher of the Marburg School who engaged in a more detailed discussion of the phenomenological concept of intuition. His critique of the alleged immediacy and absoluteness of "originarily giving intuition" displays certain similarities to Heidegger's substitution of understanding for intuition; and in both cases, I believe the critique is justified. Husserl himself had to realize that he could not attain his ultimate philosophical goals, his "dream" of grounding a rigorous scientific philosophy in the immediacy of intuition.

One can observe a renewed interest in "intuition" in the younger members of the Marburg School, who swore off any commitments to this school after 1912 (the year of Cohen's departure from Marburg) in following their own paths. It was Nicolai Hartmann who attempted, as late as 1912, to combine, from a Neo-Kantian perspective, the transcendental with the phenomenological methods in a systematic methodological edifice. According to Hartmann, what the transcendental investigation lays out for itself beforehand with the "problematically" given scientific cognition of experience, must be, previous to that, "described" in its own character. However, his allegation that the *factum* of the sciences presupposes the merely naïve cognition of objects, a cognition which might be guided by principles but is not aware of these principles, cannot secure the status of an independent method of description in the sense of phenomenological description. Heinz Heimsoeth saw this when, in his correspondence with Hartmann, he pointed out a problem that seems to arise in the descriptive clarification of pure givenness:

> It seems to me that the task of the descriptive method would be, rather, to *reverse,* to renounce all attempts at concept formation, at grasping of principles . . . by simply *indicating* what everyone can see, what is there, what is given. (In this way, I think, the phenomenologists want to construe their science.) I agree with you that the object, as it is given, implies its categories; but I do not agree that a method which posits this object purely as givenness before our eyes, which *demonstrates* (aufweisen) it in its peculiarity and determinacy, ought to be interested in pursuing these categorial grounds in the object in any way (*auch nur im Ansatze*). (Heimsoeth 1978, 137; letter of 21 November 1912)

These reflections, which criticize the idea that the object could be interesting for a philosophical analysis only as determined by thought or by principles, have their historical basis in Heimsoeth's encounter with the phenomenologists Alexander Pfänder and Moritz Geiger, whose lectures he attended at the University of Munich. In the same letter, he gives an account of these lectures: "Compared to the intuitive and primitive nature of the things that are given there, I feel terribly *empty* with my constructive brain which is always only interested in 'standpoints' and is empty of all concrete insights" (Heimsoeth 1978, 135).

It is likely that this feeling was widespread and contributed to a displacement of Neo-Kantianism in favor of a—more or less methodologically conscious—philosophy operating on phenomenological grounds. Even Cassirer is likely to have been influenced by this contemporary mood, in his advancement of Marburg "Leibnizianism." Regardless of how one wants to interpret Cassirer's relation to Kant and Neo-Kantianism, it is clear that he makes use of (as Ernst Wolfgang Orth has termed it) "operative conceptual allusions" to Kantian intuition—as in the expressions "intuitive concept" and "myth of forms of intuition"—without thematizing them. In so doing, he "recalls the seemingly known, only to open up entirely new dimensions of understanding" (Orth 1988, 51). For instance, in the third volume of the *Philosophy of Symbolic Forms*, Cassirer takes up without further elucidation the Kantian distinction between intuition and concept, only to attribute discursivity to intuition in the sense that "it never stops at the particular but strives toward a totality it never achieves in any other way than by running through a manifold of elements and finally gathering them into *one* regard" (Cassirer 1963, 288/1964, 338). Even if the concept already functions this way in intuition, all conceptual relations "are realized over and over again in separate concrete structures (*Gebilden*)," which "condense into *forms* (Gestalten) of intuitive reality" (Cassirer 1963, 319/1964, 338). Last but not least, this holds for aesthetic intuition, which is characterized just as a concept is—that is, as the "basic form of differentiation and unification, but which is not carried out in the medium of thought but in pure *Gestalt*" (Cassirer 1985, 100–101). What is crucial here is the distance from Cohen's critique of the Romantic ideal of art, which Cohen sees resurrected in Benedetto Croce's aesthetics. While Croce identifies "the intuitive or expressive cognition with the aesthetical or artistic appearances" and declares them to be independent of intellectual (logical) cognition (Croce 1905, 1, esp. 12), Cohen again insists that in grounding art in intuition, the meaning which "concepts of scientific cognition" have for art is neglected (Cohen 2005a, 30 ff.). In post-Neo-Kantian times, however, intuition once again regains a genuinely philosophical relevance in the philosophy of *art*.

TRANSLATED BY SEBASTIAN LUFT

NOTES

In the case where English translations of original German texts are available, these are given first below, followed by the original source. The pagination of original German editions is also given in the above citations: Hence, where two years of publication are listed in this essay, the available translation is being cited and referenced first, while the German pagination follows. Where only one year is listed, the citation has been newly translated for this essay.

1. From Husserl's more precise definition of these roots (*rhizómata*), the difference between this form of phenomenological radicality and that of Gilles Deleuze and Félix Guattari in their concept of the "rhizoma" comes clearly to the fore.

2. Pieper also criticizes the development of the methodological basic principle of "originarily giving intuition" as orientated to the experience of perceptual objects (Pieper 1993, 135ff.); yet he does not do so with the intention of furthering the problem in a phenomenological context, but in the course of a complete destruction of the Husserlian program.

3. Heidegger also comments that Husserl's "tendency to aim at . . . complete clarity, that is, at so-called 'phenomenological evidence' . . . is dangerous" (Heidegger 1992, 238).

4. Cf. also Natorp's review of Husserl's *Ideas I* (Natorp 1973b, 36–60): "Also the '*intuitus*,' the insight or internal seeing, can only be understood to mean the intuiting/looking into (*das Hineinsehen . . . in*) of something discretely posited through deliberate delimitation into (*in*) the original continuity, from which and in which it only arises for this positing thinking . . .'"

5. As Natorp declares in a letter of 1915, this conception comes closest to his own, yet he attempted "to grasp it more precisely and to answer it" (quoted in Holzhey 1986, 443).

6. It is conspicuous that in Cohen's *Logik der reinen Erkenntnis* (*Logic of Pure Cognition*), the beginning is made with an unreflected "we": "*We begin with thinking*" (Cohen 2005b, 13). If, contrary to this, Heidegger's Kant-interpretation gives primacy to intuition ("Knowing is primarily intuiting. . . . Thinking . . . , according to its inherent structure, serves that to which intuition is primarily and constantly directed" [Heidegger 1997, 15–16/1973, 21]), then this occurs from the very start in the light of an existential self-interpretation of the philosophizing subject (Cohen's "we") as finite: "That a finite, thinking creature can 'also' think is an essential consequence of the finitude of its own intuiting" (Heidegger 1997, 17/1973, 24). The thesis of the primacy of intuition in human cognition is an expression of the insight into the finitude of the human being.

7. I can only hint at Rickert's attempt to construe all thinking as "heterothetical," that is, as a co-thinking (*Zusammendenken*) of a logical and an a-logical (intuitive) moment.

BIBLIOGRAPHY

Cassirer, Ernst. 1963/1954. *The Philosophy of Symbolic Forms,* vol. 3: *The Phenomenology of Knowledge.* Trans. Ralph Manheim. New Haven and London: Yale University Press. / *Philosophie der Symbolischen Formen. Dritter Teil: Phänomenologie der Erkenntnis.* Oxford: Bruno Cassirer.

———. 1985. "Mythischer, Ästhetischer und Theoretischer Raum." In: Ernst Wolfgang Orth and John M. Krois, eds. *Symbol, Technik, Sprache. Aufsätze aus den Jahren 1927–1933.* Hamburg: Meiner.

Cohen, Hermann. 2005a. *System der Philosophie,* vol. 3: *Ästhetik des Reinen Gefuehls = Werke,* vol. 8. Hildesheim: Olms.

———. 2005b. *System der Philosophie,* vol. 1: *Logik der Reinen Erkenntnis = Werke,* vol. 6. Hildesheim: Olms.

———. 2005c. *Das Prinzip der Infinitesimal-Methode und seine Geschichte = Werke,* vols. 5/I and 5/II. Hildesheim: Olms.

Croce, Bendetto. 1905. *Aesthetik als Wissenschaft des Ausdrucks und Allgemeine Linguistik. Theorie und Geschichte.* Trans. Karl Federn. Leipzig: no publisher.

Gadamer, Hans-Georg. 1972. "Die Phänomenologische Bewegung." In: *Kleine Schriften (III): Idee und Sprache.* Tübingen: Mohr/Siebeck.

Heidegger, Martin. 1988/1989. *The Basic Problems of Phenomenology.* Trans. Albert Hofstadter. Bloomington: Indiana University Press. / *Die Grundprobleme der Phänomenologie,* 2d ed. = *Gesamtausgabe,* vol. 24. Ed. Friedrich-Wilhelm von Hermann. Frankfurt: Klostermann.

———. 1992. *Grundprobleme der Phänomenologie = Gesamtausgabe,* vol. 58. Ed. Hans-Helmuth Gander. Frankfurt: Klostermann.

———. 1993. *Phänomenologie der Anschauung und des Ausdrucks. Theorie der philosophischen Begriffsbildung = Gesamtausgabe,* vol. 59. Ed. Claudius Strube. Frankfurt: Klostermann.

———. 1996/1993. *Being and Time.* Trans. Joan Stambaugh. Albany: SUNY Press. / *Sein und Zeit,* 17th ed. Tübingen: Niemeyer.

————. 1997/1973. *Kant and the Problem of Metaphysics*. Trans. Richard Taft. Blooming-ton: Indiana University Press. / *Kant und das Problem der Metaphysik*, 4th exp. ed. Frankfurt: Klostermann.

Heimsoeth, Heinz. 1978. *Nicolai Hartmann und Heinz Heimsoeth im Briefwechsel*. Ed. Frida Hartmann and Renate Heimsoeth. Bonn: Bouvier.

Held, Klaus. 2003. "Husserl's Phenomenological Method." Trans. Lanei Rodemeyer. In: Donn Welton, ed. *The New Husserl: A Critical Reader*. Bloomington: Indiana University Press.

Holzhey, Helmut. 1986. *Cohen und Natorp*, vol. 2: *Der Marburger Neukantianismus in Quellen. Zeugnisse kritischer Lektüre. Briefe der Marburger. Dokumente zur Philoso-phiepolitik der Schule*. Basel and Stuttgart: Schwabe.

Husserl, Edmund. 1974. *Formale und Transzendentale Logik* = *Husserliana*, vol. XVII. Ed. Paul Janssen. The Hague: Nijhoff.

————. 1981/1987. "Philosophy as Rigorous Science." Trans. Quentin Lauer. In: Peter McCormick and Frederick A. Elliston, eds. *Husserl: Shorter Works*. Notre Dame: Notre Dame University Press. / "Philosophie als Strenge Wissenschaft." In: Thomas Nenon and Hans Rainer Sepp, eds. *Aufsätze und Vorträge (1911–1921)* = *Husserliana*, vol. XXV. Dordrecht, Boston, and Lancaster: Nijhoff.

————. 1983/1976. *Ideas Pertaining to a Pure Phenomenology and to a Phenomenologi-cal Philosophy. Book I. General Introduction to a Pure Phenomenology*. Trans. Fred Kersten. Dordrecht, Boston, and London: Kluwer. / *Ideen zu einer Reinen Phäno-menologie und Phänomenologischen Philosophie. Allgemeine Einführung in die Reine Phänomenologie* = *Husserliana*, vol. III/1. Ed. Karl Schuhmann. Dordrecht, Boston, and London: Kluwer.

————. 2001/1992. *Logical Investigations*. Trans. J. N. Findlay. London and New York: Routledge. / *Logische Untersuchungen* = *Husserliana*, vols. XVIII, XIX/1, and XIX/2. Ed. Ursula Panzer. Dordrecht, Boston, and London: Kluwer.

Kant, Immanuel. 1998/1976. *Critique of Pure Reason*. Trans. Paul Guyer and Allen W. Wood. Cambridge: Cambridge University Press. / *Kritik der Reinen Vernunft*. Ed. Raymund Schmidt. Hamburg: Meiner. (Quoted here as "KrV"; the letters "A" and "B" before pagi-nation indicate the first edition of 1781 and the second edition of 1787, respectively.)

Kroner, Richard. 1924/25. "Anschauen und Denken. Kritische Bemerkungen zu Rickerts Heterothetischem Denkprinzip." *Logos* 13.

Landgrebe, Ludwig. 1949. *Phänomenologie und Metaphysik*. Hamburg: Schröder.

Lazarus, Moritz. 1878. *Das Leben der Seele in Monographien über seine Erscheinungen und Gesetze*, 2d ed. Berlin, vol. 2.

Natorp, Paul. 1912a. "Kant und die Marburger Schule." *Kant Studien* 17 (1912).

————. 1912b. *Allgemeine Psychologie nach Kritischer Methode, Erstes Buch. Objekt und Methode der Psychologie*. Tübingen: Mohr/Siebeck. (Note: No other volumes of this work ever appeared.)

————. 1973a. "Zur Frage der Logischen Methode" (1901). Reprinted in: Hermann Noack, ed. *Husserl. Wege der Forschung*. Darmstadt: Wissenschaftliche Buchgesellschaft.

————. 1973b. "Besprechung von Husserls *Ideen zu einer Reinen Phänomenologie*" (1917/18). Reprinted in: Hermann Noack, ed. *Husserl. Wege der Forschung*. Darm-stadt: Wissenschaftliche Buchgesellschaft.

————. 1981/1887. "On the Objective and Subjective Grounding of Knowledge." Trans. L. Phillips and D. Kolb. In: *Journal of the British Society for Phenomenology* 12(3). / "Ueber Objective und Subjective Begründung der Erkenntniss." In: *Philosophische Monatshefte* 23.

Orth, Ernst Wolfgang. 1988. "Operative Begriffe in Ernst Cassirers Philosophie der Symbolischen Formen." In: H.-J. Braun, H. Holzhey, and E. W. Orth, eds. *Über Ernst Cassirers Philosophie der Symbolischen Formen.* Frankfurt: Suhrkamp.

Pieper, Hans-Joachim. 1993. *"Anschauung" Als Operativer Begriff. Eine Untersuchung zur Grundlegung der Transzendentalen Phänomenologie Edmund Husserls.* Hamburg: Meiner.

Spiegelberg, Herbert. 1971. *The Phenomenological Movement. A Historical Introduction,* 2 vols. The Hague: Nijhoff. (Volumes are referred to as 1971/1 and 1971/2 in essay.)

Ströker, Elisabeth. 1992. *Zu Husserls Werk. Zur Ausgabe der Gesammelten Schriften.* Hamburg: Meiner.

Tugendhat, Ernst. 1967. *Der Wahrheitsbegriff bei Husserl und Heidegger.* Berlin: De Gruyter.

2

The Hermeneutics of Perception in Cassirer, Heidegger, and Husserl

Rudolf Bernet

We all know that hermeneutics was not born in the twentieth century. Nevertheless, it is undoubtedly the case that the idea of a hermeneutic philosophy is most familiar to us in the form given to it by Heidegger, Gadamer, and Ricœur. Moreover, this new hermeneutics is inseparable from the major issues of twentieth-century philosophy—the definitive overcoming of a sensualist or rationalist theory of knowledge; the recognition of the multiple forms of symbolic mediation of the intentional relationship between subject and object; the reevaluation of the link between theoretical and practical philosophy; and finally, a new definition of philosophical knowledge in the face of the growing split between the natural sciences and the human sciences. These issues are not new, however, and their simple enumeration is sufficient to recall the problematic of Kant's three *Critiques*. This first impression will only confirm itself in the course of our enquiry, which will focus in particular on the 1920s as the decisive period for twentieth-century hermeneutic philosophy. Through a new reading of Kant (which is inseparable from its Hegelian shadow), a hermeneutic of objective spirit (Cassirer) and a hermeneutic of the finitude of Dasein (Heidegger) assert their ambitions and rapidly head toward a confrontation, which is still being discussed.

Heidegger's hermeneutics is born in a historical context essentially marked by the rivalry between Neo-Kantianism and phenomenology. It is well known that Heidegger and, soon after him, Gadamer, took part in this debate which animated the philosophical *milieu* of Freiburg no less than Marburg. However, it has perhaps not been sufficiently noted that this battle between the phenomenologists and Neo-Kantians was not unrelated to the fact that the phenomenological movement was itself already divided between, on the one hand, a cognitivist, essentialist, and transcendentalist tendency, and, on the other, a practical (or more precisely poetic), existentialist, and hermeneutic tendency. It is while fighting on these two fronts—that is to say, against the first generation of phenomenologists and the Neo-Kantians (of all tendencies)—that Heidegger developed his hermeneutic approach to fundamental ontology. Even accepting that Heidegger's cause was philosophically important and justified, one cannot help thinking that he is often mistaken about his adversaries. How can one consider Husserl's early philosophy as the expression of a simple theory of knowledge, based on a dualist ontology? And how can one go so far astray as to claim that the thought of Cassirer is a typical example of an epistemology essentially concerned with the status of the natural sciences?

However, Heidegger's remarks on Cassirer's *Philosophy of Symbolic Forms* do more than simply assimilate it with Neo-Kantianism, and the discussions at Davos between Heidegger and Cassirer are not simply about the correct reading of Kant. It seems to me that their disagreements over the finitude of the subject, the relationship between activity and passivity in its comportment, productive imagination and language, philosophy in relation to ethics and religion, etc., primarily refer back to the problematic of a philosophy which claims to be hermeneutic. Today's reader quickly realizes that Heidegger's criticisms cannot excuse him from having to pay close attention to the work of Cassirer, which has lost nothing of its contemporary relevance. Paying the same attention to Heidegger as to Cassirer, however, such a reader also cannot dismiss Heidegger's critical remarks or consider them null and void.[1] If one really wants to escape a simplistic polemic, one has to recognize that in the dispute between Heidegger and Cassirer, two conceptions of hermeneutics confront one another, conceptions that it is still difficult to choose between. Moreover, can one choose between two types of hermeneutics without first reflecting upon what it is that separates them from phenomenology, to which both Heidegger and Cassirer continually refer? Is it not this common appeal to Husserl's phenomenology that best allows us to measure the gap which separates them?

In what follows, we will attempt to show how Cassirer endeavored to hold himself back from the supposed necessity of choosing between Husserl and Heidegger. For this reason, we will begin our enquiry into Cassirer's hermeneutics by examining his conception of symbolic perception. Only then will we take on the much larger questions of the relationship between a hermeneutic of subjective experience and a hermeneutic of the works of objective spirit, the problem of accounting for the plurality of symbolic forms and their possible unification, and finally, the problem of evaluating the status of hermeneutic knowledge itself.

A Hermeneutic Conception of Perception

We will begin by seeking to place the analysis of perception within the systematic and rigorous (though sometimes in its details ambiguous) construction that is *The Philosophy of Symbolic Forms*. We know that the first volume of this work deals with language, the second with myth, and the third with the symbolic function that is common to all symbolic forms, as well as science as a particular symbolic form. In addition, Cassirer analyzes, in a particularly profound manner, the symbolic forms of religion, art, and technology. These different symbolic forms are the result of a "meaning-giving" (*Sinngebung*) or symbolic "comportment" (*Verhalten*) of the "subject" or "consciousness," which in turn have multiple modes of functioning.[2] Cassirer distinguishes three types of such functioning or symbolic comportment—"perception" (*Wahrnehmung*), "intuition" (*Anschauung*), and "cognition" (*Erkenntnis*). Each of these types of subjective comportment is governed by a different symbolic function: One perceives according to the category, or rather symbolic function of "expression" (*Ausdruck*); intuition is accomplished in the symbolic register of "representation" (*Repräsentation* or *Darstellung*); and cognition obeys the rules of "signification" (*reine Bedeutung*). Corresponding to these different modes of subjective comportment, which are determined by the different symbolic functions, are objective correlates which are nothing other than the different symbolic forms already mentioned. Thus, Cassirer places the comportment of expressive perception parallel with myth; representational intuition, with language; and cognition that articulates itself through significations, with science. We will see that this correlation between, on the one hand, the different types of symbolic comportment of the subject, and on the other, the different symbolic forms which form the realm of objective spirit, has the effect of setting the hermeneutic analysis of the *Philosophy of Symbolic Forms* on a circular path. Journeying indefinitely between the *terminus a quo* and *terminus ad quem* of the symbolic life of the spirit, Cassirer's hermeneutic forbids all immediate access to the subjective origin of objective culture. The course of this hermeneutics of the symbolic function is thus a living testament to the originary character of the symbolic mediation that it strives to illuminate.

Within this general framework, perception thus appears as a subjective comportment which is determined by a specific symbolic function, and is only accessible via the detour of the hermeneutic analysis of a particular symbolic form of objective spirit. It is striking to note that Cassirer wished to make a distinction between perception in the strict sense of the term (*Wahrnehmung*), and perception in a broader sense (*Anschauung*). The first form of perception is expressive in nature, and is chiefly encountered in a form of existence which is tied to the symbolic form of myth. The second form of perception is more evolved, because it makes use of articulations that are proper to the function of representation, and develops closer connections with the symbolic form of language. In what follows, we will focus on the analysis of this last form of perception in order to emphasize its hermeneutic character.[3]

Just as Merleau-Ponty will after him, Cassirer proposes a middle way between an empiricist or sensualist analysis of perception, and a rationalist or intellectualist one. Rereading Kant's first *Critique* in the light of his third *Critique*, he claims that content and form constitute an indivisible whole in perception. It is true that a given can be apprehended under different forms, but it is no less true that the form is itself a given; and it is a form in the sense of Gestalt psychology—at once a sensible figure and a function of differential articulation. That which appears in perception is a phenomenon which is immediately meaningful and appears according to its meaning. The perception of an object is only possible if it is accompanied or even arranged by this work of a schematizing productive imagination, which Cassirer terms symbolic activity or function.

Always concerned to be in dialogue with others, Cassirer wanted to make clear what it was that separated his conception of the sensible phenomena from those of Husserl and Heidegger. As one might expect, the *Husserlian* conception of *hyle* and *morphe* and of their possible synthesis, finds no favor in his eyes[4]: For Cassirer, a given deprived of noetic apprehension is a nonsense. The confrontation with *Heidegger* is more interesting since, as we will see, Cassirer and Heidegger share the conviction that to see is to see according to a mode of vision (*Sicht*), and both refer to Kant's schematism. However, their conceptions of the transcendental imagination and of schematism differ on essential points. For Heidegger, Kant's schematism corresponds to the elaboration of an *a priori* cognition of an ontological sort, and is deeply marked by the finitude of Dasein. Cassirer proposes a more classical interpretation, notably insisting upon the fact that Kant's chapter on schematism ought not be isolated from the chapters dealing with the *Grundsätze* and the distinction between phenomena and noumena, and that it develops what he calls a "phenomenology of the object."[5] Cassirer is thus led to dispute the claim that the symbolic function of the productive imagination has an exclusively temporal sense, that it refers to a sense of being irreducible to objects, and that it is marked by an insurmountable finitude.

This dispute has important consequences for the problematic of perception. For Heidegger, the unity of perception and imagination is the sign of a fundamental dependence of the formative activity of the understanding on sensibility. For Cassirer, on the contrary, it represents the possibility of its emancipation. For Heidegger the meaning of a sensible phenomenon is given to the subject,[6] for Cassirer, this primitive givenness must give rise to an activity of symbolic formation, which leads to an objective meaning being conferred upon the phenomenon.[7] It is precisely because Cassirer understands perception as a symbolic comportment, the nature of which is to surpass itself toward a more objective determination of the world, that Heidegger's insistence on finitude and passivity seems to him to be a sign of the confinement of subjective life to a primary mode of comportment, i.e., to the mythic and the exclusively practical. The issue debated by Heidegger and Cassirer at Davos is thus located within a hermeneutic analysis of perception, and directly concerns the mode of givenness of the meaning which is apprehended and interpreted in perception. For Cassirer, the meaningful articulation of the world presents itself under the aspect of an objective and universal symbolic form, which results from a symbolic function that is pure spontaneity (*Geist*). For Heidegger, the world is a signifying network in which Dasein is itself entangled, one that it will eventually transform, but which it can never form in the sense of a transcendental constitution. That is not to say that Heidegger is less "subjectivist" than Cassirer; we will see that, quite the contrary, Heidegger unremittingly reproaches Cassirer for leaving in the dark the question of the subjective (existentiell and existential) foundation of the system of objective spirit that is constituted by the symbolic forms.

But let us return once more to the specific issues of Cassirer's "true phenomenology of perception" (*wahrhafte Phänomenologie der Wahrnehmung*) (224/193), issues which, moreover, are revealing in regard to what we have called his hermeneutics. Like Heidegger (but apparently prior to having read him),[8] Cassirer tirelessly reiterates that perception in the sense of representational intuition (*Anschauung*) is a seeing (*Sehen*) that is made possible by a symbolic vision (*Sicht*)[9]:

> For there is no seeing and nothing visible which does not stand in some mode of spiritual vision. . . . A seeing and a thing seen outside of this "sight," a "bare" sensation preceding all formation, is an empty abstraction. The "given" must always be taken in a definite aspect and so apprehended, for it is this aspect that first lends it meaning. This meaning is to be understood neither as secondary and conceptual nor as an associative addition: rather, it is the simple meaning of the original intuition itself. (156–157/134)

Just as in Heidegger, this vision or *Sicht* is compared to the Platonic idea (*eidos*) (282/241), which is described as a framework allowing for an "interpretation" (*Deutung*) of what one sees (335/286), and is said to determine the direction and goal toward which the apprehension of the meaning of a perceptual given tends (214/184, 236/203, 320/273–274, 337/288). Thanks to it, perception is capable of "reading" (*Lesen*) the meaning of that which appears, and even "spelling out" (*Buchstabieren*) data individually and separately (222/191, 281/242). It allows us to conjointly perceive, act, and speak—as the empirical research on aphasia, apraxia, and agnosia shows, each pathology revealing a deficit of this *Sicht* and, importantly, a deficit of the subject's ability to pass from one *Sicht* to another (238ff./205ff.).

We cannot go into the detail of Cassirer's analyses, which are extremely well researched, rich in historical observations and critical discussions, and attest to an erudition and breadth of horizons which are simply astounding. Rather, we want now to concentrate on deepening our understanding of the symbolic function of this *Sicht,* which makes seeing a hermeneutic experience. For Cassirer this *Sicht* is a symbolic function or order which, without arising from sensible givens, nevertheless binds itself to them to the point that it forms a whole with them, that is to say, a phenomenon impregnated with its meaning. In order to characterize this whole of sensible and meaning, of visible and of light, Cassirer introduces the term "symbolic pregnance" (*symbolische Prägnanz*) which he defines as follows: "By symbolic pregnance we mean the way in which a perception as a sensory experience contains at the same time a certain non-intuitive meaning which it immediately and concretely represents" (235/202).

The appearance of the phenomenon is thus indelibly marked or impregnated by a symbolic "order" (*Ordnung*) which gives it its meaning. In other words, only that which is signitive, and signitive through a certain relationship or according to an order of meaning, can appear. If the diversity of orders of meaning can be examined as such by a "philosophy of symbolic forms," this does not exclude that these symbolic forms are inseparable from sensible givens (at least at the level of symbolic function that is termed "representation"). The forms "impregnate" the given and the given "represents" the form. Changing the form or the *Sicht* thus requires a familiarity with "analogy" and "metaphor": The subject must endeavor to "transpose," "transform," or "translate," the phenomenon which, in appearing according to another meaning, appears otherwise and becomes another phenomenon.

With his conception of "symbolic pregnance," Cassirer once again situates himself precisely midway between Husserl and Heidegger, which is to say, between the doctrine of categorial intuition and the analysis of understanding as a mode of being of an individual Dasein. (This does not, however, prevent all three thinkers from appealing to Plato.) Even though Heidegger wished to align Husserl's categorial intuition with his own conception of transcendence and ontological difference, it is indisputable that for Husserl categorial intuition is a matter of an intuitive, intentional act directed toward an ideal object. It is true that this ideal object is a non-empirical object which exceeds the power of sensible intuition, but this in no way means that for Husserl categorial intuition is the condition of possibility of perception. As a *sui generis* intuition of an ideal object, categorial intuition is also not a sensible perception impregnated with a non-intuitive meaning of the sort Cassirer talks about. Husserl thus distinguishes himself from both Heidegger and Cassirer in that his interest in the appearance of a non-sensible object does not at all lead him to doubt that sensible perception can by itself give a meaning to that which appears to it. On the other hand, however, Husserl shares with Cassirer the conviction that the categorial form is something objective, the validity of which is general and, as a consequence, irreducible to the experience of an individual subject. It is precisely on this point that Heidegger separates himself from both Husserl and Cassirer, by considering the *Sicht* an *a priori* of sensible perception which is not at all objective but which characterizes, on the contrary, the mode of being of an individual subject.[10] The *a priori* of sensible perception—the light which makes visible that which appears—is thus for Heidegger neither the intentional experience of a transcendental subject (Husserl), nor a universal form of objective spirit (Cassirer), but the existential world of an individual subject marked by its facticity.

To summarize, we can say that Cassirer is innovative with respect to Husserl in stressing that sensible perception is inseparable from what Husserl analyses under the form of a "categorial intuition," and which he himself calls a "*Sicht*." Thus, on this point Cassirer agrees with Heidegger against Husserl. However, Cassirer also agrees with Husserl against Heidegger in understanding the symbolic forms as ideal *objects,* and it is thus that he accuses Heidegger of having given a purely "anthropological" description of the *Sicht.*

Cassirer's theory of "symbolic pregnance," which turns sensible perception into a hermeneutic experience, is a theory of the unity of the sensible given and its meaning that emphasizes a reciprocal dependence between the sensible phenomenon and the symbolic order which determines its visibility. Seeing is a seeing and understanding *according to, via, by detour through,* and thus implies what Heidegger calls "the hermeneutic 'as'" (*das hermeneutische "Als"*) (*SuZ* § 33). However, one can only truly speak of hermeneutics to the extent that a given can be interpreted according to different points of view or different *Sichten.* Thus, Cassirer is careful to specify that what deserves to be called "hermeneutic" in a perception—the unity between the sensible given and the symbolic form—is not a unity of confusion or of "expression," but a unity of distinction and determination, which he terms a unity of "representation." As an experience fashioned by the symbolic function of representation, hermeneutic perception situates itself halfway between, on the one hand, an expressive or mythic mode of perception which is delivered over to the occult powers of the thing and its metamorphoses; and on the other hand, a mode of scientific perception which depends *only* on a formal and autonomous symbolic system, and thus frees itself from any dependence upon a pregiven reality. In hermeneutic perception, the meaning is not confused with a concrete sensible, but neither does it detach itself to the point of attaining the logical autonomy of a formal system of pure signification.

But what does "representation" mean for Cassirer, and what is it to perceive according to the symbolic function of representation? Among the numerous definitions and descriptions given in *The Philosophy of Symbolic Forms,* the reader who is familiar with Husserl, Heidegger, and above all Derrida, will perhaps be most responsive to the following formulation: "For no content of consciousness is in itself merely present, or in itself merely representative; rather, every actual experience indissolubly embraces both factors. Every present content functions in the sense of representing. Just as all representation demands a link with something present in consciousness" (232/199).

Hermeneutic or representational perception thus addresses itself to a given insofar as the given is enmeshed in a network of references. These references deserve to be called intentional, even if they are not really of a subjective order. Nothing is given as simply present; the event of the presence of a given sets off a "vibration" (*Schwingung*) (259/222) that reverberates and awakens new givens, which announce themselves in the distance (*Ferne*). Perception traverses and, at the same time, deepens the distance which separates the present from the absent. It is the symbolic function of representation that mediates the relationship between the present and the absent; representation which employs the linguistic sign is only a particular case (but as we will see, a highly significant one) of that function of representation which operates within all perception. That function of representation which is common to perception, image-consciousness, and the manner in which a sign refers to a signified, effaces the opposition between "presentation" (*Gegenwärtigung*) and "re-presentation" (*Vergegenwärtigung*) on which Husserl's entire theory of perception rests. Inspired mainly by Gestalt psychology, Cassirer considers the relationship between the whole and the part to be a paradigmatic example of the functioning of "representation." Perception becomes representational because it is animated by a "hunger for forms" (*Gestaltenhunger*) (141/121) which impels it toward a "dynamic" unification of the visible and invisible under the direction of a "center" of interest or a symbolic form which enables a globalization of phenomena. Hermeneutic perception moves in a field or horizon wherein anything can become representative of anything else, as well as of the form of the whole itself. The presence of a phenomenon is thus a function of the network of representations at the point where vertical and horizontal refer-ences intersect. The presence of a phenomenon depends on the manner in which it presents other phenomena, as well as on the symbolic form which is common to them and which determines the general kind of their mean-ing: "For now there is no longer any absolutely isolated thing; every element that is engaged with others in such a common movement bears in itself the general law and form of that movement and is able to represent it for con-sciousness" (258/223).[11]

Thus the color of a wall can be perceived in function of the material with which it has been constructed, or in function of the light in which it bathes; it can represent an architectural style, an epoch, or a town; or it can make one think of Vermeer's "little patch of yellow wall" so celebrated by Proust, or of the Wailing Wall. Thus, hermeneutic perception is representational because it is *analogical.*

However, Cassirer is not content to describe how a phenomenon refers to other phenomena. Above all, he is interested in exploring the different symbolic dimensions which mold this function of representation that is at work in hermeneutic perception. He devotes a chapter to each of the differ-ent forms of the representational function—space, time, and the unity of the thing and its properties. He shows how the presence of a "here" represents a "there," how the presence of a "now" is indissolubly bound to the represen-tation of the past and the future, and how multiple, changing properties are assembled into a representation of the unity of the subsistent thing. Without going into the detail of these analyses, let us note that Cassirer strives in each case to show that neither the multiplicity and changing character of the rep-resentational relations, nor the fusion of these symbolic forms with sensible givens, compromises in any way the stability of the symbolic order of space, time, and the subsistence of things. On the contrary, for him, this stability is the result of the non-coincidence of a place, an instant, and a thing with themselves. Understood as representation, this non-coincidence creates dis-tinctions and differences that have a definite value. Instead of threatening the constancy and general value of the meaning of the order of the sensible, the variety and multiplicity of these representational relations are, quite the contrary, a necessary condition of the emergence of unity and identity in the field of phenomena. Prior to the concept and in a different way, representa-tion establishes "the unity of recognition" within sensible perception.

Such a description of hermeneutic perception, marked by the symbolic function of representation, nevertheless remains incomplete so long as the close connection which unites perception with language has not been clari-fied. To use Heidegger's terms: the analysis of the hermeneutic "as" calls for an analysis of the apophantic "as" (*SuZ* § 33). Here again, Cassirer situ-ates himself midway between Husserl, who affirms that language is only an unproductive reflection of intentional experiences,[12] and Heidegger, who declares: "*We see what one says about the matter.*"[13] For Cassirer, linguistic expression comes neither before nor after hermeneutic perception, since linguistic expression and perception are both rooted in the same symbolic function of representation:

> The question of whether the articulation of the intuitive world must be conceived as preceding or following the genesis of articulated language—the question of whether the first is the cause or effect of the second—must here be regarded as falsely formulated . . . Neither of them, in a purely temporal sense, "arises" from the other: rather they are like two stems springing from the same spiritual root. (133/114)

> The more closely we follow the special paths taken by the universal function of representation and recognition, the more clearly their nature and specific unity will be revealed to us—and it will be increasingly evident that it is ultimately one and the same fundamental achievement by which the spirit rises to the creation of language and the intuitive world view, to the discursive understanding and objective *intuition* of reality. (136/117)[14]

But what exactly is the nature of this language that is the twin of hermeneutic perception? Like the latter, it must be situated halfway between the realm of myth and the realm of science. It is thus a language that is neither "mimetic" nor purely symbolic. By virtue of its articulation it surpasses the "mimetic" or "expressive" language of primitive man and children, but by virtue of its adherence to sensible phenomena, it cannot claim the universal scope of the "symbolic" language of science. It is an "analogical" language which functions in the same way as the representational perception that we have termed "hermeneutic" perception. The hermeneutic nature of this perception and of this language is thus bound up with their analogical character, with the way in which they seek a unity of meaning without abandoning the multiplicity of references, and with the way in which they explore an intermediate space between the sensible and the logical. Their hermeneutic nature is due to their being open to a free play between the signifier and the signified, instead of reducing the one to the other as do (each in their own way) myth (or schizophrenia) and science.

Method and Status of a Hermeneutic Philosophy

Is the evidence provided by our analysis of a hermeneutic mode of perception in Cassirer sufficient to allow us to say that *The Philosophy of Symbolic Forms* is a hermeneutic philosophy? What then would be the field of investigation marked out by this hermeneutics, and what in its method would distinguish it from both Husserlian phenomenology and Heidegger's hermeneutic of Dasein's facticity? To what degree would it announce a hermeneutic epoch of philosophy itself, a new age of hermeneutic reason?

As regards the method followed by Cassirer, Heidegger's critique, formulated in his 1928 review of the second volume of *The Philosophy of Symbolic Forms*, and then forcefully reaffirmed in the encounter at Davos in 1929, is revealing. According to this critique, Cassirer focuses too exclusively on the analysis of the symbolic forms of objective spirit, and totally neglects the way in which their significance is rooted in the existence of an individual subject.[15] Cassirer's response is no less interesting: he says he focuses on objective expressions of subjective activity because they make possible communication between humans, and are thus the guarantee of an enlightened rationalism and a responsible humanism.[16] For Heidegger, the learned analysis of the symbolic forms in which our culture is registered is the work of an "idle"[17] philosophy that creates nothing new and recoils before the facticity of human existence. Cassirer, for his part, says he is concerned by the ethical and political consequences of what appears to him to be an extreme form of irrationalism and individualism—much closer to religion than to the grand tradition of philosophy. We know that he was not entirely wrong on this point, but in order to better understand what is at issue in the debate, we should distrust the overly simple and covertly ideological images employed by the protagonists and their communities of the faithful. If we were to believe them, then the debate is a struggle between a philosophy anchored in the *Aufklärung* and a form of mystical and anti-humanist militant fundamentalism—a struggle that raises issues comparable to those which divided Erasmus and Luther, Goethe and Hölderlin, Kant and Jacobi, etc.[18]

As concerns Cassirer's hermeneutic method, Heidegger is certainly not wrong to remark that the way in which Cassirer characterizes the subject of the formative activity that produces the symbolic universes of language, myth, art, and the sciences, is singularly lacking in precision.[19] However, at first sight nothing obliges us to follow Heidegger further when he claims that this imprecision is a direct result of the absence of a "radical ontology of Dasein in the light of the question of Being in general."[20] Cassirer himself offers us a simpler and more illuminating explanation when he refers to the "reconstructive" (*rekonstruktiv*) method of Natorp's psychology, which he summarizes in these terms:

> We can never expose the immediate life and being of consciousness as such. But it is a significant task to seek a new aspect and meaning for the unhalting process of objectivization by exploring it in a twofold direction: from *terminus a quo* to *terminus ad quem* and back again. In Natorp's

opinion, it is only by a continuous back and forth, by this twofold direction of method that the object of psychology can be made visible as such. (63/53)[21]

We know, furthermore, how much Natorp appreciated Husserl's introduction of the concept of "noema"[22] in *Ideas I*, and that Cassirer refers to the correlation between "noesis" and "noema" when he pays homage to Husserl's phenomenology in *The Philosophy of Symbolic Forms*.[23] We can, in addition, recall the importance of the problematic of the "*Leitfaden*" in *Ideas*, and that of the "*Rückfrage*" in Husserl's later work. Husserl thus shares with the Neo-Kantians (but not with Heidegger) the conviction that access to transcendental constituting subjectivity can only be attained by a detour through what it constitutes. The examination of transcendental life cannot proceed without the support of the regional ontologies, even if it must go beyond them. The origin only reveals itself in retrospect, and to an analysis that constantly "zigzags" back and forth between the beginning and the end, or—to put it in the words of Cassirer and Heidegger—between the *terminus a quo* and the *terminus ad quem*.

Thus it could be that Heidegger's critique, rather than identifying a fundamental deficit in Cassirer's philosophy, actually brings to light precisely its hermeneutic character. And undoubtedly, it would not be unfair to employ this hermeneutic back-and-forth between the subject and culture to cast a critical eye upon the project of fundamental ontology. In any case, it is certain that Cassirer, before Ricœur, insisted upon the necessity of approaching the life of the subject by relying on the evidence of its works. This detour is inevitable and indispensable as long as one emphasizes, as Cassirer consistently does, the symbolic nature of reason. It follows from this that the subject's relationship to itself is always already mediated by culture and, most notably, by the language it shares with other subjects. The subject is immersed in the work of the symbolic imagination, well before the meaning-saturated givens with which it finds itself presented, make themselves noted and allow the subject to recognize itself in them.

Equally, this hermeneutics of Cassirer has the great merit of making clear that objective spirit fragments itself into a multiplicity of symbolic forms or universes. If the analysis of each of these symbolic orders makes possible a return to their subjective principle, it is also true that this principle appears in a different way in each case. Consequently, it is not enough to emphasize that the life of the subject is regulated by the same forms as the world in which it lives; it must be added that there are different worlds and thus different ways to live. Apprehending itself across a plurality of symbolic forms, the subject, according to Cassirer, endlessly seeks its own unity. Here again, this hermeneutics that is open to dissemination runs up against Heidegger's critique. Heidegger criticizes precisely this lack of unity and suggests that this multiplicity of symbolic forms is to be understood through its foundation in Dasein's existence. Cassirer's reaction is not slow in coming: he suspects that the hermeneutic of Dasein promotes a new metaphysical "monism."[24] The project of founding the various meanings of being in the facticity and finitude of an individual subject's existence makes even less sense for Cassirer given that Heidegger seems content to examine a purely practical mode of this existence. Thus, their disagreement pertains not just to the method for approaching the subjective principle of the world; it concerns, more fundamentally, the conception of the mode of being of the world and of the subject, and also entails a different comprehension of the nature of philosophical knowledge.

For Cassirer, the hermeneutic method of moving back and forth between the multidimensionality of the world created by the various symbolic forms and the forms of life (*Lebensformen*) which correspond to them, does not in any way compromise the ideal objectivity of these forms. Despite their multiplicity and diversity, the symbolic forms represent universally valid forms of order, unmarked by any contingency or arbitrariness. These symbolic forms are ideal objectivities resulting from the auto-objectivation of an equally ideal subjective principle termed "spirit" (*Geist*). Cassirer's hermeneutics thus seems to be compatible with conceptions of intentionality and constitution that scarcely differ from those developed by Husserl's transcendental phenomenology. On closer examination, however, its strictly Kantian conception of the transcendental subject is out of tune with Husserl's phenomenology. Indeed, the determination of *Geist*—the subject which realizes itself in the symbolic forms—remains quite formal. It is a principle which above all functions as the condition of possibility of those ideal objectivities which are the symbolic forms, and it is quite unclear what connection it has to the actual experiences of a subject which is at once transcendental and individual. Husserl had already noted this before Heidegger, as the letter he wrote to Cassirer in 1925 after reading the second volume of *The Philosophy of Symbolic Forms* demonstrates. In this otherwise very complimentary letter, Husserl reproaches Cassirer for not having pursued his investigation into the different conceptions of the world and their historical sequence to the point of inquiring into the genesis of the transcendental subject itself, and for neglecting to question the transcendental signification of facticity.[25]

Heidegger's critique goes much further. However, under the guise of an alliance with Husserl against Cassirer in the name of a phenomenological conception of the subject, this critique ends up being turned against Husserl as well. What is ultimately at stake in Heidegger's criticism of *The Philosophy of Symbolic Forms* is nothing other than the *finitude* of the subject. This problematic was already at the center of the disagreement between Heidegger and Cassirer over Kant's philosophy. Examining the *Critique of Pure Reason* as well as the *Critique of Practical Reason,* Cassirer holds, in opposition to Heidegger, that man, according to Kant, is at once the citizen of the *mundus sensibilis* and the *mundus intelligibilis,* and that Kantian reason represents precisely the call to transcend the self so as to be immersed in the realm of the universal. The symbolic forms with their ideality and general validity are, for Cassirer, striking evidence of the possibility and meaning of such a transcendence of the "personal" (*persönlich*) towards the "trans-personal" (*überpersönlich*).[26] Thus, beyond this quarrel over the right way to read and extend the thought of Kant, it is the question of the status of philosophy itself which is at stake. It is not just that Cassirer does not share Heidegger's taste for receptivity, anxiety, death, and the nothing; it is that Cassirer is incapable of recognizing in these figures of human finitude genuine philosophical and, more precisely, ontological value. The hermeneutic of symbolic forms and the hermeneutic of Dasein differ thus, not only with respect to their object, but equally with respect to their philosophical status.

In undertaking a "critique of culture" (*Kritik der Kultur*) (*PSF* I, 11/80), *The Philosophy of Symbolic Forms* indisputably introduces a hermeneutic turn into the philosophical thought inspired by Neo-Kantianism. The project of a philosophy of the natural sciences is transformed into an analysis of the "understanding of the world" (*Weltverstehen*) that Cassirer takes good care to distinguish from a "*conceiving* of the world" (*Weltbegreifen*).[27] This philosophy of symbolic life within the world studies the forms of "significations" (*Bedeutungen*) as they operate in the experience both of the human world and of nature, and it deciphers therein the reflection of that universal constituting principle it calls "spirit" or "reason." *The Philosophy of Symbolic Forms* brings to light the diversity of symbolic orders, and shows how they are all traversed and articulated by the same basic symbolic functions. Commentators have not failed to emphasize that the link which connects the symbolic forms such as language, myth, and science to each other, lends itself to a double reading: synchronic and logical, or diachronic and genetic. They are nevertheless struck by the fact that the place of philosophy among these various symbolic forms remains particularly unclear.[28] This lack of precision is not accidental and, on the contrary, leads us back to the vital question of the relationship between hermeneutics and finitude.

Even if Heidegger did not immediately realize it, his hermeneutic of Dasein's finitude necessarily leads not only to the recognition of the finitude of Being's manifestation, but also of the finitude of the thought solicited by this manifestation. If, in order to inquire into the meaning of Being, philosophy slips into the skin of a finite Dasein—and Dasein's existence is characterized precisely by the fact that it cannot shrink from the question of its own being—then one cannot see how philosophy can escape from the fate of human finitude. Even though Cassirer was skeptical about Heidegger's claim to have detected a movement of recoil before the finitude of the subject in Kant's treatment of the transcendental imagination, it seems to me incontestable that *The Philosophy of Symbolic Forms* traces an analogous recoil before the view that philosophy is but one symbolic form among others. Divided between Kant and Hegel, *The Philosophy of Symbolic Forms* seems, in the end, to be drawn up from the viewpoint of absolute knowledge. It describes a system of symbolic forms from a vantage point that is a "view from nowhere." It is thus a philosophy that remains hermeneutic so long as it is concerned with perception, language, or world pictures, but ceases to be so when it turns its attention to itself. It is a philosophical hermeneutics, but not a hermeneutic philosophy. In distinction from a philosophical hermeneutics, hermeneutic philosophy is committed to the onerous task of thinking its own finitude. Properly understood, this does not mean—as Cassirer seemed to fear—that it has to abandon philosophy for religion. It does mean, however, that it can no longer shrink before the question of the scope, value, and validity of philosophical knowledge, as well as its place among the forms of objective spirit. Cassirer's recoiling before the recognition of finitude, a recognition that risks ending up affirming a philosophical relativism, must continue to be a question for us. At stake is the credibility of hermeneutics.

TRANSLATED BY PAUL CROWE

NOTES

1. I will mention only one example of this tendency, which is quite widespread among those who are committed to rehabilitating the importance of Cassirer's philosophical hermeneutics: J. M. Krois, "Cassirer's Unpublished Critique of Heidegger," *Philosophy and Rhetoric* 16, no. 3 (1983): 147–159.

2. Cf. particularly, E. Cassirer, *Philosophie der symbolischen Formen*, vol. 3: *Phänomenologie der Erkenntnis* (Darmstadt: Wissenschaftliche Buchgesellschaft, 1964), 67; *Philosophy of Symbolic Forms*, vol. 3: *The Phenomenology of Knowledge*, trans. Ralph Manheim (New Haven: Yale University Press, 1957), 57. Hereafter, throughout the essay, all numbers between parentheses refer to this text—unless otherwise specified (*PSF* I, *SuZ*). The first number refers to pagination in the German text, and the second to the English translation. We use the abbreviation *PSF* III in the following notes.

3. One would have to reread Merleau-Ponty's *Phenomenology of Perception* to illuminate this distinction between an expressive (mythic or animist) perception and a quasi-linguistic perception, requiring as it does a structuralist analysis of the system of differential traits and symbolic references that it involves. This would not only allow us to properly assess the immense debt this text owes to Cassirer, but

would also be useful to clarify certain passages, the obscurity of which seems to be due precisely to the absence of a clear distinction between these two modes of perception.

4. *PSF* III, 228ff./196ff.

5. Cf. the review of Heidegger's *Kantbuch* by Cassirer, "Kant und das Problem der Metaphysik, Bemerkungen zu Martin Heideggers Kant-Interpretation," *Kanstudien* 36, no. 1 (1931): 8ff. and 18ff.

6. Heidegger speaks of a *"Grunderfahrung der Angewiesenheit auf Gebung"*: Martin Heidegger, *Kant und das Problem der Metaphysik* = GA 3 (Frankfurt: Klostermann, 1991), 297; *Kant and the Problem of Metaphysics,* 4th ed., trans. Richard Taft (Bloomington: Indiana University Press, 1990). The *Gesamtausgabe* volume contains appendices with Heidegger's notes on this book, his review of volume 2 of the *PSF,* documentation of the conversations between Heidegger and Cassirer at Davos in 1929, as well as Heidegger's remarks on the reviews of his book by Cassirer and Odebrecht. It will be cited hereafter as GA 3. The English translation has only the Davos material in an appendix. Where possible, the page numbers of the English translation will follow those of the German text. Heidegger's review of *PSF* II has been translated in *The Piety of Thinking,* trans. James G. Hart and John C. Maraldo (Bloomington: Indiana University Press, 1976), 32–45. Where the reference is to this text the page number for the translation will be preceded by PT.

7. *PSF* III, 173–174 n. 1/149 n. 4.

8. Published in 1929, *PSF* III was completed, according to Cassirer, in 1927 (ix/xvii). Furthermore, all of his references to *Sein und Zeit (SuZ)* are to be found in the notes, no doubt added after Cassirer's text had already been written.

9. *PSF* III, 155/134, 185/158, 187/160, 212/183, 232/200, 265/227, 282/241, 295ff./253ff., 318/273. Cf. *SuZ* §§ 31–32.

10. Cf. *SuZ* § 31: "Die mit der Erschlossenheit des Da existential seiende Sicht *ist* das Dasein . . . nach den Grundweisen seines Seins."

11. Cf. also *PSF* I, 31ff./ 97ff., 37ff./ 102ff.

12. Cf. *Ideas Pertaining to a Pure Phenomenology and to Phenomenological Philosophy,* vol. 1, trans. F. Kersten (The Hague: M. Nijhoff, 1982), § 124: ". . .the stratum of expression [. . .] is not productive"; "An appertinant intuitional medium is present which, according to its essence, has the distinction, so to speak, of mirroring every other intentionality according to form and content."

13. *Prolegomena zur Geschichte des Zeitbegriffs, Marburger Vorlesung Sommersemester* 1925 = GA 20 (Frankfurt: Klostermann, 1979), 75: "Wir sehen, was man über die Sache spricht"; *History of the Concept of Time: Prolegomena,* trans. Theodore Kisiel (Bloomington: Indiana University Press, 1992), 56.

14. Cf. also *PSF* III, 19/15.

15. GA 3, 265ff., 288ff./180ff.

16. GA 3, 292ff./183ff. Cf. also E. Cassirer, "'Geist' und 'Leben': Heidegger (An Unpublished Manuscript)," *Philosophy and Rhetoric* 16, no. 3 (1983): 164–166.

17. GA 3, 291/182.

18. Cf. E. Cassirer, review of the *Kantbuch,* cit. above, note 5; J. M. Krois, "Cassirer's Unpublished Critique of Heidegger," *Philosophy and Rhetoric* 16, no. 3 (1983):

147–159; J. M. Krois, "Aufklärung und Metaphysik. Zur Philosophie Cassirers und der Davoser Debatte mit Heidegger," *Internationale Zeitschrift für Philosophie* 2 (1992): 273–289.

19. Cf. GA 3, 265/PT 41: "What about the task [. . .] of working out the ontological understanding and mode of being of that which, indefinitely enough, is sometimes called 'consciousness,' sometimes 'life,' sometimes 'spirit,' sometimes 'reason'?"

20. Loc. cit.: "The interpretation of the essence of myth as a possibility of human Dasein remains accidental and directionless as long as it is not founded on a radical ontology of Dasein in the light of the problem of Being in general."

21. Cf. also *PSF* I, 21/88, 25ff./92ff. This quote is a direct response to the objection Heidegger had made at Davos: "In the first lecture, Cassirer used the expressions *terminus a quo* and *terminus ad quem*. One could say that for Cassirer the *terminus ad quem* is the whole of a philosophy of culture in the sense of the elucidation of the wholeness of the forms of the shaping consciousness. For Cassirer, the *terminus a quo* is utterly problematical. My position is the reverse: The *terminus a quo* is my central problematic, the one I develop" (GA 3, 288/180).

22. Cf. Natorp's review of Husserl's *Ideas I*: "Husserls Ideen zu einer reinen Phänomenologie," *Die Geisteswissenschaften* 1 (1914): 426ff. Reprinted in *Logos* 7 (1917/1918): 224–246.

23. *PSF* II, 16/12. Cf. also Cassirer's letter to Husserl (10 April 1925): "Ich bin über-zeugt, dass sich die Gemeinsamkeit der Aufgaben und der Überzeugungen noch schärfer herausheben wird, wenn ich nunmehr an die Ausarbeitung des *dritten* Bandes der *Philosophie der symbolischen Formen* herangehe. [. . .] Dass ich hierbei wieder auf Grundfragen der Phänomenologie zurückgeführt werden muss, sehe ich schon jetzt—und gerade in den Tagen, in denen Ihr Brief eintraf, hatte ich mich wieder aufs neue mit den *Ideen zu einer reinen Phänomenologie* beschäftigt und in ihnen—insbesondere in den Erörterung über 'Noesis' und 'Noema'—ganz neue Beziehungen zu meiner eigenen Problemstellung entdeckt." (Letter preserved in the Husserl Archives at Leuven.)

24. Cf. the review of the *Kantbuch* by Cassirer (op. cit., 16): "Indem Heidegger alle 'Vermögen' der Erkenntnis auf die 'transzendentale Einbildungskraft' zu beziehen, ja auf sie zurückzuführen versucht, bleibt ihm damit nur eine *einzige* Bezugsebene, die Ebene des zeitlichen Daseins zurück. [. . .] Kant vertritt nirgends einen derartigen 'Monismus' der Einbildungskraft."

25. "Ihr Buch lässt, wie Sie selbst wissen, abgesehen davon, dass es nur erster Anhieb sein konnte, ungeheure Probleme offen. Vor allem: die Idee und Form einer mythischen Weltanschauung, und jeder sonstigen zur Einheit einer Gesamtan-schauung sich verflechtenden universalen Intentionalität einer vergemeinschaf-tet dahinlebenden Menschheit, charakterisiert zunächst ein historisch faktisches Gebilde. Historische Genesis steht aber unter Wesensgesetzen. Es gilt aus dem 'ABC' der transzendentalen Strukturen und darunter denjenigen der Genesis tran-szendentalen Lebens die notwendigen Stufen der konkreten Entwicklungstypik einer Menschheit überhaupt verständlich zu machen: die Entwicklungstypik der geltenden und doch nicht endgiltigen Weltanschauungen, ebenso die Typik aller universalen Scheine und Verirrungen in der Stufe der schon erwachten Vernunft.

Dazu natürlich und auf anderer Seite die Probleme der Faktizität als solcher, die der 'Irrationalität,' die, wie mir scheint, nur behandelt werden können in einer erweiterten Methode der Kant'schen Postulate." (Letter of 3 April 1925.)

26. Cf. E. Cassirer, "'Geist' und 'Leben': Heidegger (An Unpublished Manuscript)," op. cit., 165. Cf. also GA 3, 276/173, 286/179; review of the *Kantbuch,* op. cit., 9ff.

27. "The philosophy of symbolic forms is not concerned exclusively or even primarily with the purely scientific, exact conceiving of the world; it is concerned with all the forms assumed by man's understanding of the world. It seeks to apprehend these forms in their diversity, in their totality, and in the inner distinctiveness of their several expressions" (*PSF* III, 16/13).

28. Cf. J. M. Krois, "Problematik, Eigenart und Aktualität der Cassirerschen Philosophie der symbolischen Formen," in Braun, Holzhey, and Orth (eds.), *Über Cassirers Philosophie der symbolischen Formen* (Frankfurt: Suhrkamp, 1988), 20–21; E. W. Orth, "Operative Begriffe in Ernst Cassirers Philosophie der symbolischen Formen," in Braun, Holzhey, and Orth (eds.), ibid., 53.

3

Reconstruction and Reduction: Natorp and Husserl on Method and the Question of Subjectivity

Sebastian Luft

Paul Natorp's influence on the development of Edmund Husserl's phenomenology, especially on the transcendental reduction and genetic method in Husserl, has been vastly underestimated. Husserl's contemporary, Natorp (1854–1924) was an exact observer and critic of Husserl's philosophical development from before the publication of his *Logical Investigations* (1900/1901, hereafter LI) and up to Natorp's death. Moreover, Natorp was the single contemporary philosopher with whom Husserl had the most intimate contact, as is witnessed to by their extensive correspondence.[1] Natorp provided the "interface" through which Husserl came into contact with the Neo-Kantianism that was then prevalent in Germany philosophy, as well as with Kant himself.[2] As Husserl acknowledged after his transcendental turn, it was his discussions with representatives of the transcendental tradition—i.e., the Neo-Kantians—that aided him in developing a full-fledged *transcendental* phenomenology. His closest ally among these erstwhile opponents was undoubtedly Natorp.[3]

The relation between phenomenology and Neo-Kantianism remains to a large extent an untold story, though the intersections between both schools are extensive. But to tell this story will prove decisive for the development of twentieth-century philosophy and beyond, and disentangling the many strands of these interactions has more than just historical merit. The present essay can only be the beginning of this story, and will focus on the relation between Natorp and Husserl and the most important issue that fueled their discussion. This issue is that of the status of transcendental philosophy, especially as it purports to be the method proper for the analysis of *concrete subjectivity*. The original impulse to undertake such an endeavor came, interestingly, from Natorp, whose philosophical psychology—in contradistinction to other brands of psychology, such as Brentano's "descriptive psychology"—intended to carry out such an analysis within the framework of the "Marburg" transcendental method inaugurated by his teacher Hermann Cohen. In so doing, however, Natorp was already in a sense going beyond Cohen's methodological confines. He found in Husserl a kindred spirit in such an attempt, as shall be shown.

While Husserl was striving to develop his own philosophical method and school—this tendency called the "phenomenological movement" is akin to what was frequently called the "movement back to Kant"—he nevertheless with one eye, and competitively, peered at the Neo-Kantians. Husserl's philosophical method of phenomenological reduction and his turn to transcendental phenomenology were developed in close discussion with Natorp. This was so much the case that many of Husserl's followers believed, upon reading *Ideas I* (1913), that he had become a Kantian himself and had thereby fallen back into the naïve or speculative idealism that phenomenology had supposedly overcome once and for all.[4] However, it is more appropriate to say that the influence that representatives of the Neo-Kantian tradition exerted on Husserl helped him come into his own. Natorp's influence on Husserl also extends to the very way phenomenological description should be carried out. As has been argued by Iso Kern in his *Husserl und Kant* (1964)—the first study to address this topic—and again more recently by Donn Welton in *The Other Husserl* (2001),[5] the development of Husserl's later genetic phenomenological method is inspired by Natorp's concept of a "reconstructive" analysis of consciousness. Put more strongly—Husserl would have been unable to attain this late stage without Natorp's influence.

Hence, this paper will claim that Natorp was the decisive factor that led Husserl to develop both the phenomenological reduction and his later genetic phenomenology. Although their philosophical presuppositions and education, as well as their understanding of the nature of philosophy, were quite different from the outset,[6] Natorp and Husserl were working on parallel problems and in close proximity, which enabled them to benefit from each other. For his part, Natorp was attempting to draft a philosophical psychology that intended to counter the "objectifying" tendency of the transcendental method developed by his teacher Hermann Cohen. This was called for, according to Natorp, in order to recapture the concrete life of the subject. And indeed, the same philosophical motivation lay behind Husserl's phenomenology and its call to the "things themselves." Yet it was, ironically, Husserl who exploited and executed the project for which Natorp strove but himself later abandoned (and the many attempts on the part of Neo-Kantians to "overcome" their original positions would be another, perhaps final, chapter of the story that is only begun here). Thus, the relation between Natorp and Husserl does not point to a simple one-sided "learning" of one from the other; instead, it bespeaks a genuine *symphilosophein* on issues which were commonly held to be vital for doing transcendental philosophy. Especially in the light of Husserl's later self-interpretation, phenomenology is conceived (in line with Natorp) as critical philosophy and is committed to transcendental idealism—as the ultimate scope of his philosophical project demonstrates, when it finally does justice to the concrete subject and its lifeworld—i.e., a world of culture.

Husserl knew what he owed to the Neo-Kantians: "After having learned to see Kant from my own perspective, I am now able, and especially in the last years, to receive rich instructions from Kant and the true Kantians," Husserl writes to Ernst Cassirer in 1925.[7] By the time Husserl composes the *Crisis* in 1936, however, he again obfuscates most traces of contemporary influence and mentions only the most outstanding philosophers in the modern Western tradition (Descartes, Kant, the British Empiricists) as having had any significant impact on him.[8] One reason for this omission may have been the historical fact that after Natorp's death and the emigration of many German philosophers of Jewish descent after 1933—Cassirer among them—the Neo-Kantian movement had all but died off in Germany. Nevertheless, as of 1913 Husserl had shared with the Neo-Kantians an agreement on the fundamental issues of philosophy—points of convergence which Husserl's first presentation of phenomenology in the *Logical Investigations* of 1900/1901 had explicitly shunned. There are certainly immanent reasons for Husserl to widen his philosophy from a descriptive psychology to a full-fledged transcendental phenomenology—first in a static, and then in a genetic register. But there is a somewhat unhealthy tendency in Husserl scholarship to ignore, or at least downplay, the influences Husserl was exposed to early in his career, especially if they issued from thinkers outside of the Brentano School. Exposing the intersections between Natorp and Husserl will help to rectify a skewed view of Husserl and the influences he incorporated into his mature system. But this paper is not just about Husserl; instead, we shall focus on the philosophical issues *common* to Husserl and Natorp. Rather than playing one off against the other, this discussion will demonstrate how the accommodation of certain theoretical elements in both thinkers led to a richer account and philosophically more satisfying theory of subjectivity in its "concreteness," within the framework of transcendental philosophy.

Hence, in this paper Natorp's and Husserl's theories of subjectivity and their respective methods for analyzing it shall be compared. Their philosophical disciplines are termed, respectively, psychology (Natorp) and phenomenology (Husserl). I would like to point out differences and also draw out commonalities, but most importantly to show how both are working on the same project—namely, an attempt to analyze subjectivity in its most *original concreteness*. Both Natorp's method of reconstruction and Husserl's method of reduction add decisive elements to such a theory. Although Natorp rejects any experience of the life of the subject through reflection (or "introspection"), Husserl takes over, in a modified way, the former's idea of a reconstructive method which he employs for a *genetic* account of subjectivity. Hence, this debate is also about the methodological principle of *phenomenology*—which, as it turns out, cannot restrict itself to pure intuition alone. For a phenomenological account of subjectivity, this is an insight of the highest importance.

While Natorp is critical toward his own method and in the last step of his philosophical development moves toward a "general unifying logic"—a doctrine of categories that unifies both "objectifying" and "subjectifying" tendencies—it is, ironically, *Husserl* who actually carries out Natorp's "grand vision" of a truly philosophical psychology. Natorp's method and conception of psychology proved a dead end for Natorp himself, but had a lasting importance for Husserl's late conception of subjectivity, which needed to be framed in a genetic register in order to capture subjectivity's "full concretion." Husserl's mature phenomenology, thus, can rightfully be considered phenomenological *as well as* Neo-Kantian. Husserl thus recasts the method for analyzing subjectivity in a way that cannot remain strictly phenomenological in the traditional sense of pure description. His mature method goes beyond the common scope of phenomenology with the help of the methodological tools that he took over from Natorp. Husserl was able to adopt Natorpian elements because both shared in principle the same goal—to analyze the concreteness of subjectivity *without* succumbing to a pre-transcendental, naïve philosophy of "existence."

The following sections will develop these issues by following the historical order in which Husserl and Natorp interacted with each other between the 1890s and 1924—the year of Natorp's death—though Natorp's influence can be discerned up until Husserl's death in 1938.

Natorp's Theory of Reconstruction and Husserl's Method of Reduction

Natorp's Position: Subjectivation versus Objectivation

Since Natorp's position was already well established by the time Husserl developed his phenomenology, it deserves to be discussed first. Natorp drew the conclusion of the Marburg reading of Kant, especially for the discipline of psychology. He presented his theory in an article of 1887, "Ueber subjective und objective Begründung der Erkenntniss" (On the Subjective and Objective Grounding of Cognition) as well as in his short book *Einleitung in die Psychologie nach kritischer Methode* (*Introduction to Psychology According to Critical Method,* hereafter EP) of 1888. This concept of psychology was further developed in the completely reworked *Allgemeine Psychologie nach kritischer Methode* (*General Psychology According to Critical Method*, hereafter AP) of 1912.[9] As mentioned, the problems with this conception later led Natorp to abandon his psychology altogether and to develop, in his late work, what he called a "general logic." In this late conception of logic—which was sketched in his posthumously published lecture-courses, *Vorlesungen über praktische Philosophie* (*Lectures on Practical Philosophy*, 1924) and *Philosophische Systematik* (*Philosophical Systematic*, 1954)—Natorp comes close to Cassirer's conception in the *Philosophy of Symbolic Forms*. One could even make the claim that Cassirer's philosophy was but the execution—with some important modifications—of Natorp's sketch of a philosophical systematics; and that, in this respect, both Natorp and Cassirer moved beyond the Neo-Kantian project of a science which lays ultimate foundations, the *Grundlegungswissenschaft* inaugurated by Hermann Cohen.

The Marburg Neo-Kantian position can be best characterized by the so-called *transcendental method*.[10] This method, first explicated by Cohen in his interpretations of Kant's *Critique of Pure Reason*, was further developed by Natorp and exploited for the discipline of philosophical psychology. Natorp's early work defined this task as filling a gap in the framework of Cohen's transcendental method. This is to say, what Natorp means by "psychology" is not an empirical discipline but a sub-discipline under the rubric of transcendental philosophy. Husserl understands it, quite correctly, as "aprioric psychology."[11] How does this fit in with the transcendental method, and what is the transcendental method about?

The starting point of philosophy, for Cohen, is the given reality as a *factum*. However, the *factum*—Cohen claims—is primarily the *factum* of the positive sciences (*das Faktum der Wissenschaften*). The *factum* is not a *factum brutum*, but itself cognition.[12] After all, Neo-Kantianism arose in the midst of the scientism of the second half of the nineteenth century, when there was seemingly nothing left for philosophy to do apart from providing a foundation or explanatory basis for the activities of the positive sciences. However, Natorp insists—and this is where his own thinking sets in—that the *factum* is in effect a *fieri*, i.e. something that is *made* through cognizing acts in the sciences: What is ascertained in the sciences is the product of theoretical activities. Through these activities the scientist explains the world as governed by *a priori* laws. The world is in this sense *constructed* through cognizing activities. We shall see, however, that the scope of Natorp's epistemology already goes beyond this limitation to scientific cognition. The term Natorp uses is *Erkenntnis*, which has the known ambivalence of meaning both explicit, specifically scientific or philosophical "cognizing," as well as simply "knowledge" as that *which is known*—and it is *both* meanings that Natorp wants to grasp.[13]

Hence, the transcendental method is about giving a logical justification regarding the conditions that govern the construction of reality through subjective, cognizing acts. The construction of reality is the deed of the scientist, but the philosopher thematizes the *a priori* conditions that factor into this construction of reality. Insofar as these cognizing acts ascertain something *lawful* through their activity, these laws can be called "objective." In short, the transcendental method of constructing reality can also be called "objectifying": It is about constructing objective reality through subjective acts, insofar as they cognize something objective, something with the character of a *law*. The law is a subjective production but, as objective and "fixed," is *no longer* subjective. Subjectivity thus becomes *objectified*; it is *in* objectifications that we find subjectivity. The method of objectivation—i.e., the transcendental method—is about the objective founding and constructing of knowledge. Knowledge, insofar as it can be called scientific knowledge, has the character of lawfulness. Laws, in turn, are not fleeting or dynamic, but static and abstract vis-à-vis their appearances in the subject. This is precisely what makes them "objective."

Natorp goes on to argue, however, that not just cognizing ascertainments with the character of laws are objectifying: Subjective life as such is objectifying, although it may not always be lawful. This becomes most visible in utterances. All judgments are objectifying insofar as they claim *something*. This is the character of "objectifying cognizing (*Erkenntnis*), scientific *as well as* prescientific: [. . .] to make objects out of appearances (*Erscheinungen*)."[14] In other words, the transcendental method can and in fact must be expanded to cover not only objectifying acts in the sciences, but all activities of a subject which are objectifying *in one way or another,* and of which lawful cognizing in the *emphatic* sense of *Erkenntnis* is the highest (and thus the norm for all other judgments). In this respect, Natorp claims that his constructive method proceeds teleologically—beginning *genetically* with the lowest form of objectifications in everyday utterances (which have no explicit truth-claims), up to the highest forms of objectifications in scientific discourse.[15] Thus, to sum up: The transcendental method of constructing reality in *Natorp's* interpretation is about ascertaining objectifications and their conditions by means of subjective acts, precisely by *objectifying* them. With this turn to the subjective, however, Natorp is already departing from Cohen's transcendental method, for which the objective laws alone are of interest.

What then, asks Natorp, about the subjective "side" of things? Where do subjectivity and its study, psychology, stand in regard to this project? The method or process of objectivation raises a significant question: If all subjective acts *objectify* in a given way, then what about the specifically *subjective* character of these acts? What happens with subjectivity? If subjectivity is objectified in the construction of reality, and if all subjective activities are objectifying, what about those pertaining to subjectivity itself? Obviously they, too, will be objectifying.[16] The result of this objectification is that subjectivity will be treated in the same, constructive way—the result is psychology as a scientific discipline, which in this sense is not different from biology, which objectifies biological affairs. However, in so doing, that element which precisely makes for the subjectivity of the subject—its dynamic, fleeting, concrete life—is lost. There can be, according to Natorp, *no direct description* of the subject in its genuine state of living, since every thematization is objectifying. As Natorp adds dramatically, that which makes the subject a subject is "killed."[17] In thematizing the subject one thus deals, metaphorically speaking, with a corpse instead of a living being. *All* traditional psychology supposedly proceeds in this way: It ascertains *facts* about subjectivity, and in this process loses the subject. The "spirit" of the subject vanishes in thematizing it, for thematization is objectivation. Thus it seems that psychology, at least in the sense of a description of psychic states of affairs, is rendered impossible from the outset. That is indeed Natorp's answer, *unless* one construes psychology as a philosophical discipline which pays heed to the special character of subjectivity: This is the task that Natorp set for "transcendental psychology."

What is needed, then, for a philosophical psychology is a method which allows for a thematization of subjectivity that is *not* objectifying or constructive. This method is now the opposite of construction; rather, it is reconstructive. The method which is opposed to objectivation—namely subjectivation—is that of a *reconstruction* of subjectivity by going back, regressively, from its objectifications. Whereas the objective method focuses on the relation between an opaque subject which constructs objectivity and this objectivity itself, the subjective method turns 180 degrees and looks at the relation to the subject. As such, it is the *inverse method* of objectivation, and Natorp also speaks of it as a "turning inside out" (*Umstülpung*) of objectification. Whereas construction proceeds teleologically toward objective laws, which are abstract and unifying, the reconstructive method is genetic: It goes back to that which has constructed reality—the dynamic structures of consciousness, subjectivity's concrete life. Whereas objective laws are always mediated through constructions, the method of reconstruction goes back to the *immediateness* of subjective appearances, to conscious phenomena. It is about a "reconstruction of the immediate in consciousness."[18] Natorp also calls these conscious givennesses "phenomena." Thus, quite phenomenologically, the reconstructive method is about a recovery of the phenomena of consciousness which are otherwise only objectified. In EP of 1888, Natorp even uses the term "reduction" for this move: "Thus for all spheres" of consciousness, he writes—for instance, "scientific representations as well as unscientific representations such as phantasy, but also the regions of feeling, desiring, willing"—"the same task is posed, [namely,] that of a reduction of the always already and in some way or other objectified representation to the immediate of consciousness."[19]

Before asserting critical questions, one should point out the valid philosophical motivation for this move: In his insistence on the difference between objectifying (constructive) and subjectifying (reconstructive) methods, Natorp clearly intends to preserve the radically different character of subjectivity vis-à-vis the sphere of objectivity. The distinction between subjectivity and objectivity is so strong that it can almost be considered an "ontological difference." It is about doing justice methodologically to "subjective *qualia*" which, if one were to treat them in an objectifying manner, would vanish precisely *in* their qualitative character as the dynamic, concrete life of the subject.[20] It is not so much that Natorp denies *any* access to subjectivity; rather, he merely warns that in *describing* consciousness one is already objectifying it. But this does not mean that consciousness, in its genuine character, cannot be *thematized* altogether; this thematization simply cannot be a *direct* description, but rather must be a reconstruction. It is not descriptive as such, but explanatory: It retroactively explains subjectivity in going back from its objectivations and explaining the specifically subjective moments which were involved in a given objectivation. Whereas objectification is teleological, subjectification is a "reverse teleology": It is a *causal* reconstruction of objectifications.

Hence, "objectivating" and "subjectivating" methods are nothing but opposite movements on an identical line.[21] One can proceed positively and reach the objectivations in construction, or move in the opposite, negative direction in order to "undo" the objectifications into subjective structures. The method of subjectivation is about regaining the dynamic, flowing subjective life *from which* fixed, crystallized objectivations have been constructed. Thus, on the side of objectivation there are *laws,* which are unified and abstract. On the side of subjectivation there are *phenomena,* which are plural and manifold and concrete because they have not been objectified—and these must be preserved as such by the subjective method. Subjective life cannot be directly described but only reconstructively explained. The only "positive" and irreducible structure of consciousness (*Bewußtsein*) that one can discern is the *fact that it has (something) conscious* (*Bewußtheit:* "conscious-ity").[22] This having (something) conscious, Natorp calls subjectivity's fundamental character of "relation" (*Verbindung* or *Relation*). Thus, the fundamental trait of subjectivity is *having (something) conscious,* yet this "something" has always already been objectified. The pure relation of *being-conscious-of,* however, is the original structure of subjectivity into which one cannot further inquire.[23]

Husserl's Critique: Natorp's Reconstructive Method is Blind to Intentionality

Husserl first discusses Natorp's position in the first edition of the *Logical Investigations*. Here he is critical of several points in Natorp's account, most famously that of the "pure ego"—of which, however, Husserl later says that he "has learned to find it."[24] Hence Husserl's rejection of Natorp's notion of the pure ego is a moot point for the Husserl of the *Ideas* of 1913. As he adds in the second edition of the *Logical Investigations* (also 1913), Husserl left this passage (§ 8 of the Fifth Investigation) nearly unchanged for the sake of documenting a historical and (according to him, at least) dated debate—because Husserl, being originally "metaphysics shy" with regard to the question of a pure ego, had allegedly moved on in the intervening years. Thus, what Husserl calls "pure" ego in his early critique of Natorp is nothing but the latter's concept of *Bewußtheit*. The fact of having (something) conscious, Husserl holds (in full agreement with Natorp), has a necessary relation *to whom* something is conscious. Hence, the concept of *Bewußtheit* implies a pure ego as "unifying referential point."[25] This is the only positive discernable moment of subjectivity, but as such, it is empty or indescribable for the reasons mentioned above. Hence it is "pure" of any kind of descriptive content—it is a mere *center* of any conscious relation. In Husserl's reading, this center is nothing that can be "seen" (intuited), but it must be assumed as an idea. If it cannot be intuited, however, its status is highly problematic. Yet, Husserl suggests, if we leave these "metaphysical" questions aside we *can* describe subjective acts—"lived experiences" (*Erlebnisse*)—regardless of how we may *characterize* them. No matter how we determine them within a putative philosophical "system," the fact is we *have* subjective lived experiences and experienced phenomena. Thus, Husserl already at this stage presupposes a certain methodological *epoché*, which leaves aside questions regarding a pure ego (as well as the question of the object of experience) and focuses on that which we experience and describe, the "in-between"— i.e., intentional acts in their *relation* to their fulfillments. The "relation" of *Bewußtheit* that Natorp exposes is, to Husserl, none other than that of *intentionality*—intentional acts and their *fulfillments*.

Hence, Natorp holds that consciousness is fundamentally a relation, while Husserl fleshes out this relation. The fact that relation is the basic character of consciousness does not mean that this relational character cannot be described. To say that consciousness is a relation is far too general; thus Husserl writes in the margin of his copy of Natorp's *Allgemeine Psychologie*:

> Consciousness is not, as in Natorp, as such relation. The fact that all relating occurs *consciously* is not to say that all relation is *within* consciousness.

And further, the ego's relating itself to the object is not to say that consciousness itself is a relation, as if the ego would posit itself in relation to the object, as if it would posit "right" in relation to "left."[26]

Thus, Husserl's point is that relation is not merely a structure *within* (rather than *of*) consciousness as always intending *something*. The character of intentional consciousness is that it relates itself to something, no matter how one wishes to characterize that something (as a meant object, a meaning, a content, etc.); and this relation is not something immediately and evidently seen but can only be known by reflection *on* this relation: "What the *relation* between ego and intentional object (as objective [*gegenständliche*] relation) presupposes, as fundamentally relative, is reflection on the lived-experience and reflection with identification of ego and object."[27] Thus, precisely *in* the process of objectification there are experienced phenomena or appearances and corresponding lived experiences which can be reflectively described *in* the process of experiencing them.

Accordingly, Husserl notes beside a passage in Natorp's *Einleitung in die Psychologie:* "The appearances *before* objectivation are [supposedly] the problem? No, the appearances *of* the objectivations, I would say, are the problem, maybe even the appearances *before,* but first and foremost, especially the appearances *in* the objectivation."[28] In other words, no matter how one characterizes objectivation and its difference vis-à-vis subjectivation, the fact is that even in objectivations there are lived experiences that "have" phenomena, and these can be described, *not* just reconstructively but reflectively precisely *in* the process of constructing objectivity. Thus, Husserl disregards these supposedly "metaphysical" questions of the fundamental character of subjectivity as "relation" and as pure ego, and simply focuses on the phenomena that are seen in reflection. However, in "simply" focusing on the realm of intentionality, Husserl implicitly criticizes the relation to the pure ego as a pointless addition. Instead of reflecting on the relation between *Bewußtheit* and ego—which Natorp himself says cannot be described, and which is therefore an empty notion—Husserl focuses on the relation *of Bewußtheit* itself, i.e., on that which is conscious. The ego is hence to be found "in the object" it intends and, on the level of description, there is nothing wrong with this.

As Konrad Cramer claims, Husserl was very well aware of the theoretical problems with Natorp's construction, and *not* going along with Natorp in this respect was therefore a deliberate decision: "If there should be difficulties with Natorp's theory that cannot be alleviated by means of his own approach; if, furthermore, the reasons for the emergence of these difficulties are representative of a whole tradition of theories of consciousness, then this will protect Husserl's objective conception of ego at least from *that* suspicion that he was theoretically naïve."[29] Husserl purports to be "naïve" in a "positive" sense of focusing on the "things themselves" given in *Bewußtheit,* regardless of any "interpretations" of their ontological or "metaphysical" status.

By thus leaving aside the question of the pure ego—the subjective, essentially opaque "side" of the constructive process—Husserl at the same time avoids the problem of having to describe this subjective side or in general of having to take a position on it. To express it in his later terminology, in the *Logical Investigations* Husserl focuses only on the *progressive* side of the constitutive process (in Natorp's terminology, "construction") of world constitution. And "within" the noetic side there is no place for a pure ego other than perhaps as an idea—a "unitary ego" corresponding to the "unity of the object." But more importantly, this is also about the methodological tools to be employed for describing consciousness—a concept which, at this point in Husserl's development (and as a legacy of Brentano), can be called "consciousness without a subject." The method Husserl employs is that of phenomenological description based on direct evidence: Again, in his later terminology, it is a static description of lived experiences in their intentional "functioning."

This method, Husserl claims, is in no way speculative or indirect (i.e., reconstructive), but is directly based on evidence in phenomenological introspection or reflection. This is to say, Husserl goes along with Natorp's method of construction in his analyses of intentionality, only that Natorp was blind to this very intentionality *in* this process, due to the restriction Natorp placed on describing subjectivity *as* objectifying. Husserl rather focuses on the intentional elements precisely *in* the process of objectification. This description is in no way especially difficult or mysterious: One merely has to avert one's eyes from objects as transcendent and focus on the acts in which objects are given in psychic immanence. This description tacitly employs an *epoché* from the object as transcendent, as well as from a pure ego from which these acts supposedly come forth. In fact, it is in this context that Husserl first introduces the phenomenological reduction, in 1907: The reduction means primarily going back to pure immanence, into a sphere that can be described purely and in evident intuition.[30]

Metaphysical Implications of Natorp's Transcendental Method for Husserl's Transcendental Turn

The "pure ego" that Husserl was able to "find" by 1913 due to his transcendental turn was, of course, the "transcendental subject."[31] This is not the place to reconstruct Husserl's development between 1901 and 1913.[32] But here one can point out some metaphysical implications in Natorp's method to which Husserl was receptive, once he opened up toward "transcendental questions."

Natorp's method of construction was, after all, a *transcendental* method in the sense of tracing the conditions of possibility of the construction of cognition in subjective "deeds." Natorp tried to emphasize this transcendental aspect by directly opposing the methods of objectivation and subjectivation. This move suggested a critique of Cohen's method, as well as implying that not only were the two methods (supposedly) radically opposed, but so were the *domains* or *spheres* to which they pertained—namely, objectivity and subjectivity. We have called this Natorp's "ontological difference." This could be seen by the fact that Natorp denies any direct access and description of subjectivity, because any such description would *nolens volens* revert to the method(s) of objectification. Another way of phrasing this is that the "objectifying" language pertaining to reality and its cognition cannot be applied to a sphere that is utterly different from reality. If subjectivity, in a manner which is indescribable for us, *constructs* reality, then it cannot be of the same *ontological kind* as reality itself. The subject that constructs objectivity is not itself objective but—*transcendental.* Because it is transcendental, it cannot be *described* by means and methods of objectivity. Although Natorp's actual *execution* of a subjectifying method may have serious problems, as Husserl will point out, one can retain the metaphysical implication of his theory. It was this implication that Husserl was shying away from in his first draft of phenomenology as "descriptive psychology."

It is clear that Husserl would be critical of the term "construction." Already in the *Logical Investigations,* however, he does use the term "constitution" to refer to the activities in the sphere of intentional life. One can understand this use of constitution entirely free of metaphysically loaded implications: Objectivities constitute themselves in intentional acts; objects are intended in certain (types of) acts and have their ways of giving themselves or appearing in certain ways of experience. However, a "metaphysical" overtone is inevitable if one *generalizes* this structure—as Husserl indeed does later—to say: Reality *in general* or *as such* (and not just its cognition) is constituted in intentional acts, in the immanence of subjective life. In other words, subjectivity *constitutes* objectivity—and this relation is, furthermore, a *correlation* that is valid for all types of subjective experience: The correlation is *a priori.* This at the same time marks a "fundamental essential difference" between "*being as lived experience* and *being as object*,"[33] and can be termed (as we have also termed it for Natorp) an "ontological" difference. Thus, if one posits a "correlational *a priori*" between constituting subjectivity and constituted objectivity (as the world in which I am also an object), then the question as to the "ontological" status of this "primal" subjectivity arises: That which constitutes the world cannot in itself be a worldly entity. Husserl's transcendental turn can also be interpreted as *admitting* this "metaphysical" consequence of the theory of constitution. To be sure,

(Husserlian) *constitution* is not (Natorpian) *construction,* but both share the idea that the two "regions"—i.e., the constituting and the constituted, the subjective and the objective—are radically different in nature, whether or not one wants to label this difference "ontological." While there are certainly more motives that factor into Husserl's transcendental turn, it is safe to say that it is this "metaphysical" implication that Husserl embraced as he came to characterize his phenomenology as "transcendental idealism." Transcendental idealism means, in the phenomenological sense (which Husserl also calls "constitutive idealism"), that being is only being insofar as it is experienced by a real or ideal subject—and that this subject, insofar as it constitutes being, cannot in itself *be* in the sense of worldly being. This state of affairs is later, in the *Crisis,* treated as the famous "paradox of subjectivity."

Husserl's Method of the Transcendental Reduction as a Reconstruction of the Natural Attitude

Seen from this perspective, it is conceivable that Natorp's idea of methods that are specific to objectivity and subjectivity, respectively, becomes attractive again for the transcendental Husserl. One element of subjective (intentional) analysis that Husserl deems fundamental to this analysis—and which Natorp flatly denies—is *reflection* in order to access this intentional life. This presupposes, however, a primal way of subjective life prior to reflection—a life that is "straightforward" (*geradehin*), that experiences the world and as such constitutes it. The latter is certainly in line with Natorp's idea of the method of objectivating being through construction: The scientist, like any normally living human being—Natorp also speaks of "natural consciousness"[34]—"constructs" reality, yet without any explicit knowledge of the transcendental elements which make this constructing possible, as conditions of possibility *of* construction. In Natorp, all normal execution of life (and not just science, as Cohen would construe it) is objectifying, and thus knows nothing of subjectivity's constructing deeds which would have to be reconstructed. For Husserl, however, simple reflection is already capable of accessing this constructing subjective life in intentional acts. That means, however, that normal life is directed at *objects* and not at the intentional life that *constitutes* them: It lives in a state of blindness with regards to intentional life. As of *Ideas I,* Husserl calls this way of life the *natural attitude.* It is characterized as being unaware of the subjective life that intentionally constitutes reality as it is experienced. This sphere of intentional life can, consequently, only be accessed by a *radical break with the natural attitude.*[35] This break is one key element of the phenomenological reduction. What emerges, hence, is a new attitude—namely, the phenomenological attitude of the philosopher who has broken with the natural attitude. The natural and phenomenological attitudes are thus two absolutely distinct ways of viewing the world: The natural attitude lives in a state of naïveté with regard to constituting intentional life; the phenomenological attitude thematizes precisely this life, and studies how it constitutes the world in which the human being lives *in* the natural attitude.

In short, the transcendental reduction as a break with the natural attitude can be interpreted as a *reconstruction* of how the natural attitude has come to be constituted through intentional life. It reconstructs how it has "happened" that normal human beings encounter the world as "fixed" and "complete" *after* a process in which it has been constituted—a process which, significantly, is never actually brought to a halt but is merely "bracketed" for the sake of investigation. It is clear, however, that this philosophical method must be fundamentally different from the natural attitude. The latter is guided by a certain "metaphysical" belief, namely that the world exists independently of any experiencing subjectivity (and as such, it is a "naïve metaphysics"). Husserl calls this the "general thesis" of the natural attitude. Life in the natural attitude is not itself a method, like the method of a given science. However, it is Husserl's claim that the positive sciences themselves rest on this tacit base of the general thesis—they are "sciences of the natural attitude." That is, they have developed certain "objectifying" methods, but they share with the natural attitude of everyday life a belief in the subject-independent existence of the world. This echoes Natorp's levels of objectification, which begins genetically with everyday quotidian utterance and culminates in the objectifications of scientific judgments. Furthermore, Husserl also sees the need of a wholly different "method" of inquiry into subjectivity after a break with the natural attitude. On the one hand, the thematization of intentional life that has constituted the world—now we can say, the world of the natural attitude—is about describing how precisely this world *in* the natural attitude has arisen *in* and *through* these intentional acts. On the other hand, the term Husserl uses to access this sphere of immanence—namely, "reduction"—already implies that there must also be a genuine method that is adequate to what he also calls the "depth sphere of transcendental life."

It is thus from here that Husserl, after *Ideas,* is in general attracted to Natorp's method of reconstruction. As we shall see, however, Husserl is also critical of a crucial aspect of it, due to the theory of transcendental constitution that he developed in the meantime.

The Reduction Overcomes the Problem of Natorp's Method of Reconstruction

Let us turn back to Natorp briefly. So far, his theory of reconstruction as the method for an *a priori* psychology has remained a sketch. His psychology

reconstructs subjectivity by going back from "fixed" and static objectifications to the dynamic, flowing life that has constructed the former. The
method of reconstruction, thus, goes the *opposite* way of construction; it is
its simple inversion. But so far this is mere theory. How is it actually carried out, and what new element does this *a priori* psychology *add* to the
transcendental method? If it is merely reconstructive and, as such, comes
after the accomplished work of construction, is there anything significant
that this subjectifying method can add to the transcendental method? The
answer is negative. Natorp's *Allgemeine Psychologie* is, as he points out, at
least in the presentation of 1912, merely a sketch—a "foundation of the
foundation" of psychology.[36] But this psychology is never actually carried
out, and for a simple reason—there *remains* essentially nothing to be done.
What can it mean to follow the same constructive path in a negative, reconstructive direction? And what can it mean to "undo" constructions, other
than to point out that subjective life is radically different—namely, in its
dynamic and flowing character—from its objectivations?[37] Indeed, Natorp
conceived of his psychology as "philosophy's last word"[38]—but his attempts
to enunciate this last word lead him to completely modify his method.[39]

As Husserl sees it, however, Natorp's reconstructive attempt is not fundamentally flawed; rather, Natorp's mistake is that he does not carry it through
to the end. It is, as we have seen, Natorp himself who tries to make a case
for the radical difference between the spheres of objectivity and subjectivity.
However, the "panmethodist," as Natorp has been called,[40] does not transfer
this substantive difference to the methodological level. Natorp is rather a
"methodological monist": The methods of construction and reconstruction
are, for him, essentially the same and differ merely in their direction. Had
Natorp acknowledged the *ontological* difference he emphasizes so strongly,
and then accounted for it on the *methodological* level, then the thematic
object of investigation would also by necessity have had to be different as
well. In other words, an ontological dualism stands here against a methodological monism, and this methodological monism was then translated into
an ontological monism, regardless of the fact that Natorp himself insisted
on the radical difference between subject and object.

Husserl's theory of the phenomenological reduction can now be seen to
solve Natorp's dilemma. Instead of presenting a method of subjectivation
and then claiming any analysis of its very subject-matter (namely, subjectivity) as a "no-go," Husserl precisely accounts for the difference between
objectivity and subjectivity on the *methodological* level. This allows Husserl
to avoid the *problem* altogether by shifting to a different level of reflection—
from the natural to the transcendental attitude. If one concedes that a different method of analysis is possible—one which does not take the existence
of the world for granted but studies its constitution in subjective acts—*then*

one can acknowledge that the "structure" (to avoid the term "object") to be studied also is by necessity radically different. However, in keeping with this radical difference, this structure is to be analyzed by a method which is, in equal measure, radically different. Thus Husserl writes in the margin of his copy of Natorp's *Allgemeine Psychologie*:

> The opposition of object-subject that is at play here finds its comprehensive resolution only through the phenomenological reduction, viz., in contrasting the natural attitude—which has givennesses, entities, objects as pregiven—with the transcendental attitude, which goes back to the *ego cogito*, i.e., which passes over to absolute reflection, which posits primal facts and primal cognition, i.e., absolute cognition of possible cognition that has nothing pregiven but that is purely self-having cognition (*sich selbst habendes Erkennen*).[41]

Thus, the distinction between the natural attitude as objectifying intentional tendency *and* the reflective, transcendental attitude which studies the constitution precisely *of* the natural attitude, is Husserl's solution to the problem that Natorp had posed but was himself unable to solve. Acknowledging this difference, however, makes way for a genuine study of subjectivity *as* constituting intentional life. Husserl also calls the way reduction pursues a "regressive analysis" (or simply "regression," *Rückgang*)[42] since it goes back from the "finished," constituted world as it is experienced in the natural attitude to constituting, subjective life.

Let us look at an example of how this works in Husserl, in contrast to Natorp. In Natorp, the objectifying method proceeds teleologically in constructing reality; the reconstructive method, since it is a mere inversion of the former, proceeds causally (although Natorp points out that subjectivity itself is not causally determined).[43] Nevertheless, since both methods are essentially the same, there is no other way in which to reconstruct subjective data than such a causal manner. To Husserl, however, causality is but one way of explaining processes in the world: It is a naturalistic type of explanation in accordance with the methods of the positive sciences (in the "naturalistic attitude"). However, if one concedes that subjective life, seen in its own domain and with the adequate "attitude," is not objective, then one can also apply a different method of analyzing it, the "personalistic attitude": This is where the classical phenomenological distinction between causality and motivation comes into play. Motivation is that type of "causality" which applies specifically to subjective life.[44] A "reduction" to this subjective life by means of attaining a different level of reflection and a subsequent regression into this life allows for an investigation of subjectivity in its true way of functioning, for instance, by using motivational structures as guiding clues.

Consequently, subjectivity is conceived of as a sphere of experience that can only be accessed in its genuine nature by a *break* with the natural attitude, and this entails a break with the *methods* of the natural attitude. Indeed, this break opens up a whole new region of experience in which nothing of the natural attitude is lost, but merely comes to be seen from a radically new perspective: Not the world, but that consciousness which *has* world as its intentional *relatum,* is absolute being. This makes possible what Husserl envisions, with phenomenology, as a universal "transcendental empiricism." Although this would be a *contradictio in adiecto* for a Kantian, it was, ironically, Natorp who first envisioned it, though from his standpoint he was unable to take advantage of its discovery. Whereas the very consequence of Natorp's psychology is to render such a study impossible, it is Husserl who exploits it in his transcendental phenomenology. Interestingly, in his reflections on the idea of a "universal empirical science of consciousness" in 1926—when he had already reached his mature, genetic standpoint—Husserl mentions Natorp's "grand premonition" of such a universal psychology as a laudable exception vis-à-vis all other (!) imperfect attempts at a "pure psychology."[45] Yet Natorp's sketch of a psychology proper—unlike the interesting epistemological reflections that accompanying it—has not, for essential reasons, been able to contribute to any actual psychologically valid insights, while Husserl's has. As Helmut Holzhey sums up his comparison: "Natorp's groundwork of a philosophical psychology supplies us only with modest contributions to a theory of subjectivity, contributions that are oriented to traditional psychological dispositions. Husserl's phenomenological analyses present incomparably richer material and have accordingly, also in the positive science, been more intensely received."[46]

Natorp's Epistemology and Husserl's Phenomenology Form a Correlation

At the outset it was suggested that Husserl's and Natorp's ideas together can yield a richer insight into the nature of subjectivity. With regard to Natorp's psychology, however, we have seen that it is ultimately flawed. The only reason it was worth acknowledging *seemed to be* that it aided Husserl in developing first his concept of transcendental phenomenology as the science of transcendental subjectivity, and then (as we shall see later) in his draft of a genetic phenomenology. One can nevertheless retain an aspect of Natorp's theory which in fact complements Husserl's—a feature which is, indeed, for the most part lacking in Husserl. It is this aspect that can potentially *enhance* Husserl's phenomenology—and it was, in fact, taken up by the late Husserl. (It is worth mentioning that Cassirer took a similar and very fruitful path in his draft of a "philosophy of symbolic forms," in which Natorp's theory was his explicit point of departure.[47]) This aspect is, curiously, Natorp's interpretation of the transcendental method—i.e., the method of objectivation.

As has been shown in preceding sections, the methods of objectivation and subjectivation (or epistemology and psychology) form a correlation. As correlative methods, what they have in common is that they are both to be carried out in a transcendental register. They are both about the "grounding of cognition" in objective and subjective senses, respectively. Given that the psychological method has nothing substantial to contribute to an account of the subject and that, consequently, any "hint" of the subject is only to be found (according to Natorp) *in* its objectivations, then it might be appropriate to call Natorp's objectivating epistemology a "psychology in disguise." After all, it *does* thematize subjectivity—albeit only *ex negativo*, as objectivated in its constructing activities, and primarily with regard to the logical justification of the conditions of possibility of not only scientific but also everyday cognitions.[48] Transcendental epistemology identifies the logical and functional principles at work in cognizing activities and thought-contents[49] of the thinking subject. As mentioned, it is about *fixed* laws of cognition vis-à-vis the *dynamic* life of the subject, or more precisely, the lawfulnesses *in* subjective cognitions. This is why epistemology's task (namely, discerning these laws in the acts of cognition) is primarily linked to construction in the positive sciences and only secondarily to "natural consciousness." But indeed, it is also about the "structures"—which can be called "logical" or "lawful" only in a vague sense—that govern everyday judgments and thoughts. Still very much in the tradition of a formal conception of the *a priori*, Natorp's epistemology thematizes the forms of thinking rather than the actual (intentional) thought processes that phenomenology analyzes—what Scheler famously termed the "material *a priori*."

In this sense one can say that what Natorp provides is, however mediated, nevertheless an account of subjectivity—to be sure, one lacks the concreteness of a direct description of subjectivity that the phenomenological account is capable of. Yet his epistemology thematizes—to use Natorp's term *Bewußtheit*—the basic relational character of consciousness *with regard to the object of cognition*. The relation as such and in its "inner functioning" are not analyzed—that would be an account of intentionality—rather, this objectively oriented epistemology discerns the *a priori* preconditions *of* the processes in intentional acts *in* their objectifying activities, i.e., in their relation to the object. As such, this epistemology takes place within a transcendental framework and remains close to Kant's objective deduction in the B-edition of the *Critique of Pure Reason*.[50] It is a transcendental account of consciousness with regard to the *object* of cognition (and of experience in general), and this object can only be grasped as a fixed entity—the constructed object or law that is constructed by subjective activity. Psychology goes backward, inverting this objectivating tendency, but stops short of delving into the depths of subjectivity—the subject is a pure *a priori* principle and as such an eternally distant, ideal point.[51]

Husserl, however, has shown that it *is* possible to trespass this threshold when one practices the reduction and attains a different perspective from which to analyze subjectivity in its proper nature. In *this* sense, both accounts form a correlation insofar as—in Husserl's terminology—Natorp thematizes the transcendental-*noematic,* Husserl the transcendental-*noetic* aspect of subjectivity. In other words, Natorp's epistemology is not only about a construction or constitution of objectivity in general; it is also a *formal genetic account* of how objectivity has become "constituted" from simple acts up to the highest forms of judgment. Furthermore, this objectivity differentiates itself into distinctive spheres of objectivity; following Kant, it is not only about the constitution of theoretical and scientific cognition, but of "all other regions of objectivation: ethical, aesthetical, and religious."[52]

Although Natorp never carried through with his program, this "noematic" account of the "objectifying" tendency of subjectivity was the starting point for Cassirer's account of the different symbolic forms. It might have also been an inspiration for Husserl's later draft of an ontology of the lifeworld with its different sub-forms (the so-called "special worlds") as ways in which transcendental subjectivity "enworlds" itself—the "worlds" of science, of everyday life, of art, etc. Thus, Husserl also looks at the noematic side of constitution. The transcendental-noetic account proper, on the other hand, is represented in the phenomenological psychology which Husserl also calls "egology," meaning the specifically egoic structures of the acts of the *ego.* It is also concerned with the *cogitatum,* but this *cogitatum* is always already embedded in a sphere of objectivity or, more simply speaking, a sphere of "meaning"—a "world." Constitution is ultimately a constitution of worlds as horizons of meaning, and instead of focusing on the constituting process that forms the world, one can look at the world as a *product* of constitution, and that means, as something that *always already has been* and *is always and at every moment* in time being-constituted. Although Husserl's transcendental method is primarily interested in world-constitution and more specifically in different "spaces of meaning," it is an insight of his late theory of passive genesis that these meaningful contexts have not been constituted by a self; rather they are worlds which a self has been endowed with, and can only be taken-over as given horizons of objectivities. This is to say, "world" is something that is constituted by transcendental subjectivity, but this subjectivity is properly speaking an intersubjectivity embedded in a history of world-constitution.

The methods of Husserl and Natorp thus form a correlation insofar as, on the one hand, Husserl thematizes subjective, constituting activities as the accomplishments (*Leistungen*) of transcendental subjectivity. As constituting intentional acts, they constitute *something*. This something, however, is ultimately a world, which is not something a single subject does by itself but rather an intentional activity that has always already been carried out by a community of subjects, and to which the individual merely contributes. On the other hand, Natorp's method thematizes the objective forms *into which* these accomplishments flow as they construct reality. As objectified constructs, however, they have already formed and become differentiated into spaces of meaning—the spheres of science, ethics, aesthetics, and religion (here Cassirer would add myth and language). These in turn have formed specific formal conditions that need to be adhered to when carrying out specific acts—acts of (scientific) knowledge, ethical acts, etc. These would be transcendental-noematic questions—in a manuscript where Husserl takes this Neo-Kantian position, he calls them "*a posteriori* questions of a 'transcendental' kind"—such as: "What would a *world* have to be like in order for it to be accessible for human cognition?"[53]

The Husserlian account can thus be called phenomenal or even dynamic, whereas the Natorpian account is structural or "functional" (as Cassirer has called it)—both present *two sides* of one coin. Whereas the Husserlian account takes place within egology as a "first philosophy," Natorp's account can be considered (as Husserl would have it) as a "last philosophy."[54] This indicates that such a "last philosophy" is not at all excluded from the horizon of Husserl's philosophy. Rather, Natorp's "last philosophy" points to a sphere of questions which Husserl sensed would have to be answered at some point—spheres which he clearly anticipated.[55] To pursue such a "correlative" transcendental inquiry, then, seems to be a fruitful path of further research, and it shows how Husserl's phenomenological and Natorp's critical accounts can be reconciled, yet also stimulate each other.

Husserl as the Executor of Natorp's Reconstructive Method in Genetic Phenomenology

Let us focus now on the Husserlian method, i.e., on the transcendental-noetic analysis of subjectivity in its intentional process of world-constitution: What has been thematized thus far is an account of subjectivity *insofar as it constitutes world*. As directed at the world, Husserl also calls this type of intentional analysis "progressive." This method as investigating the world-constituting activities of subjective accomplishments is the first and foremost task of phenomenological (as intentional) analysis.

However, it was Natorp who criticized this method as remaining on the level of a "static Platonism," in his review of *Ideas I*.[56] Natorp believed that in this method the transcendental ego was treated like a Platonic, i.e., *static and unchanging* idea, and that Husserl did not consider the human subject in its dynamic and ever-changing character. Instead, Natorp insists that world-constitution is a *genetic* process that proceeds in essential "levels of consciousness."[57] Put on the defensive, Husserl replies to Natorp in a letter of June 1918 to the effect that "already for more than a decade,"[58] he has "overcome the level of static Platonism" and has posed "the idea of transcendental genesis" as the main theme of phenomenology.[59] Indeed, Husserl asserts that analysis of subjective intentional acts—purely in their "progressive" tendency of constituting—grasps merely the uppermost stratum of this intentional life. Subjectivity, however, when seen in its fullest dimensions is a "thick" and dynamic structure, of which a purely static description catches merely an "abstract" layer and not its full "concretion." Although, methodologically, static analysis is the first,[60] one cannot remain there; it is first *for us* but not *for itself,* to employ the Aristotelian distinction. Rather, the phenomenological observer has to delve into the dynamic, genetic depths of subjective life in a *regressive* analysis.

Since this regression is not to be understood in a causal or any other "mundane" manner, it proceeds backward according to the genuine structures of transcendental subjective life. And as such, Husserl's regressive analysis actually goes the "subjectifying" way, and thereby fulfills Natorp's original idea—namely, to actually observe subjective *genesis* from a new standpoint (after the reduction). Husserl himself refers to the Neo-Kantian transcendental method interchangeably as "regressive" and "reconstructive," and claims that the Neo-Kantians (and he means mainly Natorp) never truly understood their own project correctly: "All regressive, 'transcendental' method in the specific sense of regressive—often used by Kant and most prominently preferred in Neo-Kantianism—operates with presuppositions that were never systematically sought for, never scientifically established and, especially, that were not grounded on a pure, transcendental basis."[61]

This regressive move is a "regression to origins, namely a transcendental phenomenological inquiry into the constitution," that is, into the "*origins of objectivity in transcendental subjectivity,* of relative being of objects out of the absolute [. . .] in the sense of consciousness."[62] This regression, however, is a move back to dimensions of transcendental life that lie—genetically as well as logically—*prior* to the acts in the "here and now" viewed in static analysis. It is not simply a regression back to subjective life as such (something that Natorp would reject). Rather, it goes further back and *beyond current* subjective life as witnessed in the "lived present," and back into the passive ("hidden") dimensions of subjectivity—dimensions for which Husserl uses different notions such as latency, the unconscious, "sleeping" subjectivity, etc.[63] This implies that a regressive analysis regresses into spheres that *cannot* be made intuitively evident in the lived present of the subject (for instance, certain past primal institutings). There can be, accordingly, no *direct description* of these spheres, but only a certain explanation or "interpretation." Structurally, one can discern certain eidetic "laws of genesis," but sedimented phenomena *in* this genetic process can only be retroactively explained and consequently interpreted. The phenomenological *Urmethode* of intuition finds its limits in the realm of "passivity." In a remarkable passage, Husserl concedes that actually *all* genetic analysis is based on interpretation; the passage concludes as follows: "This [type of genetic inquiry] is 'interpretation,' but obviously it is not arbitrary, but an unfolding (*Auseinanderwicklung*) of an explicatable intentionality. Or rather, such unwrapping (*Aufwicklung*) is *from the very start* interpretation; and all intentional analysis, all self-clarification (*Selbstverständigung*) of consciousness that finds its expression in 'description,' is interpretation."[64]

What kind of original evidence can this interpretation be based on? If these "depth structures" of subjectivity cannot be accessed directly, but only regressively, and hence cannot described but only explained or interpreted, then the method of making such structures evident can only be a *reconstruction*. Although Husserl prefers the terms "regression" or (as just cited) "interpretation," there can be no doubt that this type of consideration might equally be called a "reconstruction": And Husserl at certain places does indeed use this term.[65] What is at stake, however, is more than a merely terminological issue (to whatever extent Husserl may have adopted a Natorpian term). It is about a *significant modification* or *transformation* of the very principle of phenomenology: It is a tacit acknowledgment that the conception of intuition is too narrow, so that Husserl broadens the scope of phenomenological descriptive analysis by allowing the use of reconstructive or regressive analysis as an interpretation rather than a direct description of intuitively evident phenomena. This is called for because these phenomena in genetic analysis *are* not and cannot be *made* evident in direct intuition. This insight would have been quite foreign to the Husserl of *Ideas I* with its "principle of all principles": "that every originary presentative intuition is a legitimizing source of cognition, that everything originarily (so to speak, in its 'personal' actuality) offered to us in 'intuition' is to be accepted simply as what it is presented as being, *but also only within the limits in which it is presented there*."[66]

As Kern states, this "type of phenomenology"—namely, the type employed in genetic analysis—"Husserl also calls 'explanatory' in opposition to the descriptive character of static [analysis]. 'Explanatory' science to Husserl essentially goes beyond the realm of the intuitive. In this sense, he concedes explicitly a non-intuitive, constructive element for *genetic* phenomenology."[67] To allow "genetic" dimensions to become at all thematic for phenomenological analysis requires a modification of the phenomenological method from a purely descriptive account of static intentionality to a *genetic* dimension of subjectivity based on reconstruction or interpretation. Thus, it was again Husserl who saw the "hidden truth" in Natorp's method, and it was this that he exploited after his turn to genetic phenomenology. Indeed, the regressive or reconstructive method with which Husserl was familiar was *proposed* by Natorp already in texts of the 1880s. Though this proposal was *opposed* by Husserl at the time, yet it is fair to say that he came to know of this option through Natorp, and that it heightened his awareness of the possibility of a genetic dimension of transcendental analysis—a possibility that Natorp proposed in his draft of an *a priori* psychology from the very start.

Husserl did not admit to this methodological shift, and instead presented it as a flowing development. Yet, given his original resistance to Natorp's regressive psychology, this seamless development is not as continuous as Husserl himself presents it. It is no exaggeration to say that Husserl's mature form of philosophy as genetic phenomenology would not have been possible without Natorp's interventions. Husserl might have stayed true to the "letter" of phenomenology in his later work, but in the actual execution of his analyses he overstepped the boundaries which he had previously set himself.

Conclusion

This paper attempted to reconstruct parallels between Natorp's psychology and Husserl's phenomenology with the intent of showing how each influenced the other's attempts to produce a method that would yield a rich account of subjectivity. Husserl and Natorp were on parallel tracks and dealt with similar issues, despite coming from different traditions. Following their philosophical instincts, they were each attempting to reach the "primal concreteness" of the subject. At a certain stage in this continuing discussion, Natorp had a view that was superior in certain respects to Husserl's, because he was willing to consider "metaphysical" questions regarding the ego that Husserl refused to broach. However, as of Husserl's transcendental stage—which was influenced by Natorp—Husserl in turn went beyond Natorp in overcoming the restrictions imposed by Natorp. Indeed, it was the transcendental reduction that "cashed in" on Natorp's wish to have direct access to the life of the subject—a wish which Natorp deemed unrealizable. Moreover, elements of this continual *Auseinandersetzung* then factored into Husserl's late recasting of phenomenology as a genetic analysis of transcendental consciousness. Hence, this comparison should help to highlight some of the important features of each thinker's views and how they influenced one another in their concrete work. It also shows that many insights taken to be "possessions" of phenomenology proper have been inspired in decisive ways by Neo-Kantianism.[68]

Finally, what is at stake in this discussion between Natorp and Husserl—and which still is at the heart of the discussion concerning *phenomenology itself*—is the question of what method is to be employed for an analysis of subjectivity. Largely unacknowledged by Husserl, the deepening of the intuitive by a "reconstructive" method breaks with the methodological paradigm of self-giving evidence which is sometimes believed to be the "holy grail" of phenomenology. Indeed, one can hardly underestimate the importance that this discovery had for Husserl's method, as well as for a reassessment of his phenomenology as a whole. But its importance is also due to the fact that Husserl strove, in the 1920s, to develop a philosophical system inspired by the idealistic thinkers of the first half of the nineteenth century. Whether openly admitted or not, Husserl's genetic phenomenology is influenced by the idea of a "history of self-consciousness" as professed by the German Idealists—a kinship which he dimly felt through his interaction with the Neo-Kantians. And since Husserl came into contact with the *latter* tradition by way of Natorp, a tradition so different from the one in which he came of age philosophically, the present essay intends to contribute no less to reopening a philosophical dialogue between phenomenology and Kantianism in general, than to recovering the dialogue between Husserl and Marburg Neo-Kantianism in particular. If the sketch of a Natorp-Husserl relationship which is provided here is in any way convincing, it should be clear that there are intricately connected and provocative dialogues which philosophers, particularly since the Second World War, have wrongly considered to be concluded.

Appendix: Works of Natorp Studied by Husserl

"Ueber objective und subjective Begründung der Erkenntniss." *Philosophische Monatshefte* 23 (1887): 257–286.
Einleitung in die Psychologie nach kritischer Methode (hereafter EP). Freiburg: Mohr, 1888. (In Husserl's library under the signature: BQ 326.)

Both texts, which appeared at nearly the same time, deal with the same issue of the possibility of a "subjective grounding" of cognition, vis-à-vis Hermann Cohen's critical (constructive) epistemology (the "Transcendental Method"). The 1887 essay is a programmatic text which emphasizes the possibility of a "subjective" direction of transcendental-philosophical research—a possibility that Cohen ruled out.

• Husserl studied both texts in the course of composing *Logical Investigations* (cf. esp. Hua. XIX/2, pp. 372–376).

• New excerpts in 1904 (?) and October 1909 on EP, on the occasion of Natorp's visit to Husserl in Göttingen on 17 October 1909. (Archive signature: K II 4/98–110.)

Allgemeine Psychologie nach kritischer Methode. Erstes Buch: Objekt und Methode der Psychologie (hereafter AP). Tübingen: Mohr/Siebeck, 1912. (Archive signature: BQ 342.)
"Philosophie und Psychologie." *Logos* 4 (1913): 176–202. (Archive signature: SQ 111.)
Originally intended as a new edition of EP (1888), the AP is rather a new work that is roughly three times the length of EP. Some sections, however, are taken over *verbatim* from EP; Husserl marks these passages in the margins of his copy of AP. Again, Natorp's book and article appeared at nearly the same time. His article lays out again the project of a philosophical psychology—a topic with which the AP deals explicitly—in programmatic terms.

• Both texts studied by Husserl in August and September 1918, in Bernau.[69]
• In the winter semester of 1922–1923, Husserl holds a seminar on Natorp's AP (cf. Archive signature N I 26, class notes by the Dutch philosopher H. J. Pos). At this time, Husserl also rereads sections of the EP from 1888, in order to compare Natorp's earlier and later positions on a transcendental psychology.
• H. J. Pos writes an article in reaction to Husserl's seminar, on "the methodological difference between Natorp and Husserl concerning subjectivity": "Het methodisch verschil tusschen Natorp en Husserl inzake der subjektiviteit," *Tijdschrift voor Wijsbegeerte* 19 (1925): 313–330.

NOTES

I would like to extend my gratitude to Christopher Arroyo, Thane M. Naberhaus, and Donn Welton for their valuable comments on earlier versions of this text. A shorter version of this essay was presented at the 33rd Annual Meeting of the International Husserl Circle, Fordham University, New York, June 2003. I would like to thank the conference organizer, John J. Drummond, for giving me the opportunity to present my ideas on that occasion, and all the participants of the meeting who provided me with important feedback. I would also like to thank Ullrich Melle in his capacity as the director of the Husserl Archives in Leuven (Louvain), Belgium, for granting me permission to quote from unpublished material in Husserl's *Nachlass*. Finally, thanks to Celeste Harvey for her help with grammar and style.
  1. See his correspondence with Husserl, published in *Husserliana*-Dok. III/V. (The edition of Husserl's critical writings, the *Husserliana* (The Hague: Kluwer,

1950ff.), will be cited hereafter as "Hua." with volume numbers in Roman and page numbers in Arabic numerals.) Husserl and Natorp as well as their families were on friendly terms. Their later correspondence seemed to center primarily around university business, especially hiring affairs, where both more than once asked for, and trusted, the other's good judgment. For example: One of the reasons for Heidegger's call to Marburg was Husserl's recommendation to Natorp and Natorp's high opinion of what later has been called the "Natorp-Bericht," Heidegger's excerpt on his (never published) work on Aristotle. (Heidegger's "Natorp report" is published as "Phänomenologische Interpretationen zu Aristoteles (Anzeige der hermeneutischen Situation)," in *Dilthey-Jahrbuch* 6 (1989): 235–269.) Natorp and Husserl viewed each other as the most distinguished representatives of the Neo-Kantian and phenomenological movements, respectively. At least up to 1923, Husserl read Natorp's writings time and again (cf. the appendix at the end of this paper) and remembers Natorp's "grand vision" of a philosophical psychology in a manuscript from 1926, cf. Hua. XXXIV, 4. Also, Natorp was an engaged reader of Husserl's publications, wrote penetrating reviews (of *Logical Investigations* and *Ideas I*) and quoted them in his own writings. For an account of Natorp's discussion of Husserl's philosophy, cf. U. Sieg, *Aufstieg und Niedergang des Marburger Neukantianismus. Die Geschichte einer philosophischen Schulgemeinschaft* (Würzburg: Königshausen & Neumann, 1994), esp. pp. 413–416. (All translations in essay and notes, unless otherwise noted, are the author's.)

2. Regarding the relationship between Husserl and Kant as well as Neo-Kantianism, cf. the extensive study dedicated to this topic by I. Kern, *Husserl und Kant. Untersuchung über Husserls Verhältnis zu Kant und zum Neukantianismus = Phaenomenologica* 16 (The Hague: Nijhoff, 1964), to which I shall refer time and again in this chapter.

3. Though Husserl felt, especially in his late Göttingen and Freiburg years, somewhat closer to the Southwest School of Neo-Kantianism—especially to Rickert, whom Husserl succeeded in Freiburg in 1916 (cf. Husserl's lecture *Natur und Geist* of 1927, Hua. XXXII, as well as the highly instructive introduction by M. Weiler)—he was nevertheless over the entire Halle, Göttingen, and Freiburg periods in closest contact with Paul Natorp. It should also be noted that it is striking that Husserl never mentions Hermann Cohen (1842–1918), the perceived head and founder of the Marburg School of Neo-Kantianism and arguably one of the most renowned philosophers in Germany at the turn of the century. This is most likely due to a biographical fact: In his later philosophy, especially after the turn of the century, Cohen had turned to an exploration of the Jewish roots of modern moral philosophy and was an ardent proponent of the project of a Jewish state and the question of preserving the Jewish identity. After his retirement from Marburg, Cohen moved to Berlin where he worked at the Center for the Study of Judaism, where Theodor Herzl also worked (cf. H.-L. Ollig, *Der Neukantianismus,* Stuttgart: Metzler, 1979, 32–34). An irritable man, Cohen despised Jewish converts such as Husserl, who together with his wife was baptized—like many Jews in the (nonetheless quite secular) German *Reich.* Cohen's disdain for Husserl is revealed in a letter to Natorp of 23 August 1914, where he writes: "Der oesterreichische Konvertit ist auch so eine geschwollene

Eitelkeitsfigur, ohne Aufrichtigkeit & Wahrhaftigkeit." "The Austrian convert is also a blown-up figure of vanity, without a sense of honesty and truthfulness." (Quoted in H. Holzhey, *Cohen und Natorp,* vol. 2: *Der Marburger Neukantianismus in Quellen,* Basel and Stuttgart: Schwabe, 1986, 430). Cohen makes this statement in the context of his fight against anti-Semitism *within* the Jewish community, which has to become, he believes, more "positive" (loc. cit.), instead of denying its Jewish origins—as the Husserls had done. According to the late Karl Schuhmann, with whom the author corresponded about this passage, there can be "no doubt" that it is Husserl that Cohen is referring to here. Cf. also Cohen's letter to Natorp of December 1908 (ibid., 369–370), where he warns Natorp of Husserl, and suggests "einige Reserve und nicht vollkommene Vertrauensseligkeit": "some reservation and not complete gullibility."

4. Cf. the account of this split within the phenomenological movement in L. Landgrebe, "Husserls Phänomenologie und die Motive zu ihrer Umbildung," in *Der Weg der Phänomenologie* (Gütersloh: Mohn, 1978), 27–28; cf. also the note on Natorp at loc. cit., footnote 22. In 1929 Heidegger, during the Davos debate with Cassirer, claims that Husserl had "in a certain sense fallen into the arms of the Neo-Kantians between 1900 and 1910." It is interesting that Heidegger dates this influence in the *first* decade of the twentieth century, i.e., before the publication of Husserl's *Ideas I* in 1913, which is usually seen as inaugurating Husserl's transcendental turn. Cf. "Davoser Disputation zwischen Ernst Cassirer und Martin Heidegger," in M. Heidegger, *Kant und das Problem der Metaphysik,* 4th ed. (Frankfurt: Klostermann, 1973), 247. Although one could think that Heidegger's phrasing "falling into the arms" is a bit strong, it is the intention of the present paper to show that Husserl in fact not only came close to Neo-Kantian (or simply Kantian) thought by 1910, but that by 1913 he explicitly embraced this philosophical tendency and came to more and more disregard, sometimes even belittle, his origins in the Brentano circle.

5. I. Kern, *Husserl und Kant. Eine Untersuchung über Husserls Verhältnis zu Kant und zum Neukantnianismus* (The Haag: Nijhoff, 1964); and D. Welton, *The Other Husserl: The Horizons of Transcendental Philosophy* (Bloomington: Indiana University Press, 2000), esp. 443 n. 38.

6. Husserl's background was, of course, in mathematics, and he slowly worked his way into philosophy by way of Brentano's psychology. Natorp's background was partly in mathematics as well, but besides being formally trained as a philosopher, he also held a degree in classics. His scholarship with respect to Greek philosophy, especially Plato, is considered solid and careful, although not unproblematic in respect to its *philosophical* claims. Cf. the second edition (1921) of Natorp's influential *Plato's Theory of Ideas: In Introduction to Idealism* (originally published in 1902), with its famous "Metacritical appendix": ed. with an intro. V. Politis, trans. V. Politis and J. Connolly (Sankt Augustin: Academia, 2004).

7. Hua.-Dok. III/V, 4. Cf. also Husserl's letter to Natorp from June 1918, Hua.-Dok. III/V, 135–138, esp. 137, ll. 9–39.

8. In Husserl's late manuscripts, he deals less and less with any other philosophers and, by the 1930s, with literally none of his contemporaries, except for (as with Heidegger and Scheler) in a polemical context. Another reason for Husserl not

mentioning any Neo-Kantians (e.g., in the *Crisis* of 1936) might be due to the fact that by the mid-1930s Neo-Kantianism can be said to have nearly vanished from the European continent. In terms of influence, the movement had seen its final day as a philosophical school of any importance after 1918 (the end of World War I and the year of Cohen's death) and even more so by 1924 (the year of Natorp's death). For instance, Windelband and Rickert are mentioned in passing in a manuscript of the *Crisis* period, but here in the framework of a dated debate (cf. Hua. VI, 344). In the letter quoted in note 7 (above), from 1925, Husserl calls Neo-Kantianism "*totgesagt*" (moribund), but indicates that Cassirer (and not Nicolai Hartmann, who had inherited Natorp's chair) is one of the only ones that has kept this heritage alive.

9. Cf. the appendix to this essay for an overview of the relevant publications of Natorp's in Husserl's research.

10. For a comparison of the transcendental and the phenomenological methods (esp. Natorp and Husserl), cf. Helmut Holzhey's contribution to the present volume, "Neo-Kantianism and Phenomenology: The Problem of Intuition."

11. Cf. BQ 326, Husserl's copy of *Einleitung in die Psychologie*, title page. Here Husserl writes: "Apriorische Psychologie Korrelat der apriorischen Erkenntnistheorie." The latter is what is discussed above as the method of "objectivation."

12. Cf. Holzhey's essay in the present volume.

13. In including also pre-scientific cognizing as part of constructing activity (of the *fieri* of consciousness), Natorp already goes significantly beyond Cohen's "Marburg paradigm," cf. Sieg, *Aufstieg*, 414: "Vielmehr gelte es [for Natorp], den subjektiven Charakter aller seelischen Phänomene hinreichend zu berücksichtigen. Dies bedeutet eine entscheidende Erweiterung des philosophischen Konzepts der 'Marburger Schule,' die sich bislang ausschließlich mit der objektiven Begründung bereits vorhandener wissenschaftlicher Erkenntnis beschäftigt hatte."

14. AP, 193, emphasis added. Cf. also ibid.: "Dass nun diese Rekonstruktion eine wirkliche und nicht ganz leichte Aufgabe ist, wird gerade dann besonders klar, wenn man sich vergegenwärtigt, wie unmittelbar und unvermerkt die Objektivierung alles [!] Subjektiven sich zu vollziehen pflegt. Schon jede Benennung, jede Fixierung des Blicks, man möchte sagen jeder Fingerzeig, jede noch so entfernt auf ein Erkennen gerichtete Funktion schließt wenigstens den Ansatz, den Versuch einer Objektivierung ein."

15. Cf. AP, chap. 10 (229ff.), where Natorp presents a first "sketch" of this genetic account. The operative term for the levels of *Erkenntnis* is, interestingly, "*Potenz*" (potency), the central notion Schelling uses in his ("reconstructive") history of self-consciousness in, for instance, the *System des transzendentalen Idealismus*. Cf. Husserl's reflections on *Potenz* in the manuscript pages between pages 244 and 245 of BQ 342.

16. This has led K. Cramer to argue that Natorp's theory renders self-consciousness essentially impossible. (Cf. K. Cramer, "'Erlebnis.' Thesen zu Hegels Theorie des Selbstbewusstseins mit Rücksicht auf die Aporien eines Grundbegriffs nachhegelscher Philosophie," in *Hegel-Studien* 11 [Bonn: Bouvier, 1974], 537–603, esp. 556–569.) However, the way the argument proceeds in the present essay hopes to show that the reconstructive method for subjectivity does not *want* to claim any

such accessibility. To *accuse* Natorp of this omission, as Cramer does, is thus to misunderstand his intentions. Rather, Natorp claims that self-consciousness "takes place," "occurs," on a level deeper than that of explicit, objectifying knowledge. What Natorp wants to *preserve*, precisely through this methodological *caveat*, is something like pre-reflexive self-awareness, which is close to Husserl's paradigm of intuition as foundation for the phenomenological method. For an account of pre-reflexive self-awareness from a phenomenological point of view, and a critique of the so-called "Heidelberg School" (of which K. Cramer was part), cf. D. Zahavi, *Self-Awareness and Alterity: A Phenomenological Investigation* (Evanston: Northwestern, 1999), esp. 31–37.

17. Cf. AP, 191.

18. AP, 199.

19. EP, 89.

20. It seems that Nagel's arguments against the "various forms of reductionism— behavioristic, causal, or functionalist," aim at the same intention that Natorp is pursuing in his philosophical psychology (T. Nagel, *The View from Nowhere,* New York and Oxford: Oxford University Press, 1986, 15). This lead cannot be pursued here. For a comparison between Husserl and Nagel, cf. M. Ratcliffe, "Husserl and Nagel on Subjectivity and the Limits of Physical Objectivity," *Continental Philosophy Review* 35 (2002): 353–377.

21. CF AP, 200: "Der zweifache, gleichsam Plus- und Minussinn des Erkenntnisweges, vom Subjektiven zum Objektiven und zurück, entspricht der zweiseitigen Bedingtheit der Erkenntnis, durch die Erscheinung einerseits, den 'Gesichtspunkt' der Einheit des Mannigfaltigen andererseits. Die subjektivierende Erkenntnis deckt sich demnach mit der objektivierenden nach dem ganzen Umfang des zu Erforschenden, aber ist der Richtung nach ihr diametral entgegengesetzt."

22. This is how Dermot Moran translates this term in his *Husserl's Phenomenology: An Introduction* (London and New York: Routledge, 2006).

23. Cf. AP, 24, where Natorp names the three "moments" of subjectivity: (1) the *content* of consciousness, (2) the *ego* which *has* the consciousness, and (3) the *relation* between both, i.e., the *Bewußtheit*, which can best be rendered as "the fact of having (something) conscious," or literally, "conscious-ity." Only this last, however, is the "irreducible" moment in consciousness—and this is the topic of psychology (cf. AP, 27ff., § 3).

24. Hua. XIX/2, 374, footnote.

25. Hua. XIX/2, 372: "einheitlicher Beziehungspunkt." One can question already at this point whether this is a fair reading of Natorp. The pure ego is something Natorp mentions, however, it does not play a significant role in his account. Whereas Husserl's argument shuns any concept of a "pure" ego and focuses instead on what he calls the "empirical" ego, i.e., the ego's actual life as (intentional) experience-of(-something).

26. BQ 342, 27.

27. Ibid., 26.

28. K II 4/104a (Husserl's excerpts from 1904 or, more likely, 1909).

29. K. Cramer, "'Erlebnis,'" 548.

30. Cf. Hua. II, 44. Cf. also ibid., 5: "That which is transcendent (not really [*reell*] immanent) I may not use. For that reason [!] I must perform the *phenomenological reduction;* I must *exclude all that is posited as transcendent*" (trans. L. Hardy).

31. The pure ego is not coextensive with the transcendental ego. In his analysis of the constitution of the ego as person in *Ideas II*, the "pure ego" is the lowest level of egoity in its pure function as "ego pole" and as "radiating center" (*Ausstrahlungszentrum*) of acts (cf. Hua. IV, 97). However, from the way the transcendental ego is introduced in *Ideas I* (cf. Hua. III/1, § 33, 66ff.), it is clear that Husserl in this period uses "pure" and "transcendental" ego nearly interchangeably. Cf. also the insightful passage in ibid. at page 124, where Husserl mentions the difficulties with the "pure ego" and makes a reference to *Ideas II*. It is precisely in this passage where, in the footnote, Husserl makes reference to the discussion with Natorp on the issue of the pure ego. For a support of this reading of pure and transcendental ego, cf. Welton, *The Other Husserl*, 230.

32. A full-scale study has been devoted to this reconstruction by J.-F. Lavigne, *Husserl et la Naissance de la Phénoménologie* (Paris: Presses Universitaires de France, 2002).

33. Hua. III/1, 87. It is in this context that Husserl also uses the term "constitution."

34. AP, 194. The way Natorp describes this "natural consciousness" is incidentally quite similar to Husserl's account of the natural attitude: "Dem natürlichen Bewußtsein gilt es [. . .] als selbstverständlich, daß die Gegenstände zuerst da und gegeben, das Wahrgenommenwerden oder Erscheinen sekundär sei."—"It is a matter of course for natural consciousness that firstly objects are there and given, whereas the being-perceived and the appearing are secondary."

35. I am leaving aside here the question of "normal" and "phenomenological" reflection. When I mention earlier in this passage that "simple reflection" suffices to access intentional life, it certainly does not mean that it suffices in order to thematize subjectivity in its universal dimension after the transcendental reduction. For the latter, a radical reflection and a break with the natural attitude are necessary. For a discussion of this distinction cf. Hua. I, § 15, 71ff.

36. Cf. AP, vi. The published work of 1912 is volume one of a projected two-volume series and as such merely a "*Grundlegung der Grundlegung*" ("grounding of a grounding"). The planned but never completed second volume was to contain the actual execution of psychology under the title "General Phenomenology," although Natorp concedes that he is not sure if he can also lay out the "systematic of the unities of lived experience" (*Systematik der Erlebniseinheiten*) (ibid., vii) in this second part. It is, in other words, the most crucial part of his psychology that he leaves open at this point—and eventually abandons! In general, the *Allgemeine Psychologie* was considered a work of remarkable density, originality, and acumen. It was discussed, apart from members of the Marburg School (for instance, by Cassirer in his *Philosophy of Symbolic Forms*), by representatives of phenomenology and experiential psychology. A. Reinach and L. Binswanger applauded its philosophical quality, though they also pointed out the problematic elements of Natorp's sketch. Cf. Sieg, *Aufstieg und Niedergang*, 416–417.

37. It is not in itself a critique to point out that re-construction is itself a form of

construction, as Heidegger seems to suggest in his critical discussion of Natorp's psychology in his lecture from the *Kriegsnotsemester* 1919. (Cf. *Zur Bestimmung der Philosophie* = GA 56/57, Frankfurt: Klostermann, 1987, 107; cf. also the whole of § 19c, 107–109.) Natorp would immediately concede that reconstruction is constructive, albeit negatively. What is more problematic is what this further implies, i.e., that there is no real difference *on the methodological level* for Natorp's insistence on the difference between subjectivity and objectivity. But this is not Heidegger's point, which is moot for Natorp.

38. Cf. "Philosophie und Psychologie," in *Logos* 2/4 (1913): 176–202, here 202. This formulation already indicates a shift of perspective away from psychology being a mere "parallel" discipline of epistemology.

39. This modification was not so much a giving up of the reconstructive method as it was Natorp abandoning the notion of an invertedness of constructive and reconstructive methods. This led him to a radicalization of the reconstructive method. The change in Natorp's method can already be seen in his review of Bauch's Kant-book of 1918 (cf. footnote 13), and is further carried out in his lectures on "Allgemeine Logik" of 1920 (part of which is published by W. Flach and H. Holzhey, in *Erkenntnistheorie und Logik im Neukantianismus,* Hildesheim: Olms, 1980, 226–269) and in his posthumous works *Vorlesungen über praktische Philosophie* (Erlangen, 1925), and *Philosophische Systematik* (edited from the *Nachlass* by H. Natorp in 1958, and reprinted Hamburg: Meiner, 2000; cf. also the fine introduction by H.-G. Gadamer (ibid., xi–xvii), who was after all a student of Natorp's). Natorp's late development clearly distanced him from Neo-Kantianism in the "classic" sense; for an account of this development cf. J. Stolzenberg, *Ursprung und System. Probleme der Begründung systematischer Philosophie im Werk Hermann Cohens, Paul Natorps und beim frühen Martin Heidegger* (Göttingen: Vandenhoeck & Ruprecht, 1995); as well as C. v. Wolzogen, *Die autonome Relation. Zum Problem der Beziehung im Spätwerk Paul Natorps* (Würzburg: Königshausen & Neumann, 1985). Finally, cf. also Massimo Ferrari's essay in the present volume, "Is Cassirer a Neo-Kantian Methodologically Speaking?"

40. Gadamer has also called him "the most rigorous methodological fanatic of the Marburg school," in his introduction to Natorp's *Philosophische Systematik.*

41. BQ 342, 22: "Der Gegensatz Objekt-Subjekt, der hier überall spielt, findet erst seine verständliche Aufklärung durch die phänomenologische Reduktion bzw. in der Kontrastierung der natürlichen Einstellung, aus der natürlichen Reflexion, die Vorgegebenheiten, Seiendes, Objekte im Voraus hat, und der transzendentalen Einstellung, die auf das *Ego cogito* zurückgeht, also in die absoluten Reflexion übergeht, die die Urtatsachen setzt und Urerkenntnis, also absolute Erkenntnis von möglicher Erkenntnis, die nichts vorgegeben hat, sondern sich selbst habendes Erkennen ist."

42. Cf., e.g., Hua. VII, 382.

43. AP, 209.

44. For Husserl's account of motivation as "fundamental law of the spiritual world," cf. Hua. IV, 211ff. (§§ 54–61).

45. Cf. Hua. XXXIV, 4.

46. Helmut Holzhey, "'Zu den Sachen selbst!' Über das Verhältnis von

Phänomenologie und Neukantianismus," in *Sinn und Erfahrung. Phänomenologische Methoden in den Humanwissenschaften*, ed. M. Herzog and C. F. Graumann (Heidelberg: Springer, 1991), 3–21, here 18.

47. I have tried to show this in greater detail in my "A Phenomenology of Subjective and Objective Spirit: Husserl and Cassirer," *New Yearbook for Phenomenology* 4 (2004).

48. As D. Welton has suggested to me (in electronic correspondence), this may be an interesting application of Kant's principle that the unity of the subject is to be found in the unity of the object; cf. *Critique of Pure Reason*, B 136ff.

49. Cf. the Natorp quotation on page 11 of Holzhey's "Zu den Sachen selbst!," as well as his discussion on pages 11 and 12.

50. Cf. *Critique of Pure Reason*, B 129ff. Natorp himself points out that this distinction is the decisive difference between his own and Husserl's position in his penetrating review of Husserl's *Ideas I*. This review first appeared in 1913, but was reprinted in 1917/1918 (*Logos* VII: 224–246), and again reprinted in *Husserl = Wege der Forschung* XL, ed. H. Noack (Darmstadt: Wissenschaftliche Buchgesellschaft, 1973), 36–60, here 41. Cf. also Sieg's comment to this difference, *Aufstieg und Niedergang*, 414–415.

51. Cf. AP, 199: "'unendlich ferner Punkt'"—"'infinitely distant point.'"

52. AP, 198. In his famous review of Bauch's Kant-book, Natorp defines philosophy as follows: "Ist doch Philosophie überhaupt nichts anderes als das Bewußtsein der zentral begründeten *Einheit*, der *unzerstückten, nie zu zerstückenden Ganzheit* des Kulturlebens."—"Indeed, philosophy is nothing but the consciousness of the centrally founded *unity*, of *the unsevered, never to be severed unity* of cultural life." Cf. "Bruno Bauchs 'Immanuel Kant' und die Fortbildung des Systems des Kritischen Idealismus," in *Kant Studien* 22 (1918): 426–459, here 426, emphasis added.

53. Hua. VII, 383.

54. Hua. VII, 385.

55. In Husserl's discussion of the transcendental and phenomenological methods, he himself presents the two as correlative or at least compatible, although the phenomenological method goes deeper. In this account, the transcendental method as regressing to "logical origins [. . .], leading back to logical beginnings and principles" (Hua. VII, 382), is presented as comparable to the eidetic reduction that calls for a deeper inquiry into the origins *of* these origins—i.e., the *transcendental* reduction. Thus, he goes on: "*These* origins of cognition, the *logical* ones, call for a further regress to origins, namely a transcendental phenomenological inquiry into the constitution of that which is referred to as objective in these principles: the *origins of objectivity in transcendental subjectivity*" (ibid.). Cf. also the discussion of this passage in the following section of the present essay.

56. Natorp compares his and Husserl's methods esp. in his review of *Ideas I*, cf. op. cit., 37–38 and 54ff.

57. Cf. AP, 229ff.

58. Hua.-Dok. III/V, 137.

59. As both Kern and Welton argue, what Husserl had in mind with this retrospective self-interpretation were most likely his analyses of inner time-consciousness,

which Husserl first presented in his lecture course of 1904/1905 (published in Hua. X). This discussion is not crucial for the above train of thought, and hence need not be broached here; cf. Kern, op. cit., 348, and Welton, op. cit., 198ff.

60. Cf. Husserl's reflections in his text on "static and genetic phenomenological method," especially with regard to the question of *Leitfäden* (guiding clues), Hua. XI, 336–345.

61. Hua. VII, 370; cf. the subsequent passage where Husserl reflects on the relation between (his own) progressive and regressive methods.

62. Loc. cit.

63. These concepts are familiar from Husserl's late reflections on the problems of passive genesis, cf. Hua. XI and XV.

64. A VII 13 / 62b. I am indebted to R. Sowa of the Husserl Archives in Leuven for bringing this passage to my attention; it is now published in Hua. XXXIX, 2.

65. Cf. a list of these and more passages in Kern, op. cit., 370–372.

66. Hua. III/1, 43–44 (trans. Kersten), emphasis added.

67. Kern, op. cit., 370.

68. To be sure, there are still many other areas of philosophy where Husserl drew heavily from the Neo-Kantians—and not exclusively from the Marburg School, though I have focused on them here. One would also have to mention Husserl's reflections on the philosophy and theory of science; reflections that he carried out mostly in conversation with the Southwest School of Neo-Kantianism, especially Windelband and Rickert (cf. Hua. XXXII). Finally, Husserl was also heavily influenced by volume 2 of Cassirer's *Philosophy of Symbolic Forms,* which deals with mythical thought.

69. This was—*nota bene*—*after* Husserl penned his *Bernau Manuscripts* on time. The latter were written on the occasion of two visits to Bernau in the Black Forest, in the late summer of 1917 and the spring of 1918 (cf. the editors' elucidations, Hua. XXXIII, xx).

4

The Neo-Kantian Heritage in Gadamer

Jean Grondin

Heidegger [hat] meinen eigenen Denkversuchen nachgesagt, ich hätte die Erstprägung durch meinen Lehrer Natorp nie ganz überwunden. Vielleicht hatte er recht. Auf jeden Fall sollte das nicht nur negativ klingen.

Heidegger made the critical comment about my philosophical endeavors that I never fully overcame the first influence I received from my teacher Paul Natorp. Maybe he was right. At any rate, this shouldn't sound only negative.

—HANS-GEORG GADAMER, 1985

A Neo-Kantian Background and Upbringing before 1923

Hans-Georg Gadamer (1900–2002) was the founder, with Paul Ricœur (1913–2005),[1] of modern-day hermeneutics. As a close pupil of Heidegger he came to view Neo-Kantianism largely through the prism of Heidegger, that is, as a "theory of knowledge" that would follow, as a second-degree reflection, the fact and success of science, of which it would only strive to reconstruct the presuppositions. But Gadamer should have known better.

Before he met Heidegger in 1923, and quickly became a "Heideggerian" of sorts, Gadamer had the privilege of studying with some of the finest Neo-Kantian thinkers of his time, in Breslau (1918–1919) as well as in Marburg (1919–1923). After being lured to philosophy from the field of German studies in 1918 by the largely forgotten Neo-Kantian Eugen Kühneman, he attended for three semesters the lectures of Richard Hönigswald, the leading figure of the "Breslau School" of Neo-Kantianism. When his father, a professor of pharmaceutical chemistry, was named professor in Marburg in 1919, Gadamer followed him and had the opportunity to intensify his philosophical studies with the most heralded Neo-Kantians of his time—studies for which Hönigswald's schooling offered an excellent preparation (as Gadamer reminisced in his 1977 autobiography). In Marburg he had close, indeed intimate contact with Nicolai Hartmann from 1919 to 1923, and beyond. His first publication was a critical essay on Hartmann's *Metaphysics of Knowledge,* penned in 1923.[2] It is on Hartmann's advice that Gadamer submitted his dissertation on Plato to Paul Natorp, a towering figure of the Marburg School of Neo-Kantianism. Hartmann also invited his protégé Gadamer to write a paper for a *Festschrift* for Natorp's seventieth birthday in 1924—incidentally, Natorp died on 17 August of that year—quite an honor for a twenty-four year old.[3]

In a letter to Husserl on 30 November 1922, Natorp expressed his satisfaction with Gadamer's thesis.[4] Submitted at the tender age of twenty-two, this 116-page dissertation was completed quite early, yet not extraordinarily so for the times. (Heidegger, by comparison, completed his doctorate at the age of twenty-three, in 1912.) At that age, Gadamer was still "impressionable," and Heidegger's ascendancy with him would soon confirm this. Nevertheless, before he met Heidegger, Gadamer already enjoyed a more than respectable philosophical upbringing that was marked, if not dominated, by Neo-Kantianism.

In my biography of Gadamer and a few other essays I have focused, to the extent that the sources permit, on the encounters Gadamer had with his Neo-Kantian teachers before he met Heidegger in 1923.[5] New insight into these encounters will certainly become possible when the compilation of Gadamer's *Nachlass* is completed in the *Deutsches Literaturarchiv* in Marbach, in 2010 or so. Earlier letters from and to Gadamer, as well as his student essays, will shed more light on this Neo-Kantian background.

In the present essay, I would like to address the issue from a somewhat different angle. The question I would like to discuss is whether there were any lasting influences of Neo-Kantianism on Gadamer and his hermeneutics as a whole. I will argue that this is the case, even if this heritage remained hidden to a large degree.

A Mostly Hidden Heritage, but Hidden by Gadamer Himself

Gadamer was very generous in acknowledging, in various tributes which were largely written after *Truth and Method,* his admiration for some of his Neo-Kantian teachers, most notably Natorp and Hartmann. But he was far less forthcoming in recognizing their lasting impact on his thought. In an important autobiographical sketch of 1973, he readily dismissed his first essays on Hartmann and his contribution to the Natorp *Festschrift* (1923–1924) as "documents of his immaturity"[6] and "quite impertinent stuff" (*recht vorlautes Zeug*). Nonetheless, some Gadamer scholars have found these essays to be, on the contrary, quite prophetic. His critique of the notion of system in the Natorp *Festschrift,* as well as the notion of a "critical destruction of the philosophical tradition"[7]—obviously borrowed from Heidegger's lecture-courses, which Gadamer was then following—anticipated some intuitions of his later work. Yet the mature Gadamer did not think these essays had that much philosophical value—perhaps because he thought, and wanted his readers to believe, that he only found his philosophical bearings after meeting Heidegger. (And perhaps in the process Gadamer also forgot that his early essays of 1923 and 1924 already carried the traces of his recent encounter with Heidegger.) This could be the reason that Gadamer did not take them up in the edition of his completed works, in ten volumes. (Or "assembled" works: *Gesammelte Werke,* not *Gesamtausgabe.*) Here he even changed his mind, since the original prospectus for his *Gesammelte Werke,* issued by the publisher in January 1985, specifically announced that these essays would be published in the fourth volume: They were not included in that volume when it came out in 1987.

Furthermore, Gadamer was rather selective in what he said about his Neo-Kantian teachers. He alluded to Richard Hönigswald's influence in his self-presentation of 1973,[8] but did not devote any tribute to him in his *Philosophical Apprenticeships,* which are devoted to the great teachers he had. In that volume, Gadamer's tribute to Natorp relates a few anecdotes about the "silence" of which Natorp was capable, but says precious little about a philosophical debt to his thought—to Natorp's Plato-interpretation, more specifically. The same could be said with regard to his tributes to Hartmann.

When Gadamer published *Truth and Method* in 1960, his introduction highlighted three models for his work: Husserl, Dilthey, and Heidegger. Gadamer praised the first for the rigor of his phenomenological descriptions, the second for the breadth of his historical perspective, and the last for combining both. There was no mention of his Neo-Kantian teachers—most of whom, needless to say, also displayed the highest rigor and historical scope. It is thus no surprise that "Neo-Kantianism" was also skipped over in the various historical perspectives the book offered on the evolution of philosophical thought in the twentieth century—though in all fairness, it must be noted that there was little historical interest in Neo-Kantianism back in 1960. Nonetheless, the history of the problem of understanding in the book's second section started with Schleiermacher, Ranke, Droysen, and Dilthey before leaping to Husserl, Count Yorck, and Heidegger's perspective, where Gadamer hailed an "overcoming of the epistemological approach."[9] The perspective that was here expressly "overcome" was that of Dilthey, but one can surmise that the whole Neo-Kantian outlook was also engulfed in this overcoming. Regardless, the fact remains that Neo-Kantian perspectives on the notion of *Verstehen* and on the cultural sciences—say, those of Windelband and Rickert, to whom one could add the names of Max Weber and Ernst Cassirer—were not deemed worthy of consideration. If they had been, one can easily guess that they would have been dismissed because they focused too much on the idea of "method." Heidegger was here, for Gadamer, the great "liberator."

When Gadamer discusses Neo-Kantianism elsewhere, it is mostly to hammer home the point that its "epistemological" perspective was too narrow and needed to be overcome. In his more autobiographical essays and interviews, Gadamer often pointed out that for him the Neo-Kantian stress on "epistemology" was out of touch with the spirit of the times after the First World War. In his eyes, Neo-Kantian professors were pursuing the same kind of academic, meticulous work they had carried on before the war, failing to grasp that the absurd *Materialschlachten* (trench-warfare) of the Great War had shattered the scientific optimism that fueled Neo-Kantianism. What the war had destroyed for Gadamer—and his entire generation— was the idea that science offered the only truth and could lead humanity to a promised land of peace, prosperity, and happiness. The intellectual disorientation that followed the First World War thus attracted young intellectuals to figures that stood outside the "mainstream" of Neo-Kantianism; for instance, to the existentialism of Kierkegaard and the promise of a new realism in phenomenology that Heidegger drew upon, when he spoke of the necessity of a "destruction" of the ontological tradition in order to return to the insurmountable historicity of human existence. It is this new beginning that Gadamer found appealing. Even though Heidegger's own "theory of science" in the introduction to *Being and Time* displayed, for the careful eye, quite a few affinities with Neo-Kantian apriorism, Heidegger promised to do away with the Neo-Kantian obsession with epistemology. There is no question that this was also the perspective that carries Gadamer's conception of twentieth-century thought in *Truth and Method,* and is confirmed in his later autobiographical sketches. In short, Gadamer portrays Neo-Kantianism (1) as a chapter to be overcome, because of its too-narrow focus on epistemology, (2) as an episode in his upbringing that had no lasting impact on his thought, and (3) as a perspective that was successfully blown away by Heidegger's "hermeneutics of existence," whose lead Gadamer claimed to follow.

Given Gadamer's scant references to the influences of Neo-Kantianism on his thought, it is a daunting task to question his self-portrait. But there are some who noticed that Neo-Kantianism left a lasting imprint on Gadamer. And Heidegger was among them.

Herkunft ist Zukunft: Heidegger on the Neo-Kantian Influence in Gadamer

Even now, relatively little is known about what Heidegger thought of Gadamer. The soon to be published correspondence between the two will certainly change that. But there are clear indications that Heidegger believed his pupil did not entirely overcome his Neo-Kantian background. This must have irritated Gadamer to some extent, since he felt that he was indeed following in the footsteps of Heidegger. And this might have led Gadamer to downplay his Neo-Kantian heritage, in *Truth and Method* and elsewhere. Yet Heidegger—who had a strong Neo-Kantian upbringing of his own, with two theses written under the supervision of the Neo-Kantian, Heinrich Rickert—always felt that Gadamer remained at heart a Neo-Kantian.

A hint of this was given by Gadamer himself in a book review published in the *Philosophische Rundschau,* which was quoted at the beginning of this essay. Heidegger, Gadamer said, reproached him for not having overcome his *Erstprägung bei Natorp*—i.e., the first formation he received from Natorp. That is an impression Heidegger had early on, and first impressions being what they are, it lasted. In a letter to Karl Löwith in 1923,[10] Heidegger described Gadamer as "a student of Hartmann," "originally Hönigswald—Natorp—now enthusiastic devotee of Hartmann—in this semester attached to me—well-versed—full of academic gossip—very impressionable." He already viewed him quite critically: "for now, I see nothing at all positive about him," "repeats concepts and propositions—but is just as helpless as his 'master' [Hartmann is intended]. I will certainly intervene if it looks he will do a quick *Habilitation.* Now he is writing a review of Hartmann's *Metaphysics*—he got the ideas from me—until now he has not had the slightest idea of philosophy." The irony, or cruelty, of this letter is that is was written on 23 August 1923, the very day Gadamer left Heidegger's cabin in the Black Forest after having spent nearly four weeks there with his wife (from 29 July to 23 August)! On the one hand, Heidegger had enough respect and affection for Gadamer to invite him to his house for almost a month (!), on the other, he acidly wrote to Löwith that he saw nothing positive about this new pupil who had been a devotee of Hönigswald, Natorp, and Hartmann.

In my biography of Gadamer, I described with some detail the critical distance Heidegger maintained in the Marburg years (1923–1928) toward his pupil Gadamer, who for his part was always eager to prove himself to his master.[11] When his major work *Truth and Method* came out in 1960, Gadamer hoped he had finally proved himself to Heidegger, whom he invited many times to Heidelberg, and had elected to the Heidelberger Academy of Sciences (such honors were rare for Heidegger in Germany, given his involvement with National Socialism). Heidegger had contributed an essay for Gadamer's *Festschrift* in early 1960, but reacted quite icily to *Truth and*

Method itself. Gadamer was somewhat miffed when he initially received no response from his teacher, not even a friendly acknowledgment on receipt of the volume. He first heard of Heidegger's reaction through the French psychoanalyst Jacques Lacan, who told Gadamer of a visit he paid to Heidegger. They had met in a *Weinstube* in Freiburg and while he escorted Lacan to his hotel, Heidegger passed by a bookstore that happened to display Gadamer's book in the shop window. "That is a book you must read," Heidegger said to Lacan. Gadamer was relieved, and intensified his contacts with Heidegger in the following years.

Yet in his judgments to others, Heidegger appeared quite critical of Gadamer. In a letter to Otto Pöggeler in January 1961, he wrote: "You will have seen by now Gadamer's book. When he speaks of the relation of my thought to Husserl, he commits gross mistakes, which can of course only be corrected through a careful philological work."[12] In a later letter, he would bemoan the conclusion of Gadamer's work: "It is indeed curious (or odd, weird: *merkwürdig*) to see how Gadamer takes up the metaphysics of Being at the end of his book without further examination, and understands language as a transcendental determination of Being."[13] One might guess that Heidegger may have detected here a secret Neo-Kantian heritage in his pupil. Otto Pöggeler himself echoed Heidegger's feeling when he wrote to him that he was also taken aback by Gadamer's general cultured "urbanity," confirming the impression Heidegger had garnered in 1923:

"In Chantilly, I experienced something strange. Gadamer also came, having been invited by the *patres* to Chantilly (the *patres* organized the conference in Chantilly). He gave there a *causerie*, that is, he told stories—in French—about his life, from his beginnings with Natorp up to his teaching in Heidelberg. There it dawned upon me—something I had not understood before—why Gadamer looks for such positions such as the presidency of the Hegel Society and why he goes from one conference to the next. It is that he needs such a platform; for him today, philosophical questions are almost no life problems anymore, they are things that have to be developed and about which he has to tell stories in a very cultivated and highly spiritual way. For this, he needs each time his public, and since conferences are his element, he accomplishes astounding things—doesn't shy away from any strain and nothing exhausts him."[14]

Natorp again, and again Heidegger's grumbling about Gadamer's versatility and cultured demeanor. There is no doubt Heidegger associated Neo-Kantianism with this "superficial" sense of culture he found in Gadamer and which he had also encountered in the learned Cassirer.

But on a more fundamental level, was Heidegger right in suspecting that there was a Neo-Kantian heritage in Gadamer? I will argue that he was, by focusing on the following aspects that reveal a more or less tacit Neo-Kantian bent in Gadamer: (1) his interrogation of the "validity claim" of the human sciences, which sounds much more Neo-Kantian than Heideggerian; (2) his reliance on the humanistic tradition to understand this truth claim; (3) the preponderance of the notion of "consciousness" (*Bewußtsein*) which Gadamer retained—much to the ire of Heidegger, who will have suspected a Neo-Kantian bias here; (4) Gadamer's understanding of the history of philosophy as a "history of concepts" (*Begriffsgeschichte*), which aims to replace the "history of problems" (*Problemgeschichte*) of Neo-Kantianism by drawing lessons from Heidegger's conception of *Destruktion;* and (5) his notion that language constitutes the bed-rock of our experience of Being—an idea that Gadamer defends by drawing on (and criticizing) Cassirer, but also Hönigswald and Natorp.

The Validity Claim of the Humanities

To be sure, Gadamer repeatedly assures us that the truth-claim of the humanities cannot be understood through the idea of method, or through this idea alone. Yet the entire inquiry of *Truth and Method* is devoted to the question of the *validity claim* of the human sciences (*Geisteswissenschaften*) that enables them to enjoy scientific respectability. As he puts it on the first page of his book: "In understanding tradition not only are texts understood, but insights are acquired and truths known. But what kind of knowledge and what kind of truth?"[15] Method is not the key, we are told, but what Gadamer seeks is not only a mere description of this truth-experience, but also the ground of its "legitimacy": The following investigations, he states, "are concerned to seek the experience of truth that transcends the domain of scientific method wherever that experience is to be found, *and to enquire into its legitimacy.*"[16] Isn't Gadamer presupposing here something like the "fact" of an experience of truth in the human sciences, just as the Neo-Kantians presupposed the *Faktum der Wissenschaft,* i.e., the validity of scientific knowledge and raised the philosophical question of their legitimacy? The parallels are indeed striking, all the more so since Gadamer did not hesitate, in the foreword to the second edition in 1965, to use a quintessentially Kantian formula to frame the question to which his book was the answer: *Wie ist Verstehen möglich?* "How is understanding possible?"[17] And again he relied on Kant, and silently on his Neo-Kantian teachers, when he asserted that with this question he in no way (that is, no more than Kant) wanted to "prescribe what modern science must do," but only wanted to ask a philosophical question—that is, one of legitimacy or justification.

Certainly, Gadamer often claimed that he wanted to overcome the "epistemological model"—obviously present in the preceding formulations—and to follow the lead of Heidegger by saying that understanding is not a mode of knowing, but more basically a "mode of Being" of human existence.[18] Nonetheless, there are decisive passages and sections in *Truth and Method* where the basic question is framed in clearly epistemological terms, most notably when Gadamer formulates—in a key chapter on prejudices as "conditions of understanding"—"the central and epistemologically fundamental question for a truly historical hermeneutics" as follows: "What is the ground of the legitimacy of prejudices? What distinguishes legitimate prejudices from the countless others which it is the undeniable task of critical reason to overcome?"[19]

This appeal to critical reason as well as this epistemological framing of his fundamental question rings far more Neo-Kantian than Heideggerian. There are thus reasons to believe that the "overcoming of the epistemological question" is not absolute in Gadamer. But one will again notice that explicit references to Neo-Kantians are missing in this context. Heidegger is the preferred reference, yet the question is not always his.

The Reliance on Humanism and Its Notion of Culture

The same can be said of Gadamer's robust "rehabilitation" of the humanist tradition at the outset of *Truth and Method,* in order to address the legitimacy-issue of the humanities. This *rehabilitation* is obviously directed against the disrepute into which the basic tenets of the "humanistic tradition" fell in the wake of the "Kantian" revolution. By this, Gadamer means that notions such as common sense and judgment, which had earlier enjoyed an "epistemological" relevance (i.e., they were understood as sources of truth and guidance), were bereft of their validity when the natural sciences were put forward by Kant as the only reliable form of knowledge. Gadamer detects here a blindness to other modes of knowledge, a one-sidedness that continues to pervade our culture, in that methodical "science" is established as the only mode of knowing. In this downgrading of the epistemological virtue of common sense and judgment, the humanities lose the ground, Gadamer argues, upon which they could establish their claim to knowledge. This claim lies in the fact that the knowledge gained in the human sciences is one that pertains to the culture of good judgment, taste, and indeed, to the education (*Bildung*) of the self. This notion of *Bildung* is obviously crucial: The knowledge of the humanities is less one that yields objectified knowledge of the outside world, than one that serves to build and to cultivate the self. The broadening of horizon that it brings about enables one to call into question one's own limited perspective, thus elevating one into a form of larger, more "universal" knowledge which Gadamer deems specific to the humanities.[20] This is the cultural formation that is achieved by the humanities and that is misconstrued, according to Gadamer, if one understands it from the model of methodical knowledge.

The "rehabilitation" of the humanistic tradition is thus intended against the disfavor into which it fell in light of the methodical conception of science exemplified by the exact sciences of nature. But it can also be seen, albeit through a slight "over-interpretation," as a rehabilitation of the humanistic tradition *against Heidegger.*[21] There is, of course, no ounce of Heidegger-criticism in this section—*Truth and Method* is still very careful about this, fearing perhaps the master's reaction.[22] But it is no secret that Heidegger published a *Letter on Humanism* after the Second World War, in which he expressed his belief that the humanism of the West—i.e., the focus on man as the privileged vantage point from which to understand Being— was responsible for the desolation wrought by the "technological" age. This is an issue that Gadamer does not really discuss in *Truth and Method.* Yet he makes no bones about relying on the tradition of humanism and its idea of culture in order to better understand the contribution of the humanities to the field of knowledge. Gadamer was perhaps (?) unaware of the critical relation of his ideas to Heidegger's destruction of humanism, but it cannot have escaped the notice of Heidegger himself—there was Gadamer again with his cultured humanism!

But what is fascinating to note in the present context is that this defense of cultural knowledge in the humanistic tradition was by no means foreign to the Neo-Kantians themselves (as Heidegger also knew quite well). Indeed, the Neo-Kantians who reflected extensively on the humanities— most notably Windelband, Rickert, and Cassirer, but there were others— strove to establish their relevance as forms of knowledge by heralding precisely their "cultural value" and their contribution to the formation of the human spirit. To be sure, Gadamer did not take fondly to their vocabulary of "cultural values"—Heidegger had made him allergic to this talk of "value" and *Kulturwissenschaften.* But for all intents and purposes, Gadamer's defense of the validity-claim of the humanities by relying on their cultural import was *in re* strikingly similar to that of the Neo-Kantians, who were also aware in many cases—Hönigswald[23] and Cassirer especially—of their debt to the humanistic tradition. Of this, Heidegger was also aware. But Gadamer, yet again, failed to acknowledge this proximity in *Truth and Method.* His pronouncements on Windelband, Rickert, and Cassirer in this context sound quite defensive,[24] but cannot really hide a hidden solidarity in the *Sache.* To be sure, then—another trace of the Neo-Kantian heritage in Gadamer becomes visible.

Sticking to Consciousness (*Bewußtsein*)

Needless to say, Gadamer's *answer* to the "epistemological" question facing the human sciences *did* differ from the one offered by most Neo-Kantians, in that Gadamer tended to downgrade the importance of the "knowing subject" and elevate that of the *Wirkungsgeschichte*, i.e., the effective history in which the subject stands. This is indeed a specific tenet of Gadamer's conception. (Even if one could relate it to the autonomy Neo-Kantians such as Nicolai Hartmann bestowed upon the "history of problems," the *Problemgeschichte*, to which we shall turn shortly.) And this was certainly influenced by Heidegger's stress on the *Seinsgeschick* or "destiny" of Being.

Yet it is striking that Gadamer's key concept here is that of a "*conscience of this historical consciousness*," a *wirkungsgeschichtliches Bewußtsein*—a frighteningly longish notion, even in German. It is however a subtle notion, in that it "fuses" into one concept (1) the idea that one's consciousness is influenced, penetrated, carried by a (more or less opaque) history, and (2) the imperative that one has to develop a consciousness of precisely this being-influenced-by history. This "reflective" consciousness, if one can call it that, amounts to the consciousness that our consciousness is more a "being" than an explicit "consciousness," i.e., that it is not entirely transparent to itself, as most philosophies of consciousness in the idealistic mold would have it. As Gadamer would put it after *Truth and Method*, our consciousness is "more Being than consciousness" (*mehr Sein als Bewußtsein*,[25] echoing a famous word-play by Karl Marx on the German notion of *Bewußtsein*, which literally means a "conscious Being"). But it is precisely of this that one needs to develop a specific consciousness, Gadamer argued.

The aim of this consciousness was unmistakably to "humiliate" consciousness' claim to self-transparency and help it recognize its debt to history (on which the humanities thrive). This decentralization of man—"understanding," Gadamer stated, "is to be thought of less as a subjective act than as a participation (*Einrücken*: implication) in an event of tradition"[26]—was Heideggerian in inspiration, but sticking to the notion of consciousness most certainly was not. It is a notion Heidegger wanted to do away with in his famous destruction of the ontological foundations of modern consciousness. According to Heidegger, man would seek, through this almost "subliminal" notion of consciousness, to escape his own temporality by establishing his understanding as the *fundamentum inconcussum* of all reality. We are not first and foremost *Bewußtsein*, Heidegger said, but *Dasein*—that is, projected for a brief time in the breathtaking event of Being. The far-reaching thesis of the later Heidegger was that the history of the West was marked by a total oblivion of this experience of Being, which the notion of "consciousness" was meant to cover up, as it were. No wonder he was taken aback when he saw that Gadamer held on to *Bewußtsein* at precisely the same moment he appeared to be learning from him. This is perhaps what Heidegger meant when he suggested that Gadamer never surmounted the first formation he received through his Neo-Kantian teachers. In this respect, Gadamer was indeed less "radical"—i.e., less "destructive"—than Heidegger.

From the Neo-Kantian History of Problems to the History of Concepts

Gadamer would claim to follow the inspiration of his master in his recurrent critique of the Neo-Kantian "history of problems" or *Problemgeschichte*.[27] It is well known that the Neo-Kantians were keen observers of the history of "philosophical problems": Cohen, Natorp, Hönigswald, Cassirer, and Hartmann were all first-rate historians who left impressive marks on scholarship, and not only in Kantian studies. Yet they were all wary of the first great theorist of the historical development of philosophical thought: Hegel. That towering idealist had, in their eyes, a misguided tendency to conceive of the history of philosophy as a teleological process leading to his own philosophy. History of philosophy could not be carried out in this manner, they believed, though they nonetheless maintained that the evolution of philosophical thought was necessarily historical.[28] One of the prime examples of this perspective was to be found in Cassirer's impressive four-volume study *Das Erkenntnisproblem,* on the "problem of knowledge" as it evolved throughout the history of philosophy. This outlook had the upshot of bestowing philosophical relevance on the practice of the history of philosophy, which had begun to blossom in the nineteenth century. It was also nourished by the more or less Hegelian presupposition that contemporary philosophy needs to take into account the history of its own problems.

Gadamer encountered this practice of the history of philosophy in the teaching and work of his teachers Natorp, Hönigswald, and Hartmann. Yet he came to view it as a too abstract view of the history of philosophy. The main criticisms he directs against it are (1) that this conception presupposes that there are quasi-eternal questions in the history of philosophy which are treated differently by successive philosophers, and (2) that this *Problemgeschichte* can be objectively described by the contemporary historian, as if he himself did not stand in a historical tradition that affects his very reconstruction of the "classical problems." In Gadamer's opinion, it is naïve to believe that ancient authors confronted the "same" problems we confront. As a case in point, he often alludes to the problem of freedom: The word had a meaning in antiquity, serving to distinguish a slave from a "free citizen," but it was quite a different issue that modern authors associated with it when they believed that the notion of freedom was called into question by the law of causality in modern science. It is pointless, Gadamer argues, to assume one eternal and insoluble problem of freedom throughout the history of philosophy: "The question is: is there such a thing as '*the* problem of freedom'? Is the question of freedom really one and the same for every epoch?"[29] Gadamer unmasks what he sees as a "dogmatization" inherent in the idea that there are eternal philosophical problems.[30] There is only a philosophical problem, Gadamer contends, if one is confronted with an actual question one is truly asking: Every question is thus motivated.[31] By this, Gadamer accomplishes two things: (1) he gives an even more historical bent to the history of philosophy, by stating that it is not marked by the same set of recurring problems; and (2) he insists on the fact that our view of philosophical problems is deeply rooted in our own present: We only recognize problems or questions that are still our own. In so doing, Gadamer historicizes both the object (alleged "problems") and the subject (namely historians) of the history of philosophy.

This critique of *Problemgeschichte* surely stems from Heidegger, who criticized the "eternal" problems of the Neo-Kantians in the name of his own *Destruktion* of the philosophical tradition, a practice of "destruction" that the late Gadamer would claim to make his own, and would try to defend against some of its misconceptions (most notably in his later debate with Derrida). *Destruktion,* Gadamer basically argued, was by no means intended as a negative "destroying," in the sense of annihilation, of the philosophical tradition.[32] Heidegger's aims were only positive, he contended: *Destruktion* is "always a process of criticism directed at concepts that no longer speak to us,"[33] so that it becomes necessary to remove (*de-struere*) the layers (*strues*) that have been added on those ossified concepts in order to return to the "original experiences" concealed behind these layers. *Destruktion* is thus a method that enables one to return to the original meaning of a concept that has been covered up by the tradition. Applied to the history of philosophy, this conception opens the way to what Gadamer called the "history of concepts," the *Begriffsgeschichte,* obviously coined as an alternative to the *Problemgeschichte* of the Neo-Kantians.

What this *Begriffsgeschichte* strives to uncover is the history of the various *usages* of philosophical concepts, by relating them to the living language and questions out of which they sprang. It is indeed a conception of philosophy that Gadamer himself strove to practice. Its critical meaning is clear: There are no eternal "philosophical problems," as the Neo-Kantians believed (perhaps succumbing in this to an unacknowledged Hegelianism); in philosophy one only encounters philosophical concepts that have a history in the sense that they have to be related to the living languages they come from. This is a conception of the history of philosophy, and its concepts, that Gadamer shared with Joachim Ritter and which led to the creation of the famous *Historical Lexicon of Philosophy*—the "Ritter," as it is now known.[34]

The first question one can ask is whether this conception does justice to the full meaning of what Heidegger understood by *Destruktion.* Can Heidegger's undertaking be reduced to *Begriffsgeschichte* in the sense of Gadamer? This is by no means certain. One gets this impression because Gadamer strongly tends to minimize the "destructive" aspects of Heideggerian *Destruktion,* when he claims that it was only intended as a shaking-up of hardened concepts that need to be translated into fluid language. Yet when one reads *Being and Time,* it is obvious that *Destruktion* was aimed at the "history of the ontological tradition" in order to lay bare the "ontological prejudices" that commanded it—for instance, an unquestioned understanding of Being as presence could be "deconstructed," as it were, as an inauthentic mode of understanding. This presupposed, in turn, that there was a more authentic understanding of Being to be had. This sense of *Destruktion* is toned down by Gadamer. For Heidegger, there was always more to *Destruktion* than mere *Begriffsgeschichte* as a means of doing the history of philosophy.

Secondly, one can also question whether Gadamer's *Begriffsgeschichte* is so foreign to the Neo-Kantian *Problemgeschichte* after all. There is no doubt that there are no "eternal" free-floating problems for Gadamer, since all concepts are rooted in language. But Gadamer does retain the idea that there is in the course of history something like an autonomous and continuous development of problems, independently of the authors who treated them. This is one of the basic tenets of his notion of *Wirkungsgeschichte,* according to which we always stand in a stream of tradition of which we are more or less aware. Does not the "autonomy" and relative "stability" of *Wirkungsgeschichte* parallel the autonomous *Problemgeschichte* of the Neo-Kantians?

Furthermore, it can be argued that the Neo-Kantians were no less aware than Gadamer, that every *Problem-* or *Begriffsgeschichte* has to be written anew from the vantage point of the present. It indeed functions as the necessary historical recapitulation that has to precede every philosophical treatment of an issue (be it called a "problem" or a "concept," and the difference here is also very thin). The stress on language is perhaps more peculiar, yet by no means exclusive to Gadamer. But one will note in this regard that Gadamer does not speak of the history of philosophical *words,* but of philosophical *concepts.* That the way of philosophy is that of the concept was a strong Neo-Kantian conviction. So in this too, Gadamer may have been closer to Neo-Kantianism than he was willing to admit.

Language as the Unfolding of Being

The last section of *Truth and Method* is devoted to the issue of language as the fundamental "element" or "medium" of hermeneutical experience. It is also in this section of the book that Gadamer alludes to the Neo-Kantians more frequently than elsewhere—as could hardly be avoided, given the attention they bestowed on the subject. This was the case with Hönigswald, one of the great precursors of the philosophy of language, but in this respect largely forgotten. His momentous book *Philosophie und Sprache* had the bad fortune to appear in 1937 (in Basel), at a time when he was about to leave Germany and a Jewish thinker of his stature was a *persona non grata* in his homeland. It was widely ignored after the war, when Heidegger all but dominated the philosophical landscape, but Gadamer graciously quoted this work by Hönigswald in *Truth and Method*,[35] as well as Cassirer's better-known works on language as a "symbolic form." It is no surprise that Neo-Kantian thinkers should be interested in language, since Kant in his "Copernician revolution" set forth the thesis that the way the world is viewed and constituted depends on the way we categorize it. For Kant, this took place through our *a priori* concepts, but his Neo-Kantian followers had no difficulty in applying his intuitions to the schematizing function of language: Our view of the world is invariably framed by language, the *a priori* of understanding.

This is a thesis Gadamer *appears* to make his own when he states that language determines, in a fundamental fashion, the hermeneutical act of understanding—i.e., when he states that there is no understanding without some form of language. But while asserting this seemingly Neo-Kantian thesis, Gadamer develops a *critique* of the Neo-Kantian conception of language—that of Cassirer, more specifically. The Neo-Kantians, he argues, are certainly right in recognizing that language determines our worldview, but this conception risks reducing language to a "subjective power" or a "form" that only shapes our view of things. Language is far more than that, according to Gadamer: It is not only a subjective scheme imposed upon the world from the outside; it describes the way the world *is* and presents itself. The restriction of language, by Cassirer, to a mere "symbolic form" thus constitutes for Gadamer "an abstraction that has to be thoroughly rectified for our purposes."—"Verbal form and the content that is transmitted cannot be separated in the hermeneutical experience."[36]

Gadamer's notion of language can indeed only be understood as a correction of Cassirer's conception, which he deems too subjectivist, tied as it is to the notion of a "spiritual power" of intelligence that would be content with putting the matter of experience into form. Against this subjectivist view, Gadamer defends a further-reaching thesis which has seldom been fully understood: Language is not only the form of our understanding, it is also the unfolding of Being itself.[37] The linguistic presentation of the world is not to be misunderstood as our subjectivist input in the world, it is rather the world that presents itself in the light of language. To establish this, Gadamer draws upon the medieval metaphysics of Being (Heidegger saw this perfectly in his above-quoted letter to Pöggeler) according to which Being, Beauty, and Truth are "transcendentals," that is, universal *predicates of Being* as such. This is relevant for hermeneutics, Gadamer argues, because we have to cease viewing truth, language, and being as notions that are "created" by the human mind. Rather, he contends, these notions relate to and stem from the things themselves. If the metaphysics of the transcendental notions of Being is useful in this context, it is because "it conceives *knowledge as an element of being itself* and not primarily as an activity of the subject. That knowledge is *incorporated in Being* is the presupposition of all classical and medieval thought."[38] Knowledge is incorporated in Being? This means that knowledge does not stand *in front* of Being, that it would strive to conceptualize through its subjective notions. No, language is already the unfolding of Being itself. At the end of *Truth and Method*, Gadamer illustrates this point through the seldom noticed example of the poem and its "ontological" implications. When a poem says something, it lets us take part in a truly ontological experience of what is.[39] In the best of cases, we are so taken by what is "said," that we don't even notice the words: The thing is so present! It is in this way that the world we experience is language.

In his letter to Pöggeler, Heidegger appeared puzzled by this reference to the medieval *Seinsmetaphysik* that Gadamer would have taken over *ungeprüft*, "without further ado." Heidegger had good reason to be, since this was not a perfectly Heideggerian insight Gadamer was espousing. It could very well be that Gadamer was also following here, albeit silently, some of his Neo-Kantian masters and most specifically Paul Natorp's later philosophy. This is a point that has recently been made, most convincingly, by Jürgen Stolzenberg.[40] In late essays of 1993, Gadamer himself recognized that the "late Natorp finally, finally thought he had found the real key of our experience in language."[41] In his *Philosophical Systematics* of 1922, which the young and brash Gadamer probably wanted to criticize in his piece on "The Notion of System in Philosophy" in the Natorp *Festschrift* of 1924, Natorp is looking for the ultimate foundation of our experience, which he finds in the fact that our *Verstehen* (understanding) experiences the world as an event of meaning that occurs through the "mystery of language."[42] (This last is Natorp's expression.) Language thus gains a fundamental status in that it reveals that the world is already fraught through and through with meaning. It is the world that is meaningful, yet this meaningfulness only appears through the mystery of language and our understanding. Stolzenberg rightly speaks here of Natorp's (and Gadamer's) "hermeneutically grounded ontology": The self-presentation of Being occurs in the immemorial mystery of language. Both Gadamer and Natorp would share a common conviction about the "speculative nature of language": What language "reflects" (*speculare*) is Being itself, but this reflection is not a mere reduplication of what is, since "what is" only comes to the fore in language, thus hinting at a meaning of Being that precedes subjectivity.

This "hermeneutically grounded ontology" was also perceivable in Natorp's late reading of Plato. The rationality that the philosopher Plato wants to uncover is not a subjective bestowing of meaning upon a senseless matter, it is the rationality of the world, the *Hen kai pan* ("the One through the Many") that is already a characteristic of the world, even if it only shines through in the intelligence of our *logos*. Indeed, the notion of *logos*—present in the very title of Natorp's 1920 "Metacritical Appendix" to his earlier book on Plato[43]—is a precious reminder of this in that it alludes first and foremost to the secret rationality of the world itself, yet *at the same time* to our understanding and linguistic experience of this world.

This "shining through" of the meaning of the world in our language is certainly what seduced Gadamer in the *Seinsmetaphysik*, the metaphysics of Being of the Middle Ages, which was also a *Lichtmetaphysik*, a metaphysics of light: What shines forth through the light of language is the nature of Being itself. Small wonder then that Heidegger, who insisted more willingly on the self-concealing of Being, was amazed by Gadamer's sudden appropriation of this *Seinsmetaphysik* at the end of *Truth and Method*. But perhaps it was not so sudden after all. It was prepared by Gadamer's tacit dialogue with his great teacher Paul Natorp, whose early influence, as Heidegger surmised, he never entirely overcame. And as Gadamer suggested in 1985, perhaps Natorp's lasting influence on him was not such a bad thing.

NOTES

The epigraph is from H.-G. Gadamer, "Book Review of C. von Wolzogen, *Die autonome Relation. Zum Problem der Beziehung im Spätwerk Paul Natorps, 1984*," *Philosophische Rundschau* 32 (1985): 160.

1. On the important differences between Gadamer's and Ricœur's conceptions of hermeneutics, see my recent piece "De Gadamer à Ricœur. Peut-on parler d'une conception commune de l'herméneutique?," in G. Fiasse, ed., *Paul Ricœur: De l'homme faillible à l'homme capable* (Paris: Presses Universitaires de France, 2008), 37–62.

2. H.-G. Gadamer, *Metaphysik der Erkenntnis. Zu dem gleichnamigen Buch von Nicolai Hartmann*, in *Logos* 12 (1923/24): 340–359.

3. H.-G. Gadamer, "Zur Systemidee in der Philosophie," *Festschrift für Paul Natorp* (Berlin/Leipzig, 1924), 55–75.

4. E. Husserl, *Briefwechsel*, vol. 5 (Boston/London: Dordrecht, 1994), 161.

5. See J. Grondin, *Hans-Georg Gadamer: A Biography* (New Haven: Yale University Press, 2003); "Gadamer vor Heidegger," in *Internationale Zeitschrift für Philosophie* (1996): 197–226; "Der junge Gadamer und Richard Hönigswald," in W. Schmied-Kowarzik, ed., *Erkenntnis—Monas—Sprache. Internationales Richard-Hönigswald-Symposion Kassel 1995*, Studien und Materialien zum Neukantianismus, vol. 9 (Würzburg: Königshausen & Neumann, 1997), 159–170.

6. H.-G. Gadamer, *Selbstdarstellung*, in H.-G. Gadamer (hereafter, HGG), *Gesammelte Werke* (hereafter, *GW*), vol. 2 (Tübingen: Mohr Siebeck, 1986), 48; translated as "Reflections on my Philosophical Journey," in L. E. Hahn, ed., *The Philosophy of Hans-Georg Gadamer* (Chicago and LaSalle: Open Court, 1997), 7.

7. Textually in HGG, *Metaphysik der Erkenntnis. Zu dem gleichnamigen Buch von Nicolai Hartmann*, in *Logos* 12 (1923/24): 350.

8. Loc. cit.

9. An "epistemological" approach he already criticized in Gadamer's early Hartmann review (*Metaphysik der Erkenntnis*, 357). One can suspect here an early, indeed immediate Heideggerian influence.

10. Quoted in Grondin, *Hans-Georg Gadamer: A Biography*, 109–110.

11. This is confirmed in the precious recent recollections by K. K. Cho, "The Way of Philosophy as *Paideia*: Heidegger and His Two Disciples in Heidelberg," in *Philosophy and Culture* 1: Comparative Thinking (May 2007): 1–39.

12. Letter of Martin Heidegger to Otto Pöggeler of 7 January 7 1961 (quoted from *Martin Heidegger/Otto Pöggeler Briefwechsel 1957–1976*, K. Busch and C. Jamme, eds., forthcoming): "*Sie werden inzwischen Gadamers Buch auch schon gesehen haben. Was das Verhältnis meines Denkens zu Husserl betrifft, sind einige grobe Irrtümer unterlaufen, die freilich nur durch sorgfältige philolog. Arbeit beseitigt werden können.*"

13. Letter of Martin Heidegger to Otto Pöggeler of 11 January 1962 (ibid.): "*Merkwürdig is ja auch, wie Gadamer am Schluss seines Buches die Seinsmetaphysik ungeprüft aufgreift, die Sprache als eine transzendentale Bestimmung des Seins fasst.*"

14. Letter of Otto Pöggeler to Martin Heidegger of 28 December 1964 (ibid.): "*In Chantilly erlebte ich noch etwas Seltsames. Gadamer kam auf die Einladung der Patres hin auch nach Chantilly (die Patres hatten die Tagung in Royaumont organisiert). Er gab dort eine Causerie, d.h. er erzählte—auf Französisch—aus seinem Leben, von den Anfängen bei Natorp bis zu seiner Heidelberger Tätigkeit. Hier ging mir zum ersten Male auf, was ich bisher nicht verstanden hatte—warum Gadamer solche Ämter wie das eines Präsidenten der Hegelvereinigung sucht und warum er Tagung auf Tagung absolviert. Er braucht eben eine solche Plattform; philosophische Fragen sind für ihn heute kaum noch Lebensprobleme, sondern etwas, was ausgearbeitet wird und wovon er dann auch in sehr gebildeter und höchst geistreicher Weise erzählen muss. Dafür braucht er dann auch jeweils sein Publikum, und weil er auf Tagungen in seinem Element ist, leistet er Erstaunliches, scheut er keine Strapazen, ermüdet ihn nichts.*"

15. HGG, *Truth and Method*, 2nd rev. ed., trans. J. Weinsheimer and D. G. Marshall (New York: Crossroad, 1989), xxi.

16. Ibid., xxii (my emphasis).

17. Ibid., xxx.

18. Ibid.

19. Ibid., 277 (modified translation: Gadamer speaks of the *zentrale, erkenntnistheoretische Grundfrage* and not only of the "fundamental epistemological question," as the translation, albeit elegantly, puts it). Since my sole purpose here is to point out a possible Neo-Kantian heritage, I will not discuss the soundness of Gadamer's

answer to this question—i.e., the problematical appeal to the "sorting-out" function of "temporal distance"—which I discuss and criticize in J. Grondin, *The Philosophy of Gadamer* (London: Acumen, 2002), 84–90.

20. Ibid., 17: "This is what, following Hegel, we emphasized as the general characteristic of *Bildung:* keeping oneself open to what is other—to other, more universal points of view. It embraces a sense of proportion and distance in relation to itself, and hence consists in rising above itself to universality." On this notion of *Bildung,* see my essay "Gadamers ungewisses Erbe," in G. Abel, ed., *Kreativität. XX. Deutscher Kongress für Philosophie. Kolloquiumsbeiträge* (Hamburg: Meiner Verlag, 2006), 205–215.

21. See my "Gadamer on Humanism," in L. E. Hahn, ed., *The Philosophy of Hans-Georg Gadamer* (1997), 157–170.

22. This will change after the death of Heidegger, but also after Habermas' important 1979 lecture on "Gadamer's urbanization of the Heideggerian province." From that point on, Gadamer will be more keen on highlighting what distinguishes his approach from that of Heidegger.

23. Compare R. Hönigswald, *Die Philosophie von der Renaissance bis Kant* (Berlin-Leipzig: De Gruyter, 1923); *Die Renaissance in der Philosophie* (München: Reinhardt, 1931); and *Denker der italienischen Renaissance* (Basel: Falken, 1938); as well as E. Cassirer, *Individuum und Cosmos in der Philosophie der Renaissance* (Berlin: Teubner, 1927, repr. Darmstadt: Wissenschaftliche Buchgesellschaft, 1987), now in Cassirer's *Gesammelte Werke,* vol. 14 (Hamburg: Meiner, 2002).

24. E.g., *Truth and Method,* xxix: "Nor did I propose to revive the ancient dispute on method between the natural and the human sciences. It is hardly a question of different methods. To this extent, Windelband and Rickert's question concerning the 'limits of concept formation in the natural sciences' seems to me misconceived. The difference that confronts us is not only in the method but in the objectives of knowledge." Windelband and Rickert would certainly agree that there was *also* a difference in the objectives of knowledge.

25. *GW* 2, 10, 247; *GW* 4, 346.

26. *Truth and Method,* 290.

27. See, e.g., Gadamer's piece on *Begriffsgeschichte als Philosophie* (1970) in *GW* 2, 77–91; and the more recent *Die Philosophie und ihre Geschichte* (1998), in HGG, *Hermeneutische Entwürfe* (Tübingen: Mohr Siebeck, 2000), 69–96.

28. The last presentation of this differentiated conception was offered by Nicolai Hartmann, *Der philosophische Gedanke und seine Geschichte* (Berlin: Verlag der Akademie der Wissenschaften 1936; repr. Stuttgart: Reclam, 1977).

29. *GW* 2, 82.

30. Ibid.

31. Ibid.

32. See Gadamer's three essays on *Destruktion* in D. P. Michelfelder and R. E. Palmer, eds., *Dialogue and Deconstruction: The Gadamer-Derrida Encounter* (Albany: SUNY Press, 1989).

33. Ibid., 99.

34. J. Ritter, ed., *Historisches Wörterbuch der Philosophie,* 13 vols. (Basel: Schwabe

Verlag, 1971–2007). This edition was completed when the twelfth and last volume appeared in 2005; the thirteenth volume, which appeared in 2007, is an index. It has recently been revealed that Gadamer was originally tapped as a co-editor of this famed historical lexicon. See M. Kranz, "Gelehrte Geschäfte. Warum Hans-Georg Gadamer nicht Herausgaber des *Historischen Wörterbuchs der Philosophie* wurde," *Zeitschrift für Ideengeschichte* 2 (2008): 95–111, which draws on the unpublished correspondence between Ritter and Gadamer and explains the prosaic reason why Gadamer did not become an editor in the end: his financial demands were too high. See also A. Cammann, "Die Wahrheit will Methode haben," in *Frankfurter Allgemeine Zeitung,* 10 December 2008.

35. *Truth and Method,* 404 (*GW* 1, 408).

36. *Truth and Method,* 441 (*GW* 1, 445).

37. See J. Grondin, "La thèse de l'herméneutique sur l'être," *Revue de métaphysique et de morale* 2006 (no. 4), 469–481.

38. *Truth and Method,* 458 (*GW* 1, 462).

39. *Truth and Method,* 489 (*GW* 1, 493): "In a Poem, the coming to language that occurs is like a participation in relations of order [i.e., in an order of Being] through which the 'truth' of what is said is supported and guaranteed."

40. See his "Hermeneutik und Letztbegründung. Hans-Georg Gadamer und der späte Natorp," in I. M. Fehér, ed., *Kunst, Hermeneutik, Philosophie: Das Denken Hans-Georg Gadamers im Zusammenhang des 20. Jahrhunderts* (Heidelberg: Universitätsverlag Winter, 2003), 63–74.

41. *GW* 8, 401, 431 (quoted by J. Stolzenberg, op. cit., 64).

42. Quoted by J. Stolzenberg, op. cit., 67.

43. P. Natorp, "*Logos—Psyche—Eros,*" *Metakritischer Anhang* (1920), in *Platos Ideenlehre. Eine Einführung in den Idealismus* (1st ed., 1903; 2d ed., 1921) (Hamburg: Felix Meiner Verlag, 1961), 457–513.

PART 2

The Nature of Transcendental Philosophy

Interpreting Kant Correctly:
On the Kant of the Neo-Kantians

Manfred Kühn

The Question of Kant and the Rise of Neo-Kantianism

Immanuel Kant was without any doubt the most important philosopher of the eighteenth century. Furthermore, the old adage that one may philosophize with Kant or against him, but that one cannot philosophize without him seems to be as true as ever. This is so even if some contemporary philosophers, such as Richard Rorty, who would like to set aside "the notions of 'foundations of knowledge' and of philosophy," as "revolving around the Cartesian attempt to answer the epistemological skeptic," also want to set aside Kant. Rorty has tried to persuade us that a "post-Kantian" culture is possible and desirable, and that we need to "see philosophy neither as achieving success by 'answering the skeptic,' nor as rendered nugatory by realizing that there is no skeptical case to be answered. The story is more complicated"—but we do not, he assures us, have to go down the road of Kant (and Hume).[1] Perhaps this is an option. Or perhaps Rorty's easy pragmatism is a form of anti-Kantianism that takes neither Kant nor philosophy seriously. That, in any case, is how I would characterize it.

But regardless of whether Kant is avoidable, Rorty is not the first—nor will he be the last—to try to avoid him. Toward the end of the eighteenth century there were many who felt that it was necessary to "go beyond Kant." This call was so acute that Kant felt it necessary to state unequivocally on 7 August 1799, with regard to Fichte's *Wissenschaftslehre*, that all such recent philosophical developments had little to do with his own critical philosophy. Kant wrote that Fichte's "*Theory of Science* was a totally indefensible system," and that he was very much "opposed to metaphysics as defined by Fichte." He urged philosophers not to go "beyond" his critical philosophy, but to take him at his word. This appeal was not heeded, and philosophy took a decisive turn away from Kant in the works of Fichte, Schelling, Hegel, and those who followed them.

The philosophical situation changed again, however, with the rise of a new philosophical orientation that is usually described as "Neo-Kantianism." Klaus-Christian Köhnke has done much to show how this new movement was really the result of a slowly emerging confluence of many "heterogeneous currents," in which none of the "active participants" initially understood themselves to be part of a "comprehensive movement."[2] Notwithstanding this, Otto Liebmann's *Kant and the Epigoni* of 1865 remains a good starting point for any description of the movement, and it certainly marks the time when unwitting participants in the movement became conscious of the fact that they were "Neo-Kantians"—i.e., thinkers who felt that it was necessary to return to Kant.[3] Liebmann attacked Fichte, Schelling, Hegel, Schopenhauer, and their successors as speculative dogmatists; his motto was "Back to Kant." He believed that the fundamental ideas of Kant's transcendental philosophy were true, and he argued that it is important to understand the spirit of Kant's philosophy in order that we may continue to develop it. But this said, he did not follow Kant slavishly.

For Liebmann, the notion of pure experience is nothing but a prejudice. Experience must be understood as dependent on transcendental conditions. Indeed, he argued that the "original fact" of consciousness forms the basis of any science and its object. Arguing against Darwin's notion of a life force, he claimed that this "life force" is not an *a priori* concept but a gap in our conceptual framework (*Begriffslücke*) that must ultimately remain a riddle to us. Put differently, Liebmann understood reason in a rather un-Kantian way as a product of nature, and argued in an even less Kantian fashion that there must be something analogous to reason in nature itself. He also rejected Kant's notion of the "thing-in-itself" as something that is non-spatial and lies behind or beyond appearance. In this regard, Liebmann writes that the

"thing-in-itself" haunted the minds of all the epigones. To the idealists it was "absolute ego, universal ego, the absolute, [or] absolute spirit" and was known to intellectual intuition or evolved in dialectical trichotomies; with Herbart it appeared as a multiplicity of spaceless realities . . . with Fries it was the object of "a speculative faith," with Schopenhauer it was the transcendental will . . . in fact, it is in the end a dogmatic chimera which is not entitled to lead even a pseudo-existence in words . . . So away with it.[4]

Even in this divergence from Kant, Liebmann's *Kant und die Epigonen* was very important for the further development of the Neo-Kantian movement. The Neo-Kantians "all reject[ed] the unknowable ground of experience. The notorious thing-in-itself."[5]

Wilhelm Windelband characterized Liebmann not only as one of the most outstanding thinkers of the second half of the nineteenth century, but also—despite his disagreements with Kant—as "the most faithful of all Kantians." If this is faithful, one might well wonder what is unfaithful. Though Liebmann claimed that he was going "Back to Kant," it was clearly not the historical Kant to which he returned. The same is true of all the other Neo-Kantians: Their relationship to Kant was rather "loose," and thus their common philosophical outlook, insofar as it exists, cannot be reduced to this relationship.[6] Indeed, one might justifiably argue that the question "Which Kant do you take yourself to be 'returning to' or 'going back to'?" does not go to the central core of their philosophical convictions.[7] Still, I would argue that their view of Kant is at the very least a symptom of some of their most fundamental philosophical problems.

There are certainly differences between the views of Kant propagated by Alois Riehl and those of, say, Wilhelm Windelband, Heinrich Rickert, or members of the Marburg School. In spite of all similarities, these views of Kant will not be entirely compatible. Accordingly, it is necessary to differentiate between the views of Kant held by different Neo-Kantians, though in this paper I will concentrate far more on the similarities, trying to determine whether there was such a thing as "the Kant of the Neo-Kantians." To this end, I shall first take a closer look at the Marburg School—that is, at Hermann Cohen (1842–1918), Paul Natorp (1854–1924), and Ernst Cassirer (1874–1945)—trying to make out the common features of their interpretations of Kant. I will then attempt to determine whether the results of this discussion can be extended to the Baden School, though here I will restrict myself to the discussion of Heinrich Rickert (1863–1936)—the so-called "systematizer" of the doctrines of the Baden Neo-Kantians.[8] For the Baden no less than the Marburg Neo-Kantians, it will be necessary throughout the essay—and perhaps strangely, on first glance—to relate their interpretations of Kant to their valorizations of Plato. And it will be from Plato, then, that we will later turn to Lotze, Nietzsche, and the vicissitudes of Neo-Kantian theories of "value." I will conclude the paper with some reflections on Heidegger and the decline of the Neo-Kantians—and on why their decline has not coincided with a decline of Kant.

Toward the Marburg Kant, via Plato

In 1912, on the occasion of Hermann Cohen's seventieth birthday, there appeared two essays in *Kant-Studien* which are very important for understanding how the Marburg School saw itself. The first was by Cassirer and was titled "Hermann Cohen und die Erneuerung der Kantischen Philosophie" (Hermann Cohen and the Renewal of the Kantian Philosophy), the other was Natorp's "Kant und die Marburger Schule" (Kant and the Marburg School). Both essays make clear how little the Marburg thinkers were ultimately interested in historical and philological Kant-scholarship, and how much they were concerned with making Kantian ideas fruitful for their own goals. The historical Kant was of little consequence to them. As for all Neo-Kantians, "to understand Kant" meant "to go beyond Kant." Nothing less than "the renewal of Kantian philosophy" was at issue, and this did not necessarily have much to do with the Kant of the eighteenth century.

Cassirer found it important to admit that "Cohen, in building his own system, departed in particular points" very far "from Kant's own results," and that one could really only claim that "the methodological consciousness (*das methodische Bewußtsein*) that motivates all his particular achievements, had become clear and mature only through the rigorous (*wissenschaftliche*) working through (*Durchdringung*) of Kant's basic works."[9] And this is actually very little. The claim that Cohen's "methodological consciousness" was shaped by Kant does not mean that Cohen was a "Kantian" in any sense whatsoever. Taken literally, it does not even mean that he was interested in any fundamental way in the "continuation of the Kantian system" (*Weiterbildung des Kantischen Systems*).[10]

What this negative result *does* mean for Cassirer, however, is that Cohen "did not think of understanding Kant as a concern of interest-free special historical scholarship (*abgelöste Fachgelehrsamkeit*)," but that he had formulated his own position regarding the basic problems of philosophy that had to be seen as lying "outside the circle of interest of any 'Kant-philology.'"[11] For Cohen and his followers the task was to "philosophize in the spirit of Kant"—not to repeat Kant. To deal with Kant always also meant "meta-critique" and "taking sides systematically." The main concern in this was, according to Cassirer, to "retain the 'objective meaning' of Kantian idealism." This was, he said, possible only through "science as the genuine and indispensable correlate of the transcendental method (*Methodik*)," because otherwise Kant might come dangerously close to the psychological idealism of representation à la Berkeley. We should not talk of the given, and we can speak of it only insofar as it does not consist in the "material determination of objects, but in the logical structure of principles."[12]

For Cassirer, as for Cohen, this opposition between the "material determination of objects" and the "logical structure of principles" is more or less identical with the opposition between psychological idealism à la Berkeley and Kant's transcendental method. It is the opposition between naturalism and Kantian idealism. Cohen saw that Kant's transcendental idealism had to be radicalized and made even more distinct from psychological idealism. This meant that all the merely psychological elements had to be purged from Kant. This "is the original turn of Cohen's interpretation and *critique* of Kant."[13] Kant should have been clearer about the fact that the principles and axioms of mathematics are the real foundation for natural science. He should not have descended to a level where the causal interactions "of any sort of existing things" are of any consequence. Cohen by contrast developed "such assumptions about the reality of things in a universal and ideal connection of truths and their relation of mutual dependence" without ever appealing to existing things. Only after he had made these ideal dependencies clear, did he "apply" them to mundane objects. Cohen is concerned with "pure logic" in the Husserlian sense—in fact, he must be understood as having "first and in complete clarity and convincingness" worked out this ideal of a pure logic.[14] While Cohen recognized something as "given," it is "something higher" (*ein Gegebenes höhere Stufe*), something that "does not consist in the material determinedness of things, but in the logical structure of principles and ideas."[15] What is given is ultimately always a problem that needs to be solved. Appealing to Cohen's *Kant's Begründung der Ethik*, Cassirer endorses the view that it is "the law itself" that must be identified with "the thing in itself." Put differently, "reality must be thought as *conceptual* thought, not as an intuitively visible representation, as the sign of value in a cognitive normativity (*Erkenntnisgeltung*)."[16] Cohen perfected, in this way, "Lotze's category of valuation or worth (*Geltungswert*)."[17]

Cassirer is also endorsing here Cohen's rejection of Kant's radical distinction between intuition and understanding as two basic faculties of the human mind—a distinction which is reflected in the Transcendental Aesthetic and Transcendental Logic. Cohen had explicitly characterized this distinction as a sign that Kant was "lowering himself toward empiricism and sensationalism."[18]

Natorp viewed things very much the same way. According to him, the "core" (*Kern*) or "indestructible basic content of Kant's philosophy"—the part that must be "held onto" and which must still be "realized in all its purity"—is idealism. Accordingly, the "transcendental method" is nothing but the "method of idealism" or the "method of an infinite."[19] It is "pure idealism,"[20] and it is also an absolute idealism insofar as it "decisively excludes all factors that are foreign to thought from thinking, and does not allow any court of knowledge (*Erkenntnis*) that would be outside of knowledge."[21] It is just this insight that prevents the Kantian method from degenerating into subjectivism. In Kant's works certain claims could still appear to be subjectivist, but the consistent application of Kant's transcendental method eradicates this completely. Transcendental idealism has absolutely nothing to do with subjective idealism. In fact, it consists in the complete rejection of subjectivism.

Natorp saw clearly that in making such claims he came close to the "great idealists, especially Hegel."[22] But, on closer inspection, such claims are really not Hegelian either; they are better characterized as "Platonic." And Natorp admitted this openly, saying: "we, in fact, connect Plato and Kant, just as Hegel did; and from this deep and important agreements result which extend even to the details."[23] Accordingly, the agreement with Hegel was less important than the point of departure from Plato. For Natorp, the Marburg School remained "entirely within the line of development that leads from Plato to Kant, and from Kant finally to a pure and developed methodological idealism" such as is still being developed by the Marburg Neo-Kantians.[24] Plato and Kant are the representatives of all "true philosophy"; they are signposts for future development. It is objective idealism that is the only true alternative to naturalism and psychologism.[25] How important Plato was for Natorp's understanding of Kant can be seen from his controversial book on Plato, in which he argued that there was an absolute need to recover for his age the "understanding of idealism, which—I have to say it—has been lost," even though there were few that would agree with him. "One might have thought," he continued, "that this recovery had long been completed, since there had already been expended the amazing work of trying to understand Kant." There had to be, he felt, "very special difficulties that obviously prevented agreement, in spite of such ardent efforts."[26] Natorp explicitly names Cohen as the one who opened his eyes to Kant and Plato.

In his "Metacritical Appendix" of 1920, Natorp found it necessary to defend himself against the accusation that he had transformed Plato into a Kantian before Kant—and even into a Marburg Kantian. He argued:

> Anyone who can overlook the features in Plato that point forward to Kant, and in Kant the features that point back to Plato, must have equally misunderstood both. Anyone who thinks that it is even possible for a Marburg thinker to try to prove that Plato is a Kantian in the Marburg fashion, willfully misconstrues the entire meaning of the philosophical efforts that characterize and the philosophical efforts that are honored with the name "Marburg School." No age, no school, no individual will ever be able to give expression to what has timeless and eternal effects beyond all the borders of schools and individual characters, and which is made possible by the time [in which he lives], the working community of which everyone is part, and his individual nature.[27]

Though the individual expression should not be identified with the timeless and eternal, Plato's concept of the *epikeina*—that is, the *agathon-kalon-sophon* which ultimately point to an ultimate and inexpressible unity—does substantially coincide with Kant's concept of the transcendental.[28]

And here Natorp certainly writes in the spirit of Cohen, who had said: "It is the inestimable value of the Leibnizian idealism that it rejuvenated the original Platonic thought (*Urgedanke*) in thinking and reason, as compared with feeling and sensation, more distinctly and clearly than did Descartes—namely, that nature must be discovered in consciousness and that matter must be constituted in thinking."[29] In his late *Commentary on Kant's Critique of Pure Reason,* Cohen also takes great pains to point out where Kant takes his point of departure from Plato, suggesting that Kant should have pursued his "world-historical connection with Plato" further.[30] If we were to conclude from this that Cohen was more interested in the further development of idealism and not just in the further development of transcendental idealism, we would certainly come close to the truth; and in his *Aesthetics* of 1912 (the same year as the essays with which we opened this section), Cohen himself maintained that "philosophy is Platonism."[31]

Therefore, every true philosopher must somehow also be a Platonist. For this reason alone, it should not come as a surprise that the Kant of the Marburg School exhibits such decisively Platonic features that some might mistake him for Plato himself. Since their philosophical view—in conscious opposition to psychologism and naturalism—expressed a struggle against sensationalism and an attempt to uncover the non- or super-sensible, the Marburg Neo-Kantians found Plato most congenial. As Cohen's essay "Platons Ideenlehre und die Mathematik" (Plato's Theory of Ideas and Mathematics) makes clear, their most fundamental problem was epistemological or logical—it concerned the "original thought of Platonism" (*den Urgedanken des Platonismus*)."[32] The Marburg Kant leads to or, perhaps better, is based on Plato. To understand Kant correctly, then, means to see him within the Platonic tradition. So it is that Köhnke echoes the criticism Natorp considered necessary in his "Metacritical Appendix"—namely, that "it is not always easy to decide whether Cohen and his school Kantianized Plato more than they Platonized Kant or vice versa."[33] The answer is, of course, that "more" and "less" make no sense in this question: The Marburg Kant and the Marburg Plato are fused into one in the idea of a "transcendental idealist" or a "transcendental Plato" which also has some Hegelian, Husserlian, and—perhaps most importantly—Lotzean features. Ultimately, it is the Marburg School's problems that define what Kant and Plato must have meant.

We may, of course, also ask *which* Plato or *which* Platonism forms the basis of the Marburg Kant-interpretation. It was certainly neither the Renaissance Neo-Platonism of Ficino nor the *urkundlich vorhandene* Plato which the Marburgers' contemporaries had carefully reconstructed using historical and critical methods.[34] Therefore a study such as Karl-Heinz Lembeck's *Platon in Marburg,* which discusses the reception of Plato by Cohen and Natorp, is certainly of some interest. Ultimately such studies will not do justice to the "Marburg Plato," however, without paying careful attention to the "Kantian features" of this figure—just as a study of the "Marburg Kant" will not do it justice without a close consideration of his debts to Plato.[35] Cohen's

"Theses on Plato" are thus not supposed to be measured by the historical Plato but by Plato's original thought. Given these circumstances, it was perhaps not surprising that the relevant secondary sources "were hardly discussed" in Marburg, and philological accounts of Plato were not even found "worthy of critique."[36] Similar things could be said about the Marburgers' view of Kant. To understand Kant correctly means to go beyond him—that is, to apply his method to problems that he may have had no idea of. Just as the Marburg School rejected the idea of anything "given" in epistemology, so for them there is no "given" Kant: He needs to be "produced" or "constructed"; and only such a "construction" will give the correct interpretation of what Kant was about, no matter what he may have said.

Wolfgang Marx once observed: "We can best see how the Marburg School understood itself as a research program based on a common ground that transcends all the differences . . . if we look at their reception of Plato."[37] If we substitute "construction of Plato" for "reception of Plato," we may say that this is also revealed in their understanding of Kant.

Decisive Aspects of the Marburg Kant

The following features are the most salient characteristics of the Marburg "construction" of Kant:

1. Logicism, or the idea that the beginning of all thinking must be found in thinking, is prominent. According to Cohen, there cannot be any *Vorinhalte* or "prior material" in logic. Thinking may not be understood in such a way that it has an origin which lies outside of logic. "Pure thinking must exclusively produce within itself pure knowledge. In other words, the doctrine of logic must become the doctrine of knowledge."[38] Thinking is ultimately synthesizing. "To continue to hold the prejudice of *the given*" is "the gap in the determination of synthesis." And thus a hindrance to the originality and presuppositionless autonomy of thinking. Therefore it "cannot exhaust" all the characteristics of thinking.[39] In this sense, Cohen intends to develop and clarify the super-empirical character of the foundation of all science. At the same time, "the thinking of logic" is the "thinking of science," that is, the thinking of the mathematical-natural sciences for Cohen.[40] "The thinking of knowledge can really only be described, discovered, measured, and chiseled out using the problems of scientific knowledge."[41] Whether this means that the Neo-Kantians transformed the mathematical sciences into the "eternal logos," as Max Horkheimer claimed, I do not want to decide here, but I will say that I find it doubtful. This much is certain: What interests Cohen are not the "subjective" contents of consciousness, but "objective" thoughts. As an enemy of subjectivism, he is investigating the *Geltungszusammenhang* of

principles and propositions. In trying to remove the concept of a knowing subject from philosophy, thought becomes a "presuppositionless autonomy" which can dispense with any material or anything given. From this follows a logical purity of thought that is more reminiscent of Plato than of Kant.

2. Put differently, philosophy must be anti-empirical and anti-subjectivist.[42] It must proceed *a priori*. Kant was important as an anti-psychologist, but he did not go far enough—therefore, all elements in Kant that are perceived to be psychologistic need to be excised from him. Therefore:

a) The metaphysical deduction of the categories is really superfluous. Kant's proof that there are just twelve categories was neither necessary nor successful. The concerns of the Transcendental Deduction are much more important.

b) The Transcendental Deduction does not prove the Principles of Experience. Rather it receives its validity from these principles.

3. Therefore, the distinction between the Transcendental Aesthetic and the Transcendental Logic has to be eliminated, and space and time have to be understood as supernumerary categories (Kant had deduced twelve), rather than as "forms of intuition." These forms of intuition are nothing but remnants of empiricism: The *a priori* is exhausted by thinking.

4. Even ethics must ultimately be reduced to logic. Without logic there cannot be any ethics. It also is based on supra-sensible ideas or values that cannot be reduced to sensibility.

All these features serve to entirely eliminate any fundamental role of sensibility in knowing and thinking. One might say that this view of Kant "defangs" Kantian philosophy by eliminating one of his most fundamental concerns—namely, to demonstrate the limits of pure reason or pure thinking, or to insist that intuitions without concepts are blind and that concepts without intuition are empty.

Toward the Baden Plato, via Kant

The question I would like to investigate now is whether this Marburg *construction* of Kant *in accordance* with Plato can also be found in the Baden School. To do so, I will again depart from two representative, relatively late papers which attempt to outline the nature of this strand of Neo-Kantian thinking. Both date from 1934, and were written by Heinrich Rickert. The first is entitled "Thesen zum System der Philosophy" (Theses about the System of Philosophy), which was conceived as a summary of the most important features of Rickert's thought; the second has no title but is usually referred to as "Die Heidelberger Tradition und Kants Kritizismus (Systematische Selbstdarstellung)" (The Heidelberg Tradition and Kant's Criticism).[43]

Rickert was no less opposed to subjectivism and naturalism than the Marburg Neo-Kantians were, but the thinkers he primarily opposed seem to have been Nietzsche and Kierkegaard, and what he perceived as their attempts to dismiss philosophy as a "science" by claiming that thinking must be "particular," as it is based on "life" or "existence."[44] Rickert argues that philosophy must give an account of the whole of the world. This means that neither a form of subjectivism (which is restricted to the knowing subject), nor a form of realism (which restricts itself to known objects), can suffice. Indeed, both known objects and the knowing subject must be part of such a philosophy—and this is the sense of "what is called, since Kant, 'transcendental idealism.' Both the subject and the object are taken into consideration in order to understand how the entirety of the world (*das Weltganze*) is constituted."[45]

In a move that seems to depart radically from the approach of Cohen, Natorp, and the early Cassirer, Rickert then finds that such an ontology must start with experience. However, he makes immediately clear that this does not mean that we should start with a kind of "sensationalism." Any kind of sensationalism, including "hyletic sensationalism," is to be rejected. And this is significant since "hyletic sensationalism" is, on Rickert's interpretation, the position held by Kant; he also calls it the "sensationalism of pure content."[46] While all that can be known and "which we do not produce ourselves" is indeed always connected with sensible states, it is not identical with them. Nor does it mean that the sensible or the material is what is "immediately" available. In fact, what is immediate is something "non-sensible" and "protophysical."[47] Even when we speak of mental states, we must speak of sensible and non-sensible understanding (*Verstehungen*), and the non-sensible is just as original as the sensible perception. In fact, the material or the stuff of the sensible "disintegrates" at the very first step we make to characterize it in any way.[48] If only for this reason, philosophy—at least insofar as philosophy wants to be the science of the whole of the world—"cannot be restricted to the forms and principles of the psycho-physical world of the senses."[49] In his later essay, Rickert uses "sensible" and "intelligible" to talk about these two aspects, and then argues that this distinction leads to the conception of two worlds—namely, that of "a real, perceptible world of sense on the one hand and an irreal, understandable world in its determination by values"—and that this is what makes possible the question of the possibility of a unified world. We must ask "whether there does not belong to this world of things that is partially sensible and partially intelligible another world that . . . cannot be reified" because it is "prior to any objectification." This world, which should not be thought of as a transcendent realm, must be understood again in accordance with the difference between the known object and knowing subject. And the knowing subject must be thought as determined by the "value of truth," and not by causality.[50]

Accordingly, "apart from the partly sensible and partly intelligible world of objects, there is a third world that is prior to any objectification and is a world in a proto-physical sense. It must be recognized as ontologically independent. And it is investigated by a discipline that may be called proto-physics." Rickert supposes that the unity of these three worlds may be found in a fourth world that is not given and transcendent, guided by "values," which may be understood in accordance with the "Platonic 'idea' of the good in the supersensible ground of the world."[51]

If anything, this is an even "higher" version of Platonism than we have found in the Marburg School. Even though there is considerable difference in the details, we may say that in its main features, Rickert's Neo-Kantianism—just like that of the Marburg School—was construed in accordance with a definite view of Plato. And furthermore, Rickert and his colleagues in the Baden School were no more guilty of the "mistake" of confusing Kant and Plato, than the Marburgers were: The Baden Neo-Kantians were also interested in developing a "transcendental Platonism" in a positive way.[52]

We may also say—with reference to the preceding section—that the Baden Neo-Kantians (1) were nearly as strong "logicists" as the Marburg School, and (2) rejected "empiricism," "subjectivism," and "naturalism" as vehemently as they did. Accordingly, the Baden School rejected any elements in Kant they perceived to be "psychological," such as his supposed "hyletic sensationalism." Furthermore, (3) it was judgment and thinking that interested Rickert in Kant, more than the Transcendental Aesthetic: He ultimately saw in its details little more than an expression of hyletic sensationalism, though he also saw that Kant's distinction between the sensible and the intelligible worlds (in the *Inaugural Dissertation*) expressed the old Platonic *chorismos* of *aistheta* and *noeta*. It is thus that Rickert claims, mistakenly, that "the *a priori* is not sensible" and yet belongs to appearances.[53]

There is, however, a fundamental difference between the Marburgers and Rickert with regard to what forms the ultimate foundation of all philosophizing. Whereas Cohen and Natorp emphasize logic and epistemology, the words that are most prevalent in Rickert are "ontology" and "values." Whereas Cohen tried to show that morality and religion must ultimately be reduced to logic, Rickert argued that values lay at the very basis of even theoretical thinking:

> The opposition of theoretical and practical reason in Kant indicates also the opposition of *reality* and *value*. Theoretical reason is directed toward the real, practical reason toward a value . . . or, we might also say a valuable end (*wertvoller Zweck*), for value and end cannot be separated according to Kant. A valueless end would be no end for the practical human being. To escape the Kantian dualism, we have therefore the task of finding a

principle which produces the unity of reality and value—something that Kant himself tried

—not in the first *Critique,* but in the *Religion within the Limits of Mere Reason.*[54] Ultimately then, it is all a matter of faith—in values. And as we have already seen, it was Plato who first recognized the centrality of values for all human endeavor.

Lotze and the Vicissitudes of Value

To be more precise, however: Neither Plato, nor Kant, nor Rickert invented the notion of values in the requisite sense—that honor goes to Rudolf Hermann Lotze (1817–1881). Largely unknown today, Lotze spent most of his life (from 1844) teaching at the University of Göttingen. His philosophical thinking was, in large measure, a revolt against the Hegelian view that there is an objective spirit or mind. As Lotze put it:

> There is no real subject, no substance, no place in which anything worthy or sacred can be realized except the individual ego, the personal soul; beyond the inner life of the subjective spirit with its consciousness of ideas . . . its effort to realize them, there is no superior region of a so-called objective spirit, the forms and articulations of which are in their mere existence more worthy than the subjective world.[55]

While he wanted to affirm "universal moral Ideas of an absolute good, just, and beautiful," and even argued that such ideas are necessary for moral judgment, Lotze also held that these ideas were really indemonstrable and a matter of philosophical faith. They are, he argued, postulates of practical reason, not independently real entities. They seem to be such independent entities but, like Kant's ideas of reason, they have an "as if" character. In doing so, Lotze assimilated values to "ideas" in the Kantian sense, giving moral right and wrong the same status as the notions of "God," "freedom," and "immortality." They are all part of a Platonic "realm of values" which cannot be demonstrated, but which constitutes a necessary presupposition of moral thinking.

But one could argue that Rickert was indebted to Lotze not only for the notion of "value," but also for the idea that Kant and Plato needed to be connected—and that Lotze had a similar influence on Cohen and other Marburg thinkers. Lotze's influence on Germans in the latter half of the nineteenth century should not be underestimated. A historian of the era cites an American thinker who claimed, in 1912, that it "may safely be said that there are now few thinking men over forty-five in Germany who are not indebted to Lotze for mental poise, intellectual tastes, or elements of a general culture which enable them to look beyond their own individual department of activity."[56] Surely one of the most central aspects of this "mental poise" had to do with Lotze's widely discussed theory of value. But it was not just Germans who were indebted to him: George Santayana wrote his thesis on Lotze in 1889, with Josiah Royce as supervisor—and Royce had studied under Lotze himself. William James and Bernard Bosanquet were also clearly influenced by him, and Albrecht Ritschl—a theologian of great influence in the United States—cannot be understood without him. In Britain T. H. Green, R. B. Haldane, and Alfred North Whitehead were impressed by him.

But perhaps Lotze's most significant influence is deflected through Nietzsche, with whom "values" are usually most closely associated: I believe it could be shown that Nietzsche's attack on values was largely provoked by and directed at the theory of value propagated by Lotze and the Neo-Kantians who followed him. But regardless, the Nietzschean onslaught certainly precipitated a crisis in Neo-Kantianism. Among the Neo-Kantians some, like Rickert, tried to rebut Nietzsche; others more or less endorsed a Nietzschean view. Most famous among the latter was Hans Vaihinger, whose book *The Philosophy of 'As If': A System of the Theoretical, Practical, and Religious Fictions of Mankind* was published in 1911 and translated into English in 1924. According to Vaihinger, "it is precisely the 'As-if' theory that forms the meeting point of Kant and Nietzsche."[57] Vaihinger argued not only for the value of fictions, but also for the fictional character of values.

What is perhaps the strangest aspect of the Neo-Kantians who critiqued Nietzsche, is that they did not reevaluate the notion of value per se, but objected rather to any biologistic (dare I say naturalistic?) foundation for values. This is especially clear in Rickert's 1912 paper "Lebenswerte und Kulturwerte" (Values of Life and Culture), in which he argues against "fashionable" attempts to found values on their apparent usefulness in serving "life," and to ground them in "culture." Values, Rickert insists, cannot be founded in life or in nature. Nietzsche is "just one biologist among many," and "biology does not only *not* contain any factors which would be suitable to the imposition of norms (*Normgebung*), but *any* connection of conditioned connections with values is contrary to the spirit of modern biology and still belongs to a pre-scientific age." Furthermore, the biological realm is from the beginning covered with values (*Wertakzenten*), and this is only to be expected from the point of view of a willing human being, who must posit himself as the end.[58]

One early twentieth-century historian of the problem of values has argued thus:

> the concept of value is not "discovered" as something entirely new . . . the entire [historical] development is pressing toward the view that this concept is ultimately the most adequate expression of the main features found

in what was always the same solution. Anyone who believes that all philosophical work has always been concerned with a very small number of identical problems—perhaps even just one problem—[that is,] with certain original antinomies (*Urantinomien*), of which one cannot say to whom they first occurred; [anyone who believes this] will also believe that the ideal of a philosophical history of philosophy must be to hear in all philosophical doctrines the same antinomies and the same eternal tensions.[59]

This framing of the problem suggests that the problem of normativity has been around forever: The words "value" and "normativity" may be new, but the phenomenon they characterize is eternal—or as old as humanity—and the theory that is developed from these words is a definite improvement over earlier theories. If such a view were taken, we might indeed be justified—with Rickert and those who unwittingly followed him—in seeing Kant as answering the problem of normativity. I would argue, however, that this would be a mistake that arises from seeing Kant from the point of view of a transcendentalized Platonism.

The Question of Kant and the Decline of Neo-Kantianism

Did the Neo-Kantians interpret Kant correctly? If by "correct interpretation" we mean that they were faithful to the Kantian texts, the answer must clearly be "no." Their interpretation is absolutely inadequate as an attempt at interpreting Kant's own intentions. But as we have seen, this was clearly not their goal. They did not mean to obey the letter of Kant's texts, but the spirit of his thinking. There can be hardly any doubt that Kant himself would have objected to them in the same way that he objected to Fichte and others who were trying to go "beyond" his thought and argued that they should not be bound by the letter of Kant's works. This objection would hardly have worried the Neo-Kantians.

The Neo-Kantians meant to apply Kantian principles and methods to what they considered to be the problems of their day, and they were trying to advance philosophical discussion in this way. Did they succeed in doing this, i.e., did they succeed in employing Kantian methodology in the discussion of the problems of their time? Here, the answer is not so clear. At least, the answer is not an unqualified "no." I do believe that their appeal to Kant in trying to counter psychologism, subjectivism, and naturalism was at least to some extent promising. Kant's transcendental method, concerned as it is with the *a priori* conditions of possibility of experience, does appear to me to offer a robust alternative to such views. Indeed, it might be said that this project is still ongoing. While there are some who are busy trying to "naturalize" Kant, there are others who try to develop Kantian ideas as an antidote to naturalism.

However, the Neo-Kantians clearly went too far in trying to eliminate sensibility as a source of knowledge altogether and arguing that knowledge originates from the understanding alone, since this denies one of Kant's most fundamental distinctions. At least, this is what Martin Heidegger argued. In his lecture-course of the winter semester 1925–1926 in Marburg, entitled *Logik—Die Frage nach der Wahrheit* (*Logic: The Question concerning Truth*), he pointed out that the Marburg attempt to dissolve the distinction between intuition and thinking—and thereby to reduce the Transcendental Aesthetic to the Transcendental Logic—was a fundamental mistake. Heidegger suggested that this made it impossible for them to understand the Kantian project, precisely because the Transcendental Aesthetic and Kant's discussion of space and time is fundamental to the first *Critique*.[60] In a later Marburg lecture-course (winter semester 1927–1928) on the "phenomenological interpretation" of Kant's *Critique of Pure Reason*, Heidegger argued that "the transcendental aesthetic has an independent and central significance in the entirety of the *Critique*, or in the entirety of the problem of ontological or metaphysical knowledge."[61] Still, he recognized the Marburg view as "the most penetrating and significant scientific interpretation of Kant in the nineteenth century"; and while he thought that it "runs as counter to Kant's intentions as is at all possible," he also claimed that it was nevertheless "guided by a genuine philosophical motive." The Marburg Neo-Kantians were right in seeing that Kant had "not explicitly brought to light the unity" of the Transcendental Aesthetic and the Transcendental Logic. This was, of course, something that he himself intended to do, and it was for this reason that Heidegger thought the Marburg school had advanced Kant-interpretation "more than all attempts at mediation."[62]

Heidegger was mistaken, however: It is not that Kant simply failed to bring to light, in an explicit way, the unity of the Transcendental Aesthetic and the Transcendental Logic. It is rather that Kant thought sensibility and understanding to be radically different faculties that cannot be brought together. While he had mused at one point that there may perhaps exist a "common root" of these faculties, Kant never thought that this could be made out by us. Heidegger claimed that he could make out this common root. Cohen and Natorp, on the other hand, did not think that this common root could be identified with any psychological faculty, as this would have involved them in the kind of psychologism they wanted to avoid. So, though Heidegger believed that he was solving the problem that neither Kant nor the Marburg Neo-Kantians could solve, he actually posed an entirely different problem. He was, in other words, using Kant just as much for his own purposes as his predecessors had. Though it might appear that "Heidegger's approach is similar to Cohen's, since both of them aim to surpass Kantian dualism by stressing the transcendental dimension of the *Critique* as a process of production," such a view covers up the fundamental dissimilarity of their projects.[63] Heidegger was concerned with doing ontology and metaphysics; Cohen was engaged in epistemology and the foundation of science. While both of them were doing violence to the historical Kant, they were one-sided in different ways. Heidegger's critique of the Marburg Kant may have gotten at something important, but his own view of Kant was just as much a construction as the view he criticized.

Heidegger's construction of Kant may have been an important achievement in the context of his time, just as the construction of Cohen and Natorp was an important achievement in their time—but they are both constructions. One might argue that any interpretation of any important philosopher at any time is to some extent a construction or, as it is more fashionable to say today, a reconstruction: There is then no such thing as "interpreting Kant correctly," if this requires a faithful account of what Kant really meant. Perhaps this is so. The different contexts of the effective history (*Wirkungsgeschichte*) of any text clearly play a role that is difficult to overestimate in a philosophical understanding of the history of philosophy. But there are different ideals. First, there is the ideal of a philologically rigorous and historically contextualized interpretation of a thinker which takes his historical situatedness seriously. Philosophical scholars who follow this ideal try to identify and reformulate, with increasing precision, what the thinker under discussion may have meant. Second, there is the ideal of constructing or reconstructing what a thinker has said in such a way that it takes on specific relevance to contemporary problems—i.e., problems that are decidedly not that thinker's own. Each of these ideals gives rise to different methods and approaches, and each gives rise to different ideas of what it means to "interpret correctly." While I have a decided preference for the first way of approaching Kant and other magisterial figures, I understand the attraction of the second ideal as well.

One of the things I hope to have shown in this paper is that the Neo-Kantians followed the second approach. And one of the reasons why the Neo-Kantians' popularity has diminished is that their problems are no longer our problems. Kant, to the contrary, seems to have continued relevance for us. The same holds for Plato. And that is one of the tests—if not the only test—for what endures as a philosophical text.

NOTES

1. Richard Rorty, *Philosophy and the Mirror of Nature* (Princeton: Princeton University Press, 1979), 6.

2. Klaus-Christian Köhnke, *The Rise of Neo-Kantianism: German Academic Philosophy between Idealism and Positivism* (New York: Cambridge University Press, 1991), 137.

3. I do not disagree with Köhnke's claim that Liebmann marks not the beginning, but the end of the Neo-Kantian programmata (ibid., 138)—but I would like to argue that he marks the end of the beginning, and not the beginning of the end.

4. Liebmann, *Kant and the Epigones*. I quote in accordance with Köhnke's translation in *The Rise of Neo-Kantianism*, 141.

5. Thomas E. Willey, *Back to Kant. The Revival of Kantianism in German Social and Political Thought, 1860–1914* (Detroit: Wayne State University Press, 1978), 37; cf. I. M. Bochenski, *Modern European Philosophy*, trans. D. Nicoll and K. Aschenbrenner (Berkeley: University of California Press, 1956), 88–93.

6. See Manfred Pascher, *Einführung in den Neukantianismus* (Munich: Wilhelm Fink Verlag, 1997), 11.

7. Indeed, a similar question may be asked of anyone who is dealing with Kant: "Which Kant do you take yourself to be agreeing or disagreeing with?" or "Which Kant do you think you are following or avoiding?" One might, of course, object that this quest is in significant respects similar to that "research into the life of Jesus" (*Leben-Jesu Forschung*) which, as Albert Schweitzer's historical investigations showed, tends to futility: There were as many views of Jesus as there were scholars engaged in researching his life. And there may indeed be as many views of Kant as there are Neo- and other Kantians—or for that matter, anti-Kantians.

8. I will not discuss Riehl in this context.

9. See Ernst Cassirer, "Hermann Cohen und die Erneuerung der Kantischen Philosophie," *Kant-Studien* 17 (1912): 252–273, 252.

10. Wolfgang Marx, *Transzendentale Logik als Wissenschaftstheorie. Systematisch-kritische Untersuchungen in Cohens Logik der reinen Erkenntnis* (Frankfurt: Vittorio Klostermann, 1977), 16.

11. Cassirer, "Cohen und die Erneuerung der Kantischen Philosophie," *Kant-Studien* 15 (1912): 252–273.

12. Ibid., 257–58.

13. Ibid., 255 (emphasis added).

14. Ibid., 256–257.

15. Ibid., 258.

16. Hermann Cohen, *Kants Begründung der Ethik* (Berlin: Dümmler, 1877), 28–29; Cassirer, "Cohen und die Erneuerung der Kantischen Philosophie," 267.

17. Cassirer, "Cohen und die Erneuerung der Kantischen Philosophie," 269.

18. See Hermann Cohen, *Kommentar zu Kants Kritik der reinen Vernunft* (Leipzig: Meiner Verlag, 1917), 22.

19. Paul Natorp, "Kant und die Marburger Schule," *Kant-Studien* 17 (1912): 200.

20. Ibid., 204.

21. Ibid., 207. I translate *Erkenntnis* as "knowledge," though the editors of the Cambridge Edition of Kant's Works have chosen "cognition." There are several reasons for this. The most important is that I have looked at eighteenth-century German translations of works by Hume, Hutcheson, and other English philosophers, and such translations consistently render "knowledge" with *Erkenntnis*. If eighteenth-century German thinkers considered *Erkenntnis* to be the best equivalent for "knowledge," I do not think that twentieth-century English-speakers should

correct them—and this quite apart from the fact that *Selbsterkenntnis* cannot be rendered as "self-cognition," etc.

22. Paul Natorp, "Kant und die Marburger Schule," 211.

23. Loc. cit.

24. Ibid., 216.

25. "Naturalism" and "psychologism" are clearly the enemies, and Natorp's understanding of "Kant" and "Plato" is determined by his need to formulate an answer to them—as Cassirer made very clear.

26. Paul Natorp, *Platos Ideenlehre. Eine Einführung in den Idealismus* (Leipzig: Felix Meiner, 1903), 4–5.

27. Ibid., 462–463.

28. Ibid., 465.

29. Hermann Cohen, *Kritik der theoretischen Erkenntnis*, 40.

30. Cohen, *Kommentar*, 121; see also 11, 21, 24, 42, 120, 169, 218.

31. Hermann Cohen, *Ästhetik des reinen Gefühls*. Part 1: *System der Philosophie. Dritter Teil* (Berlin: Bruno Cassirer, 1912), 245.

32. Marburg: Elwert, 1879.

33. Köhnke, *The Rise of Neo-Kantianism*, 192. Köhnke discusses Cohen, Kant, and Plato extensively on pages 178–197, paying special attention to Cohen's 1867 *Plato's Theory of Ideas Developed Psychologically*.

34. See Paul Natorp, "Zum Gedächtnis Kants, 1804–12. Februar—1904," 301. I find this transcendental Platonism especially questionable because it was connected from the very beginning with a certain kind of mysticism. While this mysticism had in Cohen mainly Jewish sources, one must also speak of a Germanic and nationalistic mysticism in Natorp that is less than fortunate. Apart from much that is admirable, such as Natorp's fight against those who try to use Nietzsche to undermine Kant, and his somewhat emotional desire for a goal that would extend beyond the "dark clouds of the day" and "lend an eternal and transcendent meaning to our life," there are also in him some nearly comical thoughts which, given subsequent history, do not sound all that comical: "In our nation (*Volk*)," Natorp writes, a force has been hidden that "allows us to go back to the very foundation of the soul, to descend to the deepest sources of the life of the soul—that allows us to recover an originality and proper selfness (*Selbsteigenheit*) of feeling, willing, and thinking as history has not seen it for many centuries." And it was precisely Kant who was supposed to have made this grandiose "descent" or made it possible. I rather doubt it.

35. Karl-Heinz Lembeck, *Platon in Marburg. Platon-Rezeption und Philosophiegeschichtsphilosophie bei Cohen und Natorp* (Würzburg: Königshausen & Neumann, 1994).

36. Ibid., 5.

37. Marx, "Die philosophische Entwicklung Paul Natorps im Hinblick auf das System Hermann Cohens," 86.

38. Lembeck, *Platon in Marburg*, 13.

39. Ibid., 28.

40. Ibid., 19.

41. Ibid., 57.

42. Wolfgang Marx, "Die philosophische Entwicklung Paul Natorps im Hinblick auf das System Hermann Cohens," *Zeitschrift für philosophische Forschung* 18 (1964): 486–500; reprinted in *Materialien zur Neukantianismus Diskussion* (Darmstadt: Wissenschaftliche Buchgesellschaft, 1987), 66–86.

43. I will quote from Heinrich Rickert, *Philosophische Aufsätze*, ed. Rainer B. Bast (Tübingen: Mohr Siebeck, 1999).

44. Rickert, "Thesen," *Philosophische Aufsätze*, 319.

45. Ibid., 320.

46. Rickert, "Die Methode der Philosophie," *Philosophische Aufsätze*, 128. It is perhaps interesting that besides Kant, Rickert also mentions Husserl as a representative of this position in a special footnote.

47. Ibid., 129.

48. Ibid., 139.

49. Ibid., 151

50. Rickert, "Thesen," *Philosophische Aufsätze*, 321–322.

51. Ibid., 322. I skip the conclusions about the meaning of life that Rickert draws on the basis of this four-fold structure of the world into psychophysical, intelligible, proto-physical, and metaphysical "being." I will also say nothing about how values are grounded in his theory of culture.

52. See G. Gabriel, "Frege als Neukantianer," *Kant-Studien* 77 (1986): 84ff., 101.

53. Rickert, "Geschichte und System der Philosophie," *Philosophische Aufsätze*, 310.

54. Rickert, "Systematissche Selbstdarstellung," *Philosophische Aufsätze*, 400.

55. I quote in accordance with Willey, *Back to Kant*, 51.

56. Willey, *Back to Kant*, 41.

57. Hans Vaihinger, *The Philosophy of 'As If': A System of the Theoretical, Practical and Religious Fictions of Mankind* (1911), 313n.

58. Rickert, "Lebenswerte und Kulturwerte," *Philosophische Aufsätze*, 54 (emphasis added).

59. Fritz Bamberger, *Untersuchungen zur Entstehung des Wertproblems in der Philosophie des 19. Jahrhunderts. I. Lotze* (Halle: Max Niemeyer, 1924), 2.

60. Martin Heidegger, *Logik. Die Frage nach der Wahrheit.* (Frankfurt: Vittorio Klostermann, 1995), 269ff. He also makes similar points in his Davos discussions with Cassirer. For more on this, see Daniel Dahlstrom, "Heideggers Kant-Kommentar, 1925–1936," *Philosophisches Jahrbuch* 96 (1989): 343–366; Christopher Macann, "Heidegger's Kantinterpretation," *Critical Heidegger*, ed. Christopher Macann (London and New York: Routledge, 1996), 97–120; E. W. Orth, "Martin Heidegger und der Neukantianismus," *Man and World* 25 (1992): 421–442.

61. Martin Heidegger, *Phenomenological Interpretation of Kant's Critique of Pure Reason*, trans. Parvis Emad and Kenneth Maly (Bloomington: Indiana University Press, 1997), 53.

62. Heidegger, *Phenomenological Interpretation of Kant's Critique of Pure Reason*, 54. See also Claude Piché, "Heidegger and the Neo-Kantian Reading of Kant," in *Heidegger, German Idealism, and Neo-Kantianism*, ed. Tom Rockmore (New York: Humanity Books, 2000), 179–208.

63. Piché, "Heidegger and the Neo-Kantian Reading of Kant," 207.

6

The Highest Principle and the Principle of Origin in Hermann Cohen's Theoretical Philosophy

Jürgen Stolzenberg

If one wants to characterize the philosophical oeuvre of Hermann Cohen in a way that does justice to both its philosophical-historical meaning and Cohen's self-understanding, then it should be described as working through a double task. This task consists, on the one hand, in a defense of Kant's philosophy against interpretations it had received in the course of its rediscovery, after the post-Kantian idealistic systems lost their persuasiveness. On the other hand, the task consists in a rehabilitation of Kant's philosophy in order to contribute to the re-grounding of philosophy as a theory of science. Indeed, from the beginning Cohen characterized and legitimated his undertaking of Kantian interpretation as "a combination of the systematic and the historical task" (Cohen 1987b, iv).

This assertion of Cohen's, however, is itself in need of interpretation. Already in the preface to his first draft of a systematic reconstruction of Kant's theoretical philosophy—the first edition of *Kants Theorie der Erfahrung* (*Kant's Theory of Experience*)—Cohen emphatically called attention to this connection between the historical and systematic tasks as a connection which, for its part, stands under the signature of "systematic partisanship" (Cohen 1987b, v). This also means that the return to the original Kantian text propagated by Cohen, and the announced rebuttal of the "adversaries" of Kant "through simple citations" (Cohen 1987b, iv) from the textual inventory of the *Critique of Pure Reason,* could only derive their sense and force from a systematic interpretation with respect to the entirety of the Kantian critique of reason.

Cohen placed this interpretation under the thesis, "*Kant discovered a new concept of experience*" (Cohen 1987b, 3). The first edition of *Kants Theorie der Erfahrung* clarifies, although not until its end, what this new concept of experiences consists in.[1] Namely, it consists in the totality of synthetic propositions, which form the content of mathematics and the pure natural sciences.[2] The peculiarity of this reduction of the Kantian notion of experience, for which the relation to sense-data given in intuition is constitutive (a relation that is obviously excluded by Cohen), and which is also constitutive for the theoretical program of the Kantian critique of reason as a whole, is obvious. That is to say, if the field of objects to which philosophy is to correspond is limited at the outset to the mathematical-natural sciences, then Kant's central concern for a critique of traditional metaphysics must lose all meaning and all interest. These restrictions, however, are no less clear than the reasons that Cohen gave for this purpose. They are precisely the reasons with which he sought to defend Kant's philosophy against its critics and "antagonists," especially those who came from the field of psychology.[3]

Cohen's critique has its basis in the thesis that psychology is not in the position to accept the rank of an ultimately ground-laying (*letztbegründenden*) theory, due to its status as an empirical science; for, as an empirical science, it may attain only hypothetically ultimate elements of consciousness. Since this is the case, psychology cannot be recognized as the foundation for the interpretation of an epistemology which aims at an ultimate grounding (*Letztbegründung*), as Cohen's interpretation construes Kant's theory of knowledge.[4]

It is crucial for Cohen's reconstruction of Kant that he targeted his critique not only against the psychologistic interpretation of Kant, but against Kant himself. His underlying thesis is that Kant's theory of knowledge is, in its central elements—such as the "transcendental deduction of the pure concepts of the understanding"—merely an empirical-psychological analysis of the synthesis of knowledge from subjective conditions. Hence, what Cohen deems to be Kant's goal—the grounding of the necessity and strict universality of mathematical-natural scientific knowledge from *a priori* conditions—in principle could not be achieved.[5] From this, Cohen has drawn the conclusion that is decisive for his overall approach in reconstructing Kant's philosophy, namely, to consider the "synthetic doctrine"—which Kant had posited for the *Critique of Pure Reason*—as a psychological-empirical method of reconstruction of the genesis of cognition from its subjective conditions. Thus, this synthetic method has to be shunned as inappropriate for the enterprise of an objective reconstruction of Kant's theoretical philosophy. An "analytic" or "transcendental method" has to replace it. This novel method, which Cohen construes consciously and "critically" against Kant's "synthetic doctrine," and which attempts not to create "on its own, the science of the objects of nature" (Cohen 1987a, 577), must instead start out from science as a "*factum*" and must lay bare the *a priori* conditions on which the validity of its cognitions rest.[6] Cohen saw these conditions given in the embodiment of those synthetic *a priori* laws which Kant had characterized as "principles of pure reason," and which form the basis of mathematics and pure natural science. With the exclusion of a subjective-theoretical grounding of the objectivity of knowledge, Cohen also had to reject as merely psychological the Kantian definition of the concept of the *a priori* as the origin of a concept from the sources of reason. The character of the *a priori* for Cohen became equivalent with that of necessity and universality, i.e., with the lawfulness of cognition. And since Cohen wanted to understand natural-scientific knowledge alone as "experience," it becomes understandable that Cohen conceives of the principles contained in mathematics and pure natural sciences as the principles of experience thus construed.

The "transcendental method," as Cohen termed it, through which these principles ought to be sought, is not, however, without problems. These problems will be demonstrated and clarified in the first section, through their connection to Cohen's conception of a highest principle in the second edition of *Kants Theorie der Erfahrung*. In the second section, we will pursue the question of the way in which a continuity exists between Cohen's conception of a highest principle and the central principle for the *Logik der reinen Erkenntnis* (*Logic of Pure Cognition*)—namely, the principle of origin. We shall pursue this question with the intention of addressing a misunderstanding suggested by Cohen, and at the same time shall contribute to a controversy that exists in Cohen-research with respect to the interpretation of the principle of origin.

The Highest Principle and the Transcendental Conditions of Cognition

In the following, we shall not discuss a misconstrual of Cohen's self-understanding—namely, that he supposedly linked his "transcendental method" too closely with the "analytic method" which Kant had pursued in the *Prolegomena* and also, as Cohen thought, in the *Critique of Pure Reason*.[7] Rather, we shall call attention to a problem that arises from the concept of the analytical method itself.[8] This method starts out from a proposition that is accepted as certain and as given, and inquires into the premises from which its truth follows. With respect to the demonstration of the premises, one can initially say that more than one foundation can serve as a sufficient condition. Concerning the truth of these conditions, it is also the case that none of these conditions must be true simply because their consequences are true, since true propositions can follow from false premises. Hence it follows, concerning the truth of the propositions assumed as given, or of a set of propositions assumed as given, that their truth can in no way be proven through the analytic method, unless the truth of the premises is guaranteed independently from their grounding capacity. If this is not the case, the premises must be taken as hypotheses. With respect to the truth of the premises, it follows that it is not based on their grounding capacity for true propositions, but rather that it is to be presupposed.

Hence, a charge leveled against Cohen by Friedrich Albert Lange becomes understandable: If the truth of the premises would be claimed under the condition that the premises are the explanatory ground for the presupposed experience of science[9]—and Lange imputes this claim to Cohen—then a mere tautology would be asserted, or the argument would be circular. For then the ground for the truth of a condition of the possibility of experience would consist in that it is a condition of the possibility of experience.[10]

Cohen replied to this objection in two passages—once in the context of his explication of the transcendental method in *Kants Begründung der Ethik* (*Kant's Grounding of Ethics*);[11] and again, without referring to Lange by name, in the second edition of *Kants Theorie der Erfahrung*, in the context of his explication of the highest principle of the transcendental conditions of cognition. The argumentation in this regard will be investigated more closely in what follows.

Cohen's explications of a highest principle of the conditions of cognition proceed from the question about the systematic role to be assigned to pure spatial intuition as one of the conditions of the apriority of the principles of mathematics with respect to the whole of the "transcendental system." Cohen clarifies this role with reference to the fact that the explication of valid *a priori* conditions for the principles of mathematics must not be seen in isolation, but rather with regard to a "*total* unified science," mathematical-natural science, whose basis is mathematics (Cohen 1987a, 137). Each individual transcendental condition is to be construed, therefore, not as "an encapsulated whole" but only "as part and parcel of a higher whole"; this entirety presents the "totality of transcendental conditions which, as a unity, hold together the unity of science" (Cohen 1987a, 138). Cohen understands this relation of part and whole as that of species and genus. The concept of a highest principle therefore interprets the concept of the genus of the transcendental conditions of natural-scientific cognition. Cohen has given this concept several titles, such as the "highest principle of all synthetic judgments" or also the highest "principle of experience."[12]

It is clear that in this way merely the function of a highest principle is designated, and not its content. So it remains to be asked: In what does the commonality of the transcendental conditions of the cognition of experience consist? Cohen has linked his answer to this question with his answer to the charge of circularity formulated by Lange. A variation of Lange's accusation is formulated by Cohen as follows:

> The appearance could arise that we are going in circles. We seek that which makes possible experience or synthetic judgments as necessary, and believe

that we must assert the same in a highest law as principle; this seems to contain merely a riddle, without containing a hint for the solution. We ask: What makes experience possible? And the answer is: the highest principle of experience. (Cohen 1987a, 138–139)

The argumentation with which Cohen seeks to dissolve this concern demands special attention. At first it seems as if Cohen is not preparing to refute the accusation of a circular justification of the possibility of experience. For he starts the argument with the question: What makes possible the *highest principle itself*? And his answer, "nothing other than itself" (Cohen 1987a, 139), seems to contain no discernable response to the objection of circularity and seems to leave this objection unchanged.

Yet if one follows Cohen's argument for his answer, then something becomes apparent that is striking and also in need of explanation: Cohen's explication of the content of the highest principle, from which one should be able to discern its finality and self-justification of the highest principle, is not—as might be expected, according to the requirement of Cohen's "transcendental method" and his elucidations of the notion of the genus of the transcendental conditions—an explication of the content of the concept of what is common to the *conditions* of validity of cognitions of mathematical-natural science. It is, rather, an explication of the *recognition* of the *factum* of mathematical-natural science itself—i.e., an explication of what one ultimately accepts when one takes one's point of departure from the *factum* of mathematical-natural science. What one ultimately accepts—and what Cohen now designates as the content of the highest principle—is expressed in the idea that there are in fact laws or, in Cohen's formulation, "that a law ought to reign in the field of experience" (Cohen 1987a, 139). Since Cohen conceives necessity as the modality of the validity of laws, and since the domain of mathematical-natural science is identical with that of experience, this idea can therefore also be expressed in this manner: "we want to recognize necessity in that field of our consciousness which is characterized as science, as mathematical-natural science" (Cohen 1987a, 139). What is expressed by the content of the highest principle is nothing other than the recognition of the moment of lawfulness as such, which is implied in the recognition of the *factum* of mathematical-natural science *qua* science, and that means *qua* cognition from laws. This assertion is also ultimately proven by the following assertion: "this idea, [namely,] to take as the starting point the recognition of the *factum* of mathematical-natural science . . . *posits itself* as the highest law."[13]

Several questions are to be addressed to this conception. Firstly, we must explain the conspicuous alteration of the train of thought that has arisen with the shift from the explication of the content of the general concept of the *condition* of mathematical-natural science, to the explication of the content of the acceptance of the *facticity* of mathematical-natural science. This explanation must, at the same time, shed light on whether this alteration entails a change of the conception of a highest principle itself, or whether it has only initiated the decisive, albeit non-self-evident, step to its appropriate interpretation.

Further, it is unclear in what way Cohen could intend to use this conception to refute the accusation of circularity in his justification of the possibility of experiential cognition. This requires an elucidation of the exact sense of the thesis of the self-justification and finality of the highest principle with which Cohen opposes the accusation of circularity.

To answer these questions we must once more concentrate on what it is that became conspicuous in the course of explicating the content of the highest principle. We saw this conspicuousness when Cohen presented a double description of the content of the highest principle, from which initially it is not evident how the description can be seen as the description of the content of one and the same proposition. While Cohen, according to the first description, understands the highest principle as a presentation of the generic concept of the transcendental *conditions* of mathematical-natural science determined as experience, according to the second description, he presupposes the idea of the recognition of the *factum* of mathematical-natural science as that *whose* conditions are supposed to be explicated. As he says, this idea "posits itself as the highest law" by the fact that that which is here recognized, becomes designated as a general form of the lawfulness. While thereby at first the *conditions* and what they have in common stand in view, from which the possibility of natural-scientific cognition is to be explained, the essential character of natural-scientific cognition, which should be *explained through* these conditions, is thematic in relation to the general form of lawfulness. Since the conditions and that which is conditioned, the ground of explanation and that which is to be explained are to be distinguished from one another, it must appear incomprehensible that both descriptions should count as descriptions of one and the same principle. Thus one needs to ask: How can the epitome of the conditions of the possibility of natural-scientific cognition be identified with what is their essential formal character, i.e., the character of lawfulness as such?

Obviously, this can only be seen if what Cohen calls the transcendental *conditions* of the possibility of natural-scientific cognition of experience are the *essential formal determinations* of the *logical content* of the concept of this cognition *qua* cognition from *laws*. For only then can it be said that the concept in which the commonality of all the conditions of the possibility of this cognition is thought is *identical* with the concept whereby this cognition is determined according to its essence. However, that means that

Cohen's demonstration of the conditions of the possibility of natural-scientific cognition is in fact to be understood only as the explication of the conditions of the *logical* possibility of the *concept* of this cognition, i.e., its lawful validity.

This is precisely the sense of the "content" of the "transcendental method" specified by Cohen himself, as is demonstrated in his following statement on the "content of the transcendental method":

> Experience is given; what is to be discovered are the conditions on which their possibility rests. If the conditions which make the given experience possible are found to make it possible in a way to speak of the experience as valid *a priori,* and if strict necessity and unrestricted universality can be awarded to it, *then* these conditions are to be designated as the *constitutive characteristics of the concept of experience.* . . . That alone is the sole task of transcendental philosophy.[14]

Several things follow from this. As the context shows, Cohen's transcendental method can provide no *proof* for the validity of mathematical-natural scientific cognition. The only thing that it can accomplish and provide is the *description* of those cognitions in which the formal character of lawfulness, which is proper to mathematical-natural scientific cognition, is instantiated. This character of lawfulness or lawful validity, however, is not *proven* in this manner; rather it will be accepted as factual together with the acceptance of the facticity of mathematical-natural science. That means that Cohen's thesis that the form of lawfulness of a cognition warrants the objective validity of the cognition is *proven* neither through the practice of the transcendental method nor through recourse to the highest principle. This is so because these cognitions, to which Cohen awards the status of transcendental conditions, are for their part only species of laws; and the highest principle, which should justify them—this has been shown by our analysis of this highest principle—contains nothing other than the isolated idea of the moment of lawful validity as such that is contained in all types of laws. It therefore follows that the highest principle cannot be the kind of principle from which the objective validity of the transcendental conditions could be *proven.* Rather, it achieves only the theoretically much more modest function of being the isolated expression of the unity of the moments of lawfulness and objective validity, which are contained and always already assumed in all lawful cognitions.

If one turns once more to the context in which Cohen has developed the explication of his highest principle, then the accusation of a circular grounding of the possibility of experience can be seen as a misunderstanding. It is a misunderstanding, however, of which Cohen's "serious debate" and "resolution" is itself indeed prone to, through the reference to the groundlessness of the highest principle and the recognition of the lawfulness of natural-scientific cognition that is thereby brought to expression (Cohen 1987a, 139). For this accusation cannot be settled by referring to the recognition of the *factum* of mathematical-natural science and the implied recognition of the lawful character of its cognitions, which are elevated to the content of such a highest principle. According to this critique, the circularity in the argument lies precisely in the fact that one attempts, in conjunction with a highest principle of experience, to justify the condition of the possibility of experience *from experience itself*. Instead, this accusation can only be "resolved" by showing that it has no target. In response to this, we will show that one can in no way speak of a *grounding* of the validity of experience from the highest principle, *because there is no such grounding*. What exists and what is the content of Cohen's theory of experience is solely the presentation of these laws that constitute the concept of experience concerning its assumed objective validity. The content of the epitome of these laws is expressed in the idea that they all contain the formal-invariant moment of lawfulness in which the objectivity of cognition is always already implied, and the highest principle represents precisely this content. And because there is no *grounding* for the validity of experience, no vicious circle is set in motion with the exposition of a highest principle. To be sure, it must be said that, since every cognition contains the moment of lawful validity, which is expressed in the highest principle as such, it is no longer thought to be justified through a higher proposition. Therefore, this highest principle justifies itself and can be regarded as unconditional, insofar as it can no longer have a ground of its validity that is distinct from it. However, it is not this characteristic of the highest principle, but solely its content whose consequence is that characteristic from which the accusation of circularity can be refuted.

For the same reason, the derived accusation of the impossibility of the proof of the truth of cognition for accepted, factual mathematical-natural science simply misses the point, and hence is to be rejected, because there is no such proof in Cohen's theory of experience. Thus in another passage, Cohen describes his theoretical program as follows: "The critique of cognition . . . *separates* science into presuppositions (*Voraussetzungen*) and foundations (*Grundlagen*) that are assumed *in* and *for* its laws."[15] Since these foundations are, for their part, laws in which their own objective validity is implied, and since the highest principle only contains this moment of lawfulness and this moment of the objective validity implied in it, one can in no way speak of a proof for "the justification (*Rechtsgrund*) of certainty" (Cohen 1984, 49) with respect to these presuppositions.

The Highest Principle and the Logic of Origin

In his investigation of the development of Hermann Cohen's theoretical philosophy, Geert Edel has shown in an equally meticulous and convincing manner that Cohen's main systematic work, the *Logik der reinen Erkenntnis* (*Logic of Pure Cognition*), must be read and understood as a "sum" of the systematic content of his reconstruction of Kant's theoretical philosophy, rather than as an outline of an entirely new theoretical program. If one pursues the question of the way in which Cohen's theory of a highest principle has become useful for the system of the *Logik der reinen Erkenntnis*, then one should refer to Cohen's remarks on the concept of a "logic of origin" (Cohen 2005, 31–32) and, more precisely, to his conception of a "principle of origin" (Cohen 2005, 35). From these remarks, therefore, must arise an answer to the question of how the concept of origin that is central for Cohen's logic of cognition is different from that of the highest principle and further, in which way the content—to which the quality of origin is now attributed—is more specifically determined.

Before one can turn to these questions, one must call attention to a different and more serious problem. It arises from Cohen's statements concerning the systematic function of the principle of origin. In these statements the Platonic concepts of the idea and hypothesis and Cohen's interpretation of the same are the guiding clues.[16] Thus he writes, "If the idea is primarily a hypothesis, then the category of origin is the most fundamental groundlaying (*Grundlegung*); it is the foundation (*Grundlage*) of modern science" (Cohen 2005, 597).

And with reference to the grounding function of the *Logik der reinen Erkenntnis* concerning the "unity of a system," Cohen remarks: "The unity of the system demands a central point in the foundation of logic. This methodological center is the idea of the hypothesis, which we have developed into the judgment and into the logic of the origin" (Cohen 2005, 601).

If one initially follows the Platonic concept of the hypothesis, then Cohen means by it a thesis, which presents the beginning of a line of argumentation. Here it is decisive, on the one hand, that the meaning of the thesis consists solely in its function for the argument. This thesis consists in the starting point and criterion for the truth of the propositions derived from it. It does not consist in the validity that may be attributed to it independently of this function. On the other hand, it is crucial that this thesis can be questioned and replaced by other theses if its implications contradict it or another higher-ranking assumption.[17]

This, however, results in a problem. For if one regards the concept of hypothesis as the "methodological center" of the *Logik der reinen Erkenntnis*—as Cohen seems to do in his last-cited statement—and if one understands this function to the effect that the concept of hypothesis is utilized *as an interpretament of the principle of origin*, then it appears that one can no longer speak of a continuity between the theorem of a highest principle and the conception of the principle of origin. For the characteristics of being presuppositionless, unconditioned, and necessary which Cohen had attributed to the highest principle, no longer appear to be applicable to the principle of origin interpreted as a hypothesis. In other words: If the principle of origin is only to have the status of a "ground-laying" (*Grundlegung*), conceived by thinking and in principle always subject to revision, then it is not evident how it can be understood in light of the highest principle, which Cohen previously characterized as the unconditioned and insurmountable "systematic point of culmination" (Cohen 1987a, 143) of his system of synthetic principles. Thus, one would have to go so far as to say that Cohen's interpretation of the principle of origin as hypothesis actually presents an implicit self-critique; it excludes and negates from the very start every attempt to understand this principle as the successor to the former highest principle.

The alternative that results in this way between, on the one hand, proceeding from a highest, unconditioned, and unsurpassable principle and, on the other, undertaking the exposition of a "ground-laying" (*Grundlegung*) that is only relatively final, because it is in principle subject to revision, is not only a problem for Cohen's theoretical development. This alternative also dominates the leading scholarship. While for Geert Edel, Cohen's concept of origin "can only have the status of a hypothesis and can only signify a laying of grounds (*Grundlegung*),"[18] Helmut Holzhey has interpreted Cohen's concept of origin as "an unconditioned ground in itself" and as "absolute."[19]

In order to decide between these alternatives, we have to examine whether the respective interpretations of the relation between a highest principle, origin, hypothesis, and the unconditioned (or *anhupotheton*[20]) are themselves without alternatives. We will come to the conclusion that this is not the case.

In this light, one needs to first pursue for a moment Cohen's broader implementation of his hypothesis-theorem. It arises from a thesis that Cohen had already formulated in the context of his first reconstruction of Kant. It claims that the system of principles that forms the basis of natural-scientific cognition is to be conceived as a system that is incomplete, open, and capable not only of expansion but of revision.[21] In the *Logik der reinen Erkenntnis,* this thesis appears in the assertion that "completeness" with respect to the "number of categories . . . would not be a fullness, but would form an open wound of logic" (Cohen 2005, 396). The reasoning behind this thesis can be derived from Cohen's orientation to modern mathematical-natural science, particularly from the "*factum* of becoming (*Werdefaktum*) of mathematical-natural science," as it is now called in the *Logik der reinen Erkenntnis* (Cohen 2005, 76). With this orientation, Cohen attempts to account for the circumstance that the inventory of natural-scientific cognitions cannot be seen as complete but is in the process of continuous development, expansion, or revision. According to Cohen, however, this circumstance is to be acknowledged not only for the inventory of scientific cognitions, but also for the inventory of its basic concepts and principles—that is, for all "pure cognitions," whose presentation is the theme and task of the *Logik der reinen Erkenntnis*. "The necessary notion of the progress of science," as Cohen formulated his thesis, "not only implies, but necessarily presupposes, the idea of the progress of pure cognitions" (Cohen 2005, 396).

In the present context, it is crucial to see that from his thesis that "pure cognitions" can only be awarded the status of "ground-layings" (*Grundlegungen*) which are capable of revision, Cohen has *not* drawn the conclusion that, since this is the case, the idea of the form of lawfulness as such is to be abandoned. Cohen's conclusion is rather that:

> the ultimate foundations (*Grundlagen*) of logic are ground-layings (*Grundlegungen*) whose expressions must change according to the progress of the problems and of the insights. It is a vain delusion that therefore the law, the *a priori,* the eternal would become volatilized and subjectivized; rather, the eternity of reason is confirmed in the historical nexus of ground-layings (*Grundlegungen*). (Cohen 2002b, 84–85)

This idea of the objectivity and invariability of the universal form of lawfulness is, however, precisely the idea that forms the basis of the content of the highest principle, as Cohen had posed and elucidated it in the second edition of *Kants Theorie der Erfahrung*. Consequently one might conclude that this idea of the form of lawfulness is now indeed able to interpret the content of the principle of origin. The highest principle would now have to be described as "origin," since it is thinking alone which can generate the unity of lawfulness and objectivity—and Cohen had already proposed this insight in the context of the explication of his theorem of a highest principle.

This would also make another thesis understandable, which is decisive for Cohen's conception of the principle of origin. This is the thesis that "thinking and being are the same (in their object)" (Cohen 1928, 337). If one adds Cohen's further theses, according to which "the basic form of being is the basic form of judgment," while the latter is "the basic form of thinking" (Cohen 2005, 47), then it becomes clear that Cohen's concept of being primarily designates the moment of veridical being or being-true (*Wahrsein*) contained in a judgment, which is related to an *object of cognition.*[22] Since such a judgment, according to Cohen, has the ground of its validity solely in thinking, one can say: "Being is the being of thinking. Therefore thinking, as the thinking of being, is the thinking of cognition" (Cohen 2005, 18).

This relation between thinking and being—which can be described as a relation of the creation of being in and through thinking, and which Cohen has misleadingly termed the "identity of thinking and being" (Cohen 2005, 18)—would now have to be considered as the interpretation of the content of the highest principle and at the same time as the fundamental interpretation of what Cohen, in the *Logik der reinen Erkenntnis,* has called the "principle of origin." In accordance with the initial interpretive thesis suggested above, *thinking* is therefore to be understood as "thinking of the origin" (*Denken des Ursprungs*) (Cohen 2005, 36), insofar as it is the sole origin of being, and that *theory* which presents the manners in which thinking posits being, is to be called the "logic of origin."

With this result, however, more questions appear to be posed than answered. For on the one hand, it seems that with this result one can demonstrate the *continuity* of the significance and systematic function of the highest principle with respect to the principle of origin. On the other hand, however, it must now appear entirely hopeless to use this interpretation to understand Cohen's view that the concept of origin can merely be assigned the status of a *hypothesis* in the sense of a "ground-laying" (*Grundlegung*) which is, in principle, capable of revision. For with the conception of an "identity of thinking and being," the status of the unconditioned and necessary is reinstated—a status which cannot be thought in the concept of the hypothesis, but which is nevertheless to be attributed to the highest principle. This now seems to allow for no other conclusion than that—against Cohen's explicit self-understanding—one will *nevertheless* have to assign to the principle of origin the status of a "foundation" (*Grundlage*) which must thus be called absolute and therefore an *anhupotheton.*

These conclusions, however, turn out to be premature. For the question raised above—namely, whether the indicated position has any alternative interpretation—remains entirely unanswered as yet. Consequently it has to be shown in what follows that this alternative is in fact incomplete and that, on its basis, Cohen's position cannot be adequately described.

This shall be demonstrated in two steps. It has to be shown, firstly, that one has to adhere to the idea of what is unconditioned and without presuppositions with reference to the status of the principle of origin, without being forced into assenting to the idea of it as *anhupotheton*, which Cohen denied earlier. Secondly, it must be shown that one has to adhere to the idea of the hypothesis as a "ground-laying" (*Grundlegung*) without having to assent to the idea of its revisability with respect to the principle of origin.

If one brings into more precise view, for this purpose, Cohen's explication of the concept of the *anhupotheton*, then it becomes clear that Cohen primarily highlights with it a moment that he designates—stemming from his interpretation of the status of the Platonic Idea of the Good[23]—as a position "beyond being," while he interprets this beyondness as "beyond all thinking, all cognition" (Cohen 2002a, 32). According to Cohen, such a beyondness characterizes the "medieval concept of the absolute" as the "central concept" of a "false and unscientific metaphysics," which precisely the "logic of origin" had intended to "invalidate" (Cohen 2005, 606).

One can see immediately that such an interpretation of the concept of the *anhupotheton* can, in fact, in no way count as the interpretation of the status of the principle of origin. For Cohen's formula of the "identity of thinking and being" has its point precisely in removing any claim of the independence and self-sufficiency of being from the achievement of thinking, and in attributing to the concept of being significance and meaning only as being posited or created in thinking. Nevertheless, it is not only acceptable, but mandatory, to maintain the idea of the unconditioned in order to characterize the status of the principle of origin. One has to characterize the relation of thinking and being as unconditioned because there is no instance (nor can there be) from which this relation could in itself be deduced, since this relation represents nothing other than the basic form of each and every true judgment that is related to an object of cognition. This is a basic form that must already be presupposed in every judgment that makes a claim to objective validity and from which it would have to be deduced. Thus the principle of origin has to be construed as unconditional, although not as an *anhupotheton* in Cohen's sense.[24]

Cohen's idealistic main thesis, according to which every being is being posited in thinking, also permits a use of the concept of the hypothesis as "ground-laying" (*Grundlegung*) *without* the idea of revisability—and this use, furthermore, is possible without a collision with Cohen's thesis of the revisability of "pure cognitions." At this point one may recall that the content of the principle of origin only expresses the purely empty idea of the invariant form of each of its lawful cognitions, which is objectively determined according to its content. If the principle of origin were now assumed to be capable of revision, then Cohen's undertaking of a logic of pure cognition would be entirely questionable. For then indeed the idea of the form of lawfulness, which forms the basis of Cohen's logic of cognition, would itself be rendered vulnerable. Hence Cohen could appropriately, albeit drastically, call it a "vain delusion" if "the law were volatilized and subjectivized," for the principle of origin expresses nothing other than the principle of any given law. Consequently, one can in no way meaningfully speak of a revision with respect to the principle of origin.[25]

Furthermore, one cannot say that the principle of origin could not be considered as unconditional and unrevisable (and therefore only as "hypothesis") for the reason that its distinction as principle of every law (i.e., as original positing of being attributable to thinking) would be a distinction granted to it from thinking. This would be a distinction which could in principle not make the claim to describe the "true" essence of something, and henceforth also could not be the principle of origin. This thesis is to be rejected for the reason that, on the one hand, it is not at all concerned with the description of such an essence, but only with the isolated idea of the relation of thinking and being mentioned earlier—and this is the basis of the analysis of any kind of essence. On the other hand, it is nonsensical to submit this relation to the limitation of its mere *being-thought,* for precisely this is excluded through this relation. With this idea we think not the merely *thought* relationship of thinking and being, but this relation itself, and therein the mere being-thought as a moment of its content is not only not contained, but precisely negated implicitly.

Nevertheless, the principle of origin can be understood as "ground-laying" (*Grundlegung*), and indeed in a double sense: Firstly, insofar as it represents the common form of all particular "ground-layings" (*Grundlegungen*), determined according to their respective particular contents; and secondly, in that it presents thinking in its original relation to being, which is in principle not capable of revision, and this relation consists in that being is a being created by thinking. In this sense, then, thinking is to be construed as the "ground-laying" (*Grundlegung*) of being or, what amounts to the same, the principle of origin describes the "laying of the ground" (*Grundlegung*) of being through thinking. Hence, we can say with Geert Edel that Cohen's origin is no "separated absolute, but a moment, a character or a 'quality' of thinking, which however realizes itself *in* all particular *cognitions*"[26] and which is posited by Cohen in the form of an autonomous highest principle. Against Edel's interpretation, however, one must insist that the idea of lawfulness that is expressed in this principle *cannot* as such be subject to revision, and thus that the principle of origin can only be understood as in *that* sense a hypothesis—i.e., as a "ground-laying" (*Grundlegung*) in which thinking is the ground of being.

If one looks back on the previously mentioned phrase of Helmut Holzhey, then the origin is indeed entirely "determined in itself as unconditioned ground," since a further ground, from which its validity could yet be grounded, cannot be determined. One can ask, however, whether one can also follow Holzhey's interpretation, suggested initially by Hans Wagner,[27] according to which the origin so determined can be understood as "self-determination through self-relation."[28] This is supposed to be possible in that the origin is thought as "self-relation to an Other that is grounded by this origin and differentiated from it in order to determine oneself in this self-relation to the Other in this Other."[29] Such a conception is incompatible with Cohen's notion of origin: Since with this notion Cohen meant only the idea of the form of lawfulness which is as such entirely empty of content, no ground of creation of a difference in contents can be contained in it, and it is precisely this difference that is indicated with the moment of the Other. Cohen's proposition obviously also means that indeed validity is conditioned through the origin, but all pure cognitions are only "variations" (Cohen 2005, 36) of the origin, and that means *instances,* in which pure thinking comes to presentation or to appearance: It does not mean that these instances are analytical derivatives of the origin as a self-differentiating principle. And this is also indicated by Cohen's thesis that the unity of the highest principle is not a "creative unity, but merely an ideal unity, namely the unity of the law" (Cohen 1987a, 591).

In conclusion, Cohen's principle of origin is no metaphysical absolute, but is also not a hypothesis capable of revision; rather it is the principle of the form of lawfulness, which qualifies thinking itself. This principle is indeed an ultimate principle, yet is not a principle that generates difference. Thus here as well, as so often, the truth lies in the middle.

TRANSLATED BY COLIN J. HAHN

NOTES

1. On the following, see Edel 1988, 55–51 and 88–89. On this topic, see further the investigation of Winter 1980, 103–115.

2. The corresponding assertion of Cohen's amounts to: "The goal is: the explanation of the possibility of synthetic propositions *a priori.* These form the true and entire content of experience. And this content of experience, which is given in mathematics and pure natural science . . . needs to be explained according to its possibility" (Cohen 1987b, 206).

3. On this, see specifically Geert Edel's introduction to the second edition (also in the reprint of the third edition) of *Kants Theorie der Erfahrung* (Cohen 1987a, 11*–12*).

4. See Cohen 1984, 5–6.

5. See Cohen 2001, 46; and Cohen 1984, 6. For this specifically, see Edel 1988, 384ff.

6. See Cohen 1987b, 206: As Cohen says here, "the elements have to be sought, in which the alleged apriority of the same [i.e., of the contents of natural-scientific cognition] consist. The value characteristics of the *a priori* are necessity and universality. The ground of these, however, can only be known in us, in concepts; not in the object. It is thus necessary to find the concepts in which the *a priori* must be secured, which conditions the necessity and universality of the given content of experience."

7. Thus Cohen explains in Cohen 1987b, 206: "This course [i.e., the course of the analytical methods] is clearly indicated in the *Prolegomena,* but also in the [first] *Critique.*" Cohen could reach this position because of the fact that Kant has taken some sections of the *Prolegomena,* in which he in fact carries out the analytic method, into his introduction to the second edition of the *Critique of Pure Reason.* (Thus §§ 5–6 of Kant's introduction to the second edition of the *Critique of Pure Reason* parallel

§§ 2–5 of the *Prolegomena*.) On the synthetic and analytic methods respectively, cf. Kant's explanation in the *Prolegomena*: "In the *Critique of Pure Reason* I worked on this question *synthetically*, namely by inquiring within pure reason itself, and seeking to determine within this source both the elements and the laws of its pure use, according to principles. This work is difficult and requires a resolute reader to think himself little by little into a system that takes no foundation as *given* except reason itself, and that therefore tries to develop cognition out of its original seeds without relying on any *fact (factum)* whatever. . . . the *Prolegomena* must therefore rely on *something already known to be dependable,* from which we can *go forward* with confidence and ascend to the sources, which are not yet known. . . . The methodological procedure of the *Prolegomena* . . . will therefore be analytic" (Kant 1902, 274–75; Kant 1997, 25–26: emphasis added).

8. On the following, see Baum 1986. Baum has pointed out that the "so-called 'transcendental arguments'" discussed in the Anglo-Saxon Kant literature "are a new version of the 'transcendental methods' of Neo-Kantianism" (17–18). To this one can add P. F. Strawson's critique of "transcendental psychology": Strawson's critical thesis—namely, that Kant's theory of cognition deals with an "imaginary subject of transcendental psychology" (Strawson 1966, 97)—has its forerunner in Cohen's corresponding critique of Kant. Against Strawson's critique of Kant in this regard, see Carl 1989, 125–26.

9. The concept of experience is henceforth used in the Cohenian sense.

10. See Lange 1974. Lange's accusation reads verbatim: "If one pushes the emphasis of the mere transcendental standpoint thus far, then one arrives . . . at the tautology that experience is indeed to be explained from the conditions of possible experience" (577). The avoidance of this "tautology" and the attainment of a "synthetic result" (577) is seen by Lange as given with the proof that the "categories [must] yet be something other than conditions of experience" (578). Lange sees this "more" as given in the psycho-physical "organization" (578) of humans, from which the categories are to be grounded. On Lange's interpretation of Kant, see Köhnke 1986, 233–257, esp. 251–52.

11. See Cohen 2001, 33.

12. See Cohen 1987a, 138.

13. Loc. cit.: emphasis added.

14. Cohen 2001, 32: emphasis added.

15. Cohen 1984, 6: emphasis added.

16. Cohen's interpretation of the Platonic concepts of idea and hypothesis, which is significant for his theoretical development, is found in *Platons Ideenlehre und die Mathematik*. In: *Rektoratsprogramm der Universität Marburg vom Jahr 1878,* Sonderausgabe Marburg 1879. Reprinted in Cohen 1928, 336–366. On this, see the comprehensive presentation by Geert Edel in Edel 1988, 202–03. On Cohen's reception of Plato, see further Lembeck 1991, as well as Poma 1987.

17. On the Platonic concept of hypothesis, see Wieland 1982, 150–51.

18. Edel 1991, 81.

19. Holzhey 1986, 183 and 218.

20. [Translator's note: The Greek *anhupotheton* indicates a principle that is not

to be taken as a hypothesis, but is absolutely justified. The term is used by Plato to describe the principle that is reached through dialectical reasoning, and by Aristotle to describe the principle of non-contradiction.]

21. See Cohen 1987b, 101; and Cohen 1987a, 519.

22. On the concept of veridical being, see Tugendhat 1976, 56–57.

23. See Cohen 1928, 363.

24. Contrary to this, Geert Edel has understood the quality of the unconditioned, which pertains to the relation of thinking and being, always and solely as the kind of quality that pertains to an entity located beyond thinking; such an entity would therefore have to be thought as "*anhupotheton.*" See Edel 1991, 81 et pass.

25. The quoted citation is also found in the context of the presentation by Geert Edel (Edel 1991, 76). However, since for Edel apparently the oppositions "ground-laying" (*Grundlegung*) and "foundation (*Grundlage*) given in itself," or "hypothesis" and "*anhupotheton,*" respectively, form complete disjunctions, he has overlooked Cohen's explanation that is directed against his interpretation and furthermore has held on to the thesis that the concept of the origin itself could only be thought as hypothesis. However, it is inconceivable how this interpretation could escape the (absurd) consequence of the possible self-nullification of the foundation of Cohen's logic of cognition. Against Edel's interpretation of the origin as a hypothesis capable of revision, we can also refer to a self-commentary of Cohen's from his posthumous work, the *Religion of Reason Out of the Sources of Judaism,* in which Cohen has identified the principle of origin as the "archetype of all lawfulness" and, precisely as such, as *immune* to such objections: "Reason . . . means positively the lawfulness, the archetype of lawfulness . . . and there can be no firmer, no more profound foundation than that of lawfulness. . . . [W]herever lawfulness reigns, there the domain of reason is secured. . . . Lawfulness is so weighty that against it every objection has to retreat. For what more reliable and certain basis than lawfulness could another reason offer?" (Cohen 1966, 11–12/Cohen 1972, 10–11).

26. Edel 1988, 433 (ed. Edel).

27. See Wagner 1959, 128–29. On Holzey's connection to Hans Wagner, see Holzhey 1986, xi, 183 n. 18, and 218.

28. Holzhey 1986, 183.

29. Holzhey 1986, 218. The cited formulation is a citation from Hans Wagner's *Philosophie und Reflexion,* and is identified as such by Holzhey. Wagner's thesis concerning the absolute, which forms the basis of Holzey's interpretation of the Cohenian principle of origin, reads in its entirety: "The absolute is thus essentially self-relation to an Other that is grounded by the absolute itself and differentiated by it, in order to determine in this self-relation to the Other its own self" (Wagner 1959, 128).

BIBLIOGRAPHY

Baum, Manfred. 1986. *Deduktion und Beweis in Kants Transzendentalphilosophie Untersuchungen zur Kritik der reinen Vernunft.* Königstein: Hain Verlag bei Athenäum.

Carl, Wolfgang. 1989. *Der schweigende Kant: die Entwürfe zu einer Deduktion der Kategorien vor 1781.* Göttingen: Vandenhoeck & Ruprecht.

Cohen, Hermann. 1928. *Herman Cohens Schriften zur Philosophie und Zeitgeschichte.* Ed. Albert Görland and Ernst Cassirer. Vol. 1. Berlin: Akademie-Verlag.

——. 1966. *Religion der Vernunft aus den Quellen des Judentums.* 2d ed. Darmstadt: Melzer. (*Religion of Reason out of the Sources of Judaism.* Trans. Simon Kaplan. New York: Frederick Ungar, 1972.)

——. 1984. *Das Prinzip der Infinitesimal-Methode und seine Geschichte.* (*Werke*, vol. 5/1). Hildesheim: Olms.

——. 1987a. *Kants Theorie der Erfahrung.* 3d ed. (*Werke*, vol. 1/1). Hildesheim: Olms.

——. 1987b. *Kants Theorie der Erfahrung.* 1st ed. (*Werke*, vol. 1/3). Hildesheim: Olms.

——. 2001. *Kants Begründung der Ethik nebst ihren Anwendungen auf Recht, Religion und Geschichte.* 2d rev. and exp. ed. (Werke, vol. 2). Hildesheim: Olms.

——. 2002a. *Der Begriff der Religion im System der Philosophie.* (*Werke*, vol. 10). Hildesheim: Olms.

——. 2002b. *Ethik des reinen Willens.* 2d ed. (*Werke*, vol. 7). Hildesheim: Olms.

——. 2005. *Logik der reinen Erkenntnis.* 2d ed. (*Werke*, vol. 6/1). Hildesheim: Olms.

Edel, Geert. 1988. *Von der Vernunftkritik zur Erkenntnislogik: die Entwicklung der theoretischen Philosophie Hermann Cohens.* Freiburg: K. Alber.

——. 1991. "Kantianismus oder Platonismus? Hypothesis als Grundbegriff der Philosophie Cohens." *Il Cannocchiale* 1–2: 59–87.

Holzhey, Helmut. 1986. *Cohen und Natorp.* Vol. 1. Basel: Schwabe.

Kant, Immanuel. 1902. *Kants gesammelte Schriften.* Vol. 4. Berlin: Reimer. (*Prolegomena to Any Future Metaphysics.* Ed. Gary Hatfield. Cambridge: Cambridge University Press, 1997.)

Köhnke, Klaus Christian. 1986. *Entstehung und Aufstieg des Neukantianismus: die deutsche Universitätsphilosophie zwischen Idealismus und Positivismus.* Frankfurt: Suhrkamp. (*The Rise of Neo-Kantianism: German Academic Philosophy Between Idealism and Positivism.* Trans. R. J. Hollingdale. Cambridge: Cambridge University Press, 1991.)

Lange, Friedrich Albert. 1974. *Geschichte des Materialismus und Kritik seiner Bedeutung in der Gegenwart.* With an introduction by Alfred Schmidt. Frankfurt: Suhrkamp.

Lembeck, K. H. 1991. "Cohens frühe Platon-Deutung und seine Quellen." *Il Cannocchiale*: 89–116.

Poma, Andrea. 1987. "Il Platone di Hermann Cohen." *Annuario Filosofico* 3: 211–242.

Strawson, P. F. 1966. *The Bounds of Sense: An Essay on Kant's 'Critique of Pure Reason'.* London: Methuen.

Tugendhat, Ernst. 1976. *Vorlesungen zur Einführung in die sprachanalytische Philosophie.* Frankfurt: Suhrkamp.

Wagner, Hans. 1959. *Philosophie und Reflexion.* Munich: E. Reinhardt.

Wieland, Wolfgang. 1982. *Platon und die Formen des Wissens.* Göttingen: Vandenhoeck & Ruprecht.

Winter, Eggert. 1980. *Ethik und Rechtswissenschaft. Eine historisch-systematische Untersuchung zur Ethik-Konzeption des Marburger Neukantianismus im Werk Hermann Cohens.* Berlin: Duncker & Humblot.

7

Transcendental Logic and Minimal Empiricism: Lask and McDowell on the Unboundedness of the Conceptual

Steven G. Crowell

Introduction: Empiricism in the Shadow of Hegel

In the preface to *Mind and World,* John McDowell describes his work as "a prolegomenon to a reading" of Hegel's *Phenomenology.*[1] He also remarks that Robert Brandom has decisively shaped his thinking by "forcing me to get clear about the differences, small in themselves, that transform for me the look of our wide measure of agreement" (MW ix). These remarks are linked, for both the agreement and the differences can be seen to reflect different aspects of the *Phenomenology of Spirit,* which Hegel characterizes both as the "science of the *experience* of consciousness" and also as the "ladder" to the science of logic.[2] The agreement between Brandom and McDowell consists in their mutual embrace of what the latter calls the "unboundedness of the conceptual"—the recognizably Hegelian "refusal to locate perceptible reality outside the conceptual sphere" (MW 26). Thinking does not stand on one side of a divide whose opposite side would be a merely given, perceptible world, alien to the concept. What is perceived already belongs within what Wilfrid Sellars called "the space of reasons." The differences between Brandom and McDowell, in turn, stem from something like different assessments of the relation between the *Phenomenology* and this unbounded conceptual realm.

For Brandom, the conceptual order is unbounded because the content of experience is not a mental representation, located in an individual mind, but a function of socially mediated commitments and entitlements incurred by participants in the game of giving and asking for reasons. The indexicality of perceptual consciousness is explained causally as reliable differential responsiveness to the environment. Expressed as a report, perception serves no justificatory role but is merely an "entry move" into the realm of inferentially governed conceptual relations.³ Hence, for Brandom, the *Phenomenology* would be less important as a "science of the *experience of consciousness*" than as a "ladder" to the "self-movement of the concept" as expounded in Hegel's *Logic*. For McDowell, however, who conceives the unboundedness of the conceptual as the basis for a "minimal empiricism" (MW xi), it is the *Phenomenology*'s treatment of experience—an experience that is not superseded by the advent of absolute knowledge—that constitutes its importance. As Hegel himself insisted, "nothing is *known* that is not in experience."⁴ If Brandom's third-person approach to the unboundedness of the conceptual tracks Hegel's move beyond individual consciousness to Absolute Spirit, McDowell embraces a first-person internalism: "How can we understand the idea that our thinking is answerable to the empirical world, if not by way of the idea that our thinking is answerable to experience?" (MW xii) These differences are reflected in different interpretations of Sellars' "Empiricism and the Philosophy of Mind." Brandom sees that essay as a "dismantling of empiricism," while McDowell maintains that Sellars' aim is "to rescue a *non-traditional* empiricism from the wreckage of traditional empiricism."⁵ In traversing the *Phenomenology*'s "pathway of doubt" and "way of despair," does Hegel then *dismantle* empiricism's claim that experience plays a role in the justification of knowledge, or does he *reinvent* it by showing how consciousness arrives "at a point at which it gets rid of its semblance of being burdened by something alien"?⁶

Having raised this question we shall immediately let it drop, and set aside any thought of adjudicating the dispute between Brandom and McDowell through a reading of Hegel's *Phenomenology*. The reference to Hegel serves only to link this well-known contemporary dispute to an earlier one which is, at present, far less well known. For the question of whether empiricism is compatible with the thesis of the "unboundedness of the conceptual" is one way to formulate the issue that separates the two main schools of Neo-Kantianism. Both the Marburg School, founded by Hermann Cohen and carried forward by Paul Natorp and Ernst Cassirer, and the Baden or Southwest German School, founded by Wilhelm Windelband and developed by Heinrich Rickert and Emil Lask, read Kant through the lens of German Idealism, especially through Fichte and Hegel.⁷ In Marburg this led to something like Brandom's expressivist inferentialism. Cohen's *Kants Theorie der Erfahrung*, for instance, identifies experience not with mental processes but with the *judgments* generated in the course of scientific investigation, together with their systematic inferential linkages. And for Natorp, Kant's entire Transcendental Aesthetic is a misbegotten project, since space and time are concepts, not intuition, and sensibility makes no independent contribution to knowledge.⁸ Baden Neo-Kantianism, on the other hand, developed a more expansive concept of experience—one that suggests less a dismantling of empiricism than a value-theoretical recasting of its central tenets along the lines of McDowell's normative approach to perceptual content. Heinrich Rickert, for instance, is happy to acknowledge that "perception" is "the mode of knowledge in which a mere fact is established," but he adds that such perception is always "more" than mere "givenness"—perception is "experience," that is, meaningful. Even in perception what is given has form—at very least, the "form of givenness"—and such form is a moment of value and of normativity. For Rickert the object of perception, "that which is cognized, i.e., affirmed or acknowledged in the judgment, must be located in the sphere of the ought (*Sollen*)."[9]

This confluence of the old and the new raises the question of whether the Neo-Kantians may have something to contribute to the contemporary debate over empiricism in the shadow of Hegel. The present essay explores that possibility by staging an *Auseinandersetzung* between McDowell and the Baden Neo-Kantian, Emil Lask (1875–1915). Lask's views on what he calls "the limitlessness of truth" (*die Schrankenlosigkeit der Wahrheit*) overlap with McDowell's idea of the unboundedness of the conceptual in significant ways, while challenging it, *avant la lettre,* in ways that are equally significant.[10] The point of departure for this *Auseinandersetzung* will be Kant's idea of transcendental logic, since both Lask and McDowell acknowledge a debt to this aspect of Kant's thought. In the *Critique of Pure Reason* Kant distinguishes between "pure general logic," which "deals with nothing but the mere form of thought," and "transcendental logic," which "should contain solely the rules of the pure thought *of an object*."[11] If the former provides an account of the conditions under which thought can be consistent with itself, the latter "is a logic of *truth*. For no knowledge can contradict it without at once losing all content, that is, all relation to any object, and therefore all truth."[12] In Kant, this yields a theory of categories—i.e., a theory of those concepts derived from the forms of judgment ("pure understanding") which, together with the *a priori* intuitions of space and time, govern all empirical (perceptual) content. In thus thematizing the necessary connection between the spontaneity of conceptual thought and the receptivity of sensibility, transcendental logic is a theory of empirical cognition. And this, as we have seen, is how McDowell understands his own project.[13]

Following Sellars, McDowell argues that what is given perceptually cannot play a role in justifying empirical knowledge-claims if it is understood as traditional empiricism understands it, namely, as lacking all conceptual content: "we cannot really understand the relations in virtue of which a judgment is warranted except as relations within the space of concepts: relations such as implication and probabilification" (MW 7). So McDowell's transcendental logic must articulate a "different notion of givenness" (MW 10), one that shows how thought can be constrained "from the outside" without conceiving that "outside" as outside the logical space of concepts altogether. The challenge is to say how the world can be independent of our thinking while still having a rational—and not merely causal—bearing on what we think. And this was Lask's challenge as well.

Lask too is concerned with the conditions for a minimal empiricism. His *Kategorienlehre* aims to show how the world can stand in *normative* relation to our thought, and so constrain it. Like Sellars and McDowell, Lask understands that this cannot be accomplished if the world is conceived as an "extralogical" given, bereft of rational structure. Transcendental logic must begin by acknowledging the "supremacy of the logical" (*Allherschaft des Logischen*), the idea that nothing "given" lies outside the scope of reason. But this must not be allowed to degenerate into "*Panlogism*," the idea that knowledge is *nothing but* the coherence of an inferentially structured system of concepts—in McDowell's phrase, a "self-contained game" (MW 5).[14] For Lask, categorial "forms do not refer dialectically to one another, they refer to their material"—a material that is discovered in experience (LP 54/63). Thus, while the principle that accounts for the applicability of concepts to the world is "to this extent a purely *empirical* one," such material is already "intelligible material" and so can stand in a justificatory and not merely "exculpatory" relation to thought (LP 53/63).[15] Like McDowell, Lask wishes to establish the unbounded scope of the logical within experience (*Panarchie des Logos*) while avoiding an anti-empiricistic coherentism, or *Panlogism*.

Before exploring these similarities, however, we should note the dissimilarity that provides the basis for an *Auseinandersetzung*. In arguing that the content of perceptual states is already intelligible, McDowell embraces Kant's claim that this content has the structure of a *judgment:* "In experience one takes in, for instance sees, *that things are thus and so*. That is the sort of thing one can also, for instance, judge" (MW 9). Perception has this structure because "experience has its content by virtue of the drawing into operation in sensibility of capacities that are genuinely elements in a faculty of spontaneity"—i.e., "conceptual capacities" (MW 46–47, 10). In his Woodbridge Lectures, McDowell explains this idea in terms of Kant's Metaphysical Deduction, where Kant writes that "the only use which the understanding can make of concepts is to judge by means of them."[16] For McDowell also, conceptual capacities are essentially capacities for judging: Even if "judging is not the only mode of actualization of conceptual capacities," it "can be singled out as the paradigmatic mode."[17] Thus he can adopt a version of Kant's idea that "the same function which gives unity to the various representations *in a judgment* also gives unity to the mere synthesis of various representations *in an intuition*."[18] Though perception is not judgment, "in visual experiences conceptual capacities are actualized with suitable modes of togetherness"—namely, the truth-functional "modes of togetherness" found paradigmatically in judgments—to enable perception to serve a justificatory role.[19]

For Lask, on the contrary, a logic that focuses on "our conceptual capacities"—on our capacity to judge—cannot do justice to the logical relations between experience and thought. In taking the forms of judgment as a clue to the discovery of the categories, Kant's Metaphysical Deduction "is a thoroughly consequent development of the idea that the formal-logical domain represents an analogical copy of object-hood (*Gegenständlichkeit*)."[20] But such an approach remains on the level of "quasi-transcendence" (LU 359/423); the experiential content it has in view is not that of *perception*—which opens onto the world ("object-hood") as such—but one that is already mediated by cognitive structures. This sort of content or meaning is "separable" from the subject only in the way that propositional content is separable from its psychological or linguistic tokens, not in the way that the world is subject-transcendent. To reach the world, transcendental logic must adopt the "standpoint of genuine transcendence," demonstrating how objects themselves have a logical structure, or meaning, "prior to all contact with subjectivity" (LU 351/414, 360/425). Only so can perception of the world serve as a rational constraint on empirical knowledge-claims. McDowell's view betrays the same blindness that, according to Lask, Husserl's does: By stopping short at *intentional* content—i.e., the object as represented in a certain way by the subject—Husserl provides only a phenomenology of truth-claims, not a principled account of their justification.[21] In a letter to Husserl, Lask agrees that "the type of intentionality you advocate" is an improvement over "all consciousness-in-general concepts," but he denies that phenomenology is the "sole point of departure for a scientific philosophy." Or better—"one might rightly hold it to be the sole point of departure, but only indeed a point of departure."[22] Transcendental logic is not primarily "gnoseological"—an account of cognition, of the subjective uptake of the world as intentional content—but "aletheiological," an account of what objects themselves *are* "in truth" (LU 358/423). For Lask, the scope of the logical within experience is unbounded not because our conceptual capacities are actualized in perception, but because the *objects perceived* belong within the space of reasons. Lask calls this *Logosimmanenz* (LP 201/245).

From Lask's perspective, McDowell's minimal empiricism fails to show how the world belongs within the space of reasons. From McDowell's perspective, however, Lask must explain how things in the world, just as such, can stand in normative relation to our thinking if these are *not* "relations within the space of concepts: relations such as implication and probabilification" (MW 7). Our task, then, is to assess Lask's distinction between judgment-logic and object-logic and to see whether, in the absence of such a distinction, McDowell can move from the idea that *experience* is a source of empirical justification, to the idea that *the world* provides rational constraint on our thought.

The Two-World Theory and the Space of Reasons

Lask's thesis of the limitlessness of truth arises from his understanding of what is philosophically decisive in Kant's "Copernican revolution" (*Kopernikanische Tat*). Kant's transcendental logic is not merely a critical epistemology that proposes to "investigate cognition itself before investigating the objects," since this would make him a mere "epigone of Descartes or Locke" (LP 25/28).[23] Nor is it, as the Marburg Neo-Kantians held, essentially a "theory of science."[24] Rather, the "revolutionary achievement" that makes Kant the "founder of a new epoch" in philosophy is "the transformation of the concept of being into a concept of transcendental logic" (LP 25/28). What this means can best be appreciated, according to Lask, by contrasting it with the way philosophy has hitherto been pursued—that is, by contrasting the older "ontological" orientation with a new "aletheiological" one (LU 358/423).

The ontological orientation of all previous philosophy is evident in the persistence of "two-world" theories. Beginning with Plato, the "totality of the thinkable" is always divided into two mutually exclusive types—for instance, "the sensible and the intelligible, appearance and true reality, appearance and idea, matter and form, . . . nature and reason, nature and freedom, temporal and eternal" (LP 5/5). Characteristic of all such dualisms is the thought that these types are types of *entity*. Form, for instance, is "non-sensible being" (*Nichtsinnlich-Seiende*); nature is "sensible being" (*Sinnlich-Seiende*), while freedom is "supersensible being" (*Übersinnlich-Überseiende*) (LP 13/15). Thus, all previous philosophy has held being (*Sein*) to be the highest category; what is thinkable is always *something*, a being. Given the ontological character of such two-world theories, the history of philosophy had to become a series of attempts to "bridge the gap" between the worlds. Even Kant, whose revolution spells the end of ontological philosophy in principle, did not escape it in fact. Operating with a two-world distinction between phenomena and noumena, Kant was unable to specify the world to which the object of his own transcendental inquiry—forms of intuition, categories—belonged. Categories are not phenomena—real psychological syntheses of the perceptual manifold; but neither are they noumena—entities that transcend possible experience altogether. As Lask notes, Kant's "theory of knowledge ignores his own theoretical critique of reason, his own cognition of the non-sensible transcendental forms," with the result that "the object of his own transcendental philosophy"—namely, logical categoriality—"does not . . . so to speak count for him" (LP 110/131).[25]

If Kant did not fully recognize the implications of his "transformation of the concept of being into a concept of transcendental logic," it was, according to Lask, Hermann Lotze (1817–1881) who finally overcame ontological philosophy with an altogether *different type* of two-world theory. For Lotze, the decisive distinction is not between two realms of entity but between "entities and validities, the domain of being and the domain of validity, ontic formations and valid formations, between the sphere of reality and the sphere of value, between that which *is* and *occurs* and that which *holds* without having to be" (LP 5/5). The distinction between the world of validity (*Geltung*) and the world of being (*Sein*) is revolutionary because it acknowledges the very different sorts of relation that define each world: *Ontic* relations obtain between entities, while *normative* relations obtain between logical forms. The realm of being "consists in what is spatially extended and temporally passing, whose elements are thingly and are causally connected" (LP 15/17);[26] the realm of validity is not thingly or causally connected, rather it is inferentially governed. To see that a conclusion "follows" from its premises is to recognize a "valid implication" (*Geltungsfolge*), a "distinctive sort of complex (*Verwicklung*) within the domain of the atemporal that cannot be compared" to relations between entities, because it manifests a "moment of value and, further, of normativity" (LP 16/18, 9/10).

For Lask, then, Kantian categories cannot be understood from an ontological perspective at all since, as normative, their nature is to hold rather than to be. As a logic of truth, transcendental logic has the task of showing how the two worlds—one governed by non-normative relations (e.g., causes), the other by normative relations (e.g., reasons)—stand toward one another. In doing so it becomes an account of "being in the sense of truth"—a clarification of what entities "in truth" are, where "truth" designates the necessary connection between the ontic (*Sein*) and the normative (*Gelten*). Thus transcendental logic enacts the shift from an ontological to an "aletheiological" orientation.[27]

Where does McDowell's project fall within Lask's aletheiological two-world framework? Because the world of "that which *holds* without having to *be*" is, among other things, a space of reasons, McDowell's central claim—that what is perceptually experienced already belongs within the space of reasons—bears close resemblance to Lask's aletheiological account of what entities "in truth" are. But how close a resemblance?

McDowell begins with the problem of justification: How can perception play a role in justifying empirical judgments? Since justification is a matter of providing reasons, perception can justify only if what is perceived bears a rational, and not merely a causal, relation to our thinking. For McDowell this means that it must be able to stand in the "relations of implication and probabilification" that govern the space of reasons. But the object perceived belongs to "nature" in a broad sense, and so it might seem to stand within an altogether different "logical space." In recent centuries, for instance, nature has come to be seen as a "realm of law," closed under strict causal relations (MW xv). More generally, however, the problem arises from the plausible assumption that "whatever the relations are that constitute the logical space of nature, they are *different in kind* from the normative relations that constitute the logical space of reasons" (MW xv). If relations in these two logical spaces are different in kind, this can lead to a "familiar philosophical anxiety about empirical knowledge"—namely, the thought that experience *must* play, but is *precluded* by its nature from playing, a justificatory role (MW 15). If the object of perception belongs to nature conceived as a realm of causal law, its relation to my thought can only be a causal one. My belief could be *explained* as "the result of an alien force, the causal impact of the world," but this would not constitute a *justification* of it (MW 8). On the other hand, if I opt for some form of coherentism and deny that perception plays a role in justifying my belief, it can appear that thought loses its grip on the world and becomes a "frictionless spinning in the void" (MW 11).

McDowell calls this a "transcendental anxiety,"[28] and if we are to locate his position within Lask's framework we need to attend to what "transcendental" means here. In *Mind and World*, McDowell's understanding of Kant's "transcendental story" (MW 41) conforms to Lask's: In principle, Kant's thesis that "objects of possible experience" are constituted through the operation of our "conceptual capacities" shows how what is perceived can belong within the space of reasons. But Kant embedded this insight in an ontological two-world theory—a distinction between phenomena and noumena—under the mistaken belief that one can take a "sideways-on view" of experience. A sideways-on view of experience is distinguished from a view of experience from within by the fact that it circumscribes thinking and experience "within a boundary" while holding "the world outside it" (MW 34). Thus McDowell found it necessary to extract Kant's genuine achievement—namely, to have shown "from the standpoint of experience itself" that "reality is not located outside a boundary that encloses the conceptual sphere" (MW 41)—from his "transcendental story."

In writings subsequent to *Mind and World*, however, McDowell revised his understanding of the term "transcendental," using it to denote Kant's genuine achievement and not his two-world theory. In the "Précis of *Mind and World*," for instance, "transcendental" characterizes "any philosophical thinking whose aim is that there not be a mystery in the very idea of objective purport"[29]—and this is just what Kant's idea of experience as co-constituted by sensibility and understanding does. On this new understanding, the distinction between phenomena and things-in-themselves does not pick out two ontological regions, but two different *stances* toward entities as a whole: "Considering things as things in themselves is considering the very things that figure in our knowledge, but in abstraction from how they figure in our knowledge."[30] To consider them in terms of how they figure in our knowledge, in turn, is just to move from an ontological to an aletheio-logical understanding of the two worlds, and on such an understanding the distinction between the space of reasons and "nature" is not an ontological distinction. It is one that both Lask and McDowell call "transcendental" or "philosophical."

To speak "transcendentally," McDowell explains, is to "speak as a phi-losopher"; and "when we speak as philosophers we do not start to speak about a new range of objects" but "of the same objects, under a special mode of consideration"[31]—namely, in consideration of how they figure in our knowledge. The contrast here seems to be the following: When I am not philosophizing, I speak about objects of experience in an *intentio recta*—for instance, I describe their real properties and relations. When I construct philosophical theories of experience in an ontological register, I remain within this *intentio recta*—for instance, I attempt to solve philosophical puzzles by identifying the real properties and relations thanks to which different ontological types ("mind" and "world") can engage one another. To speak transcendentally, however, is to abandon the *intentio recta*: I no longer consider the real properties and relations of entities, but rather the conditions that enable such entities to be given meaningfully within expe-rience. For instance, in ordinary and scientific inquiry I encounter enti-ties (myself included) as belonging to nature, and I explore whatever real relations they are discovered, in experience, to have. But I can also reflect on what it is for entities to be available in this way—namely, as *open* to inquiry and thus as standing in *normative* relation to my thought. In doing so, I speak "transcendentally." I do not introduce another set of entities (e.g., mental representations) to explain how my thought can be of the world; rather, I consider entities in light of the normative or rational relations that constitute them as *meaningful*. To speak of "meaning" here is not to posit an object other than that which is perceived in *intentio recta*. Philosophy does not uncover some real property of objects that is particularly resistant to scientific investigation. Rather, as Lask puts it, the term "meaning" is a "mere philosophical *epitheton*" that designates the object as correlate of the aletheiological stance (LP 102/123).

Like Lask, then, McDowell insists that transcendental thought does not remove the anxiety about justification by explaining how the gap between two putative ontological regions (the normative and the natural) can be bridged, but by showing why this anxiety need not arise.[32] Theories that remain within an ontological register—for instance, information theories and some forms of cognitive science—try to remove this transcendental anxiety by constructing an account of how, in fact, the two ontological regions are connected. Others, such as the set of theories McDowell calls "bald naturalism," attempt to escape the anxiety by denying that "the contrast that poses our difficulties, the contrast between logical spaces, is genuine" (MW 73). Such theories deny that the space of reasons is *sui generis,* and so seek ways of restating it in the language of the space of law. McDowell's transcendental thought, in contrast, retains the distinction between the normative and the causal but denies that it cuts in the way that ontological two-world theories believe. The space of law is not nature as such, but only one form of "intelligibility" in which nature can be approached (MW xix; 70). This is precisely to approach nature as a whole in terms of the ways in which it can present itself as meaningful, and so as already entailing a relation to norms. Thus the space of reasons is not one ontological region ("the mind") distinct from another ("the world"); it is equivalent to the aletheiological stance toward the ontological, the totality of entities, as such.

According to Lask, Kant shows that "the real order (*das Seinsgebiet*) is not a thoroughly sensible-'aposteriori' . . . alogical mass lacking in significance; it does not lie altogether outside the logical, the 'understanding'; rather, logical form is embedded therein" (LP 49/57). McDowell's claim that the "real order" is "embraced" within "the conceptual order"[33] seems to make the same point. But here the decisive question arises: Is "the logical" equivalent to "the conceptual order"? Is the rational exhausted by the conceptual? On this question, Lask's object-logic and McDowell's concept-logic part company.

The Unboundedness of the Conceptual or the Limitlessness of Truth?

McDowell's idea of the unboundedness of the conceptual—the idea that the real belongs within the conceptual order—depends on the thesis that the conceptual capacities we exercise in thought—that is, in judging—are already "drawn into operation" in perception. For this reason, what we perceive will have "the kind of intelligibility appropriate to meaning" (MW 71), which explains how it can stand in normative relation to our thinking, and thus how our thinking can be accountable to the world. According to Lask, however, this view is seriously flawed, for it does not in fact show how the object perceived can stand in normative relation to our thinking. Lask agrees that the object must have "the kind of intelligibility appropriate to meaning," but to identify meaning with the form of judgment is to substitute a *representation* of the object for the object itself. On Lask's view, we do not perceive "*that* things are thus and so"; rather, we perceive the object's *being* so.

In a recent article, Charles Travis has drawn the consequences of this distinction for McDowell's claim that experience can exert rational constraint on our thinking only if it has a conceptual structure, and, since Lask does not address the issue directly, we shall let Travis move the argument forward. Suppose I perceive some meat on the rug. "Meat's being on the rug is neither true nor false. But it is a way things *count* as being just where a certain thing counts as true to think . . . One can say: the meat's being on the rug is such that for things to be that way is for a certain thought to be true." Travis continues: "*Thus* [does] the meat's being on the rug . . . also engage with normativity."[34] But this is not to say that what we *perceive* is *that* the meat is on the rug.[35] In Lask's terms, what is perceived has a *categorial*, but not a *conceptual* (i.e., predicative) structure. From the aletheiological perspective, truth is not first of all a property of judgments but is the perceived object itself as exhibiting "the kind of intelligibility appropriate to meaning." The friction between mind and world is established not by the unboundedness of the conceptual but by the limitlessness of *truth*. The rational, for Lask, is not coextensive with the conceptual.[36]

Lask's idea of the limitlessness of truth involves a distinction between "paradigmatic" (*urbildlich*) and "artificial" (*gekünstelt*) truth. The latter, identified with judgment, involves an opposition between "correctness" (*Richtigkeit*) and "incorrectness" (*Falschheit*) (LU 258/297). This opposition presupposes a "transjudgmental measure" or norm that must stand "beyond the opposition of correctness and incorrectness" (LU 300/352; 363/428), and this measure is truth in the paradigmatic sense, the object which simply is. But if this object is to serve as the norm for judgment it must have "the kind of intelligibility appropriate to meaning." Thus the object, paradigmatic truth, is equally paradigmatic meaning—being in the *sense* of truth. Anything less, Lask believes, will leave transcendental logic mired in the kind of subjectivism that gives rise to McDowell's anxiety. Lask writes: "What primarily explains the persistent dichotomization of truth and object, the copy-relation according to which truth and meaning are brought to the object" by the subject, is

> the fact that one takes one's point of departure from the—artificial—meaning of the proposition and judgment, which to be sure does not coincide with the object but can hit or miss it. Thus one fails to notice that indeed the object itself is also nothing but meaning—namely non-artificial paradigmatic meaning—and that the distance between meaning and object amounts to a distance between meaning and meaning. (LP 37/42)

To say that "the object itself is also nothing but meaning" is to speak "as a philosopher," aletheiologically—it is to characterize things in light of what makes them intelligible. And what makes things intelligible are the categories that hold of them. Because categories are validities and not entities, they are neither subjective conceptual capacities nor ontic constituents of things. Rather, to say that categories "hold" is just to say that things are in such and such ways. These "ways" are what Lask calls "form," and form is the intelligibility—the *Klarheitsmoment* (LP 64/75)—of the object itself. From an aletheiological perspective, to be an object is to be a "primordial relation" (*Urverhältnis*) between the ontic and the normative, between logical form and that of which such form holds, i.e., the "material" (LP 31/33). Hence the object is *meaningful,* being in the sense of *truth:* "Individual objects are individual theoretical meaning-structures, individual 'truths,'" and "one can say flatly: spatiotemporal objects *are* truths, physical objects are physicalistic truths, astral [objects are] astronomical truths, psychic [objects are] psychological truths, etc. To be sure, truths, unities of meaning, not cognitions, judgments, propositions; and further, truths in the paradigmatic sphere, not the sort of thing that is abstracted from scientific propositions" (LP 36/41). For Lask, then, the limitlessness of truth is not equivalent to the unboundedness of the conceptual.

To say that truth is limitless is to say that, independently of any relation to the subject's conceptual capacities, logical form belongs to the objects to which perception gives us access. Kant's thesis that being is a concept of transcendental logic means that being is not some supersensible property of things but something that holds of them—namely, a category. And what is true of being is true of all categories—"the logical extends into objects as their being, thinghood, causal necessity," and the like (LP 38/44). Because things themselves thus have "the kind of intelligibility appropriate to meaning," perceiving a thing's *being* so can bear rationally on whether I should think one way rather than another. As Charles Travis puts it: "To see the meat on the rug is just to be suitably sensitive, or responsive, to it as it then is—to the non-conceptual." If we define perceptual meaning in terms of our conceptual capacities, however, we substitute something else for the object perceived: "To see *that* the meat is on the rug I must register something else: the *instancing* by things being as they are of a certain way for things to be, meat on the rug."[37] McDowell's formulation collapses perceptual meaning into propositional meaning in just the way Lask warns us against. What can be perceived is located at some definite position in space and time, but *that* it is so is not similarly located—it is not anywhere.[38] It follows that what we see does not have a conceptual structure, and if the world exerts rational constraint on our thought, it is because what we see can be meaningful without being describable in "that"-phrases.

Lask's notion of the paradigmatic object does justice to this, but it is not without its puzzles. What can it mean to say that objects are categorially formed—are unities of the ontic and the normative—if not that in being

perceived they fall within the scope of our conceptual capacities? Lask purports tc reach beyond the intentional content of the subject's perceptual
experience to thematize the object as such, but his claim that what is perceived is a unity of logical form and material sounds suspiciously like the
Myth of the Given. Against coherentism, Lask argues that categories do not
"refer dialectically to one other" but "to their material" (LP 54/63). However, in designating this material "extralogical"—or even "irrational" (LP
65/77)—how can he fail to reintroduce a gulf between form and content,
thus reinstating the transcendental anxiety? McDowell avoids this anxiety
by insisting that the content of perceptual experience can involve nothing extralogical or non-conceptual: "We must not suppose that receptivity
makes an even notionally separable contribution to its co-operation with
spontaneity" (MW 41). But isn't Lask's "extralogical material" just such a
notionally separable contribution?

No, it is not. And it is not because—unlike McDowell—Lask does not
define "extralogicality" with reference to receptivity or sensibility. Instead,
there is a "purely functional opposition between form and material" (LP
43/49): Material is that of which a category holds. Because his account
of paradigmatic meaning makes no reference to the perceiver, Lask need
not commit himself to a debilitating alternative between taking sensibility
merely to be the result of causal processes, on the one hand, or as subordinated to our conceptual capacities, on the other. Instead, "sensible" material
is, like all material, defined by its functional role in relation to the category
that holds of it. The "irrationality" of such material derives entirely from
this role—"irrationality is not meant in the sense of the non-rational but in
the sense of the not thoroughly rationalizable (*Nichtrationalsierbarkeit*), a
sense that is grounded in the functional form/material relation" (LP 65/77).
As Lask puts it, "irrationality is not a feature that distinguishes a particular
content (*Gehalt*) from logical content, but an expression for a functional
role in respect to logical content, which is thereby conceived in the role of
form." When I think about *categories*—as I do in transcendental logic—they
are, functionally, material. Thus, in relation to the domain-category that
holds of them all and "clarifies" what they are—namely, the category 'validity' (LP 65/77)—even categories are "extralogical" and so also "irrational"
in the sense of being not thoroughly rationalizable. In this sense, writes
Lask, "*everything* is irrational, including logical content itself. For anything
that can be logically engaged (*betroffen*), all categorial material, is logically
impenetrable. But everything without exception can be categorial material"
(LP 64/75). Lask's point here is that even if sensibility makes no *independent*
contribution to the content of a perceptual state, this does not mean that the
object is "thoroughly rationalizable," i.e., nothing but the nodal point of a
set of inferential relations.

Lask thus avoids defining material in relation to subjectivity (sensibility), but this leaves open the question of how the object (the *Urverhältnis* of form and material) comes to be *available* to exert rational constraint on thinking without being a *product* of (in the sense of having the same structure as) thinking.

The beginning of an answer lies in Lask's doctrine of the "material determination" of form, through which he fleshes out the functional definition of material as that of which a category holds. Considered merely as categories—i.e., as logical form—particular categories cannot be distinguished from one another; they are nothing but "validity content" (LP 29/32). How then can we explain their *Bedeutungsdifferenzierung,* the fact that there is a *plurality* of categories? The Marburg Neo-Kantians are wrong to think that the significance of particular categories can be determined by the inferential relations between them, since in themselves they have no such relations. Lask argues instead that categories such as being, thinghood, causality, and reality can be differentiated only by reference to the material of which they hold. "Holding" is a semantic notion: "There is no validity that would not be a validity-regarding [something], a validity-with-respect-to [something]" (LP 29/32). To be valid is to hold *of* something, some material, and this material determines the significance of the category which holds of it. For instance, the category 'validity' holds, as we saw, of all other categories; it constitutes their intelligibility *as categories,* as logical form. Categories thus occupy the material position for the category 'validity' and determine its significance; that is, the very relation that obtains between them and their *own* material determines what "holding" or being valid *means* (LP 87/103). Similarly, the significance of a category such as 'causality' is determined by the specific range of material of which it is valid. On Lask's view 'causality' holds only of material that is "sensibly-existent" (spatio-temporal, thingly), and not of material that is atemporal (the mathematical, the logical, the eternal) or non-thingly (e.g., intentional consciousness). As such, the material that determines the significance of causality is already categorially formed, already includes categorial moments such as 'being', 'substantiality', or 'event-hood'. Even as material, then, it exhibits "the kind of intelligibility appropriate to meaning." To be material does not mean to be outside the space of reasons.[39]

The material that determines the significance of the categories is thus not a mere given whose relation to categoriality would be external—an "independent contribution" to the content of perception. But if categoriality is not conceptuality—i.e., if matter/form unity does not derive from our conceptual capacities—what *is* it and how does it present itself in experience? For Lask, the material determines categorial significance because the category is nothing but a certain *Bewandtnis* ("involvement," "relevance") of the material itself. The *Urverhältnis* of form and material is not a relation between two entities—there *is* nothing over and beyond the material—and so categorial form is *nothing but* a way the material is in itself deployed or involved, the way it "is." For a category to hold of some material, then, is simply for that material to exhibit certain "involvements"—structures and relations that are "categorial" because they constitute distinct regions or domains (*Gebiete*) of entities:

> What is objectivity, being, objective obtaining, actuality, reality, existence other than that particular objective involvement (*Bewandtnis*) character-izing the sensible alogical mass of content? Nothing but a sheltering, sta-bilizing integument with which the alogical is invested, as though firmly enclosed by logical content, embraced by a logical encrustation. The mate-rial is not formed and invested by cognition, however, but it is in itself engaged (*betroffen*) by logical form. (LP 59/69)

To perceive an object, then, is to be oriented toward its material by way of one or another of its involvements; the object is just the material insofar as it exhibits this or that involvement, the material *as* something.[40] But this "as" is not conceptual. The objective involvements we perceive can come to be conceptualized; that is, they can be articulated in terms of those resources, historically variable and occasion-sensitive, according to which we think about objects, judge them. But this is a further step.[41]

For example, the *category* 'causality' is a certain involvement that obtains within a certain sort of material, holds in respect of that material. I put a match to the paper and it ignites; I strike the ball with a bat and it sails over the fence; I poke pins into a doll and my enemy falls ill: In all such cases I am oriented toward some object-material by way of a certain catego-rial involvement. The category 'causality' is the intelligibility of that kind of experience. I do not *think* about the involvement but "live through" it: In everyday life the category is present to me, but in a state of "logical nudity" (LP 62/74)—i.e., it unthematically orients me toward the material in some particular way. The *concept* of causality, on the other hand, is a rule accord-ing to which we try to *characterize* that involvement in the process of think-ing about it, judging whether some given material *is* in this or that way. The "logically naked" category gets conceptually clothed, made explicit under a certain description or rule. Our concept of causality, for instance, depends on the cognitive resources available to us—something like the set of infer-ences we are entitled, in Brandom's sense, to draw from it. What counts as an instance of "causality" for us today? Must it be a uni-directional temporal event, or does future-to-present temporality ("final cause") also count? Is it merely a statistical function? Are there "historical" causes? However one may answer these questions, it is not the concept that is the transcendental unit of meaning, the ultimate instance of rationality or truth. That role belongs, instead, to the structural whole of form and material, the material in its categorial involvements. Truth is thus unlimited because there *can be* no material that is utterly alien to reason, unable to stand in a normative relation to my thought—there *can be* no material without *some* "way it is." "Being" is a category of transcendental logic.

Experience, Cognition, and the Rationality of Perception

In contrast to Kant and McDowell, Lask's transcendental logic attempts to ground cognition in the object "untouched by all subjectivity." Still, this object is not supposed to be a thing-in-itself, altogether out of reach of the subject. Lask's *argument* has established that things themselves must have the "kind of intelligibility appropriate to meaning," but without a convincing account of how this meaning is *given,* the argument remains a merely formal solution to the problem of justification. A thing's being so may bear rationally on what I should think, but it must also be given in perception *as* so bearing if even a *minimal* empiricism is to be possible. Now, on one natural way of understanding perception—namely, as an act that thematically grasps a discrete object "as" something (I see it as meat, or as meat on the rug)—it is difficult to preserve the distinction between paradigmatic meaning and conceptual meaning. Even if we accept Travis's argument that perceptual content is non-conceptual, we will need a way of capturing the difference *in meaning* between the perceptual content "meat," or "meat on the rug," and seeing *that* it is meat, or seeing *that* the meat is on the rug. The object—meat on the rug—may be non-conceptual, but on the direct-object view of perception it is hard to see how perceptual *meaning* would not have a conceptual structure. Indeed, this has led Travis to argue that experiences do not represent things as so.[42] McDowell rejects this idea—that "experience is not a case of intentionality"—as "a form of the Myth of the Given."[43] What needs to be explained, then, is how perceptual meaning has an *as*-structure without that being a *conceptual* structure.

Lask addresses this problem by distinguishing—again, in a functional way—between the correlates of two modes of meaningful givenness: "experiencing" (*Erleben*) and "cognizing" (*Erkennen*). To "experience" something is to be aware of it in a non-thematic, unreflective way; to "cognize" something is to make it thematic through a kind of reflective stance (LP 68–69/81–82). The key point is that perception is a form of experience in this sense, a non-thematic having of the thing itself as paradigmatic meaning, or truth. For this reason Lask calls perceptual experience an "immediate living in truth" (LP 160/192). In contrast, the thing itself—"the simple entwinement of the transcendent structure-elements," the totality of the material in its categorial involvements—cannot be *directly* cognized. The object, the "the goal of cognition" has, for cognition, become "a lost paradise" (LU 361/426). To understand how what is given in perception can rationally constrain our thought, then, it is necessary to clarify the relation between the meaningful content of perceptual *experience* and the meaningful content of *cognition*.

For Lask, to experience something is to "take it in" (LP 69/82), to be "absorbed" (*versunken*) in it (LP 71/84); it is a kind of "surrender" (*Hingabe*) to it (LP 158/190); it is to be a "receiver" (*Empfängerin*) of, or "locus" (*Erlebnisstätte*) for, something's presence (LP 159/190). Hence for Lask, as for McDowell, experience is not an act of the subject; it is passivity, not spontaneity: "experiencing does not 'know' what it 'does' or 'lives'" (LP 159/190). Nevertheless, the object is meaningfully given in perceptual experience and transcendental logic cannot ignore it: "the most fundamental logical problems reveal themselves only to the researcher who takes pre-theoretical life into account" (LP 154/185). To get at these problems, the philosopher must avoid "intellectualism" (LP 169/204), the tendency to "theoretize atheoretical comportment" (LP 157/172); that is, to "read judgment into immediate surrender (*Hingabe*)" (LP 165/198). Failure to avoid intellectualism leads to the impasses of McDowell's position. But how can intellectualism be avoided? In what way *is* the object meaningfully given in perceptual experience? Let us turn once more to McDowell.

What Lask calls "immediate living in truth," McDowell calls being "saddled with content." Such content is meaningful; it does not simply obtain, but presents something as obtaining—it makes a *claim*. Perceptual content has the nature of a claim because its elements exhibit the "suitable modes of togetherness" one finds in the proposition. Thus, to be saddled with content is to experience *that* things are thus and so. Subsequently, that very content can "also be the content of a judgment: it becomes the content of a judgment when the subject *decides* to take the experience at face value." In other words, judgment involves a subjective stand-taking on what is passively received in perceptual experience as the object's claim to being thus and so, and if one's perception does not go astray one is open to the world: "But that things are thus and so is also, if one is not misled, an aspect of the layout of the world: it is how things are" (MW 26).

It is clear, then, that McDowell "reads" judgment structure "into immediate surrender." At the same time, however, he acknowledges that perceptual experience is more than this: "Any ostensible seeing" of a red cube "will have more specificity to its content than just that there is a red cube in front of one, even if its content includes that."[44] Now *this* content-specificity cannot be captured in "that"-phrases; it is instead what Husserl calls the perceptual *horizon,* a holistic context in which what is "ostensibly seen" is imbricated. No account of perception can ignore perception's horizonal structure, since the meaning through which the ostensibly seen is given depends on it. Lask's distinction between *Erleben* and *Erkennen* addresses this point and thus clarifies how the object is experienced in its categorial involvements.

When Lask says that perceptual experience is a kind of "atheoretical comportment," he does not mean that it is a passive staring at something. Rather, perception is inseparable from my *practical* life—atheoretical comportment is absorption in the task at hand. I am surrendered to my writing at the computer; I am given over to scrambling eggs for breakfast; I am unreflectively hammering away while framing a house. In such activities the screen, the eggs, the hammer are perceived—not as individual, thematically grasped items but as "involved" in an horizonal whole that includes other implements within reach or out of reach; the operative textures, shapes and look of things; spatial locations oriented around my body in its activity; changing lighting conditions, and so on. I do not see "*that* the eggs are insufficiently whipped" or "*that* the hammer is too heavy"; rather, in Lask's terms, a material whole is given in a meaningful way because I "live through" its involvements: Experienced within my project or task, the categorial dimension of the material—say, the hammer's being heavy—is there as a dull ache in my arm and a difficulty in working smoothly. In my ongoing submission to the task, things are perceived as hammers, whisks, and monitors because they are *involved appropriately* for that task.

Lask here anticipates what Heidegger will call the "hermeneutic as"— "the primordial 'as' of an interpretation which understands circumspectively," i.e., the as-structure of things as they show themselves in light of some ongoing practice.[45] Heidegger contrasts such seeing-as with the "apophantic as" of judgment, the discursive *articulation* of something as something. To experience (perceive) something as appropriate for the task is not to have it thematically before one as something. Indeed, structured by the hermeneutic as, the thing's meaningful perceptual presence is really a kind of absence. The hammer *as* hammer disappears into the horizonal context; it is perceived as a hammer in a paradigmatic way only in its unreflective *use.* To "live immediately in truth" is to be atheoretically, yet normatively, guided by what is perceived—i.e., by what shows up in light of conditions of appropriateness or inappropriateness for the task at hand. Thus, what shows up can have a rational bearing on what I should think, and not merely a causal bearing on what I do think. But such experience is not yet guided by the theoretical norms of correctness and incorrectness. It thus remains to be explained how the meaning disclosed in practical experience—the world—can provide rational constraint on *cognition.*

The perceptual experience of the hammer's heaviness—that dull ache in my arm—can pass over into a disruption of my task. I become unable to go on, which leads me to reflect on my circumstances, to probe them for the source of the disruption and a way to move forward. In doing so, certain involvements become explicit—there is not enough room on this page; the eggs need more milk. Through this spontaneity, or reflective intervention of "subjectivity," Lask argues, paradigmatic meaning "becomes immanent" (LU 351/414). Becoming immanent is not yet a judgment, but it is a kind of *Erkennen*—the formation of thematic intentional content, a *representation* of the world. This representation cannot be a copy of the meaningful object given in experience; rather, the subject is "the violator of the paradigm and the originator of a certain artificiality" (LU 352/415). In cognition the subject "disrupts the *structure* of [paradigmatic] meaning," producing an "artificial, representational (*nachbildlich*) meaning" (LU 353/416; 352/415). In becoming immanent, the ontic and normative aspects of the object—the material and its categorial involvements—are "broken apart, atomized" (LU 354/418). They become "elements, artificial building-blocks for the construction of a new meaning" (LU 356/420)—that is, a representational meaning.

This, for Lask, is where concepts originate. The "artificial building-blocks" from which the "quasi-transcendent" or immanent representational meaning is constructed are something like proto-concepts, and the "isolated concepts" that become elements of judgments are "sedimentations of the meaning fragments" produced by the structural disruption of paradigmatic meaning (LU 376/445). Nevertheless, the formation of such representational meaning itself does not yet have the "suitable modes of togetherness" McDowell attributes to perception. To represent eggs *as* needing more milk when I try to get my omelette-making back on track, is not yet to cognize *that* they need more milk. For the latter, a further step is required.

What McDowell calls "the content of experience"—namely, that which becomes the "content of a judgment" when the subject *decides* to take experience at face value—Lask calls the "object of judgment-*decision*" (LU 259/299). Though this object arises, according to Lask, through an "artificial structural complication" of the paradigmatic object (LU 253/291), the object of judgment-decision—the representational meaning or intentional content constituted in practical reflection on the disruption of my submission to a task—does not yet have the structure of a judgment. To see the runny eggs, inappropriate for an omelette, as being in need of more milk is already a way of representing the total situation by highlighting certain aspects of it—the material (runny eggs) and its categorial involvements (the way eggs are supposed to be when appropriate for an omelette)—as separable elements. Doing so constitutes an object of judgment-decision, a meaning that is either "truth-accordant" (*wahrheitsgemäß*) or "truth-discordant" (*wahrheitswidrig*). The object of judgment-decision either represents the material as belonging within a categorial involvement that accords with the way it is found in the "lost paradise" of the paradigmatic object, or in one that is discordant with the paradigm. And for Lask, as for McDowell, when the subject actually *decides* whether it is truth-accordant or truth-discordant, the object of judgment-decision becomes the content of a judgment (LU 363/428).

In becoming the content of a judgment, however, the object of judgment-decision undergoes a second transformation that involves "even more complexity and artificiality" (LU 257/296): It becomes the object of "affirmation" or "negation," the object of a stand-taking on the part of the subject (LU 362/427). A judgment *that* things are thus and so can be correct or incorrect, but to have the intentional content of something *as* being thus and so (the object of judgment-decision) is neither correct nor incorrect, since no judgment has been made—it does not have the "suitable modes of togetherness" characteristic of judgments. Thus the object of judgment-decision is both cognized and perceived: I visually take in that A and B are "categorially" involved in a certain way. Subsequently I might come to judge this meaningful whole by employing the concept of "causality." In thus becoming the target of affirmation or negation, however, the object of judgment-decision is expressed in the grammar of a particular language, whose conceptual resources may be more or less adequate for capturing the categorial involvements that genuinely obtain within the material and which are perceptually represented as so obtaining in the object of judgment-decision.

This second-order complication, however, yields a content that is cognized but is no longer perceptual. Instead, what is perceived—the object of judgment-decision which is in itself either truth-accordant or truth-discordant—serves as the *measure* for my affirmative or negative expression. For instance, when I judge, incorrectly, *that* pins in the doll have caused my enemy's illness, this judgment is measured against how I perceptually represent the total situation—i.e., against a *truth-discordant* object of judgment-decision which combines the material "pins, doll, enemy's illness" with a category, 'causality', that does *not* hold of it. Thus, as such a measure, what I perceive "obligates" me to negate a judgment of causal connection—i.e., it looks to me as though there is a causal connection, but there is not. Thus, just as the perceived object is "beyond the opposition of truth and untruth," so too *perceptual intentional* content is beyond the opposition of correctness and incorrectness, the kind of truth that characterizes judgment (LU 255/294).

The correctness or incorrectness of empirical judgments, then, is not measured directly against the perceived object as such. On Lask's view, empirical justification must proceed by way of a certain coherentist detour.

Truth-*claims* are efforts to "restore the object itself" (LU 371/438) by means of conceptual resources whose measure lies not in the "unviolated" paradigmatic meaning experienced in submission to the task (hermeneutic as), but in that meaning as "atomized" in the object of judgment-decision: "After the original sin (*Sündenfall*) of cognition, the task is no longer to grasp the transcendent meaning but the immanent oppositional meaning" (LU 361/426). Is this still minimal empiricism in any recognizable sense? The only thing that keeps this effort to "restore" the paradigmatic object from being a frictionless "spinning in the void" is the fact that the world as such is *already meaningful*. What is given in perceptual experience can have rational bearing on what we think; the "simple intertwinement" of category and material is no mere extralogical given that might cause us to think in certain ways but could never justify that thinking. Even if it is not so directly, the perceived is a measure or norm for our thinking because it is the measure of the intentional content about which we decide when we judge. If we remain with McDowell's position, the world is identified with Lask calls the "object of judgment-decision." But what then serves as the measure of *its* truth-accordance or truth-discordance? According to Lask, we "live in the truth," and without this "limitlessness of truth," McDowell's "unboundedness of the conceptual" would itself be but a name for "frictionless spinning in the void."

NOTES

1. John McDowell, *Mind and World* (Cambridge, Mass.: Harvard University Press, 1996), ix. Subsequent references will be inserted in the text, abbreviated MW.

2. G. W. F. Hegel, *Phenomenology of Spirit,* trans. A. V. Miller (Oxford: Clarendon Press, 1977), 56, 14.

3. Robert Brandom, *Making it Explicit: Reasoning, Representing, and Discursive Commitment* (Cambridge, Mass.: Harvard University Press, 1994), 221–222.

4. Hegel, *Phenomenology,* 487.

5. John McDowell, "Why is Sellars' Essay Called '*Empiricism* and the Philosophy of Mind'?" (forthcoming), 1.

6. Hegel, *Phenomenology,* 49, 56.

7. See the important study by Klaus-Christian Köhnke, *The Rise of Neo-Kantianism: German Academic Philosophy between Idealism and Positivism,* trans. R. J. Hollingdale (Cambridge: Cambridge University Press, 1991). Still useful is Hans-Ludwig Ollig, *Der Neukantianismus* (Stuttgart: J. B. Metzlerische Verlagsbuchhandlung, 1970). On the relation to phenomenology see Manfred Brelage, *Studien zur Transzendentalphilosophie* (Berlin: Walter de Gruyter, 1965) and Steven Galt Crowell, *Husserl, Heidegger, and the Space of Meaning: Paths Toward Transcendental Phenomenology* (Evanston: Northwestern University Press, 2001).

8. Hermann Cohen, *Kants Theorie der Erfahrung* (Hildesheim, Zurich, and New York: Olms, 1987), reprint of the 3rd ed. (1918); Paul Natorp, *Die logischen Grundlagen der exakten Wissenschaften* (Leipzig: Verlag Teubner, 1910), 276–277.

9. Heinrich Rickert, "Zwei Wege der Erkenntnistheorie. Transscendentalpsychologie und Transscendentallogik," *Kant-Studien* 14 (1909): 169–228; here 179–80, 184. My translation.

10. Though Lask can hardly be said to receive the attention he merits, interest in his philosophy has increased in recent years—partly due to his influence on the early Heidegger, but also in part due to renewed interest in Neo-Kantian approaches to logic, knowledge, and science. Studies of the first sort include Theodore Kisiel, "Why Students of Heidegger Will Have to Read Emil Lask," *Man and World* 28/3 (1995): 197–240; Alejandro Vigo, "Sinn, Wahrheit, und Geltung: Zu Heideggers Dekonstruction der intensionalistischen Urteilslehre," *Archiv für Geschichte der Philosophie* 86 (2004): 176–208, and Steven Crowell, "Emil Lask: Aletheiology as Ontology," *Kant-Studien* 87 (1996): 69–88. Studies of the second sort include Stephan Nachtsheim, *Emil Lasks Grundlehre* (Tübingen: J. C. B. Mohr, 1992); Uwe B. Glatz, *Emil Lask: Philosophie im Verhältnis zu Weltanschauung, Leben und Erkenntnis* (Würzburg: Königshaus & Neumann, 2001); and Roger Hofer, *Gegenstand und Methode: Untersuchungen zur frühen Wissenschaftslehre Emil Lasks* (Würzburg: Königshaus & Neumann, 1997).

11. Immanuel Kant, *Critique of Pure Reason*, trans. Norman Kemp Smith (New York: Macmillan, 1968), 94 (A 54/B 78), 95 (A 55/B 80).

12. Kant, *Critique of Pure Reason*, 98 (A 59/B 84), 100 (A 62–63/B 87).

13. More precisely, McDowell proposes to investigate intentional content as such, asking "how is it possible for there to be thinking directed at how things are?" (MW xiii). We can ignore this complication, however, since "minimal empiricism" is motivated by the problem of justification, and so by a question concerning empirical cognition.

14. Emil Lask, *Die Logik der Philosophie und die Kategorienlehre*, in *Sämtliche Werke*, vol. 2 (Jena: Dietrich Scheglmann Reprintverlag, 2003), 111. This edition provides, in square brackets in the text, the pagination of the standard edition of Lask's work: Emil Lask, *Gesammelte Schriften*, vol. 2, ed. Eugen Herrigel (Tübingen: J. C. B. Mohr, 1923). Henceforth, references to *Die Logik der Philosophie* will be given in the text as LP, with the page number of the *Sämtliche Werke* edition first, followed by that of the *Gesammelte Schriften* edition: LP 111/133, etc. All translations from Lask's works are my own. As Lask uses the term, "Panlogism" refers primarily to Hegel and secondarily to the rival Marburg school of Neo-Kantianism, but we might extend it to all versions of coherentism—for instance, Davidson's or Brandom's—in order to highlight the contrast with McDowell's minimal empiricism.

15. On "justification" in contrast to "exculpation," see MW 8.

16. Kant, *Critique of Pure Reason*, 105 (A 68/B 93).

17. John McDowell, *Having the World in View: Sellars, Kant, and Intentionality*, The Woodbridge Lectures, *The Journal of Philosophy* 95/9 (September 1998), 434.

18. Kant, *Critique of Pure Reason*, 112 (A 79/B 104–105).

19. McDowell, *Having the World in View*, 441.

20. Emil Lask, *Die Lehre vom Urteil,* in *Sämtliche Werke,* vol. 2 (Jena: Dietrich Scheglmann Reprintverlag, 2003), 324. Henceforth cited in the text as LU. Citations from *Die Lehre vom Urteil* will follow the conventions described in note 14 above; so, here: LU 324/380.

21. On Husserl see LU 360/425.

22. Edmund Husserl, *Briefwechsel,* vol. 5: *Die Neukantianer,* ed. Karl Schuhmann (Dordrecht: Kluwer, 1994), 34. Letter from Lask dated 24 December 1911.

23. In this, Lask shares common ground with both Heidegger and McDowell. As the latter writes: "Against a 'Neo-Kantian' reading of Kant, Heidegger says: 'The *Critique of Pure Reason* has nothing to do with a "theory of knowledge."' I think we can make the point Heidegger is trying to make more effectively . . . by saying, not that epistemology is *no* concern of the first *Critique,* but it is no more *the* concern of the first *Critique* than it is of 'Empiricism and the Philosophy of Mind' . . ." ("Having the World in View," 437). This common ground gives way, however, when we ask what more there *is* to the first *Critique* than epistemology, for in McDowell's case "Empiricism and the Philosophy of Mind" (and so also Kant's first *Critique*) is an account of intentionality, whereas for Lask the first *Critique* is (in principle, if not in execution) an account of "being in the sense of truth."

24. See Köhnke, *The Rise of Neo-Kantianism,* 178, 230–231.

25. At LP 12/14, Lask writes that in all previous philosophy "the logical has either been subsumed into a metaphysical sphere of the Ideal, the Intelligible, Reason or Spirit, or else it is left entirely homeless." See Steven Crowell, "Lask, Heidegger, and the Homelessness of Logic," *Journal of the British Society for Phenomenology* 23/3 (1992): 222–239.

26. There is a simplification here. As Lask writes, "we must conform to the usage of our positivistically schooled age" and limit the predicate 'being' "exclusively to that sphere in which there are events and causal connections. The realm of being . . . coincides with the spatiotemporal sense-world." Lask notes dismissively that this is precisely what "the great thinkers of the past saw as the *me on*" (LP 6/7). In terms of Lotze's two-world theory, however, the realm of being includes entities of any kind—historical events, artworks, numbers, minds, and so on—each governed by distinct sorts of ontic relation.

27. The fact that Lask's philosophical approach is neither ontological nor metaphysical—he calls it "ametaphysical" (LP 8/9), since for him metaphysics concerns a distinct realm of "supersensible" entities in contrast to other kinds of entity—does not mean that it has no *relation* to ontological philosophy. On the contrary, the aletheiological perspective allows us to see precisely *how* principled divisions in the totality of "what is" are possible. It is therefore "ontological" in a sense close to that of the early Heidegger's distinction between "ontic" and "ontological"—namely, an inquiry concerned not with entities but with the being (meaning) of entities. See Crowell, "Aletheiology as Ontology."

28. John McDowell, "Précis of *Mind and World,*" *Philosophy and Phenomenological Research* 58/2 (1998): 366.

29. Ibid., 365.

30. Ibid., 469.

31. Loc. cit.

32. Ibid., 366, 367. Compare MW 85–86: "[T]he task I envision is not the one Rorty deconstructs, the reconciling of subject and object, or thought and world. My proposal is that we should try to reconcile reason and nature, and the point of doing that is to attain something Rorty himself aspires to, a frame of mind in which we would no longer seem to be faced with problems that call on philosophy to bring subject and object back together." To do so "is not to produce a bit of constructive philosophy of the sort Rorty aims to supersede." Properly understood, the transcendental standpoint makes "constructive" philosophy unnecessary.

33. McDowell, "Having the World in View," 489.

34. Charles Travis, "Reason's Reach," *The European Journal of Philosophy* 15/2 (2007): 225–248, here 227 (my emphasis at "count").

35. In another recent article, Sheryl K. Chen argues that even if we grant that we see, for instance, "that it is raining," this can only be a "justification-maker" and not justifying *reason* for our corresponding belief. Quoting James Pryor ("Is There Immediate Justification?," in Matthias Steup and Ernest Sosa, eds., *Contemporary Debates in Epistemology* (Oxford: Blackwell, 2005), 182), Chen defines a "justification-maker" as "something that *makes it* epistemologically appropriate . . . for you to believe P, rather than disbelieve P or suspend judgment." And while seeing "that it is raining" can serve that role, Chen denies that "the subject can, without begging the question, *appeal* to the fact that she sees that it is raining as *her reason* for believing that it is raining." See Sheryl K. Chen, "Empirical Content and Rational Constraint," *Inquiry* 49/3 (2006): 242–264, here 245, 259.

36. It should be noted that McDowell has recently revised his view on this point, in part in response to Travis's criticisms. In "Avoiding the Myth of the Given" (forthcoming), McDowell explicitly denies that intuitions have propositional structure: "What we need is an idea of content that is not propositional but intuitional" (4). On his current view "intuitional content is not discursive" (6)—that is, it is not "articulated" in terms of concepts and propositional structure—but it nevertheless has a "distinctive kind of unity" (5): It is "categorially unified," where a category is "a form of the kind of unity that characterizes intuitions" (7). This distinction between the conceptual/discursive and categorial/intuitive brings McDowell even closer to Lask's position. The present chapter should thus be seen as presenting some of the weaknesses of the "earlier" McDowell's position which were identified, *avant la lettre,* by Lask—the justice of whose proleptic objections can be said to be acknowledged, in part, by the "later" McDowell.

37. Travis, "Reason's Reach," 232 (my emphasis at "instancing").

38. Travis, "Reason's Reach," 238: "The meat is *in* the surroundings. To see it, look where it is. Look there, too, to see the condition it is in." But "you cannot look 'where that the meat is on the rug is.' There is no such place."

39. Lask does acknowledge material that is not already categorially formed, but even this conforms to McDowell's strictures against notionally separable contributions: The category 'being' is determined by a range of material of which we can give only a "negative characterization." A sign of our helplessness here is that we resort to terms like "the sensible or sensibly intuitable, the merely sensed or intuited, sensibily

experienceable, perceivable" when we wish to characterize it, since such terms tell us nothing about the material itself but refer only to our modes of access to it, our "psychophysical life-processes" (LP 44/51–52). We must proceed this way because such material—in contrast to that of which 'causality', for example, holds—has no further categorial formation and is thus a limiting case of "alogicality" (LP 48/56). But precisely the same thing is true of the material that determines the meaning of 'validity': What it means to "hold" of some material can only be approached by reference to our modes of access to it. Lask does not note this fact, but it is indicated in the text by his use of terms such as "clarity" and "illumination" to describe what *Geltung* means, since clarity and illumination refer to our "uptake" of what is given. It is also reflected in his emphasis on the *normative* character of validity, the claim to recognition it imposes on us—its character as an "ought." This too is a hidden appeal to something like "life-processes," this time our *moral* and *cognitive* ones (see LU 378/447). *Sollen,* then, is no less basic than *Sein;* it too is a limiting case of alogicality.

40. For cognition, this objective involvement determines how the material *ought* to be thought. Only for this reason does the category, as logical "holding," have a *normative* character at all. The category is not normative in itself but becomes a norm in the context of a certain project—that of cognition—in which it has the "value" of being the goal of inquiry. It thus determines what success or failure *means* for such an inquiry (LP 9/10).

41. Travis discusses the "occasion-sensitivity" of concepts in order to show why "that things are thus and so" does not map onto the world *tout court* ("Reason's Reach," 236–237). Correct use of a concept such as "meat" can depend on what the context is: When I am in a butcher shop it might be correct to say that a kidney is "not meat," but this may not be correct when I serve the kidney in question to my vegetarian friend. The point is that I can see the kidney on the table—its "categorial involvements," in Lask's terms—but the concepts I employ to judge what I see will not map this directly. Of course, McDowell recognizes that empirical concepts have this feature: In "active empirical thinking," he writes, "there must be a standing willingness to refashion concepts and conceptions if that is what reflection demands" (MW 12–13). But the phenomenon of context-sensitivity still attests to a difference between conceptual or discursive unity (content) and categorial or perceptual unity (content).

42. Charles Travis, "The Silence of the Senses," *Mind* 113 (2004): 57–94.

43. McDowell, "Avoiding the Myth of the Given," 8–9.

44. McDowell, "Having the World in View," 459.

45. Martin Heidegger, *Being and Time,* trans. John Macquarrie and Edward Robinson (New York: Harper & Row, 1962), 201.

PART 3

The Neo-Kantians and the Sciences

Ernst Cassirer and Thomas Kuhn: The Neo-Kantian Tradition in the History and Philosophy of Science

Michael Friedman

A central problem facing contemporary history and philosophy of science still derives from the publication of Thomas Kuhn's *The Structure of Scientific Revolutions* in 1962. In particular, Kuhn applied lessons he initially learned from early twentieth-century work in the history of science to develop a strikingly new philosophical picture of the nature of science. Directly confronting what he called the development-by-accumulation model of scientific progress, Kuhn presented an alternative conception according to which the development of science is punctuated by essentially discontinuous transitions in which the dominant paradigm that governs a particular stage of what Kuhn calls "normal science" undergoes a decisive transformation. This transformation—a "scientific revolution"—results in a paradigm which is fundamentally incommensurable with the one that preceded it. Since successive paradigms are incommensurable—the transition from Newtonian physics to relativity theory was one of Kuhn's central illustrations—then the choice between them appears not to be straightforwardly rational. Moreover, since the concepts and principles of the two paradigms have radically different meanings, it is no longer clear that empirical evidence can straightforwardly decide between them. Indeed, the very terms in which the two paradigms describe the empirical phenomena may themselves have radically different meanings.

One conclusion Kuhn drew from this picture is that there is no real sense in which the evolution of science can be seen as a process of convergence toward an ultimate single truth about reality, where succeeding theories or paradigms appear as ever better approximations to such a final truth.[1] And this conclusion, in turn, can easily be radicalized so as to result in a relativist and historicist conception according to which there is no sense of scientific progress at all: Successive theories or paradigms are simply different historically conditioned moments in a directionless temporal process, where the only notion of truth then available is an essentially relativized and historicized one. Kuhn himself strenuously resisted these particular implications of his views, hoping to replace the development-by-accumulation model and its ideal of inter-theoretic convergence with an evolutionary model of scientific progress in which successive theories become continually better adapted problem-solving tools, without thereby converging on a final endpoint. Nevertheless, this suggestion of Kuhn's has not won many adherents, and the problem dominating much post-Kuhnian work in the history, philosophy, and sociology of science has been precisely this relativist and historicist predicament: If successive paradigms, as Kuhn indicated, are really incommensurable then how can we escape the conclusion that—in fashionable parlance—"all knowledge is local"? But while this question may have become particularly acute after the publication of Kuhn's seminal work, it is not entirely new.

In the late nineteenth and early twentieth centuries, the Marburg School of Neo-Kantianism—founded by Hermann Cohen and developed by Paul Natorp and Ernst Cassirer—articulated an historicized version of Kantianism which aimed at adapting critical philosophy to the deep revolutionary changes affecting mathematics and the mathematical sciences throughout this period.[2] In particular, the development of non-Euclidean geometries appeared to decisively undermine Kant's original conception of the synthetic *a priori* character of our cognition of space, and nineteenth-century developments in mathematical physics suggested that Newtonian physics, in particular, would not be the final word. In response to these developments, the Marburg School replaced Kant's original "static" or timeless version of the synthetic *a priori* with what they conceived as an essentially developmental or "genetic" (*erzeugende*) conception of scientific knowledge. Since Kuhn, very late in his career, characterized his conception of scientific revolutions as a kind of dynamical and historicized version of Kantianism, one might naturally wonder about the relationship between Kuhn's own view and that of the Marburg School.[3] The answer, as we shall see, is both interesting and complicated.

In Cassirer's version of the genetic conception of knowledge, most fully articulated in his *Substanzbegriff und Funktionsbegriff*, which appeared in 1910, we begin with the progression of theories produced by modern mathematical-natural science in its actual historical development. This progression takes its point of departure, to be sure, from Euclidean geometry and Newtonian physics. But Cassirer and those he addressed knew, as Kant himself had not, that these constituted only a starting point and not a rigidly fixed and unrevisable *a priori* structure. Subsequent to the Euclidean-Newtonian paradigm, in particular, there has been a developmental sequence of abstract mathematical structures ("systems of order"), which is itself ordered by the abstract mathematical relation of approximate backward-directed inclusion—thus, for example, the new non-Euclidean geometries contain the older geometry of Euclid as a continuously approximated limiting case. We can thereby conceive of all the theories in our sequence as continuously converging, as it were, on a final or limit theory, such that all previous theories in the sequence would be approximate special cases of this final theory. This final theory is only a regulative ideal in the Kantian sense—it is progressively approximated but never actually realized.[4] Nevertheless, the idea of such a continuous progression toward an ideal limit constitutes the characteristic "general serial form" of our mathematical-physical theorizing and, at the same time, bestows on this theorizing its characteristic form of objectivity. For despite all historical variation and contingency, there is nonetheless a continuously converging progression of abstract mathematical structures which frames and makes possible all of our empirical knowledge. In Cassirer's new view, however—and in full agreement with Kant's original, "critical" theory of knowledge—convergence does not take place toward a mind- or theory-independent "reality" of ultimate "substantial things" or "things-in-themselves." Rather, the convergence in question occurs entirely *within* the series of historically developed mathematical structures: "Reality," on this view, is simply the purely ideal limit or endpoint toward which the sequence of such structures is mathematically converging—or, to put it another way, it is simply the series itself, taken as a whole.[5]

It is not clear, at first sight, whether or how this conception of inter-theoretic convergence relates to Kuhn's view of the matter. As we have said, Kuhn rejects all talk of convergence on a final truth concerning a mind-independent reality—but so also, as we have just seen, does the Marburg genetic conception of knowledge. Moreover, the situation becomes especially interesting (and complicated) when we observe that Cassirer's work in the history of science and philosophy—work which was directly informed by and contributed to the Marburg genetic conception of knowledge—forms an important part of the background to Kuhn's own historiography.

Cassirer began his career as an intellectual historian, and he is doubtless one of the greatest of the twentieth century. His first major work, *Das Erkenntnisproblem in der Philosophie und Wissenschaft der neueren Zeit*, published in two volumes in 1906–1907, is a magisterial and deeply original contribution to both the history of philosophy and the history of science. It is the first work, in fact, to develop a detailed reading of the scientific revolution as a whole in terms of the "Platonic" idea that a thoroughgoing application of mathematics to nature (the so-called mathematization of nature) is the central and overarching achievement of this revolution. Accordingly,

Cassirer's work is acknowledged by such seminal historians as Edwin Burtt, Alexandre Koyré, and E. J. Dijksterhuis, all of whom developed the same theme later in the century in the course of establishing the history of science as a discipline.[6]

Cassirer, for his part, simultaneously articulated an interpretation of the history of modern philosophy as the development and eventual triumph of what he calls "modern philosophical idealism." This tradition takes its inspiration, according to Cassirer, from idealism in the Platonic sense—from an appreciation of the "ideal" formal structures which are paradigmatically studied in mathematics. This idealism is distinctively modern, however, in recognizing the fundamental importance of the systematic application of such structures to empirically given nature in modern mathematical physics—a progressive and synthetic process wherein mathematical models of nature are successively and indefinitely corrected and refined. For Cassirer it is Galileo, above all, who first grasped the essential structure of this synthetic process in opposition to both sterile Aristotelian-Scholastic formal logic and sterile Aristotelian-Scholastic empirical induction. The development of "modern philosophical idealism" in the works of Descartes, Spinoza, Gassendi, Hobbes, Leibniz, and finally Kant, then consists in its increasingly self-conscious philosophical articulation and elaboration. Thus, the main philosophical implication of Cassirer's historical narrative is (not surprisingly) that the nature and character of modern mathematical physics as a whole is best represented by the Marburg genetic conception of knowledge.

Das Erkenntnisproblem exerted a decisive influence on early twentieth-century history of science, especially in its more philosophically oriented guises. It proved especially important for such writers as Émile Meyerson, Léon Brunschvicg, Hélène Metzger, Anneliese Maier, and Alexandre Koyré. And Koyré, in turn, had a particularly strong influence on Kuhn.[7] It is little wonder then, that in a text Kuhn first published in 1984, and later appended to his book on Planck and black-body radiation, he states: "The concept of historical reconstruction that underlies [this study] has from the start been fundamental to both my historical and my philosophical work. It is by no means original: I owe it primarily to Alexandre Koyré; its ultimate sources lie in Neo-Kantian philosophy" (1987, 361). Thus Kuhn, toward the end of his career, not only characterized his distinctive philosophical conception as a dynamical and historicized version of Kantianism, he also explicitly acknowledged the background of his own historiography in Neo-Kantian philosophy.

Nevertheless, there were (at least) two different strands in this early twentieth-century historiographical tradition—a more Kantian strand, associated with Brunschvicg and Maier; and what we might call a more Cartesian strand, associated with Meyerson and his student Metzger. Meyerson is the most important philosophical influence on Koyré's historiography—while Kuhn also cites Meyerson as an influence, along with Metzger, Brunschvicg, Maier, and indeed, Cassirer[8]—and the philosophical perspective shared by Meyerson and Koyré is diametrically opposed, in most essential respects, to that originally articulated by Cassirer.[9]

In the work of Cassirer and Meyerson, in particular, we find two sharply divergent visions of the philosophical history of modern science. For Cassirer, this history is seen as a process of rational purification of our view of nature: We progress from naively realistic, "substantialistic" conceptions of underlying substances, causes, and mechanisms which subsist behind the observable phenomena toward increasingly abstract, purely "functional" conceptions by means of which we finally abandon ontology and develop ever-more precise mathematical representations of phenomena in terms of rigorously formulated universal laws. For Meyerson, by contrast, this same history is seen as a necessarily dialectical progression—in something like the Hegelian sense—wherein reason perpetually seeks to enforce precisely its "substantialistic" impulse, and nature continually offers her resistance in the ultimate irrationality of temporal succession. Thus, for Meyerson, the triumph of the scientific revolution is represented by the rise of mechanistic atomism, wherein elementary corpuscles preserve their sizes, shapes, and masses while merely changing their respective positions in a uniform and homogeneous space via motion. This same demand for trans-temporal, substantial identity is represented in more recent times by Lavoisier's use of the principle of the conservation of matter in his new chemistry, as well as by the discovery of the conservation of energy. Yet in the still more recent discovery of what we now refer to as the second law of thermodynamics (formerly "Carnot's principle"), which governs the *temporally irreversible* process of the "degradation" or "dissipation" of energy, we encounter nature's complementary and unavoidable resistance to our *a priori* logical demands.

It is therefore by no means surprising that Meyerson, in the course of considering and rejecting what he calls "anti-substantialistic conceptions of science," explicitly takes issue with Cassirer's central claim in *Das Erkenntnisproblem*—namely, that "Mathematical physics turns aside from the essence of things and their inner substantiality in order to turn toward their numerical order and connection, their functional and mathematical structure."[10] And it is also no wonder that Cassirer, in the course of a discussion of "identity and difference, constancy and change," explicitly takes issue with Meyerson's views: "The identity toward which thought progressively strives is not the identity of ultimate substantial things but the identity of functional orders and coordinations" (1910, 431). Thus, in direct and explicit opposition to Meyerson's view, Cassirer insists that thought does *not* require a "substantialistic" or "ontological" identity over time of permanent "things," but merely a purely mathematical continuity over time as formulated in successively articulated mathematical structures.[11]

If I am not mistaken, this deep philosophical opposition between Meyerson and Cassirer receives a very clear echo in Kuhn's theory of scientific revolutions, particularly with regard to the questions of continuity and convergence over time. Kuhn shows himself, in this respect, to be a faithful follower of the Meyersonian viewpoint, for he consistently gives these questions an ontological ("substantialistic") rather than mathematical ("functional") interpretation.[12] Thus, for example, when Kuhn famously considers the relationship between relativistic and Newtonian mechanics, he rejects the notion of a fundamental continuity between the two theories on the grounds that the "physical referents" of their terms are essentially different; he nowhere considers the contrasting idea, characteristic of Cassirer's work, that a continuity of purely mathematical structures would be sufficient. Moreover, Kuhn consistently gives an ontological rather than a mathematical interpretation to the question of theoretical convergence over time: The question is always whether our theories can be said to converge on an independently existing "truth" about reality—on a theory-independent external world.[13]

It follows, then, that Kuhn's rejection of inter-theoretic convergence cannot be taken as a straightforward confutation of Cassirer's position. For Kuhn simply assumes, in harmony with the Meyersonian viewpoint, that there is rational continuity over time only if there is also substantial identity. Since, as Kuhn argues, the "physical referents" of Newtonian and relativistic mechanics, for example, cannot be taken to be the same, we are squarely faced with the problem of inter-paradigmatic incommensurability. Yet Cassirer, as we have seen, is no less opposed to all forms of naïve realism (and naïve empiricism) than is Kuhn. Cassirer proposes instead a generalized Kantian conception—emblematic of what he himself calls "modern philosophical idealism"—according to which scientific rationality and objectivity are secured in virtue of the way in which our empirical knowledge of nature is *framed,* and thereby made possible, by a continuously evolving sequence of abstract mathematical structures.

It is for this reason, in fact, that Einstein's general theory of relativity represents the culmination of "modern philosophical idealism" for Cassirer. In particular, his work *Zur Einsteinschen Relativitätstheorie,* published in 1921, is devoted to explaining how this theory—despite first appearances—represents a confirmation rather than a rejection of the Kantian or "critical" theory of knowledge. Cassirer begins by asserting: "The reality of the physicist stands opposite the reality of immediate perception as a thoroughly mediated reality: as a totality, not of existing things or properties, but rather of abstract symbols of thought that serve as the expression for determinate relations of magnitude and measure, for determinate functional coordinations and dependencies in the appearances" (1921, 14). And it then follows that Einstein's theory can be incorporated within the "critical" conception of knowledge "without difficulty, for this theory is characterized from a general epistemological point of view precisely by the circumstance that in it, more consciously and more clearly than ever before, the advance from the copy theory of knowledge to the functional theory is completed" (1921, 55). Whereas it is true, for instance, that Kant himself had envisioned only the use of Euclidean geometry in mathematical physics, the fact that we now employ a non-intuitive, non-Euclidean geometry in the general theory of relativity by no means contradicts his general "critical" point of view. For: "Kant also had emphasized decisively [that] this form of dynamical determination does not belong any longer to intuition as such, but rather it is the 'rule of the *understanding*' alone through which the existence of appearances can acquire synthetic unity and be taken together [as a whole] in a determinate concept of experience" (1921, 109). Hence, the general theory of relativity continues to exemplify the fundamental Kantian insight that the unity of nature as such can only be due to our understanding.[14]

It is precisely at this point, however, that I find myself in deep disagreement with Cassirer—and with the Marburg School more generally. For I believe that the Marburg tendency to minimize or downplay the role of the Kantian faculty of pure intuition or pure sensibility on behalf of the faculty of pure understanding represents a profound interpretive mistake.[15] Kant himself, on the contrary, takes the faculty of pure sensibility to have an independent *a priori* structure—given by the Euclidean structure of space and the Newtonian structure of time (or more precisely, space-time)—and this is the reason, for Kant, that all our sensible or perceptual experience must necessarily be in accordance with these forms (while it is not merely the case, for example, that we must always *think* or *conceive* nature in this way). Once this is recognized, therefore, it is by no means true that the general theory of relativity can be incorporated within the Kantian or "critical" conception "without difficulty."

Furthermore—and this is still not as well known as it should be—the logical empiricists basically agreed with Kuhn about the profoundly revolutionary character of the general theory of relativity from a philosophical point of view. The most important of their works, in retrospect, was Hans Reichenbach's *Relativitätstheorie und Erkenntnis Apriori*, which appeared in 1920—a year before Cassirer's book on relativity. According to Reichenbach (and the logical empiricists more generally), Einstein's new theory is so radically incommensurable with Newtonian theory that the Kantian critical philosophy itself needs to be radically revised: A new, revolutionary form of scientific philosophy—namely, logical empiricism—is required in the wake of Einstein's relativity theory.[16]

I agree with Kuhn—and with the logical empiricists—that Einstein's general theory of relativity is in an important sense incommensurable (not inter-translatable) with the Newtonian theory of universal gravitation it replaced. Whereas Newtonian theory represents the action of gravity as an external "impressed force" causing gravitationally affected bodies to deviate from straight inertial trajectories (moving with uniform or constant speed), Einstein's theory depicts gravitation as a curving or bending of the underlying fabric of space-time itself. In this new framework, in particular, there are no inertial trajectories in the sense which would hold within Euclidean geometry and Newtonian mechanics, and gravity is not an "impressed force" causing deviations from such trajectories. Gravitationally affected bodies instead follow the straightest possible paths or geodesics that exist in the highly non-Euclidean geometry (of variable curvature) of Einsteinian space-time; and the trajectories of so-called "freely falling bodies"—affected by no forces other than gravitation—simply *replace* the straight inertial trajectories of Newtonian theory (which are straight in the sense of both Euclidean space and Newtonian space-time).

But why does it follow that Einstein's theory and Newton's theory are incommensurable? After all, once Einstein's theory is in place, we can then derive Newtonian theory from it as an approximate special case (when, for example, we consider relatively small spatial regions that are approximately Euclidean or relatively low velocities in comparison with light); and we can thereby explain, from the point of view of Einstein's theory, why Newton's theory works as well as it does. Kuhn himself is perfectly clear about this, and he responds by insisting that this point of view is *post*-revolutionary and, in particular, uses fundamental mathematical and physical concepts that are simply unavailable from the point of view of the earlier theory: What we derive from Einstein's theory as an approximate special case, is therefore not Newton's original theory.[17] As a result, the real problem is to show how the fundamental mathematical and physical concepts of the old theory (which are thus not inter-translatable with the new theory) can nonetheless give rise to—can be replaced by—those of the new theory.

In my *Dynamics of Reason* (2001), I put the point this way (see part 2, § 3): It is clear, first of all, that Einstein's theory is not even *mathematically* possible from the point of view of Newton's original theory, since the mathematics required to formulate Einstein's theory—namely, Bernhard Riemann's general theory of geometrical manifolds or "spaces" of any dimension and curvature (Euclidean or non-Euclidean)—did not exist until the late nineteenth century. Of course this point, by itself, is perfectly compatible with

184 ■ MICHAEL FRIEDMAN

Cassirer's version of the Marburg conception—for once the necessary mathematics has been developed, we can then represent the earlier mathematical structure as a special case of the later one, which is all that Marburg-style convergence requires.

However, and in the second place, even after the mathematics required for Einstein's theory was developed, it still remained fundamentally unclear what it could mean to apply such a geometry to our sensible experience of nature in a real physical theory. One still needed to show, in other words, that Einstein's new theory is *empirically* or *physically* possible as well—and this, in turn, only became clear with Einstein's own work on what he called the principle of equivalence in the years 1907–1912. This principle, as we now understand it, states that freely falling bodies follow the straightest possible paths (or geodesics) in a certain kind of four-dimensional (semi-) Riemannian manifold; it thereby gives real physical and empirical meaning, for the first time, to this kind of abstract mathematical structure. Einstein's theory thus requires a genuine *expansion* of the space of intellectual possibilities (both mathematical and empirical), and the problem is then to explain how such an expansion is possible—since his new theory, *before* this expansion takes place, remains (in Kant's terminology) neither *logically* nor *really* possible.[18]

I cannot develop this in detail here, but my second main point in the *Dynamics of Reason* (2001) is this (see part 2, § 4): In addition to the necessary mathematical developments (i.e., the evolution of non-Euclidean geometries, as unified and completed in Riemann's work) and the necessary physical developments (i.e., the discovery of the constancy and invariance of the velocity of light, and the numerical equality of inertial and gravitational mass underlying the principle of equivalence), we still need a set of parallel developments in contemporaneous scientific philosophy to connect up the relevant innovations in mathematics and physics and thereby effect the necessary expansion in our physical or empirical possibilities.

In the case of Einstein's theory in particular, this process began with Kant's original attempt—in his *Metaphysische Anfangsgründe der Naturwissenschaft,* as well as in the first *Critique*—to provide philosophical foundations for Newtonian theory.[19] In the nineteenth century these Kantian foundations for a specifically Newtonian theory were then self-consciously and successively reconfigured: Scientific philosophers such as Ernst Mach reconsidered the problem of absolute space and motion, while others—most notably Hermann von Helmholtz and Henri Poincaré—reconsidered the empirical and conceptual foundations of geometry in the light of new mathematical developments in non-Euclidean geometry. Einstein's initial work on the principle of equivalence—which culminated, as we have noted, in 1912—then unexpectedly *joined together* these previously distinct traditions of scientific thought, and thereby led to the very surprising and entirely new empirical possibility that gravity could be represented by a non-Euclidean geometry. The crucial breakthrough came when Einstein hit upon the example of the uniformly rotating disk, for which—in accordance with the principle of equivalence—we must consider a particular kind of *non*-inertial frame of reference within the framework of special relativity: The result was a non-Euclidean physical geometry as our novel representative of the gravitational field. And Einstein was only able to arrive at this result—as he later acknowledged in the celebrated lecture *Geometrie und Erfahrung*, in 1921—by delicately situating himself within the earlier philosophical debate between Helmholtz and Poincaré, regarding the empirical and conceptual foundations of geometry.[20]

If this is correct, however, we need a more far-reaching revision of Kantian transcendental philosophy than Cassirer suggested. It is by no means true, in particular, that Einstein's general theory of relativity can be incorporated within transcendental philosophy "without difficulty"—as Cassirer indicated—since this philosophy, in its original form, is committed to the *a priori* necessary validity of both Euclidean geometry and the fundamental principles of Newtonian mechanics.[21] The only way forward, in my view, is to *relativize* the Kantian *a priori* to a given scientific theory in a given historical context (following Reichenbach in 1920) and, as a consequence, to *historicize* the notion of transcendental philosophy itself. Thus, for example, whereas Euclidean geometry and the Newtonian laws of motion were indeed necessary presuppositions for the empirical meaning and application of the Newtonian theory of universal gravitation (and were therefore constitutively *a priori* in that context), the radically new mathematical and physical framework constituted by the Riemannian theory of manifolds and the principle of equivalence defines an *analogous* system of necessary presuppositions in general relativity. Moreover, what makes the latter framework constitutively *a priori* in the new context is precisely the circumstance that Einstein was only able to *arrive* at it by self-consciously situating himself within the earlier tradition of scientific philosophy represented by Helmholtz and Poincaré—just as that tradition, in turn, had previously and no less self-consciously situated itself in relation to the original version of transcendental philosophy first articulated by Kant.[22]

The fundamental idea of the Marburg School was that it is indeed possible to continue the tradition of critical or transcendental philosophy—especially the tradition of a critical or transcendental philosophy of *science*—in the wake of quite radical revisions to the original, Euclidean-Newtonian framework for modern mathematical physics. I believe, as just explained, that this idea is still correct. In order to see this, however, we need to historicize and relativize the notion of transcendental philosophy itself. In particular,

Kant's commitment to the necessary *a priori* validity of Euclidean geometry and the principles of Newtonian mechanics was an absolutely central part of his own solution to the Newtonian problem of absolute space—and thus it was absolutely central, as well, to Kant's fundamental contention that the structures of mathematical, perceptual, and physical space are necessarily identical. Moreover, it was in precisely this way (as I have argued in detail elsewhere) that Kant was able to replace the Newtonian conception of space (infinite, three-dimensional, and Euclidean) as the divine *sensorium,* with the conception of this same space (infinite, three-dimensional, and Euclidean) as the form of our distinctly human *sensibility.*[23]

It was also precisely in this way, finally, that Kant was able to create transcendental philosophy in the first place—namely, by fundamentally transforming the metaphysical tradition he inherited in such a way that all considerations of God and divine creation could be eliminated from natural philosophy on behalf of our human "transcendental subjectivity." The tradition of scientific philosophy that arose in the wake of Kant—including the more narrowly Neo-Kantian tradition of the Marburg School and the more broadly Kantian work of Helmholtz and Poincaré—simply took this for granted: Their problem, accordingly, was to reconfigure Kant's original system in the light of developments in post-Kantian scientific philosophy, as well as in the sciences themselves.

This effort, I have argued, can indeed be brought to a successful conclusion. And when we do so, we also see how the Kuhnian problem of understanding the rationality of revolutionary transitions (involving essentially discontinuous or incommensurable scientific paradigms) can itself be successfully resolved. We see, specifically, how the decisive instance of a "scientific revolution" in Kuhn, the transition from Newtonian physics to Einsteinian relativity, is not merely characterized by what we might call *retrospective* convergent rationality—a convergence of abstract mathematical structures when viewed from the perspective of the later paradigm. More importantly, this revolution is also characterized by *prospective* convergent rationality—a convergence that was discernible from the perspective of the actual, historical evolution of concepts which made Einstein's new theory physically or empirically *possible* in the first place.[24]

NOTES

1. See especially Kuhn (1970, 206–207): "There is, I think, no theory-independent way to reconstruct phrases like 'really there'; the notion of a match between the ontology of a theory and its 'real' counterpart in nature now seems to me illusive in principle. Besides, as a historian, I am impressed with the implausibility of the view.

I do not doubt, for example, that Newton's mechanics improves on Aristotle's and that Einstein's improves on Newton's as instruments for puzzle-solving. But I can see in their succession no coherent direction of ontological development." Earlier, in chapter 9, on "The Nature and Necessity of Scientific Revolutions," Kuhn had considered the transition from Newton to Einstein in some detail, arguing that no real sense can be made of the claim that Einsteinian mechanics contains Newtonian mechanics as an approximate special case. We shall return to this example below.

2. The main works of this school include Cohen (1871) (1902), Natorp (1910), Cassirer (1906–1907) (1910). I shall confine myself here to Cassirer. For further discussion of Cassirer in relation to Cohen and the Marburg School, see Friedman (2000).

3. See, in particular, Kuhn (1993, 331–332).

4. Compare Cassirer (1910, 357): "The goal of critical analysis would be attained if it succeeded in establishing in this way what is ultimately common to all possible forms of scientific experience, that is, in conceptually fixing those elements that are preserved in the progress from theory to theory, because they are the conditions of each and every theory. This goal may never be completely attained at any given stage of knowledge; nevertheless, it remains as a *demand* and determines a fixed direction in the continual unfolding and development of the system of experience itself." (All translations from Cassirer's writings are my own.)

5. Compare Cassirer (1910, 355–356): "The change must leave a determinate stock of principles unaffected; for it is solely for the sake of securing this stock that it is undertaken in the first place, and this shows it its proper goal. Since we never compare the totality of hypotheses in themselves with the naked facts in themselves, but can only oppose *one* hypothetical system of principles to another, more comprehensive and radical system, we require for this progressive comparison an ultimate constant *measure* in highest principles, which hold for all experience in general. The identity of this logical system of measure throughout all change in that which is measured is what thought requires. In this sense, the critical theory of experience actually aims to construct a *universal invariant theory of experience* and thereby to fulfill a demand towards which the character of the inductive procedure itself ever more closely presses."

6. See Burtt (1924), Koyré (1939), Dijksterhuis (1959).

7. In addition to Koyré's book on Galileo (1939), see Meyerson (1908), Brunschvicg (1912) (1922), Metzger (1923) (1930), and Maier (1949). Kuhn was especially impressed by the new picture of the transition from medieval to modern science— the so-called scientific revolution of the sixteenth and seventeenth centuries—that emerged from this body of work.

8. Compare Kuhn (1977, 107–108): "[The proper] attitude toward past thinkers came to the history of science from philosophy. Partly it was learned from men like Lange and Cassirer who dealt historically with people or ideas that were also important for scientific development. . . . And partly it was learned from a small group of Neo-Kantian epistemologists, particularly Brunschvicg and Meyerson, whose search for quasi-absolute categories of thought in older scientific ideas produced brilliant genetic analyses of concepts which the main tradition in the history of

science had misunderstood or dismissed." In reference to the importance of properly understanding the transition from medieval to modern science, in particular, Kuhn continues (1977, 108): "That challenge has shaped the modern historiography of science. The writings which it has evoked since 1920, particularly those of E. J. Dijksterhuis, Anneliese Maier, and especially Alexandre Koyré, are the models which many contemporaries aim to emulate." Finally, in his preface to the original (1962) edition of the *Structure of Scientific Revolutions,* Kuhn writes (1970, v–vi): "I continued to study the writings of Alexandre Koyré and first encountered those of Emile Meyerson, Hélène Metzger, and Anneliese Maier. More clearly than most other recent scholars, this group has shown what it was like to think scientifically in a period when the canons of scientific thought were very different from those current today." Thus, although Kuhn does not explicitly mention "Neo-Kantian philosophy" here, we can trace the importance of its influence on his historiography all the way back to *Structure.*

9. For a more detailed discussion of relationships among Meyerson, Cassirer, and Koyré, see Friedman (2003).

10. See Meyerson (1930, 388–389); the quotation is from vol. 2 of *Das Erkenntnisproblem.* Compare also Meyerson's criticism of the "mathematical idealism" of the Marburg School (437–438), and his reference to both Cassirer (1910) and Natorp (1910) on page 423.

11. Cassirer continues the passage quoted immediately above (1910, 431) as follows: "But these [functional orders and coordinations] do not exclude the moments of difference and change but only achieve determination in and with them. It is not manifoldness as such that is annulled but [we attain] only a manifold of another dimension: the mathematical manifold takes the place of the sensible manifold in scientific explanation. What thought requires is thus not the dissolution of diversity and change as such, but rather their mastery in virtue of the mathematical *continuity* of serial laws and serial forms."

12. Here, once again, the main intermediary between Meyerson and Kuhn is Koyré: see especially Koyré (1931) for an extended defense of Meyerson against Cassirer on precisely this point.

13. Compare note 1 above. For the point about the differing "physical referents" of the terms of Newtonian and relativistic mechanics, see Kuhn (1970, 101–102).

14. Cassirer continues (1921, 109): "The step beyond [Kant] that we now had to complete on the basis of the results of the general theory of relativity consisted in the insight that in these determinations of the understanding, in which the empirical-physical picture of the world first arises, geometrical axioms and laws other than those of Euclidean form can enter in, and allowing such axioms not only does not destroy the unity of the world—that is, the unity of our concept of experience of a total ordering of the phenomena—but it truly first grounds this unity from a new point of view, in that in this way the particular laws of nature we have to reckon with in space-time-determination all finally cohere in the unity of a highest principle: precisely the general postulate of relativity."

15. For more on this issue, see Friedman (2000, 89–93).

16. For further discussion of Reichenbach (1920) and its influence on the logical

empiricists more generally, especially Carnap, see Friedman (1999, chap. 3). It is noteworthy, in this connection, that Carnap served as editor for the original publication of *Structure* in the *Encyclopedia of Unified Science,* and in this capacity wrote to Kuhn enthusiastically expressing considerable sympathy with his viewpoint; compare Friedman (2003).

17. This, in essence, is the conclusion about the fundamental divergence in "physical referents" referred to in note 13 above.

18. In particular, my argument for conceptual incommensurability in this case relies on precisely the Kantian distinction between *logical* and *real* possibility— which thereby replaces Kuhn's concern with "physical referents." Like the Marburg School, therefore, I want to confine the discussion to the conceptual realm and avoid ontology; unlike the Marburg School, however, I agree with Kuhn that purely mathematical continuity and convergence is not sufficient. I set up the problem, accordingly, by appealing to the relationship between (purely abstract) mathematical concepts and sensible experience.

19. Kant's *Metaphysische Anfangsgründe* appeared in 1786, between the first (1781) and second (1787) editions of the first *Critique.* For discussion see Friedman (2004) (2006).

20. This story is developed in Friedman (2001, part 2, § 4) and, in even more detail, in Friedman (2002).

21. Compare again note 15 above, together with the paragraph to which it is appended.

22. The point about necessary presuppositions for empirical application and meaning is just my replacement for Kuhn's appeal to "physical references" (note 18 above), and is developed in Friedman (2001). The point about further *historicizing* transcendental philosophy by locating Helmholtz, Poincaré, and Einstein within a broadly Kantian tradition, however, is new; it is developed in Friedman (2008).

23. See Friedman (2009).

24. The distinction between *retrospective* and *prospective* rationality is drawn in Friedman (2001, part 2, § 3). The account of prospective rationality, in particular, is my response to the problem of incommensurability as understood in the terms of note above.

REFERENCES

Brunschvicg, Léon. 1912. *Les étapes de la philosophie mathématique.* Paris: Alcan.
———. 1922. *L'expérience humaine et la causalité physique.* Paris: Alcan.
Burtt, Edwin. 1924. *The Metaphysical Foundations of Modern Physical Science.* London: K. Paul, Trench, Trubner & Co.
Cassirer, Ernst. 1906–1907. *Das Erkenntnisproblem in der Philosophie und Wissenschaft der neueren Zeit.* Berlin: Bruno Cassirer. 2 vols.
———. 1910. *Substanzbegriff und Funktionsbegriff.* Berlin: Bruno Cassirer.
———. 1921. *Zur Einsteinschen Relativitätstheorie.* Berlin: Bruno Cassirer.
Cohen, Hermann. 1871. *Kants Theorie der Erfahrung.* Berlin: Dümmler.
———. 1902. *Logik der reinen Erkenntnis.* Berlin: Bruno Cassirer.

Dijksterhuis, E. J. 1959. *De Mechanisering van het Werelbeeld*. Amsterdam: Muelenhoff.

Friedman, Michael. 1999. *Reconsidering Logical Positivism*. Cambridge: Cambridge University Press.

———. 2000. *A Parting of the Ways: Carnap, Cassirer, and Heidegger*. Chicago: Open Court.

———. 2001. *Dynamics of Reason*. Stanford: CSLI Publications.

———. 2002. "Geometry as a Branch of Physics: Background and Context for Einstein's 'Geometry and Experience'." In D. Malament, ed. *Reading Natural Philosophy*. Chicago: Open Court. 193–229.

———. 2003. "Kuhn and Logical Empiricism." In T. Nickles, ed. *Thomas Kuhn*. Cambridge: Cambridge University Press. 19–44.

———. 2004. "Introduction" to Immanuel Kant. *Metaphysical Foundations of Natural Science*. Cambridge: Cambridge University Press.

———. 2006. "Metaphysical Foundations of Natural Science." In G. Bird, ed. *A Companion to Kant*. Oxford: Blackwell. 236–248.

———. 2008. "Einstein, Kant, and the A Priori." In M. Massimi, ed. *Kant and Philosophy of Science Today*. Cambridge: Cambridge University Press. 95–112.

———. 2009. "Newton and Kant on Absolute Space: From Theology to Transcendental Philosophy." In M. Bitbol, P. Kerszberg, and J. Petitot, eds. *Constituting Objectivity: Transcendental Perspectives on Modern Physics*. Springer. 35–50.

Koyré, Alexandre. 1931. "Die Philosophie Emile Meyersons." *Deutsch-Französische Rundschau* 4: 197–217.

———. 1978. *Études Galiléenes*. Paris: Hermann, 1939. 3 vols.

Kuhn, Thomas. 1970. *The Structure of Scientific Revolutions*. 2d ed. Chicago: University of Chicago Press. Original edition published in 1962.

———. 1977. *The Essential Tension*. Chicago: University of Chicago Press.

———. 1984. "Revisiting Planck." *Historical Studies in the Physical Studies* 14: 231–52. Reprinted as an afterword in Kuhn (1987).

———. 1987. *Black Body Theory and the Quantum Discontinuity, 1894–1912*. 2d ed. Chicago: University of Chicago Press.

———. 1993. "Afterwords." In P. Horwich, ed. *World Changes: Thomas Kuhn and the Nature of Science*. Cambridge, Mass.: MIT Press. 311–341.

Maier, Anneliese. 1949. *Die Vorläufer Galileis im 14. Jahrhundert*. Rome: Edizioni di Storia e Letteratura.

Metzger, Hélène. 1923. *Les doctrines chimiques en France du début du XVIIᵉ à la fin du XVIIIᵉ siècle*. Paris: Presses Universitaires de France.

———. 1930. *Newton, Stahl, Boerhaave et la doctrine chimique*. Paris: Alcan.

Meyerson, Emil. 1908. *Identité et réalite*. Paris: Alcan.

———. 1930. *Identity and Reality*. London: Allen & Unwin. Translated from 3d ed., 1926 (identical to 2d ed., 1912).

Natorp, Paul. 1910. *Die logischen Grundlagen der exakten Wissenschaften*. Leipzig: Teubner.

Reichenbach, Hans. 1920. *Relativitätstheorie und Erkenntnis Apriori*. Berlin: Springer.

To Reach for Metaphysics:
Émile Boutroux's Philosophy of Science

Fabien Capeillères

> [Another direction of French philosophy consists in] a metaphysics that takes its starting point in the critique, not only of reason, but even more of science as an objective expression of the relations of reason with things. This perspective consists in getting in the presence of the sciences as given realities, in scrutinizing their elements and conditions and, if it appears that these elements are something other than facts or relations which are objectively observable, and can be related to each other through the methods of objective sciences, in searching within the sciences themselves for a support from which to reach for metaphysics. Émile Boutroux, Louis Liard, Evellin, Arthur Hannequin, Milhaud, Dunan, Brunschvicg . . . etc., took this path.
> —ÉMILE BOUTROUX

The philosophy of science of Émile Boutroux (1845–1921) occupies a paradoxical and quite specific place in the history of French philosophy. Boutroux was neither the first to develop a strong interest in this field, nor was he the one who carried forward its technical constitution. By all rights—setting Auguste Comte aside—Charles Renouvier and Antoine Cournot are the first French Neo-Kantians who should figure in a genetic and systematic study of French philosophy of science.[1] Furthermore, the metaphysical background, structure, and intention of Boutroux's philosophy bind it to Félix Ravaisson's spiritualism. This explains why Boutroux's first consideration of the sciences, his 1874 *De la contingence des lois de la nature* (*On the Contingency of Nature's Laws,* hereafter *De la contingence*), is far from providing an epistemology of a given field of physics or of the positive sciences: Rather, it is a metaphysical treatise aimed at a new foundation of spiritualism—a task which had, as a prerequisite, the limitation of a positivistic use of the mechanistic and deterministic ideals of science.

Nevertheless, within the French spiritualist movement, Boutroux developed a Neo-Kantian trend which had been initiated by his master Jules Lachelier in 1864, taken up by Paul Janet a year later, and was carried on by Léon Brunschvicg, among others. This trend possessed, among other characteristic features, two that led to a fruitful philosophy of science: The first was considering science as one of the main expressions of spiritual life, and hence as a necessary positive object of philosophy; the second was emphasis on a method which, in opposition to the idealistic speculative method, focused on the given sciences and analyzed them.

Moreover, Boutroux's sociocultural situation placed him in a highly productive, reflective, and influential scientific milieu. During his years at the École Normale Supérieure (hereafter ENS), a number of eminent French scientists were located across the street from him or even—in the case of Pasteur's lab, where Émile's brother Léon worked—in a pavilion outside the building. And if, in Boutroux's opinion, too few professors and students at ENS crossed the Rue d'Ulm, others, such as his friend Jules Tannery, nevertheless did so. Boutroux's trip to Germany after his ENS years gave him the opportunity to meet two of the most prominent representatives of early German Neo-Kantianism, Eduard Zeller and Hermann von Helmholtz. This encounter impressed on him the necessary unity of all the sciences and philosophy's essential relation to them; it also familiarized Boutroux with the latest developments in the natural sciences. Later in his career, Boutroux's inner circle included outstanding and even leading representatives of nearly all the scientific disciplines—here we name Jules Tannery, Benjamin Baillaud, Henri Poincaré, Pierre Boutroux, and the best historian of antique and contemporary sciences in his generation, Paul Tannery. All of these elements, in conjunction with the specific historical dynamics Boutroux participated in and was affected by, at least in part explain why his final consideration of the sciences in 1908, *Science et religion dans la philosophie contemporaine* (*Science and Religion in Contemporary Philosophy*), present a conception of science which is in some agreement with our interests a century after its publication.

In sum, then: Due to Boutroux's strategic position within the French educational system; his close relations with and influence on leading scientists both inside and outside of his circle; and more specifically, because of his links with French conventionalism as well as his influence on later generations of historians and philosophers of science such as Brunschvicg, Gaston Milhaud, Émile Meyerson, and Pierre Duhem: Boutroux's philosophy represents one of the main sources of a new dynamic which animated the philosophy and history of science at the end of the nineteenth century in France, and further characterized them at the beginning of the twentieth century. He promoted this new dynamic to a very important degree, and his influence was still felt by such later, seminal figures as Alexandre Koyré and Martial Guéroult.[2]

The peculiar *character* of Boutroux's philosophy of science—namely, that it seems to go progressively beyond its original metaphysical frame, yet never really reaches beyond it (and never wishes to)—as well as his specific *situation,* necessitate a particular hermeneutics.[3] A strictly epistemological or structural reading of his philosophy of science—one aimed at the restitution of a model of scientific reasoning, the architecture of science and its transformation, or the interpretation of decisive scientific achievements of the period (such as non-Euclidian geometries and thermodynamics)—would be both frustrating and inappropriate. The results of such a reading would be poor, would lack originality, and would certainly not explain the key role played by this philosopher.[4] In order to understand and fully appreciate Boutroux's thought and more particularly his philosophy of science, then, we have to develop a "constellation-analysis" built on two considerations: (1) a social and cultural history of the period,[5] and (2) a history of the intricate network of problems that shaped Boutroux's intellectual background. The center of this intellectual web was the "philosophical crisis" of spiritualism[6] which Boutroux addressed and temporarily resolved in his 1874 dissertation, *De la contingence.* There is no room here for the exposition of such a study, and the present essay can only be schematic: I will nonetheless try to indicate how Boutroux's thought is a transitional element bridging two very different trends in French philosophy, and more generally, two rather remote philosophical interests.

On the one hand, Boutroux facilitated the transition between a French metaphysical spiritualism exemplified by Ravaisson and his faithful or "true" heir, Henri Bergson.[7] Heidegger's interest in Ravaisson shows the kind of metaphysical attention this tradition still generated after the turn of the century.[8] On the other hand—and though other sources such as Renouvier, Cournot, and Vacherot should ideally be taken into account here—Boutroux linked Lachelier's spiritualism, which differed from Ravaisson's mainly in its substantial Neo-Kantianism, up with Neo-Kantian philosophers. These included epistemologists like Louis Liard, Arthur Hannequin, Poincaré, Brunschvicg, Milhaud, and Meyerson; historians of science (and sometimes active scientists) like Pierre Boutroux and Paul Tannery; and historians of philosophy such as Xavier Léon and Victor Delbos. It was this transitional aspect of his philosophy which drew most of the attention to Boutroux during his lifetime as well as today, for two reasons: (1) the rise and nature of "French epistemology" and conventionalism, and (2) the rise and nature of French Neo-Kantianism. At the intersection of these two general trends arose some specific and contemporary questions such as the static or dynamic nature of the *a priori,* its function in perception and its "psychological" status, and the role of *a priori* structures in the constitution of scientific knowledge.

Boutroux's philosophy of science shows that the meaning of his contribution to epistemological problems can only be assessed on the ground of a substantial historical and systematic contextualization. Hence, in the first part of this essay I will reconstruct the crisis of spiritualism that led to Boutroux's intervention in 1874. This crisis, which consisted in the apparent opposition between science and metaphysics, not only formed Boutroux's intellectual background, it constituted the problem he addressed by formulating an ambitious spiritualist program in his epoch-making *De la contingence*. The significance and intent of this work are unintelligible without reference to the historical and conceptual context I will delineate. It can only be understood as a metaphysical work and not, as it is often retrospectively seen, as an epistemological achievement. Furthermore, the rise of French Neo-Kantianism as a whole has its roots in this crisis which was shaped and charged by conflicting uses of German philosophy in France.

If, therefore, Boutroux's philosophy of science was embedded in a much larger metaphysical structure which imparted to it its meaning and function, it is necessary to circumscribe the place and function of Boutroux's philosophy of science within his metaphysics. The second part of this essay will therefore be devoted to that task: It will show that the dynamic interface of metaphysics and science that Boutroux contributed to also influenced his work. The intellectual distance that separates his 1874 *De la contingence* from his 1908 *Science et religion* is the result of precisely this dynamic interface. The latter work differs from the former not only in its *object*—namely the reconciliation of science and religion, rather than science and metaphysics—it also addresses a different conception of *science* which, arguably, resulted from: (1) the clarification of Boutroux's metaphysical position, owing to his confrontation with Bergson; and (2) the influence of the "Boutroux circle" (primarily Poincaré) on Boutroux himself. The second part of the essay will end with an examination of possible answers that Boutroux's work can provide to our contemporary epistemological questions, even though the spiritualist metaphysics and philosophy of nature that form the basis of his philosophy of science make it quite foreign to our problems.

In a concluding section I will suggest that, although Boutroux seemed to begin his philosophical enquiry with a critique of science, its goal was "to reach for metaphysics." Since the metaphysical spiritualist perspective was always for him the commanding viewpoint, what Boutroux gave us is truly a metaphysics of science.

Science *or* Metaphysics: The Philosophical Crisis of Spiritualism (1840–1874)

Characterizations of the Crisis in 1864: Science against Metaphysics

According to his student, colleague, and friend Léon Brunschvicg, the goal of Boutroux's formative trip to Germany in 1869 was

> easy to determine if one refers to the articles Lachelier published in the *Revue de l'instruction publique* [in 1864], on the occasion of Caro's book: *The Idea of God and Its New Critics*. The new critics are Renan, Taine, Vacherot. According to Caro, their common trait is to "dissolve all metaphysics and to deprive human thought of its leaning point in the absolute"; their common inspiration goes back to the doctrines Cousin brought back from Germany in the old days, to Kant's critique and to Hegel's dialectic.[9]

Brunschvicg's account is quite accurate, though a little biased. In order to put Lachelier, the first Neo-Kantian spiritualist and Boutroux's influential master, in the spotlight, Brunschvicg left the major problem that Lachelier's paper was more generally addressing in obscurity. This problem was the deep crisis spiritualism was striving to overcome. All trends within spiritualism acknowledged this situation. A critical and progressive spiritualist, and doubtlessly one of the most interesting philosophers of this period, Étienne Vacherot opened the first book of his *Essais de philosophie critique,* "La philosophie et les sciences" (Philosophy and the Sciences), with these words: "For anyone interested in the future of philosophical studies, it is clear that in the present days they are going through a dreadful crisis. Since the beginning of the century, philosophy has not suffered a more serious one, a more difficult one, one that puts its very existence in danger to such a degree."[10] The two most important representatives of traditional spiritualism and philosophical voices of the Sorbonne at that time, Elme Caro and Paul Janet, got involved at the same time and for the same reason. In order to understand how this crisis was perceived, one should analyze the spiritualists' descriptions of their time.[11]

Caro's analysis can be found in two complementary texts published in 1864—his inaugural lecture for the chair of philosophy at the Sorbonne, "De la situation actuelle du spiritualisme" (On the Current Situation of Spiritualism),[12] and his book, *L'idée de Dieu et ses nouveaux critiques* (*The Idea of God and Its New Critics*). His lecture, paying tribute to Caro's predecessor, the eclectic philosopher Adolphe Garnier, situated the current state of spiritualism by way of an evolutionary discussion of the problems it addressed. In Garnier's time, around 1840, the main problem was "the definition of philosophical sciences, their organization as different and separated sciences, the distinction between psychology and physiology"; by 1864 the problem had become "that of the origins: Where does the world come from? Where does man come from?"[13]

Why had the problem shifted, and why did it become that of the origins? Because of the development of the natural sciences and, above all, because of their tendency to reject any explanation other than that which they offered. Any explanation that considered anything beyond the phenomena and the mathematical and mechanical laws which linked them in a necessary and deterministic series, was considered metaphysical and therewith rejected. The dismissal of any cause but the efficient, narrowed the focus to the problem of origins: Final causes presuppose what Caro called "primordial causes," that is, God as author of the design which final causes fulfill. Caro therefore drafted the opposition of science and metaphysics in this way: "either intentional laws regulating the development of the world, or blind forces untangling in an original chaos through an infinite number of combinations—order as a manifestation of a choice, or order as manifestation of necessity—nature suppressing God or nature subordinating itself to God."[14] Caro's book played an important part in the intense and complex discussions of religion that characterized this period. But the quarrel over God and religion was not primarily assessed from a historical and political perspective; it was seen as the consequence of a much broader issue—the possibility and meaning of metaphysics.

Caro offered an explicit analysis of the crisis in his book. Although his lecture blamed "the critical spirit" for producing the general conditions of the crisis, his book made clear who was originally to blame. Kant is "the authentic father of philosophy," that is, of Taine, Renan, and Vacherot.

> The first responsibility for this general trend of minds which estranges them more and more from metaphysics, goes back to him. . . . Condemnation of metaphysics, distrust for our higher faculties, which lead further than their accurate reach, elimination of any reality that does not come from direct observation, all the critical philosophy [in Taine, Renan, and Vacherot] and even the principle of Positivism are already there in the *Critique of Pure Reason*. Hegel's influence then joined Kant's.[15]

Caro engaged in the same kind of analysis regarding the attack made in the name of science. The actual ruin of metaphysics was attempted by a positivism which was produced historically by Auguste Comte's legacy, then represented by Émile Littré; and conceptually by a strict and severe ideal of scientificity, shaped by a narrow understanding of recent progress in the natural sciences. The "new critics" heavily rely on these scientific advances by Charles Darwin, Claude Bernard, and Marcelin Berthelot:

These philosophical dispositions [against metaphysics], which are unambiguous signs of the spirit of the time, found an energetic, decisive support in the preeminence of experimental methods, which tend to replace all others and which will, as a matter of fact, become the only one on the day there will be only one science left—that of the physical world.[16]

In July and August 1864, the months between the publication of Caro's book and his inaugural lecture, Paul Janet, who held the other chair of philosophy at the Sorbonne, published a long article, "La crise philosophique et les idées spiritualistes" (The Philosophical Crisis and the Spiritualist Ideas). In his article, Janet likewise analyzed this "philosophical crisis." The designated origins of this crisis were the same as those Caro pointed to—the positive sciences and German philosophy. Janet dramatized a bit: "But more is at stake here [than a school]: an idea, the spiritualist idea. It is this idea's destinies that are threatened today by the most formidable onslaught it has had to suffer since the *Encyclopedia,* and, were it to succumb, it would bring down with it the liberty and dignity of the human spirit."[17]

In order to understand the nature of the crisis and to offer a solution, it was essential to identify the real opponent: Was it the sciences, or a given philosophical use of the sciences?

The Real Opponent: Critical and Positivist Misuses of German Philosophy and of the Sciences

Despite several ambiguous formulations, both Caro and Janet strove to put the blame neither on the genuine doctrines of Kant and Hegel nor on the positive sciences, but on an illegitimate use of both. Indeed, given Victor Cousin's use of Hegel, the genuine Hegelian doctrine could not be a threat to the spiritualist doctrine—hence Caro and Janet were more preoccupied with defending Hegel than Kant.

Following Caro,[18] Janet examined the nature of the Hegelian claims in Taine and Renan. His conclusion was merciless: "In Hegel's system, the external is the symbol of the internal, the real the symbol of the ideal. In M. Taine's system it is quite the opposite. . . . I do not find any more of the true spirit of Hegelianism in the more subtle and distinguished opinion brightly represented today by M. Renan."[19]

Concerning the second cause of the crisis—namely, the influence of the natural sciences—Caro spoke positively in his lecture of an attempt to "enlarge and complement" philosophy with the new discoveries of the sciences, and advocated an "alliance" of "spiritualist philosophy with the positive sciences";[20] he also castigated those "adventurous minds whom serious science disavows and who compromise it."[21] Janet followed the same path—again, swords are crossed with Taine, Renan, Littré, and Vacherot.[22] Hence to a certain degree, which will be assessed more objectively later, it is not the sciences that are criticized here but rather their philosophical interpretations and use by "the new critics."

What pushed traditional spiritualists to enter this arena? Only an evocation of their opponents' doctrines can give a clear idea of what they were fighting against. In order to illustrate what preoccupied Boutroux, I will briefly mention a few elements of Taine's philosophy. Concerning German philosophy, the *casus belli* is to be found in Taine's direct attack on spiritualism in 1857, in his *Les philosophes classiques du XIXe siècle en France.* Although the role of Hegelian philosophy is not absolutely clear in this book, it was nevertheless explicitly written *sub invocatione Hegeli.*[23] Furthermore, Taine's reference to Hegel was perceived as an attempt to appropriate the German legacy, thereby invalidating the evolution of eclectism and the legacies of Cousin and Jouffroy.[24] This attempt is quite clearly expressed in Taine's *L'idéalisme anglais,* a series of articles published in the *Journal des Débats* in 1860: "From 1780 to 1830, Germany produced all the ideas of our historical age and, for half a century or maybe a century, our big task will be to rethink them."[25] The publication of Kant's *Critique of Pure Reason* in 1781 and Hegel's death in 1831 here constitute the landmarks which circumscribe "the matter of all tools as well as the instrument of all work; we have to recast them."[26] Because Taine considered himself to be master of the French forge, his position represented a rejection of traditional spiritualism's genealogy, beginning with Cousin's integration of German philosophy. Furthermore, Taine's interpretation of Scottish philosophy—which constituted the background of Jouffroy's work—submitted it to a Germanization of its original content. The result, in the eyes of the traditional spiritualists, was a denial of the evolution of eclecticism which lead from Cousin to Jouffroy: Instead of an enrichment, this evolution was to be seen as an integration—the accomplishment of which was to be found in Taine. Lastly, Taine also rejected Schelling's last philosophy, which was a major reference for spiritualism.

One of the aims of Boutroux's trip to Germany in 1869 was to settle, for the benefit of another trend of spiritualism, this controversy concerning German philosophy. In 1870, while Boutroux was preparing himself to proclaim, with Zeller and Helmholtz, the death of Hegelianism and the rebirth of Kantianism, Taine and Renan published the Berlin Academy's subscription for a Hegel monument![27]

Concerning metaphysics, the core of the problem was the adoption of what was considered to be a scientific method. Taine's manifesto against spiritualism had a very clear structure: After having criticized all the historical representatives of the spiritualist trend—Laromiguière, Royer-Collard, Maine de Biran, Cousin, and Jouffroy—a summary negative chapter explained the institutional and popular success of this philosophy "in its final stage, that of a nice body, well dressed and well embalmed."[28] Then came the concluding positive chapter, "De la méthode," in which Taine explained his scientific method. It is this chapter, with similar passages from *De l'intelligence,* that spiritualists—including Lachelier in 1864 and 1872, as well as Boutroux in 1874—would quote and attack.

For Taine, the scientific method consisted in the succession of analysis and synthesis.[29] Analysis is a double translation: "to translate words by facts, that is its definition; exact translation, complete translation, these are its two parts."[30] The negative result of this translation is to suppress metaphysical entities;[31] its positive result is to leave only facts and their relations in what is considered as a mathematical formula (inspired by Condillac's *Language of Calculation*). This formula expresses a fact and a cause, whose definition is: "*A fact from which one can deduce the nature, the relations, and the modification of the other facts.*"[32] Then comes synthesis. It consists of pyramidal imbrications of more and more general formulas, regarded as what Hegel called a concrete universal. At a certain level, which Taine characterized as the "type," "we will only have a unique formula, a generative definition, out of which will come, through a system of progressive deductions, the well-ordered multiplicity of the other facts."[33] When we take into account that even God is considered a formula ("an axiom"), Taine's thought appears as a mathematical and deterministic system which superimposes Hegel (or Spinoza) and Laplace.

Taine gave analysis a chronological anteriority over synthesis. This is explicit in the final description of his method:

> we remained in the region of facts; we did not evoke any metaphysical being, we only thought about forming groups. Once these groups were established, we replaced them by the generative fact. We expressed this fact by a formula. We have united these diverse formulas in a group and we looked for a superior fact that generated them. We kept going and have finally arrived at the unique fact, which is the universal cause. By calling it a cause, we did not want to say anything else but that from its formula one can deduce all the other formulas and the formulas following these formulas.[34]

Nonetheless, he proclaimed the superiority of the synthesis. He also considered that the possibility of the ultimate synthesis, that is the perfect and total deduction, is not an ideal in the Kantian meaning of that word (or even, to remain in a closer field of reference, in the Leibnizian sense of a symbolic knowledge). As we will see, this deductive synthesis is what

Boutroux would condemn under the name of *a priori* deduction, thereby identifying "the German *a priori* metaphysics" (namely Hegel) and the scientific ideal in Taine.

Taine fully accepted the consequences of his theory. It should nonetheless be noted that his scientism did not rest on a totally deterministic conception of reality. He acknowledged two limits to determinism—chance at play between events, and the undeducibility of individuality as such.[35] If the latter is irreducible, the former can be tamed by statistics and probability; but within a given human mind, there is a definite determinism. In a letter to Cornelis de Witt dated 17 May 1864—one in which, as in his letter to Sainte-Beuve, he commented on reactions to the publication of his *Histoire de la littérature Anglaise*—Taine described the heart of his philosophical thought: "all the feelings, all the ideas, all the states of the human soul are products that have their causes and their laws, and the future of history consists entirely in the search for these causes and these laws. The assimilation of historical and psychological research to physiological and chemical research, such is my topic and my leading idea."[36] His historicism was grounded on a naturalism, and the core of this naturalism was physiology. And his metaphysical last word? "I am a determinist, in the more absolute meaning of that word, not only like Stuart Mill, but like Spinoza."[37]

The Exact Nature of the Crisis: Philosophy of Science and the Scientific Status of Metaphysics

Three different problems were interwoven, sometimes in a rather intricate way—the philosophical understanding of positive sciences, the metaphysical implications of this "epistemology," and the scientific status of philosophy and of its content, metaphysics. Mainly because of its relation to Scottish philosophy, spiritualism had for a short while attempted to keep contact with positive sciences, but even in this case it was a rather distant relationship and the sciences considered—psychology and physiology—were, at the time, rather problematic. When this relation died, the whole traditional field of philosophy of science became neglected.

Positivism, naturalism, and criticism (in Vacherot's positive meaning of that word, or even in Caro's negative sense) were only attempts to reunite philosophy and the sciences, as well as to bring philosophy onto the safe path of a science. In other words, they were *reactions* to metaphysical wanderings—as well as to the social and political institutionalization of these wanderings—rather than autonomous and spontaneous philosophical *constructions*.

Spiritualism entered a deep crisis when it neglected the necessary relation of philosophy to science, while at the same time the sciences were in a very important transitional period. It is fascinating to see how even a clear formulation of the crisis was painful for the traditional kind of spiritualist. This could be summarized by their dilemma, "science *or* metaphysics"; and because the spiritualists could not give up metaphysics, the whole status of their philosophy had become problematic. For if they were to renounce the status of a science, what was left? Another dilemma then seemed excruciating: If it is not a science, metaphysics could only be an illusion. Two other possibilities seemed to resolve the dilemma: First, scientificity could have degrees, and therefore sciences could differ not only in their objects but also in their modal status. Unfortunately, the positivistic ideal claimed a monolithic concept of science—and with it, of truth and certitude. When spiritualists attempted to profess for metaphysics a different kind of scientificity, not only were they mocked, they were also unable to confer on this science a decent intellectual status or, in other words, a respectable place in the hierarchy of the sciences. Second, metaphysics could belong to another genre of knowledge than positive sciences, a genre that would still hold a strong value. In its historical realizations, this possibility generally brought metaphysics into the vicinity of art. As we will see, Ravaisson will take that path, followed by Lachelier, and Boutroux will inherit from his mentors the idea that philosophy is not a science and that, like a work of art, it is an individualized work, not an abstract universal structure. But for philosophers like Caro and Janet, to conceive of philosophy as an art meant to identify it with literature, a possibility which they strongly objected to.

The First Programs for a Solution to the Crisis: Caro, Janet, and Lachelier (1864–1868)

Against these attacks, what did Caro offer? A strictly negative response—the criticism of his opponents' arguments. Though Caro acknowledged the necessity of a reawakening after some sort of dogmatic slumber, the constructive part of his book is a very vague program grounded on Cousin's and Jouffroy's thesis: It is a timid attempt to let the positive sciences be autonomous and to consider them as an essential field of reflection for philosophy, as well as to claim for philosophy the status of a different science. Unfortunately, the details of and justification for this position were lacking. This largely negative dimension was noticed by Janet: "The book is, generally speaking, more critical than demonstrative"[38]—and this constituted a reason for Janet's intervention in 1864. Caro's later works, although addressing other aspects of the same problem, remained negative.[39]

As noted, Janet published his article on the "philosophical crisis" in 1864—a year before Boutroux entered the ENS. Janet's diagnosis was the same as Caro's, but did he offer a consolidated or renewed philosophical spiritualism? In no way. His article ended with a proposed program: Enough with critiques; we should build "strong thoughts." His program was full of good resolutions, similar to Caro's: We shall not forget that philosophy is a science, and a science in progress; we should go back the grounds and to theoretical research; we should not allow ourselves to become "more and more isolated from the evolution of physical, natural, and historical sciences, which touch philosophical science on so many sides."[40] However, all this was much too vague to satisfy anyone, and thus left spiritualism in an even deeper crisis.

Did Lachelier's articles in 1864 introduce new elements? Their goal was to reassert God's personality and existence, as well as their function in spiritualist metaphysics—to offer for thought, knowledge, and faith a ground in the absolute. What is interesting is that Lachelier took a methodological perspective. He attacked Taine's naturalism by an examination of his concept of cause. If the only possible cause of a fact is another fact acting as an efficient cause, as Taine claimed, then he should not be able to extend his method to the explanation of the organism's functions because—according to Caro, Janet, and Lachelier—such an explanation requires final causes. Two critiques were therefore recurrent: Taine's naturalism was an ontological monism that failed to firmly delineate the gaps in the hierarchy of beings; this naturalism had, as a correlate, a methodological monism which claimed to apply scientific mechanism to all fields of knowledge.

Lachelier's correction of Caro's concept of God touched on the same strategic point. Caro tried to reclaim the classic concepts of God as first cause and Being of all beings (*Summum ens*). Lachelier specified how these conceptions were to be understood in order to avoid contradiction. The anteriority of the first cause is not chronological:

> the first cause is not from another age, but from another order than the second causes; it did not act before them to directly determine a given state of the beings, but it did not cease to act with the second causes in order to create being as such in all the series of its determinations—or rather, it is the only one acting and the others are the limits and the measure of its own operation.[41]

Second causes belong to the field of sensibility and the positive sciences, whereas the first cause is conceived of by reason and belongs to metaphysics only. It should be noted that the independence of these two orders was asserted with reference to Kant:

> If there is a principle which after Kant can no longer be contested, it is that a given state of the universe cannot start *ex abrupto*, but that it must always have its reason in a preceding state, from which it follows according to a law: hence all direct calls to divine power, concerning a specific event, can

only be used as a temporary substitute for our ignorance of natural causes, and indicate to science a lacuna that only science itself can fill. We should let science freely weave the infinite weft of phenomena: the part that is left for us is good enough, as it consists in explaining them, not physically but metaphysically, not by the cause that determines them in time but by the one that creates them in eternity.[42]

The kind of cause Lachelier attempted to bring into play in order to avoid the problems of a first phenomenal cause—"we could not care less here about Pascal's *chiquenaude*" or "flick," as he pleasantly termed it—remained, in the eyes of the "new critics," no less chimerical than a first phenomenal cause.

None of the programs suggested by these first spiritualists attempts to solve the crisis of metaphysics, then, were satisfactory. A second series of publications followed, essentially comprised of Ravaisson's famous 1868 report, *La philosophie en France au XIXe siècle*, and the discussion it prompted; Janet's manifesto, *Le spiritualisme français au XIXe siècle*, published immediately after Ravaisson's report; Lachelier's *Du fondement de l'induction*, published in 1872; and Alfred Fouillée's *La liberté et le déterminisme*, published in the following year. This sequence differed from the previous one largely because of its more positive, constructive content. If, again, none of the answers offered were really satisfying, they nonetheless delineated the structure of a problem and offered several suggestions which resulted in what was referred to as a "new phase of spiritualist philosophy."[43] Boutroux's 1874 dissertation, *De la contingence*, was the outcome and most coherent and elegant synthesis of this new spiritualism.

The Second Programs: A New Phase in Spiritualist Philosophy (1868–1873)

When Boutroux wrote a report on French philosophy in 1908 which took over exactly where Ravaisson's 1868 report had stopped, he noticed: "Something, around 1867, ended; something was soon to be born."[44] What ended is clear: Cousin died in 1867, but intellectually—having already been seriously wounded by the positivists and some of the new critics—he was finished off by both Ravaisson's and Paul Janet's genealogies of the spiritualist movement. In a complex strategy that attempted to place responsibility for the crisis of spiritualism on its eclectic origin, these authors severed eclectism from spiritualism. Cousin's head rolled from philosophical eminence into the dust of political and institutional history; spiritualism's rebirth was dated to 1840, and this new spiritualism was attributed to Maine de Biran and André-Marie Ampère.[45]

Ravaisson's book, *La philosophie en France au XIXe siècle*—considered by Boutroux to be the second reason for the reawakening of philosophical activity in France (Lachelier's lectures at ENS being the first)—offered a picture of the French philosophical landscape that looked like a strategic atlas. In his 1840 review, "Philosophie contemporaine, *Fragments de philosophie par M. Hamilton*," Ravaisson had already condemned Cousin's attempt to unite the scientific method of the Scottish school to Schelling's metaphysics and philosophy of nature; he had also installed Biran in his status as "reformer of philosophy in France."[46] References to this article allowed Ravaisson to picture himself as the continuator of Biran's work, and thus as the main representative of an authentic spiritualism.[47] He had indeed rejected "the specious parallelism one attempted to establish between the method of physical sciences and that of philosophy,"[48] but what was his constructive solution for their reconciliation?

Ravaisson started with the general opposition of materialism and spiritualism; this opposition concerns both their object and method. Materialism focuses on the matter, on the elements, and satisfies itself when the object of knowledge has been analyzed into its irreducible elements, because analysis can go no further. In the process, analysis loses the concrete individuality of the object, and its knowledge is abstract. Spiritualism addresses the form, the unity that commands the specific assembly of all the object's elements and the function each of them fulfills within the whole. Its method is not analysis but synthesis, and its model is art. Synthesis retains the concrete individuality of its object without losing its universality; individuality is not particularity. At that very general level Ravaisson already suggested an absorption of science and its methods, analysis and induction, into synthesis and art. Quoting Leibniz, he claimed that induction cannot progress without an "art of guessing," and that synthesis is the real method of invention, of creation.[49] This can only be true if synthesis is not the mere assembly of what the analysis of phenomena produced. And as a matter of fact Ravaisson redefined, with a reference to Kant that would be fruitful for Lachelier and Boutroux, the meaning of synthetic judgments:

> there are other synthetic judgments [than those which merely reassemble phenomenal elements,] by which we go beyond everything that sensitive experience presents. It is these that Kant brought to light under the name of *a priori* synthetic judgments. However, when he saw in them only an application to the objects of experience, of the sensitive conditions under which only we imagine them, perhaps he was not looking for the principle of these judgments high enough. It is not only to the laws of extension and duration that, by our *a priori* synthetic judgments, we submit the objects offered by our senses, but to superior laws, of which the laws of extent and duration are themselves doubtless only by-products.[50]

This passage is essential for our understanding of both Lachelier and Boutroux. It was at the root of a spiritualist interpretation of Kant's originally synthetic unity of apperception: It is not only a higher synthetic level than any determinate categories but also, as the "'I think' that can accompany any of my representations," it is understood as the self-reflection of the spirit, as Ampère had suggested to Biran. This passage also interprets the synthesis as a creation of the spirit: The synthesis itself is a pure act of the spirit, but it should also be noted that the senses and their content (both pure and empirical) are themselves unconscious products of the spirit. The last point here opened the possibility of considering Kant's theory as correct, although unfulfilled, and therefore as offering a superficial or popular spiritualism. Boutroux will develop this possibility, considering the forms of understanding (categories) and forms of intuition (space and time) as hypostases of the creative activity of the spirit or, more precisely, as "habits" in the Ravaissonian meaning of this term.

This conception of the synthesis was developed by Ravaisson in his exposition of the concepts of cause. His first move was to reduce the efficient cause to the final cause—the former is only a partial understanding of the latter. From the perspective of physics, this meant that movement (conceived of as physical force) is grounded on "tendency" and "effort"—both of which are teleological concepts that only gain significance when we think of them as a tendency *to* and effort *toward* something. But toward what? Perfection and intelligibility, claimed Ravaisson, in keeping with his Aristotelian inspiration. This specific determination of the "end" involved a critique of the Kantian idea as a regulative principle: This idea, as an "ideal," is for Ravaisson too abstract and in fact a product of analysis. Perfection as final cause is to be found in ourselves. In a Leibnizian (as well as metaphorical) description, Ravaisson brought all elements of thought (perceptions, memories, and the like) back to the vivifying and unifying action of a superior idea—a relative perfection that pervades and directs all our thought. The fundamental elements, like Leibniz's small, unconscious perceptions, are thought that ignores itself as such but that is pervaded and moved by a spiritual tension. "One should add that if the relative perfection of our thought is the cause of everything that happens in us, this relative perfection itself has a cause, which is absolute perfection."[51] This absolute perfection is God.

Such a metaphysical construction—one which not only referred a fact to a preceding fact as its cause or resolved it into its elements, but which related it to the action of a superior perfection—involved a specific method: "For this synthetic operation, which is . . . the philosophical method, there is a necessary principle. This principle is strictly speaking the method of high philosophy, of metaphysics: it is the immediate consciousness, in the reflection on ourselves and by ourselves on the absolute in which we participate, of the last cause or reason."[52]

Several consequences of this are important for the question of a philosophy of science. The first is that there is, *de facto,* no philosophy of science here: A philosophy of nature stands in its place and in many ways prevents it. For the expression "philosophy of nature" has the very peculiar meaning that we find, for instance, in Schelling's system after 1800, and more precisely in an interpretation of his last philosophy. This philosophy of nature is not strictly limited to a philosophy of the *laws of* nature; it is much more fundamentally a metaphysical genesis of the objects of nature as a whole. The second consequence is that this lacuna is not an accident, for at least three reasons: (1) Natural sciences do not provide the authentic laws of nature, but only mechanical causes of phenomena. Deeper than the phenomenal appearance stands the real essence—the spiritual effort which constitutes its actual cause and thus the authentic principle of a philosophy of nature. (2) As a consequence, the natural sciences—dealing with apparent causes and blind to real causes—are situated quite low in the hierarchy of knowledge. Foremost in this hierarchy now stands art, which is used as a metaphor and paradigm for the dynamics of creation as such. And (3), as a consequence of this revised hierarchy, Ravaisson has no difficulty in metaphorically suggesting a relativization of natural laws—that is, in challenging their necessity. This point will be important for Boutroux.

Ravaisson distinguished two concepts of necessity. One is absolute necessity and designates the logical necessity of the principle of reason, as well as what he considered to be a mathematical principle: That which contains something (x), also contains whatever this thing (x) contains. The other concept of necessity is a relative one. This is moral necessity, one which involves freedom and is involved in our determination to do what we believe to be the best.

From the perspective of science, nature only obeys the first, absolute necessity. But science can explain neither the real cause for a given fact, nor a progression relative to the hierarchy of beings. Spiritualism corrects this first flaw by reintroducing final causes, and the second by filling the gaps between the ontological series of beings and the different sciences which account for each order of reality, thus restoring an ontological as well as "epistemological" continuity. While filling these gaps, metaphysics inserts the second, relative necessity both at the foundation (vertically, so to speak) and between series (horizontally) of the absolute necessity that pertains in nature: "Nature is now no longer, as materialism teaches, all geometry, and hence all absolute necessity or fatality. It contains morals; nature is as mixed with absolute necessity, which precludes contingency and will, and with relative necessity, which implies them. And this is not all: morality here is the principle."[53] Although it would be inappropriate to call Ravaisson's doctrine a "philosophy of contingency"—an expression coined to characterize

Boutroux's philosophy—for him this relative necessity, as the necessity of a moral duty, presupposes a contingency at the origin of being.

Ravaisson's solution is ultimately a spiritualist providence—"everything obeys, and willingly so, a wholly divine Providence."[54] His condemnation of the fatalism attributed to the "new critics" is not entirely without grounds: If and when we can have knowledge of the historical development of providence, it is never complete; and it is this blindness which results in the misconception that providence is for us a destiny, quite equivalent to a materialistic *fatum*. But this consequence is only true from a gnoseological perspective. In the spiritualist's ontological perspective there is this tremendous difference—we are supposed to have access to the first principle, God as love, and because we find it *in* us, we participate in it both in essence and in action. In "obeying willingly" what we recognize as a divine providence—itself the result of God's free will—we transform passive obedience to a *fatum* into the realization of the freedom of spirit.

In this Ravaissonian guise of a spiritualist philosophy, how was the opposition between positive science and metaphysics solved? It figured as the exact opposite of the positivistic solution. The scientificity of the sciences is dismissed. In a rather disturbing way, Ravaisson not only instituted a gnoseological hierarchy of knowledge wherein the positive sciences held the lower place, he also added a very strong moral and social value to this classification.[55]

> It is necessary, says Pascal, to have a thought in the back of the mind and to judge everything from this perspective; while nonetheless speaking like ordinary people. The thought "in the back of the mind" which should not keep us from speaking of each specific science in its own language, that of physical appearances, is metaphysical thought.[56]

The only real science is metaphysics, as "nature can only be explained by the [knowledge of the] soul"[57] or, as Aristotle put it, because metaphysics is the science of first principles and first causes.

This program is important for us because it shows that when Boutroux was completing his intellectual development at the ENS, one of the most influential spiritualists had set up a metaphysical conceptual framework in which the orders of reality were separated by gaps which the positive sciences could not bridge. Continuity could only be restored by metaphysics—a restoration which also introduced contingency at the ground of these orders and between them. Furthermore, the hermeneutics allowed by this idea "in the back of the mind" will be important for Boutroux's understanding of Neo-Kantian epistemology as developed by Milhaud and Poincaré: Boutroux will be able to agree to their version of the synthetic *a priori* judgment, while at the same time maintaining a deeper spiritualist perspective.

Ravaisson's 1868 report was, as Boutroux noted in 1908, an important factor in the revival of philosophical reflection in France: It not only positively framed a program which many spiritualists were to take up in different ways and to varying degrees, it also provoked negative reactions which were no less important to philosophy, since they explained the diversity Boutroux tried to describe in his later report.[58]

The next publication leading us to Boutroux is Janet's manifesto *Le spiritualisme français au XIX* *siècle*, also published in 1868.[59] In it, Janet endorsed a perspective on nature that was similar to Ravaisson's: German philosophy, from which, now, "may come the salvation of spiritualism," showed that "nature, properly speaking, has no reality in itself: it is full of spirit; it is, lives, and breathes only through the spirit"; "matter, says Schelling, is sleeping spirit."[60] On this ground, Janet strives "for the reconstruction of a new philosophy."[61] The material for "a rejuvenation and a renovation" consisted in "getting closer to the sciences, of which spiritualist philosophy offers a more and more serious and careful study."[62] In the same years, Janet had claimed a scientific status for philosophy[63]—namely in his published lectures of 1865, "La philosophie: Sa définition, son caractère, son objet" (Philosophy: Its Definition, Its Character, Its Object).[64] This text addressed the question "What is science?"—but the author significantly refused to define it by any characteristics other than "free examination" and "the search for universals and causes." He rejected criteria such as consensus, verification, or certainty, considering that a "cautious opinion is a scientific state of mind."[65]

However weak Janet's consideration is here, it led to a methodological point which is extremely important in understanding Boutroux. Philosophy's legitimacy is to be established by what Janet called "the authentic critical method": "Admitting that after all perfectly certain and doubtless objects, each having its science, have been counted, listed, exhausted, [and] classified, something nonetheless remains: why should we not deal with this something?"[66] The authentic critical method can be seen, then, as an examination of the insufficiencies of the sciences on their own terrain. This was a common idea at the time, but Janet elevated it to the rank of a general method. Lachelier used it in his 1872 *Le fondement de l'induction* and, as we will see, it became an essential element of Boutroux's method in his 1874 *De la contingence.*

Furthermore, this "something"-left which constitutes the object of philosophy is, for Janet, self-reflection understood in a spiritualist way. This led Janet to debate the relations of psychology (which he separated from physiology) and metaphysics. For him psychology offered the ground of ontology. This topic, as expressed in Janet's concluding words—"philosophy, strictly speaking, consists of psychology and metaphysics tightly united"[67]—prepared the way for Lachelier's 1885 article, "Psychologie et métaphysique."

But Janet's efforts did not bring any resolution to the crisis. Although he was the official "voice" of the Sorbonne his reflection was too loose, too general; Janet's was a popular and eclectic philosophy.

Thus, Boutroux awarded Lachelier first place with regard to the awakening of philosophy; and Brunschvicg did the same a few years later. This ranking, however, is not relevant in tracing up a solution to the crisis of spiritualism. First, Lachelier's actual recasting of spiritualism was only published in 1885;[68] second, Boutroux's evaluation was grounded on Lachelier's teaching, rather than on his publications; and third, this ranking took into account the most diverse influences Lachelier exerted, and not merely his specific contribution to spiritualism. With what was probably the most anti-dogmatic, influential teaching ever provided in the French university, Lachelier's tremendous impact consisted in the revival of reflection, and not in the assertion of a doctrine. Hence two questions should be distinguished with regard to Lachelier: (1) that of his active participation in public debate—a participation which should be limited to his publications, and in particular *Du fondement de l'induction*—and (2) his influence on Boutroux, an influence that was exerted through his lectures at the ENS. I will briefly address the first issue.[69]

At first glance, *Du fondement de l'induction* can be understood as an epistemological enquiry: It researched the grounds of the operation by which we progress from the knowledge of facts to the knowledge of their laws, a transition which is also understood as the step from contingency to necessity, and from particularity to universality—this operation is the ground of science. Lachelier's first move, against Taine, was to disqualify any foundation in logic and in the principle of identity. Only a "material" principle can add universality and necessity to the knowledge of facts. On this basis, Lachelier's reflection took on a definite Kantian character, in terms of both its form and its content.

Concerning its form, the search for a ground started with the construction of an antinomy between empiricism (Hume and Mill, § 2) and eclecticism (Royer-Collard, Cousin, Jouffroy, and Janet, § 3). The solution to this antinomy was found in a "third hypothesis, introduced by Kant" (§ 4).[70] With regard to its content, this third way was derived from the consideration that

the highest of our cognition is neither a sensation nor an intellectual intuition, but a reflection, by which thought immediately seizes its own nature and the relation it holds with phenomena: it is from this relation that we can deduce the laws that thought imposes on phenomena and which are nothing other than its principles.[71]

Hence,

> if the conditions for the existence of phenomena are the very conditions of the possibility of thought . . . we can, on the one side, determine these conditions absolutely *a priori*, as they result from the very nature of our mind; and, on the other side, we cannot doubt that they do apply to the object of experience, as without these conditions there is for us neither experience nor objects.[72]

How then was induction to be grounded? Lachelier had reduced induction to two different principles: (1) the causal determination of the phenomena within a series, and (2) the teleological insertion of phenomena as parts determined by the whole. The foundation of the legitimacy of these two principles would be accomplished if one could show that they are the conditions of the given fact of human thought. The general idea is the following: "All phenomena are submitted to the law of efficient causes because this law is the only ground for the unity of the universe, and because this unity is in turn the supreme condition of the possibility of thought."[73] The interesting element is less this regression to conditions of possibility than the way in which Lachelier conceives the relations of these conditions. *At this level of his reflection*, they are not strata or layers of hierarchical ontological entities, but rather expressions of one and the same thing—a spiritual necessity. There can be no isolated phenomenon, because it would have to exist in space and time, which are systems of relations, and of sensible relations; thus phenomena are already unified with other phenomena and with the spirit in a gnoseologic web. Furthermore, "our cognition of the phenomena and the existence we confer on them are . . . , in reality, one single thing." Lastly, and *still at this level of reflection*, "thought is nothing for itself but the necessity constituting the existence of phenomena." Lachelier can therefore conclude: "in this world of phenomena, of which we occupy the center, thought and existence are only two names for universal and eternal necessity."[74]

This legitimization of the principle of causality, as the first constituent of the principle of induction, was essential for the philosophies that would succeed Lachelier's, and in particular for Boutroux's, because it offered, within a "spiritualist realism," the ground for a positive and detailed conception of the sciences. In this perspective, Lachelier's strategy in this first moment of his philosophy was quite explicit: All the doctrines he rejected were criticized because they could not account for the reality and the requirements of science.[75] In other words, the sciences built on causality are based on—or rather, express an essential constitution of—the fundamental layer of reality governed by necessity. *At this level* and *within its limits*, this universal necessity is legitimate.

This argumentative strategy and its resulting doctrine showed an important evolution of Lachelier's thinking about science. In 1864, he had ended his *Revue*-articles with harsh words: "Science, which boasts to be the only positive one, is, when well considered, only a perpetual illusion; it operates on inconsistent externals, and knows nothing of the inside and the reality of things; it laboriously gnaws the skin of the fruit while philosophy has the privilege to express its living juice and to taste its divine flavor."[76] In 1872, however, science presented the legitimate expression of the fundamental stratum on which the two other strata of reality and of the spiritualist realism that conceive them were to rest.

These two other levels are (1) that of the second constituent of the principle of induction, the law of final causes, and (2) the moral leap or *saltus* into religion. It is interesting to note that each of these levels corresponds to a specific philosophy and to a specific vision of the world. Indeed, necessity is not the last word: "the empire of final causes, while penetrating without destroying the empire of efficient causes, substitutes everywhere force for inertia, life for death, and freedom for fatality."[77] And it should also be noted that Lachelier's reflection on science remained within the limits of a philosophy of nature identical to Ravaisson's: "the true philosophy of nature is a spiritualist realism in the eyes of which all being is force, a thought that tends to a more and more complete self-consciousness."[78] Nonetheless, if religion is the omega of this philosophy, science is its alpha. Boutroux would later comment: "Whoever strives to maintain philosophy's originality," as opposed to its dissolution into diverse positive sciences, "while at the same time reestablishing and tightening its relations to the sciences and religion is, in some degree, Lachelier's disciple."[79]

Far from being an epistemological undertaking, *Du fondement de l'induction* laid the ground for the accomplishment of spiritualism's metaphysical program. It fulfilled such a goal by delimiting the metaphysical essence of the ground on which science is erected. If, looking beyond the differences related to specific answers, we focus on the general problem that *Du fondement* addressed as well as on the structure of that problem, it appears that Boutroux's 1874 work went into more detail than Lachelier's did. But the function of Boutroux's enquiry was the same—to ground a spiritualist realism by the delimitation of the sciences.

Conclusion: The Philosophical Situation of Spiritualism in 1874

Despite the diversity of the programs sketched out in preceding sections, a general spiritualist framework for addressing the crisis in French philosophy was present by the time Boutroux drafted his *De la contingence*: (1) Philosophy should reconcile science and religion with each other and with metaphysics. (2) Whatever the epistemic status of philosophy (whether an apodictic science or not), it should be an autonomous, self-sustaining field with a specific content—metaphysics. And (3), in order to remain within the limits of the concept of spiritualism and its tradition, this philosophy should be built on four "dogmas":

- The fundamental dogma was that reality is in essence constituted by the spirit.[80]
- The explanation of the general structure of reality as a stratification of the spirit formed the second dogma. The orders of reality described by the positive sciences as well as by the moral sciences were to be explained and grounded in more fundamental orders where the spirit knows itself as such and the whole process presents the progressive self-reflection of the spirit, a unified perspective that only philosophy can reach.
- The third dogma concerned the origin and the end of reality. Teleology is fundamental to spiritualism. The origin of reality is the same as its end— its first cause is an efficient cause only because it is ultimately a final cause. The spontaneity of the spirit is the lower forms of the spirit's desire for its own perfection.
- The fourth and last dogma was that all the apparent necessity within the phenomenal orders and spiritual orders, as well as their dynamics, rest on a universal contingency. Because the ground of reality is spirit and because it is conceived of as free, spiritualism was in its very idea a philosophy of contingency. "It is universal contingency that forms the true definition of existence, nature's soul, and the last word of thought," wrote Lachelier in 1872.[81]

Following up on the last page of Ravaisson's *Rapport*, which called for the future triumph of spiritualism, Janet ended his 1868 paper with these words: "then will probably come a vigorous mind which, recollecting in a new synthesis these scattered elements, will regain for spiritualist thought its strength and its splendor."[82] From his first appearance on the philosophical stage, Boutroux would be seen as such a providential man. He, after Ravaisson and Lachelier, was advancing "spiritualist realism," and they granted him their extremely powerful institutional support.

Reaching from Science to Metaphysics: Boutroux's Philosophy of Nature

Boutroux's Intellectual Development within the Context of Spiritualism's Crisis (1864–1874)

Boutroux's formative years, culminating in his dissertation on nature's laws, can be divided into three periods. The first (1863–1869) comprises his education at the ENS, a period dominated by Lachelier's teaching and Ravaisson's 1868 report; the second (1869–1870) covers his trip to Germany, the intellectual substance of which derived from his encounter with Zeller and Helmholtz; the third (1871–1874) marks a year spent in Caen with Jules Tannery, and two following years, for which most of our information stems from Jules and Paul Tannery. Lachelier published his dissertations during this time. More than artificial "periods," these divisions mark the layers constituting the thought at work in Boutroux's two dissertations. It is not possible here to enter into the detailed constitution of this stratification, but I will nonetheless try to sketch it.

Although this should probably not be given too much importance, it should be noted that even before he entered the ENS, Boutroux's first encounter with philosophy occurred in a strong spiritualist ambiance: His teacher at Lycée Napoléon (now Henri IV) was Jean-Félix Nourrisson, a preeminent spiritualist who participated in the fight against the "new critics," on Caro and Janet's side, and was later appointed to the Académie des Sciences (1870) and the Collège de France (1874).[83]

Boutroux entered the ENS in 1865. By that time, Lachelier had already altered his first conception of spiritualism, inspired by Maine de Biran and Ravaisson, by integrating Kantian elements and a Kantian methodology which led to a specifically spiritualist Neo-Kantian position, very different from both the neo-criticists (Renouvier) and the new critics (Vacherot).[84] Lachelier and Boutroux entertained very close intellectual and professional relations that developed into a strong friendship: As a student, Boutroux was among the "Normaliens" who compiled Lachelier's lectures; and during his stay in Germany, he maintained an important correspondence with Lachelier, to whom he also dedicated his Latin dissertation. Boutroux's 1921 eulogy for the master he had met fifty-six years prior is not only emotional—it ends with a sentence that pays tribute to a very deep personal influence, by mentioning that the effort to maintain philosophy's specificity, while at the same time reestablishing and tightening its relations to the sciences and religion, is characteristic of Lachelier's legacy.[85] For Boutroux, this aspect of Lachelier's philosophy should be referred to its ground—metaphysical contingency. The personal influence most strikingly appears in passages where Boutroux expounds a philosophy of contingency in Lachelier.[86] Finally, as mentioned, Boutroux considered Lachelier's teaching to be the primary cause of the general revival of philosophy in France in his time.

The second cause of this revival was, according to Boutroux's later estimate, Ravaisson's *Rapport* of 1868—a major philosophical statement that came out in the midst of Boutroux's studies. What was Ravaisson's influence? The dedication of Boutroux's French dissertation to him attests to a high personal regard, but if we turn to the eulogy Boutroux wrote for him in 1900, he describes Ravaisson's significance as follows: Firstly, Ravaisson was seminal in his philosophical practice of the history of philosophy. Secondly, his method remained fruitful—it "consists in researching the knowledge of the laws of the spirit not only in direct reflection of the I upon itself, but also in the study of relatively external objects that spirit creates for its use, such as science, art, and religion." And lastly, Ravaisson understood humanity by transcending calculation and mechanism in favor of a spiritual creation of orders of beauty, truth, and morality—and in this he should be followed. Boutroux's accomplishments fit perfectly within the limits of these philosophical characteristics he uses to describe Ravaisson.

The second "period" of Boutroux's formative years can be characterized by three intellectual gains. The first is that Boutroux's Neo-Kantian training drew closer to its German sources. Next, the question of philosophy's relation to the sciences was illustrated by Zeller's and Helmholtz's lectures and by related exchanges within the German university. Third, Boutroux's acquaintance with Zeller and his work translating Zeller's *History of Greek Philosophy* led him to explicitly formulate his own philosophy of history, while the relationship with Helmholtz familiarized him with contemporary sciences and their importance for philosophy. I will briefly summarize each of these contributions and conclude that the significance of this very short period does not rest on any authentic discovery or excursion out of the spiritualist framework established by Ravaisson and Lachelier, but rather—and no less importantly—on a much deeper and more detailed picture of what that framework should contain.

1. In 1869, on Lachelier's and Ravaisson's recommendations, Boutroux was sent to Heidelberg by the French Minister of Education, Victor Duruy. This mission contributed to a tradition of reports that punctuated the relations between France and Germany and, in particular, supported a strategic attempt by the French government to understand the German university system as well as German philosophy. The institutional motivation that drove Duruy was explicitly a scientific "Germanization of the French university," which he actively implemented after Bismarck's victory at Sadowa in 1866.[87]

The philosophical motivations that inspired Ravaisson, Lachelier, and Janet have their roots in the philosophical crisis already examined. As Brunschvicg suggested, Boutroux's trip was a reaction to Renan's and Taine's positivist attempt to ruin metaphysics with tools borrowed from German philosophy—aspects of Kant's critique and Hegel's dialectic. If it became necessary, as Taine claimed in his 1864 *L'idéalisme anglais,*[88] to rethink the seminal ideas of German philosophy, then Germany was the place to conduct this research. And if, more precisely, as suggested in the spiritualist agenda set by Lachelier and Janet, it was necessary to reclaim Kant's legacy and the metaphysically articulated unity of science and religion, then Heidelberg was a reasonable choice. Boutroux would make two important encounters there—with the Neo-Kantian philosopher and theologian, Eduard Zeller; and with the Neo-Kantian scientist, Hermann von Helmholtz.

In Boutroux's introduction to his translation of Zeller's *History of Greek Philosophy,* he presented the author as follows:

> Zeller progressively distanced himself from Hegel; and when, in 1862, he was named ordinary professor of philosophy at the University of Heidelberg, he declared in his Inaugural Lecture that German philosophy had to come back to Kant's critical research concerning the origin of our knowledge, avoiding the errors that had brought about the exclusive idealism of the post-Kantian period, and aiming at a conception of the world which had its starting point in experience alone, while continuing to subject experimental data to the control, the critique, and the elaborative action of *a priori* laws of knowledge.[89]

As Brunschvicg later noted: "In a striking coincidence with the orientation taken by Lachelier's teaching, Zeller indicated, in his 1862 opening lecture, the opportunity to *go back to Kant;* besides, he was only summarizing from a genuine philosophical point of view the motto formulated a few years before by Helmholtz in the name of the scientists."[90] It is indeed remarkable that Boutroux's seminal years coincided with this peak of the first wave of Neo-Kantianism in Germany, and that he met two of its most preeminent representatives in Heidelberg just before they both moved to Berlin.[91]

Nevertheless, this encounter with German Neo-Kantianism remained within very narrow and typical limits. Its main feature was an anti-Hegelianism, for this settled the dispute with Taine and Renan and cleared the way for Boutroux's doctrine of contingency. The positive dimension of Boutroux's Neo-Kantianism is much more difficult to assess, in particular because it evolved throughout the philosopher's career; I will therefore mention here only one general feature. There is a methodological dimension to this Neo-Kantianism that consisted in taking experience (i.e., the real, historical, and empirical sciences, as well as historical phenomena) as a starting point, as well as using reflection to correlate that first perspective with a second one, namely the *a priori.* But this is also a method that Boutroux attributed to Ravaisson and Lachelier, and Boutroux's perspective was very remote from the "transcendental method" that was soon to characterize Marburg Neo-Kantianism.

2. In a letter to Duruy dated 28 January 1869, Boutroux told the minister that in Heidelberg "one can apprehend the solidarity within all parts of science," and stipulated that each week the professors of all disciplines met

together for mutual discussions.[92] This question of the diversified unity of the sciences was not only emphasized by Boutroux as a strong and valuable characteristic of the German university, it was also formulated through the specific point of view of the collaborative unity of the positive sciences and metaphysics.[93] Because Boutroux had not yet made up his mind as to which work to translate while in Heidelberg, he indicated that he had started with a lecture given by Zeller in November, concerning "philosophy's position toward the other sciences":

> It seems to me that this is the very question we must ask concerning philosophy. One wonders if there is still a reason for its existence after the innumerable discoveries made by the exclusive use of the experimental method. Given two research procedures, one having established truth universally admitted, should not the first be given up in favor of the second? This question, addressed by one of the most important metaphysicians in Germany, appeared to me of the keenest interest.[94]

Zeller's talk, indeed, happened to be "Über die Aufgabe der Philosophy und ihre Stellung zu der übrigen Wissenschaften," a sequel to his inaugural lecture in 1862, "Über die Bedeutung und Aufgabe der Erkenntnisstheorie."[95] In the introduction to his translation of Zeller's *History of Greek Philosophy*, Boutroux would come back to this point: "in charge, as rector, of the speech for the new academic year" Zeller had explained, in perfect agreement with this new point of view, that "philosophy could not claim the role of a separate science, entirely *a priori* and deductive, which it had been allocated by the Platos and the Hegels, etc."[96]

I cannot enter here into Zeller's and Helmholtz's conception of the unity of the sciences and philosophy's role in it, but Boutroux's interest in these questions should be explained. First, as I have mentioned, within the context of spiritualism's crisis two different concerns were decisive: (1) the progressive estrangement of spiritualism from the sciences; and (2) a reunification with the sciences which would not lead to a complete disappearance of metaphysics and an absorption of philosophy into the methodology of the specific sciences (a double fate which was proclaimed by Comte's and Littré's positivism). Second, the philosophical and the institutional problems should not be kept apart: The *universitas litterarum* is—or rather, was—in France as well as in Germany, the common paradigm to conceive of both the unity of the faculties (traditionally law, medicine, philosophy, and theology) within the *university*, and the unity of all the sciences in *knowledge*. In a Sorbonne recently freed from the ministry of theology, philosophers were eager for their autonomy, if not for reclaiming a regal status, and were indeed quite reluctant to plead allegiance to positive science. Similarly the Humboldtian university, a half-century-old German university, cannot be understood without a similar reference. It only requires a reading of Helmholtz's 1862 address, "On the Relation of the Sciences of Nature to Science as a Whole," to notice how, in order to explain the diversified unity of knowledge and interdisciplinary relationships, he speaks of the structure of the university. Boutroux's double mission was therefore easy to consider as one. In addition, despite the intrinsic interest of both Zeller's and Helmholtz's understanding of this problem, it should be noted that these requirements which he found expressed and somehow embodied in Germany were constitutive of the spiritualist programs that preceded Boutroux's mission.

For this period and as far as the documents allow us to judge, Boutroux was only meticulously fulfilling the goals of this mission. One should nonetheless note that in his second year lecturing at the university of Montpellier, Boutroux gave a lecture on German philosophy in which traditional spiritualism's oversight of the importance of science became a characteristic of French philosophy, dominated by analysis; whereas the systematic unity of doctrine became a distinctive feature of German thought, dominated by synthesis.[97] The main interest of this lecture rested not so much in Boutroux's characterization of the philosophical national spirits per se, a banal feature at the time, but rather in the fact that he integrated into spiritualist philosophy Taine's conception of these national characters, without its determinist background, thereby following up, six years later, on the fulfillment of his mission!

3. When he was sent to Heidelberg, Boutroux was no neophyte with regard to history or science. He had studied under Nourrisson, a renowned spiritualist historian, and Lachelier used history in a philosophical way. Furthermore, the status of history was problematic within the spiritualist crisis as such—the eclectics' antiquarian practice of history was blamed by Janet for the crisis, as previously noted, while Ravaisson put an end to its uncritical erudition. Furthermore, given the polemic around religion, the relation between history and its religious version, theodicy, was quite sensitive.

Concerning science, Boutroux had a friend and scientific adviser at the ENS, Jules Tannery. Whatever their relation was at the time (we know more about it in later years), when Boutroux arrived in Germany, he found a situation that better suited his expectations. In a letter to Duruy he mentioned: "I sometimes listen to Mr. Helmholtz, who gives a class which I would have been happy to find at the École Normale. He talks about the general results of the sciences."[98] Boutroux, hence, attended and appreciated Helmholtz's famous "popular lectures." What else? The young philosopher could easily cultivate this relationship, as Helmholtz was famous and popularized in France.[99] When Boutroux arrived in Heidelberg, Helmholtz was at a critical moment in his career: Professor of the chair of physiology since 1858, he had just published the third and last part of his *Handbook of Physiological Optics* (1867), a volume often presented (with some justification, despite containing many anti-Kantian ideas) as the foundation of what would later be called "physiological Neo-Kantianism." In 1869, a third and substantially revised edition of this work was published. Furthermore, since 1867, Helmholtz had been working on the question of the axioms of geometry. Boutroux's presence in Heidelberg, then, is delimited by two landmarks in Helmholtz's career—his 1868 lecture "On the Facts Underlying Geometry" and his 1870 lecture "On the Origin and the Meaning of Geometrical Axioms."[100]

These historical elements suggest that Boutroux found himself in a context that was extremely favorable to his development of a spiritualist program concerned with the philosophy of the sciences. He also may have had a firsthand and early knowledge of more specific questions, such as the role of intuition in mathematics in general and in geometry in particular—questions which, when he was in the middle of his career, would be strenuously debated by prominent members of his circle (Poincaré, Tannery).

Boutroux's First Program: A Moral and Aesthetic Teleological System

In his 1874 French dissertation, *De la contingence des lois de la nature* (*On the Contingency of Nature's Laws*), Boutroux sketched the program of a rather ambitious philosophy which would solve spiritualism's crisis and set the grounds for a spiritualist conception of the world. This program can be expressed in terms of (1) its metaphysical constitution—a universe organized in hierarchical strata, starting with undifferentiated quantity and rising up to perfect spirit, namely God; (2) its fields—science, religion, morals, aesthetics, and history; and (3) its goal—freedom and intelligibility. I will briefly explain these aspects in order to precisely circumscribe Boutroux's project and explicate the place and function of his philosophy of science during this period.

"One can distinguish, within the universe, several worlds forming like stories piled up on each other. There are, above the world of pure necessity—of quantity without quality, which is identical to nothingness—the world of causes, the world of notions, the mathematical world, the physical world, the living world, and lastly the thinking world."[101] Boutroux's vision of a stratified universe resulted from his study of each level: It is because, when considered in itself, none of these worlds leads to the next without a *solution* of continuity, that they can be seen as different layers. Each of the higher levels seems to depend on the lower, concerning both its existence and its laws: The material physical object would neither exist nor be conceived without generic identity, causality, and mathematics; nor would the living being exist or be conceived without the physical elements; nor would a thinking human without life. But although these are conditions of *possibility,* no relation of *necessity* makes the superior forms dependent on the lower ones—an assertion by which Boutroux meant that the upper layers can be deduced from lower ones neither *a priori* nor *a posteriori:* "the higher elements will remain irreducible to the lower elements."[102]

Boutroux hereby rejected a genesis of reality which would explain the diversification and specification of being by means of a development governed by necessary processes in which the primary stage envelops the final stage. The gaps between strata and the rejection of an external necessity linking one stratum to another leave room for Boutroux's main thesis: The relations between the strata are contingent, and so is the global development.

Could a necessity nonetheless be at work within (and upon) each stratum? Or, in other words, are all the elements constitutive of a stratum submitted to necessary laws? In the strata where the elements are phenomena, are not the latter submitted to infrangible laws (as matter is to physical law, etc.)? Boutroux's examination of the different sciences had as its goal a demonstration that, although there are laws and they have domains of validity, they can be considered as necessary neither *a priori* nor *a posteriori.* They cannot be deduced *a priori* because, in order to do so, one would have to start from the essence of the object—but this essence is a quality that involves an infinity of quantitative degrees. Therefore no scientific law, as a fixed and determined rule regarding quantity, can be deduced from this quality.

Neither can they be deduced *a priori* from the knowing mind, because strictly rational and *a priori* formulaic modes of thought concern things-in-themselves or indemonstrable relations, and therefore cannot be immediately applied to specific things. Boutroux added: "the formula involving an experimental use contains no term that could not be explained by experience itself. It is therefore inaccurate to say that laws govern phenomena. They are not posited prior to things but presuppose them."[103] Such a statement rejects what Boutroux called a metaphysics of the *a priori*—a metaphysical position shared, in his eyes, by Kant and the post-Kantian idealistic systems.

No strict necessity can be claimed *a posteriori* for several reasons. An empirical principle is always established through a hypothetical argument, and no conclusion can overcome the contingency involved in the content of the starting point. Furthermore, no empirical principle can be identified with the nature of things: The principle is quantitative, abstract, and considers stable relations regarding fixed, immobile things—thereby missing their lively qualitative dynamics. In addition, and independent of the question of their determination by a scientific law, "beings from a given world are not in a state of absolute dependency regarding their own nature"[104]—their very nature is open to a contingent becoming.

Boutroux's conclusion was that, for strata constitutive of the universe, there exists no necessity—neither internal nor external, *a priori* or *a posteriori*. The correlate of this thesis was his doctrine of contingency: At the root of all being, at the source of any phenomenon, and at every level of being stands a radical contingency. Contingency is, so to speak, a negative principle; it does not indicate what determinate relation is at work in the universe Boutroux is describing. It opens possibilities without indicating which is actual—it could be chaos, for instance. Hence, the first principle to complement contingency is creation: The higher elements are "superimposed on the lower by a way of addition, of absolute creation."[105]

This general structure is, in its very essence, a spiritualist conception, both in its constitution in layers and in the principle of their relations. When Janet told Boutroux during his defense, "You belong with us"—that is, to the spiritualist school—Boutroux answered that he was happy to be so well understood, and that "it is Ravaisson's authority that established the very principle of this dissertation: 'all modification implies an addition of being, any phenomenon is, relative to the preceding phenomena, a true creation.'"[106]

When we turn to the question of the nature of reality and of the composition of these worlds, we are again led back to a spiritualist vision, for "the universe is not composed of equal elements, susceptible of transforming themselves into one another, like algebraic quantities. It is composed of forms superimposed on each other although related to each other, perhaps, through completely insensible gradations—that is, additions."[107]

"Form" here specifies the conception of quality that Boutroux, following Ravaisson again, opposed to quantity. Such a concept of form has nothing in common with the Kantian concepts of form; it is derived from the Aristotelian conception of *formation*, of the teleological fulfillment of a form toward its own perfection. This process involves neither a preexistence within the first stages of the principles of development, nor a simple preformation. Boutroux compared it instead to an epigenesis, "which supposes explicitly a principle of addition and perfecting."[108] It also allows for the development to be a decline or a decadence without this negative development being conceived as accidental or monstrous, thereby showing the real contingency of the process, which is at work both within each world and between them.

The omnipresence of these concepts of form and perfection show that the metaphysics Boutroux sketched in his early program is dominated by a qualitative and dynamic conception of reality, whereas his conception of positive sciences emphasized their complete dependence on quantity and stability, which they cannot exceed. It gave to the historical sciences, or what he calls the "dynamic sciences"—to which philosophy belongs, and which deal with the becoming of qualities—an overwhelming gnoseological and axiological supremacy over the positive sciences.[109]

Through this hierarchy of worlds, the scientific laws (which are quantitative) loosen their grip, not because of the complexity of the phenomena but because of the supremacy of *formation,* that is, of the *qualitative* process of creation:

> In the lower worlds, law holds such a large domain that it may almost be substituted for being; in superior worlds it is the opposite; being almost replaces the law. Hence all facts depend not only on the principle of conservation, but also and in the first place on a principle of creation. Therefore being, in none of its degrees, is known to its ground when positive sciences have achieved their work. It is known in its permanent nature and laws. It remains to know it in its creative source.[110]

At this very point, Boutroux's reflection reached its first essential goal, the critical circumscription of science. The result of this philosophical delimitation is that, in complete opposition to naturalistic and positivistic claims, the sciences cannot provide an exhaustive knowledge of being and of reality. Some room is therefore left for metaphysics: "It would devolve upon metaphysics to fill the void that philosophy of nature has left, by examining whether man could know, by another path than experience, no longer essences and laws, but true causes endowed with both a faculty for change and a faculty for permanence."[111]

What then are the real causes, the principles of this creative source? This is what falls to metaphysics to reveal. God is at the top of the hierarchy of being and the principles of the world: "By this doctrine of God's liberty is explained the contingency presented by the hierarchy of the forms and the general laws of the world."[112] Boutroux, however, refuses to use the traditional onto-theological explanation which attempts to deduce the finite and its development from the infinite, notably because this would involve bringing necessity back within the structure of being.

That God cannot be the immediate agent of the living dynamics of the universe and of its forms does not mean that he has to be removed from his status of first principle. It rather implies that he should be conceived of as a final cause instead of an efficient cause; "nature's beings . . . have an ideal to realize, and this ideal consists in getting closer to God, to resemble him, each in its own kind."[113] Here Aristotle, and Ravaisson's interpretation of his physics and metaphysics, stand in the background. The *prōton kinoun akinēton*—the "prime non-moved mover"—moves everything else in the way that desire moves, as Aristotle claimed.[114] Ravaisson Christianized this doctrine and claimed that desire was transcended in love and grace; he saw in this dynamic the accurate interpretation of necessity. Boutroux followed Ravaisson here, concerning the general dynamics: "As we ascend the scale of being, we see the development of a principle that, in a sense, resembles necessity: attraction for certain objects. The thing would seem to be led necessarily. It is not, however, driven by something already realized; it is attracted by something which is not yet given and which perhaps will never be."[115] This impulse toward perfection is, in the realm of nature, a striving toward beauty, whereas in the human world necessity takes the form of moral duty.

Such a teleology supposes that, in order to somehow conceive and realize this ideal, each being possesses a "given degree of spontaneity"[116]—a claim which deserves further explication, in the case of an inert material object, for instance. Boutroux's explanation came in the form of a strategic revival of the concept of "habit" that Ravaisson set out in his 1838 essay, *De l'habitude* (*Of Habit*). Habit, according to Ravaisson, demonstrated that matter, in the given guise of the human body, was a degradation of the spirit—a numb or sleeping spirit. He first identified habit as mechanism within the acts of spirit. But the inertia of the spirit can be explained, even in bodily habits, only by a form of spontaneity and of individuality, thereby showing the insufficiency of a mechanistic understanding. Generalizing his thesis by way of a "daring analogy," Ravaisson claimed that "all, in nature itself, is in fact *spontaneity*. And . . . I defined *nature* by *habit*."[117] Boutroux's remarkable idea in his renewed use of Ravaisson's concept is that habit offers the support, the anchorage point for the laws of nature (and in particular, for all the laws of psychology and sociology): "Animals' instinct, life, physical and mechanical forces are, somehow, habits that penetrated always deeper into the spontaneity of being. Hence these habits became almost insurmountable. They appear, from the outside, as necessary laws."[118]

This conception constituted an original renewal and radicalization of Ravaisson's doctrine, not so much because it reasserted an authentic spiritualist conception of reality, but rather because habit became a hinge which allowed for a reconciliation between the perspectives of science and metaphysics. "From the outside" we conceive of habits as the *a posteriori* laws of nature, but from the inside perspective proper to metaphysics, different and *a priori* orders appear—those of aesthetics and morality. Let us focus on nature and scientific laws.

Every stratum of being and all the laws and principles of sciences are ultimately interpreted by Boutroux in an aesthetic vein. "In each region of being, essences and laws have two aspects": "the principles of physiology, of physics, and of mathematics would not only have a material meaning and an *a posteriori* origin: they would also have an aesthetic meaning and, from that point of view, an *a priori* origin." Even "the logical experimental laws would rest, in the last resort, on *a priori* aesthetic principles"; "the principle of causality too would have an aesthetic meaning, and, from this perspective, an *a priori* origin." And necessity itself "would be, in the last resort, and in a logical language as abstract as can be, the translation of the activity exerted by the ideal upon things and by God upon its creatures. It would be the most material symbol of moral obligation and of aesthetic attraction, i.e., of necessity assented and felt."[119]

There is no clearer way to claim that the ultimate metaphysical significance of nature and of scientific laws is aesthetic, while that of thinking beings is moral.[120] The steps of Boutroux's research progressively and resolutely led to such an *Aufhebung*—the philosophy of science appeared to be grounded on the philosophy of nature, which gave way in turn to a doctrine of contingency. This doctrine of contingency then led, by way of a doctrine of creation, to a doctrine of liberty:

> according to this doctrine, the highest principles of things would still be laws, though moral and aesthetic ones, more or less immediate expressions of divine perfection, preexisting phenomena and presupposing agents endowed with spontaneity. . . . As for nature's laws, they would have no absolute existence; they would simply express a given phase, a stage, a moral and aesthetic degree of things, so to speak. They would be the image, artificially obtained and stabilized, of a model that, in essence, is living and moving.[121]

Scientific truth is, to say the least, only a half-truth.

Boutroux's Philosophy of Science beyond the 1874 Spiritualist Program

Most of Boutroux's philosophy of nature and doctrine of contingency in *De la contingence* was written in the conditional tense, denoting that this doctrine still had to be fully developed and more firmly established. Was it ever developed, and did this development lead to any significant change concerning the philosophy of nature and the philosophy of science?

Although Boutroux did not publish many books, he produced doctrinal explanations concerning his philosophy of history and his philosophy of religion, and he reexamined the question of science at least twice: In his 1892–1893 lectures, *De l'idée de loi naturelle dans la science et la philosophie contemporaines* (*On the Idea of Natural Law in Contemporary Science and Philosophy*, hereafter *De l'idée*), and in his 1908 *Science et religion dans la philosophie contemporaine* (*Science and Religion in Contemporary Philosophy*, hereafter *Science et religion*). The most striking character of these works is that Boutroux never came back to the metaphysical foundation and edification of the principles of his spiritualism. One can speculate that, in addition to a context that was dragging him away from metaphysics, he became aware of Bergson's superior achievements in these matters. Nothing that Boutroux subsequently wrote, however, would lead one to believe that he ever renounced the spiritualist metaphysics he sketched in the conclusion of *De la contingence,* and numerous passages suggest that he upheld these views until the end of his life.[122] Although he clearly toned down his juvenile enthusiasm, I believe he never significantly modified or, *a fortiori,* abandoned, the framework he inherited from Ravaisson and Lachelier, and which he considerably enriched. All his later works are, to some extent, either developments of doctrinal points that could only be suggested in the dissertation—that is, they attempt to fulfill aspects of its programmatic conclusion—or simple marginalia to the 1874 book. The writings on history and on religion belong to the first genre, whereas most of the lectures on nature and science belong to the second. A couple of examples will illustrate this continuity.

In the Gifford Lectures delivered in Glasgow in 1903, the first part of the lecture, on nature, is a summary of his 1874 dissertation. It follows the same negative argumentation directed against what he called "phenomenalist naturalism":

> If once science is established [by an experimental method and independently of metaphysics], we reflect on its conditions and its meaning, is it true that we can still make abstraction of the spirit as an original and spontaneous power? If the spirit is, in this sense, presupposed by science itself as well as by the laws of nature as science exhibits them, one can say no more that spiritual life is, from a scientific point of view, a way of being purely subjective, without grounds and without value. Spiritual life, as it begins in science, is in the perspective of science itself a reality; it is therefore in agreement with reason to ask if science by itself alone fulfills this life in its plenitude.[123]

At the end of the first series of lectures he concluded: "all phenomena envelop or suppose, in the eyes of philosophical reflection, the spirit as reality."[124]

His 1911 lecture titled "About Philosophy's Relation to the Sciences" again developed the antinomy of science and metaphysics that was Boutroux's preoccupation as early as 1870, and he gave the same answer as in 1874. The end of the talk suggested the transition to metaphysics.

And finally, when in 1916 Fred Rothwell produced an "authorized translation" of *De la contingence,* he changed the conditional tense of the conclusion into the present tense, a fact which, if Boutroux effectively looked at the translation in order to "authorize" it, could hardly have escaped his attention. I believe that this transition of Boutroux's metaphysical assertions from a hypothetical status to an assertorical one was not a linguistic oversight.

However, this continuity regarding his fundamental spiritualist position does not imply that Boutroux's conception of science did not evolve. It only means that this actual evolution had other causes than a transformation of his metaphysical position. For if we compare the picture of science painted in 1874 (or even in his 1892–1893 lectures) with the one depicted in 1908, a very important difference appears.

In 1908 Boutroux published *Science et religion,* a book that can be considered as the counterpart of *De la contingence.* In it, Boutroux reexamined science in order to solve its apparent incompatibility with religion, and in the course of his analysis he made this essential remark:

> Until recently, science was or wanted to be dogmatic. In its most rigorous parts, it considered itself as erected once and for all; in the other parts, it was looking for the same perfection. In everything, it sought to present itself under the form of a system that deduces from universal principles the explanation of particular things. Scholasticism, as a form, was its ideal. Today however no science, not even mathematics, agrees to be scholastic.[125]

In 1874—and in many regards, still in 1892—Boutroux based his analyses on such "scholastic" science, which he then believed to be an accurate description of it; whereas in 1908, he addressed a non-dogmatic science and a science in the making. What initiated such a change?

One could indeed argue that the methodological self-reflection which accompanied contemporary developments in the sciences legitimized Boutroux's attribution of this change to science. I nevertheless think that it is Boutroux's understanding which evolved, rather than an objective transformation of science, however effective that may have been. Three factors led to this change in Boutroux's thought: (1) spiritualism's crisis lost its intensity; (2) "Boutroux's circle"—and Poincaré foremost in it—exerted a strong influence by confronting Boutroux with real science in the making; and (3) further developments of spiritualism—notably by Henri Bergson and his follower, Édouard Le Roy—drove Boutroux to a more coherent position regarding his own spiritualism, and drew his attention toward its consequences: The spirit is alive in science also, and the philosophy of science should reflect this life. I will elaborate on the last two factors.

The first difference between the views expressed in his 1874 and 1908 books is that, in the later work, Boutroux investigated what he called "the scientific spirit"—not a corpus of knowledge, not the given sciences, but "intelligence, alive and flexible, developing and determining itself through the exercise and the work that the task to be accomplished requires."[126] Hence, the opposition between science (characterized by stability and steadiness) and life (always moving, becoming) nearly disappeared. At all levels of his consideration of science, Boutroux introduced the dynamics of becoming. In the sciences, he now sees the work of a personality: "And because, in fact, what exists is not precisely the science—an abstraction denoting only a goal, an absolute, hence an idea—but scientific work, which is always in a state of becoming, therefore real science cannot be separated from the scientists; and the moving and subjective life will always be one of its constitutive parts."[127] This dynamic is also part of the formal constitution of science: Among the latest categories science appropriated is "the concept of radical change, of partial or even universal evolution."[128]

This new approach was perfectly coherent with Boutroux's metaphysical position and was in fact more consistent than his first attitude; in 1874 the positivistic use of science contaminated Boutroux's understanding. I believe this clarification of his position occurred, from a metaphysical perspective, in his consideration of the strong spiritualist position developed by Bergson and Le Roy. Le Roy was a zealous Bergsonian and therefore not only manifested significant differences from Boutroux, but also either emphasized them or simply "forgot" to mention the author of *De la contingence*. However, two points should be noted. First, Le Roy saw a unity in what he called the "new philosophy":

> one can observe in the philosophical history of these last thirty years the birth and progression of two large trends. . . . The first one, psychological and metaphysical, starts with Ravaisson to reach Bergson. . . . The second, epistemological and critical, arises from Boutroux's works and continues with those of several contemporary scientists, among whom I will mention only Milhaud and Poincaré. It is the necessary confluence of these two trends that I studied in a memoir, *Science and Philosophy*. . . . It is, however, the product of this confluence that I designated under the name of *new philosophy*: the claim for the fundamental rights of the spirit, a claim based on the fact of a given contingency granted to the laws of nature.[129]

Le Roy's strategy consisted in a preliminary disavowal of Lachelier and Boutroux as transitional figures between Ravaisson and Bergson, and in the later inscription of Boutroux within this "epistemological" trend which happened to be in perfect agreement with Bergsonian spiritualist metaphysics, and which therefore—by virtue of this remarkable "confluence"—can and should be integrated as a part of the "new philosophy." The fact that this convergence led to an integration *under* the figure of Bergson is so obvious for Le Roy that he neglects to mention it explicitly! Poincaré did not fail to protest—and we turn now to him.

Le Roy's integration of Poincaré (to his displeasure) as well as Milhaud into this trend of "epistemological and critical" philosophy stemming from Boutroux pointed to an important, and I believe underestimated, role of Poincaré relative to Boutroux. As I have suggested, Le Roy's genealogy should not be taken into account without a considerable amount of critical skepticism. It shows, however, the possibility that Boutroux may have considered a similar integration; and therefore that in opposition (or in complement) to most interpretations, Poincaré had a strong influence on Boutroux's ultimate position concerning science.

Whatever the sequence of their possible mutual influences, it is incontestable that Boutroux's deepening of his conception of science in 1908 is accompanied by significant references to his brother-in-law, Poincaré. For instance, the idea that a scholastic conception of science had been shared by scientists until recently, but that it was no longer held—an idea which, as I have cited, opened Boutroux's consideration of the scientific spirit in 1908—can be found in Poincaré's 1902 introduction to *La science et l'hypothèse*.[130]

Another example: When Boutroux wanted to explain how the very concept of scientific truth underwent a drastic change, when the conception of science shifted from a dogmatic to a critical one, he referred to Poincaré: "Could science, nonetheless, in its field of competence, offer to the spirit a true certitude? Even this is contested; and certain people think that one should limit, even in its own field, the value of science."[131] In 1874, the limitation of scientific truth was a function of its external limits: From a metaphysical point of view scientific truth was only a half-truth, but within the limits of science, it was considered to be a legitimate certitude. In the above citation, Boutroux insisted twice that now the critical assessment is made from *within* the field of science; and he used an expression, "the value of science," which titled an essay Poincaré had published in the same year, and which Boutroux quoted a couple of pages later. Milhaud is also doubtless among the "certain people" who endorsed the "disappearance of that absolute that still remained in the signification of rational truth."[132]

Furthermore, these factors—Boutroux's clarification of his spiritualist position, and the influence of the scientific circle that grew up around him—should not be artificially separated. Poincaré's objection in 1902 to the illegitimate appropriation of some of his theses by Le Roy, produced a complex position. Poincaré's critique was aimed at Le Roy, but given some (nominal and real) similarities between Le Roy's and Boutroux's spiritualist positions, it also necessarily accomplished two tasks. First, it legitimated some of Boutroux's theses against Le Roy; but second, it implicitly took some distance from Boutroux. In this perspective, one can look at *La science et l'hypothèse* as Poincaré's version of *De la contingence* (or indeed of *De l'idée de loi naturelle*). This debate between Poincaré and Le Roy could not have failed to impact Boutroux.

In this regard, some pages of Boutroux's *Science et religion* seem quite illustrative. Poincaré's critique of Le Roy followed the latter's hierarchy in its reconstitution of the experimental method—from facts to laws and theories. Le Roy claimed, according to Poincaré, that "the scientist creates the fact" and blurred the difference between the "raw fact" and the "scientific fact." When Boutroux undertook to explain what a scientific fact is in 1908, he closely followed Poincaré's explanation—thereby endorsing Poincaré's critique of Le Roy.[133]

A final indication: In Milhaud's 1896 article "La science rationnelle," we find as an instance of the construction of a scientific law, "Phosphorous melts at a temperature of 44 degrees" centigrade.[134] Le Roy claimed this example and its function in his 1899 text, "Science et philosophie";[135] Poincaré commented on the same in his 1902 paper "Sur la valeur objective de la science";[136] and finally, Boutroux employed it in his 1908 *Science et religion*. Of course, each time, the meaning of the proposition was different. But once the difference in their initial approaches is taken into account, Milhaud and Poincaré are relatively close. And where did Boutroux stand? On their side, indeed.

Boutroux's ultimate understanding of science resulted, then, at least in part, from debates at the origin of what is now referred to as French epistemology.

Boutroux's Relevance for our Epistemological Interrogations

The historical and systematical contextualization of Boutroux's philosophy of science shows how, because of his external knowledge of science, his philosophy of nature, and his spiritualist metaphysics, he belonged to nineteenth century's official and traditional philosophy. Because of his transitional position, however, Boutroux is often addressed in the context of questions more characteristic of our present interests in early twentieth-century epistemology. The answers provided are necessarily, although not always explicitly, parts of interpretations which are situated on a wide spectrum that is delimited by Ravaisson's metaphysics on one side, and elements of French epistemology (Poincaré, Milhaud, Meyerson, Duhem) on the other.

In the best cases, interpreters are reluctant to carefully untangle that seemingly Gordian knot and either cut it to the benefit of one of the sides or content themselves with an ambiguous description.[137] Yet epistemological questions tend to impose interpretations situated toward the most contemporary end of the hermeneutical spectrum. Pushed beyond the limits of what should be called "interpretation,"[138] this perspective leads to an understanding of Boutroux's treatment of the sciences as an autonomous project, directly related to the development of French epistemology. The most characteristic expression of this hubris can be found in Michael Heidelberger's extreme assertion: "as his student Brunschvicg expressed it, Boutroux's doctrine is, above all, 'an examination of science for science, without reference to a prejudicial metaphysics.'"[139]

The extended historical and systematical contextualization I have offered here has no other aim than to help contemporary research circumscribe an accurate interpretative field within which to accurately assess the meaning of Boutroux's philosophy of science and his participation in the rise of French epistemology in general, and conventionalism more particularly. Hence, I would like to conclude this study with a few indications concerning the kind of answer Boutroux's work can provide to some of our present-day questions. In order to do so, I would like to first address Boutroux's Neo-Kantianism—for this problem directly leads to the much-debated question of mathematics and geometry as *a priori* synthetic judgments, as well as to the question of the possible constitutive function of *a priori* knowledge in natural sciences.

Because a denial of Boutroux's Neo-Kantianism would be historically indefensible, the question is not *whether* he upheld a Neo-Kantian position, but *what* the nature of his Neo-Kantianism was. The lectures he gave in 1894–1896 and 1900–1901 provide some helpful hints. They start with a factual statement concerning the Kantian ambiance and referring to data I have previously mentioned—Lachelier's teaching, Renouvier's Neo-Criticism, Vacherot's critique, Janet's return to Kant. Many other details and connections could be added in support of the historical accuracy of Boutroux's claim: "We, the French, entertain today a much more intimate relationship with Kant's philosophy than we did fifty years ago." Since the historical accuracy of this is obvious, my object is rather the *meaning* of this relationship. Boutroux continued: "These [Kantian] studies contributed for a part to the metaphysical awakening of our country. . . . Hence, to return to a study of Kant is not only to work as a scholar, a historian, a dilettante, it is to draw useful cognitions and forces to deal with problems confronting us."[140] At first glance, Boutroux's move back to Kant seems pragmatic, in that Kant would offer us tools for confronting problems which are ours. A second glance reveals that in fact, for Boutroux, the possible usefulness of Kantian "cognitions and forces" is grounded precisely on the fact that *our* problem happens to also be *Kant's* problem.

The first chapter of Boutroux's lectures described this coincidence. Titled

"The Kantian Problem," this chapter starts with a basic description of the problem: "How is science possible? How are morals possible? How is the agreement of science and morals possible?"[141] A few pages later, he comes to the point that interests us:

> The idea which governs Kant's research is the following: to admit that experience is the only source of our knowledge, that there is actual knowledge only when we rely on facts, and at the same time, to uphold the absolute character of morals. . . . Kant aims at drawing from experience the absolute in science and morals. This doctrine, when considered carefully, corresponds exactly to our state of mind. . . . The Kantian problem is ours. In his writings, it is all about us: *nostra res agitur.*[142]

A first determinant of Boutroux's Neo-Kantianism rests on the shared interest in a problem. A careful examination of his formulation of this problematic would reveal striking discrepancies with what contemporary interpreters of Kant would admit as "Kantian," but for now we can neglect that question.

What then are the tools that can be borrowed from Kant in order to solve our common problems? At a very general level, Kant is praised for his attempt to reconcile immanence and transcendence, and for his first discovery of the principles for this reconciliation: "First, it is the substitution of the spirit as life and activity for its conception as immovable substance and essence; second, it is the idea of a relationship between nature and spirit such that this relationship overcomes both pantheism and dualism."[143] These principles give a precise idea of what Boutroux is doing with Kant here: He continues Lachelier's spiritualist interpretation of Kant.

Can we borrow more precise and specific tools? With this question, the plot considerably thickens, and Boutroux's Neo-Kantianism reveals its very peculiar nature. Because we are addressing the problem of the reconciliation of science and morals, can we use the distinction between noumena and phenomena? In no way. Boutroux rejected Kant's claim of a strict determinism in phenomena. He also rejected the conception of noumenal freedom because, according to Boutroux, the doctrine of intelligible character is a subtle form of determinism: "one single action decides for all behavior. . . . Our liberty resumes in one single act; and its work is a whole in which no detail can be altered."[144] The noumenal-phenomenal distinction, then, is not useful.

Can we at least take a transcendental perspective on knowledge? Well—no! Such a viewpoint presupposes a methodological perspective which, through a radical redefinition of the *a priori,* cuts loose empiricism in the guise of Locke and idealism in the guise of Descartes or Berkeley.

Taking a structural approach to the understanding of knowledge, it expels from philosophy and inserts into psychology a temporal (hence, causal) interrogation. It therefore considers the question of genesis—of the "acquired" or "innate" origin of knowledge—to be philosophically irrelevant. Boutroux always dwelt within the mindset of the spiritualist genesis of knowledge. If he ever understood the Kantian meaning of transcendental, he never agreed and pulled Kant towards an odd version of the "acquired" thesis;[145] neither did he properly understand the Kantian determination of the two levels of the *a priori*—pure (the category of cause in the Analytic of the *Critique of Pure Reason*, for instance) and impure (though still *a priori*, such as the concept of force in the *Inaugural Metaphysical Principles of the Science of Nature*). Here again, Boutroux's only view of Kant was through a spiritualist lens: He only retained in Kant's *a priori* a generality that comforted his spiritualism. Following Lachelier's understanding of the "I think," Boutroux saw in the pure categories actions of the spirit (instead of functions of knowledge) and the claim that experience presupposes reason: "this result of Kant's *Critique* is still sound today."[146] The strictly functional meaning of reason's anteriority, expressed in Kant's phrase "transcendental condition of possibility," totally evaded Boutroux. Let us be more specific on this question, which is essential to the constitution of science.

In 1874, when Boutroux examined the possibility of a necessary link in scientific knowledge, he wrote:

> It would nonetheless be a necessary link, were it posited by the spirit, independently of all experience, in a causal *a priori* synthetic judgment. But the formulas that would suppose an *a priori* origin are not those that apply to given things or even to the knowledge of these things; whereas the formula really explaining the nature of given things comes from experience itself.[147]

This claim was made to dissolve a necessary link between mathematics and physics, but its immediate consequence is, for Boutroux, that there is no constitutive *a priori*—neither in Kant's meaning of "constitutive principles," nor in Reichenbach's and Friedman's sense of the former expression.[148] Did his lectures on Kant lead to Boutroux to a reconsideration? In no way. A brief evocation (1) of Boutroux's understanding of Kant's *a priori*, and (2) of *a priori* synthetic judgment will illustrate this point.

Describing the history of the dogmatic conception of science, Boutroux wrote:

> With Descartes, but above all with Kant, the scientific spirit seemed determined, in an immovable manner, by the logical conditions of science and by the nature of the human mind. . . . In Kant it was the *a priori* claim of

a necessary connection of phenomena in space and time. . . . The success obtained by the spirit led it to believe that it was from then on in possession of the eternal and absolute form of truth.[149]

Boutroux blamed Kant for opening the way, with his "*a priori* claim of a necessary connection," to what Boutroux called the "metaphysics of the *a priori*," which Hegel would fully develop; he also blamed Kant for reinforcing the scholastic conception of science and truth. One may therefore expect that, in a similar way and at almost the same time as the second generation of Neo-Kantians and the first generation of logical positivists, Boutroux would proceed to a historicization or a relativization of the transcendental *a priori*. He actually took a third way. The quotation continues: "This opinion, however, had to change when one examined the ways in which science is made, the conditions of its development and of its certitude. . . . Neither scientific spirit nor the principles of science are something given; this spirit shapes itself in the process during which science creates itself and progresses." It is not so much the very nature of new figures of science—thermodynamics, non-Euclidian geometries, Einstein's relativity—that called for a reconsideration of the constitution of science; rather it was the life of the spirit at work in science that called for such reconsideration. Hence, Boutroux's basis for his "historicization" was not the actual sciences and their epistemology, but rather the life of the spirit and its metaphysical understanding; and this "relativization" rests, as I will now show, on Ravaisson's metaphysical concept of "habit."

It is "habit" that forms the basis of Boutroux's interpretation of the Kantian transcendental *a priori*. On the page following the passage I have just cited, Boutroux added: "What we call the categories of the understanding are only the ensemble of the spirit's habits, contracted while working onto itself in order to assimilate phenomena."[150] When he qualified the categories as "habits," he did not want to simply align himself with Hume. He elaborated on Ravaisson's conception of habit as a temporary steadiness of the life of the spirit. As Boutroux had already claimed in *La philosophie de Kant,* Kant's *a priori* concepts are acquired "by an internal work" of the spirit onto itself—as are space and time, the *a priori* forms of sensibility.[151] Kant's transcendental was hence historicized because, for Boutroux, the principles of knowledge evolve in history on a path which parallels the totality of the sciences (including the *Geisteswissenschaften*). This history is that of the self-constitution of spirit. The dynamics of the *a priori* are described through the alternation of two kinds of phases constitutive of the life of spirit: (1) its progression towards figures of perfection (truth, beauty, and the good), and (2) the self-knowledge which reveals its habits to be its own temporary laws. This historicization is therefore also a double metaphysical relativization:

The transcendental *a priori* does not represent the eternal and absolute picture of human reason, it only presents temporary "working habits" of the spirit; and in turn, it does not produce eternal and absolute objective truth, but only a temporarily successful and convenient way to deal with phenomena. Finally, it should be noted that Boutroux's interpretation was made on the basis of a definitive overcoming of the Kantian transcendental *a priori,* and not on the grounds of an adaptation. For Boutroux, the accurate philosophical position is spiritualism, not Kantianism; and the spiritualist *a priori* Boutroux contemplated was a metaphysical *a priori,* not a transcendental one—it represented the anteriority of the final cause and of the superior spiritual orders.

With such discrepancies between what could reasonably be called a Kantian position and Boutroux's position, how was it possible that the latter defended positions such as the synthetic nature of mathematics—and thus took sides with more typical Kantians (against Leibnizians), who were associated with the fight for intuitionism (against logicism)? The answer to this question rests in Boutroux's conception of synthesis and in the hermeneutics allowed by his spiritualism.

Boutroux maintained a curious conception of synthesis. It is mainly negative: Everything that cannot be reduced to an analytic content is synthetic. The positive meaning of synthesis is creation—that is, the addition we have to make to an analytic element in order to reach the next level; to go from logic to mathematics, for instance, or from one given mathematical element to the next (as in $5 + 7 = 12$). Such addition is a creation of the spirit. In a Kantian context, creation cannot stand for synthesis; first because creation is not a transcendental concept, and second because it can remain within the homogeneous, whereas synthesis requires the unity of the heterogeneous. The Kantian transcendental synthesis, unlike logical synthesis, does not unify one concept to another concept whose content was not present in the first one. Rather, it unifies a pure conceptual element with its radical other—a pure sensory element. Boutroux, however, held that Kant's concept of synthesis allowed for a synthesis which would remain within the narrow limits of the understanding. Concerning the quarrel about the synthetic nature of mathematical judgment, he thought that the battle took place in a globally Kantian field. A strict empiricism (Mill) and a strict "intellectualism" or "logicism" (Calignon, Lachelas) form the external poles of an antinomy which the Kantian position resolved. In Boutroux's perspective, what separated the two broadly Kantian camps was the content of the synthesis: On one side, philosophers like Renouvier, Helmholtz, and Bergson maintained a sensory intuition, whereas on the other side people like Couturat maintained the idea of an *a priori* synthesis but strove to remain within the limits of the understanding.[152] Boutroux's classification followed the general tendency to reduce the role of sensibility to a minimum—to the point at which it even vanishes—without suppressing its *a priori* synthetic character.

Where did Boutroux stand in his own classification? Given the fact that he rejected a strictly empirical ground for mathematics, while he also emphasized the irreducibility of mathematics to pure logic, Boutroux placed himself on what he considered to be Kantian terrain. What is then the nature of the synthesis at work in a mathematical judgment? This synthesis requires an intuition. What kind of intuition? Boutroux did not qualify it, but what he called intuition is, again, negatively defined: It is that which resists purely intellectual and analytical intelligibility. Hence, in definitions: The facts that contain an infinite number of definitions and are valid for an infinite number of them, require an intuition. In demonstrations: The generalization, which is a form of apodictic induction, also requires an intuition. Is this intuition sensible or not? Boutroux circumvented this problem. He emphasized that the main interest in Kant's pure sensory intuition was the immediate solution it provided to the problem of the objective validity of mathematics and its application in physics. So we should be able to find in Boutroux' solution to the problem of the objective validity of mathematics his answer to the question of the nature of intuition.

Boutroux's solution to the problem of the objective validity of mathematics has its origin in the genesis of mathematics: "Mathematical laws require a very complex elaboration. They are known neither exclusively *a priori,* nor *a posteriori;* they are a creation of the spirit; and this creation is not arbitrary, but takes place thanks to the spirit's resources, on the occasion of (*à propos de*) and in the perspective of experience."[153] How shall we understand the terms "occasion" and "perspective" here?

He continues, in *De l'idée:* "Our mathematics represent a specific form of mathematics; others are possible and the only reason we keep to our own is because it is more simple, or more convenient for our comprehension of external phenomena."[154] The non-arbitrary character of the creation which produces the set of mathematics we prefer is here specified by way of a transparent allusion to Poincaré's conventionalism: "We should not, nonetheless, regard mathematics as a pure convention, as a simple game of the mind."[155] In his 1892 lectures, then, Boutroux's answer to the genetic constitution of mathematics and to the problem of mathematics' objective validity relies on Poincaré's conventionalism—which was first published in December 1891.[156] Boutroux even anticipated Poincaré's more precise delimitation of the nature of this conventionalism, which he published (against Le Roy) in 1902.[157]

This schematic filiation does not give a clear answer with regard to Boutroux's concept of intuition, but it situates the problem in a narrower field—namely, within the Neo-Kantianism that characterized French epistemology at the turn of the twentieth century.[158] Poincaré's distinction between four meanings of "intuition" in "Sur la valeur objective de la science," could offer a suitable guiding indication for further investigation of Boutroux's position. However, Boutroux's spiritualist position presented a remarkable hermeneutic advantage: It allowed him to have thoughts "in the back of the mind" and still speak like the scientists and more orthodox Kantians. In this perspective, Boutroux's conciliatory position was not a new form of eclectism; it rather demonstrated a tolerance based on an interpretation of Kant as a preamble to the accurate spiritualist position.

Boutroux's Neo-Kantianism is therefore quite peculiar—to the point that we would, today, likely reject such a classification without second thoughts.[159] But it should also be remembered that our contemporary understanding of Kant is the result of an enormous exegetical task that commenced when Boutroux was starting his career, and that paternity or family claims in philosophy often develop out of rather complex and strange strategies.

Conclusion: A Philosopher at the Crossroads

In every regard, Boutroux stood at the intersection of the main thoroughfares which link the nineteenth century to the twentieth. He participated in the quarrels of religion with science and republicanism. In philosophy, he efficiently promoted and negotiated many difficult transitions—from Ravaisson's and Lachelier's spiritualism to the spiritualisms of Bergson and Brunschvicg; from his masters' rather conservative political and educational opinions, to a much more democratic vision. To reclaim the legacy of Kant, Boutroux began his career as a Germanophile; for political reasons, he ended it as an enthusiastic Americanophile and a virulent and incoherent Germanophobe. His first Neo-Kantianism was doubtlessly a strategic association commended by the crisis of spiritualism in France, while his last Neo-Kantianism obeyed a more strictly philosophical demand: To participate, along with Tannery, Milhaud, Poincaré, and Meyerson (to name only a few) in new and related trends within the history of science and epistemology.

As Koyré justly noted, Boutroux was not a remarkable epistemologist. But there is a good reason for this: Boutroux was not an epistemologist at all. His first book, the 1874 *De la contingence des lois de la nature,* was a metaphysical program. His 1892–1893 lectures, *De l'idée de loi naturelle,* were a synopsis of this 1874 work, and their main importance is to indicate Boutroux's evolution during his dialogue with Poincaré. Even Boutroux's treatment of determinism can hardly be understood outside of his specific metaphysical framework.[160] In the last texts in which he dealt with science—notably, his 1908 *Science et religion*—the metaphysical program that governed Boutroux's 1874 dissertation was still present. Because of his contact with Poincaré, Milhaud, Meyerson, and Duhem, we find in Boutroux a philosophy of science that can still shed some light on our present concerns. And indeed, there *is* a philosophy of science in Boutroux—but it rests on his spiritualist psychology and philosophy of nature, and is ultimately a *metaphysics* of science.

NOTES

The epigraph is from Émile Boutroux, "La philosophie en France depuis 1867," in *Nouvelles études d'histoire de la philosophie* (Paris: Alcan, 1927), 146–147.

1. On Cournot's Neo-Kantianism from the perspective of the sciences, see in particular Dominique Parodi, "Le criticisme de Cournot," in *Du positivisme à l'idéalisme* (Paris: Vrin, 1930), 144–180; and Jean-Claude Pariente, "Criticisme et réalisme chez A. Cournot," in *L'épistémologie française 1830–1970*, ed. Michel Bitbol and Jean Gayon (Paris: Presses Universitaires de France, 2006), 213–230. For instance, Parodi considered that Arthur Hannequin (1856–1905), in his *Essai critique sur l'hypothèse des atomes* (Paris: Masson, 1896), "seems to have attempted, in a narrower field and in closer consideration to factual details and technical perspective, a work similar to that of Boutroux's" and "seems to essentially adopt the same conclusions" (*La philosophie contemporaine en France*, 3d ed. [Paris: F. Alcan, 1925], 205). It might very well be that Boutroux's precise philosophy of science is to be found in other philosophers' work, like Hannequin's. As I will later suggest, Henri Poincaré's *La science et l'hypothèse* (1902) should in that regard also deserve special consideration.

2. Guéroult, a seminal Neo-Kantian who was also essential to the development of French structuralism, considered Boutroux to be "the founder of the contemporary French school of history of philosophy" (*Dianoématique* [1933–1941; Paris: Aubier-Montaigne, 1979], 2: 20).

3. See Dominique Janicaud's introduction to his *Une généalogie du spiritualisme français* (The Hague: Martinus Nijhoff, 1969).

4. Koyré noticed this paradoxical status in "Un précurseur, un grand philosophe, Émile Boutroux" (*Un Effort* [Cairo], March 1934, 3–5), where he wrote that although "it would have been easy, and therefore unfair and sterile to criticize Boutroux's epistemology," he provided the impulse for the new historical and epistemological works of the time, and was the source of Meyerson's, Milhaud's, and Brunschvicg's works.

5. Exegeses based on (more or less) similar methodological principles are offered in four texts: The first recent article of note is Mary Jo Nye, "The Boutroux Circle and Poincaré's Conventionalism," *Journal of the History of Ideas* 1 (1979): 107–120; followed by my "Généalogie d'un néokantisme français: À propos d'Émile Boutroux," *Revue de Métaphysique et de Morale*, Néokantismes, no. 3 (1997): 405–442; then Laurent Rollet, "Retour aux origines: É. Boutroux et son cercle," in *Henri Poincaré: Des mathématiques à la philosophie* (Villeneuve d'Ascq: Presses du Septentrion, 2000), 74–132; and lastly Michel Espagne, "L'Allemagne d'Émile Boutroux," *Cahiers d'Études Germaniques* 41 (2001): 199–215, which was reissued in *En deçu du Rhin: l'Allemagne*

des philosophes français au XIXe siecle (Paris: Cerf, 2005), an important book for our understanding of Boutroux's period. All histories of French philosophy between 1850 and 1950 included a chapter on Boutroux. Among these numerous portraits, the best are in Isaac Benruby, *Les sources et les courants de la philosophie contemporaine en France* (Paris: Alcan, 1933), also published in a schematic English translation from the German edition as *Contemporary Thought of France,* trans. Ernst B. Dicker (London: Williams and Norgate, 1926); and Dominique Parodi, *La philosophie contemporaine en France* (Paris: F. Alcan, 1919). Léon Brunschvicg's sketch, "Émile Boutroux," in *Écrits philosophiques* (Paris: Presses Universitaires de France, 1951–1958), 2: 197ff. is excellent, although written from the perspective of a further evolution of Neo-Kantian spiritualism. (It is also printed as an obituary and introduction to the reprint of Boutroux's 1874 dissertation.) The first general presentation of Boutroux's thought was published in 1920: A. P. La Fontaine, *La philosophie d'Émile Boutroux* (Paris: Vrin, 1920). The peak of the literature was reached just after Boutroux's death. Around the world, five general monographs followed at least twenty substantial obituaries: José Ingenieros, *Emilio Boutroux y la filosofia universitaria en Francia* (Buenos Aires, 1922); Mathieu Schyns, *La philosophie d'Emile Boutroux* (Paris: Fischbacher, 1924), a Swiss PhD dissertation; Lucy Crawford, *The Philosophy of Émile Boutroux as a Representative of French Idealism in the Nineteenth Century* (New York: Longmans, Green & Co., 1924); Raymond Thamin, *Notice sur la vie et les travaux de M. É. Boutroux* (Paris: Firmin-Didot, 1925); and Ersilia Liguori-Barbieri, *La filosofia di E. Boutroux . . .* (Pisa: Societaèd. nazionale, 1926). Most interpretations of Boutroux prior to 1945 participated, to varying degrees, in a quarrel over the essence of spiritualism and tried to give him the features of his interpreter's specific philosophical lineage. The two most common histories of French philosophy in English are Gary Gutting, *French Philosophy in the Twentieth Century* (Cambridge: Cambridge University Press, 2001), and Alan Schrift, *Twentieth-Century French Philosophy* (Malden: Blackwell, 2006); both studies are interesting with regard to the later period they focus on (neostructuralism). The first one is inaccurate and misleading concerning my topic. Today's revived interest in Boutroux grows out of the rediscovery of Neo-Kantianism and early-twentieth-century French epistemology. Half-forgotten partisan quarrels are reenacted in contemporary discussions of Neo-Kantianism and epistemology: See, for instance, Michael Heidelberger, "Die Kontingenz der Naturgesetze bei É. Boutroux," in *Naturgesetze, Historisch-systematische Analysen eines wissenschaftlichen Grundbegriffs,* ed. Karin Hartbecke and Christian Schütte, (Paderborn: Mentis, 2006), 269–289. Heidelberger seems so annoyed by the kind of epistemology exemplified by Michael Friedman's use of Neo-Kantianism that, against all historical evidence, he denies not only Boutroux's initial allegiance to spiritualism, but also his obvious—if very peculiar—Neo-Kantianism.

6. Paul Janet, "La crise philosophique et les idées spiritualistes," *Revue des Deux Mondes* (15 July and 1 August 1864): 459–490, 718–746. Later published as a monograph, *La crise philosophique* (Paris: Germer-Baillère, 1865). I quote throughout from the 1864 essay.

7. On this filiation see Dominique Janicaud, *Une généalogie du spiritualisme français* (The Hague: Martinus Nijhoff, 1969).

8. On Heidegger's interest in Ravaisson, see Frédéric de Towarnicki's preface to Félix Ravaisson, *De l'habitude* (Paris: Rivages, 1997), 7–24. For phenomenological and Heideggerian interpretations of Ravaisson, see Dominique Janicaud, "Habiter l'habitude," and Daniel Panis, "Le mot 'être' dans *De l'habitude*," in *Les Études Philosophiques* (January–March 1993): 17–24, 61–64.

9. Brunschvicg, "Émile Boutroux," in *Écrits philosophiques* (Paris: Presses Universitaires de France, 1951–58), 2: 197ff., quoted here from the introduction to Boutroux's 1874 text, iii. Caro's quote is from *L'idée de Dieu et ses nouveaux critiques*, 7th ed. (1864; Paris: Hachette, 1883), 43.

10. Étienne Vacherot, *Essais de philosophie critique* (Paris: Chamerot, 1864), 1. In the following pages, Vacherot will appear as a "new critic," to use Caro's classification. A student and editor of Cousin, Vacherot considered himself to be, quite legitimately, a new spiritualist—but he remained misunderstood and rejected by traditional spiritualists. In a different genealogy of spiritualism—a genealogy I would favor—Vacherot would be counted as the first Neo-Kantian spiritualist. But this involves a different conception of spiritualism. It is interesting that in Benruby's rich and well-informed history of French philosophy, there is only one nominal mention of Vacherot and no section dedicated to him. On this major figure, one can read Léon Ollé-Laprune, *Étienne Vacherot* (Paris: Didier, 1898), while keeping in mind the terrible irony of that book, written on request by a *tala* (ENS slang for "cleric") who spontaneously wrote the eulogy for Father Gratry, Vacherot's first and successful opponent. See also Sudhir Hazareesingh, *Intellectual Founders of the Republic: Five Studies in 19th-Century French Political Thought* (Oxford: Oxford University Press, 2001).

11. My scope being Émile Boutroux's solution to this crisis, I will neglect authors, such as Vacherot, who played little positive role in the genesis of his philosophy, even though they might have offered both a remarkable diagnosis of the crisis and an efficacious treatment.

12. Elme Marie Caro, "De la situation actuelle du spiritualisme," *Revue des Cours Littéraires de la France et de l'Étranger*, 24 December 1864, 54–61.

13. Ibid., 56.

14. Ibid., 56–57.

15. Caro, *L'idée de Dieu*, 8–9.

16. Ibid., 23.

17. Janet, "La crise philosophique," 461. He first wrote: "A new spirit arose, the spirit of the positive sciences, which spread with an immeasurable power. At the same time a breath came from Germany which, in accordance with the genius of the moment, carried away eager souls toward pantheism's deceiving temptations. In a word—we shall not conceal it—during the last ten or fifteen years the spiritualist school suffered the most serious failure."

18. Caro wrote: "What was retained from Hegel are mental habits, critical principles, loosely linked together, but hence more powerful when it comes to the dissolution of the spiritualist beliefs"; he then mocked "the Hegelians from Paris" (*L'idée de Dieu*, 9, 20).

19. Janet, "La crise philosophique," 475.

20. Caro, "De la situation actuelle du spiritualisme," 57, 58.

21. Ibid., 58.

22. It should be noted that at this time, Auguste Comte was not as famous as it is often claimed. His recognition came through Littré's work.

23. Hippolyte Taine, *Les philosophes classiques du XIXᵉ siècle en France* (Paris: Hachette, 1857; 2nd ed., 1860; 3rd ed. 1868). See the 4th ed. (1876), x.

24. Taine's reception of Hegel has been thoroughly studied by D. D. Rosca in *L'influence de Hegel sur Taine: Théoricien de la connaissance et de l'art* (Paris: Librairie Universitaire J. Gamber, 1928).

25. Hippolyte Taine, *L'idéalisme anglais, étude sur Carlyle* (Paris: Germer Baillière, 1864), 72.

26. Ibid., 86.

27. *Journal des Débats*, 25 January 1870. Paul Janet had opened this subscription. Taine's letter underlined the political independence of the Berlin Academy and mentioned that one of the reasons for an international subscription was "the hated opposition of the Prussian government against speculative philosophy." In other words: Hegel is not the philosopher of Prussian imperialism!

28. Taine, *L'idéalisme anglais*, 289.

29. In this final chapter of *Les philosophes classiques du XIXᵉ siècle en France* both analysis and synthesis are presented as the respective (and complementary) positions of two Parisian figures, "M. Pierre" and "M. Paul." The latter's traits (pp. 345–349) are inspired by Vacherot during the difficult period following his destitution and before the publication of *La métaphysique et la science* in 1858. Vacherot was Taine's influential teacher at the ENS.

30. Ibid., 342.

31. See, for instance, ibid., 327, 328, 333, and 343.

32. Ibid., 351.

33. Ibid., 362.

34. Loc. cit.

35. See his letter to Sainte-Beuve of 30 May 1864: "I never intended to deduce the individual, to demonstrate that a Shakespeare, a Swift had to appear in a given time and a given country. I leave that to people who agree to an industrious providence, to a celestial sower who, out of goodness and prevision, drops a seed in a hole he made to that purpose. I conceive that, in each period, there is more or less the same number of gifted children, as well as the same number of hunchback or phtisical. Given this, chance works: two or three Shakespeares and two or three Swifts probably died of smallpox or big belly, two or three others were enlisted in the navy and had their heads smashed at war, etc. One more chance could very well have killed the Swift and the Shakespeare that actually lived" (Hippolyte Taine, *Vie et Correspondance*, 2d ed. [Paris: Hachette, 1904], vol. 2, 308–309). The word *hasard* is translated here as "chance."

36. Taine, *Vie et Correspondance*, vol. 2, 308.

37. Letter of 31 July 1869, in Clarisse Coignet, *De Kant à Bergson: Réconciliation de la religion et de la science dans un spiritualisme nouveau* (Paris: Félix Alcan, 1911). Also in Taine, *Vie et Correspondance*, vol. 2, 352.

38. Janet, "La crise philosophique," 462, cf. 745.

39. See Caro's lecture on "Le spiritualisme et la morale indépendante" (a discussion

with Clarisse Coignet) in *Revue des Cours Littéraires de la France et de l'Étranger,* 28 December 1867, 58; 25 January 1868, 122; 1 February 1868, 146; and 8 February 1868, 160. See also Caro, *Le matérialisme et la science* (Paris: Hachette, 1867). In his review, "Le spiritualisme liberal," *Revue des Cours Littéraires de la France et de l'Étranger,* 29 February 1868, 244, Émile Beaussire wrote: "Caro's thesis is all negative. . . . He did not intend to prove directly the truth of spiritualism, but to establish the radical impotence of materialism."

40. Janet, "La crise philosophique," 744–745.

41. Jules Lachelier, *Œuvres* (Paris: Alcan, 1933), vol. 1, 14.

42. Ibid., 16.

43. Paul Janet, "Une nouvelle phase de la philosophie spiritualiste," *Revue des Deux Mondes* 108 (15 November 1873): 363–388. Republished with a modified title ("La philosophie universitaire"), an amended first sentence, and an inaccurate date (15 October 1873), in *La philosophie française contemporaine* (Paris: Calman Lévy, 1879), 37–95; pages refer to this 1879 edition.

44. Émile Boutroux, *Science et religion dans la philosophie contemporaine* (Paris: Flammarion, 1908), 140.

45. In 1866, J. Barthélemy Saint-Hilaire published, under the title *La philosophie des deux Ampère* (Paris: Didier), letters to Biran and philosophical fragments from the physicist, with 191 pages of introduction by his son, Jean-Jacques Ampère. In his foreword (p. x), Saint-Hilaire wrote: "In one word, it seems that the elaboration of this renewing theory is made by the two [Biran and Ampère], and that in this mixture and union of such diverse minds, the parts are more or less equal."

46. Félix Ravaisson, "Philosophie contemporaine, *Fragments de philosophie* par M. Hamilton," *Revue des Deux Mondes* 24 (1840): 416.

47. Boutroux agreed to this genealogy. He wrote: "Around 1864, in France, metaphysics was languishing. Between a positivism ancillary to the physical sciences and a German metaphysics suspected of chimerical spirit, universitary spiritualism appeared above all prudent, wise, and appropriate to reassure the friends of order and tradition. For those who then read him, Ravaisson offered what many were looking for, more or less confusedly. . . . Metaphysics as Aristotle, Descartes, Leibniz, and Schelling conceived it, entered philosophy's arena" ("La philosophie de Félix Ravaisson," in *Nouvelles études d'histoire de la philosophie,* 218–219).

48. Boutroux, "La Philosophie en France," 27.

49. Félix Ravaisson, *La philosophie en France au XIXe siècle* (1868; repr. Paris: Vrin, 1983), 252.

50. Ibid., 253.

51. Ibid., 260.

52. Ibid., 261.

53. Ibid., 269.

54. Ibid., 270.

55. This form of elitism was not transmitted to Boutroux but was shared by Lachelier, as it appeared in his criticism of democracy. Ravaisson later rejected an elitist understanding of his position.

56. Ravaisson, *La philosophie en France au XIXe siècle,* 272. Blaise Pascal's exact

quotation is: "It is necessary to have a hidden thought [*pensée de derrière*] and to judge everything from there while nonetheless speaking like ordinary people [*le peuple*]" (*Pensées*, Brunschvicg 336, Lafuma 81, Sellier 125 [these numberings are used in most editions]).

57. Ibid., 272.

58. See Étienne Vacherot, "La situation philosophique en France," *Revue des Deux Mondes* 75 (15 June 1868): 963. Charles Secrétan, "La philosophie française sous le second Empire" and "La philosophie de Félix Ravaisson," *Bibliothèque Universelle et Revue Suisse* (Geneva, 1868): 192–228, 363–392. Émile Beaussire's "La liberté philosophique," *Revue des Cours Littéraires de la France et de l'Étranger,* 16 May 1868, 378–382.

59. Paul Janet, "Le spiritualisme français au XIXe siècle," *Revue des Deux Mondes* (15 May 1868): 353–385. This text is the unacknowledged rival of Ravaisson's.

60. Ibid., 370–371. Furthermore, while Lachelier had taken his Kantian turn in 1864, Janet's texts from 1865 and 1868 showed that he too had experienced a significant Kantian turn.

61. Ibid., 384.

62. Loc. cit. He referred to Caro's *Le matérialisme et la science* and Magy's *La science et la nature,* books that could not qualify as a philosophy of science.

63. Ibid., 379: "Philosophy, considered in a given perspective,"—namely, the one Janet endorsed—"is a science which, like all science, proceeds by analysis, reasoning, demonstration, a science whose conclusions are always attached to the strings of the method that produced them, which requires that one must concede a lot to dialectics—that is, to discussion of the arguments—which, in a word, is essentially rational."

64. Paul Janet, "La philosophie: Sa définition, son caractère, son objet," *Revue des Cours Littéraires de la France et de l'Étranger,* 30 September 1865, 713–722; 7 October 1865, 729–736; 14 October 1865, 752–759.

65. Ibid., 720. The massive references to Aristotle are quite illuminating—the *Analytics* do not appear!

66. Ibid., 729–730.

67. Ibid., 759.

68. Jules Lachelier, "Psychologie et métaphysique," *Revue Philosophique* (1885), reprinted in *Œuvres,* vol. 1, 167–219.

69. I have addressed the second issue in my "Généalogie d'un néokantisme français: À propos d'Émile Boutroux," *Revue de Métaphysique et de Morale,* Néokantismes, no. 3 (1997).

70. Jules Lachelier, *Du fondement de l'induction,* in *Œuvres,* vol. 1, 46.

71. Ibid., 46.

72. Ibid., 48.

73. Ibid., 52.

74. Ibid., 57.

75. Lachelier ended his discussion of John Stuart Mill's empiricism with a harsh statement: "We want to ground [*asseoir*] induction on a solid basis: let's not look for it any longer in a philosophy that is the negation of science" (*Œuvres,* vol. 1, 37).

Similarly, Cousin's eclectism conferred on induction a principle—the principle of universal order—which is ultimately "the formal condemnation of science itself" (ibid., 38).

76. Jules Lachelier, "Trois articles sur l'idée de Dieu et ses nouveaux critiques de E. Caro," in *Œuvres*, 17.

77. Lachelier, *Du fondement de l'induction*, in *Œuvres*, vol. 1, 92.

78. Loc. cit. The expression "spiritualist realism," used by Lachelier to describe his own position, is borrowed from Ravaisson: "Hence, many signs allow us to foresee a philosophical period soon to come whose general character should be the predominance of what we could call a spiritualist realism or positivism; its generative principle will be the consciousness of an existence that the spirit notices in itself, an existence that it acknowledges all other existence comes from and depends on, and which is nothing else than its own action" (*Rapport sur la philosophie en France au XIXe siècle*, 275). "Positivism" here should be understood in the Schellingian sense of "positive philosophy," not in any Comtean or neo-Comtean sense.

79. Émile Boutroux, "Jules Lachelier," *Revue de Métaphysique et de Morale* (1921); repr. in *Nouvelles études d'histoire de la philosophie* (Paris: Alcan, 1927), 31.

80. Lachelier was very explicit when, recalling the philosophical situation of the time, he wrote to Janet: "It is Ravaisson, I believe, who taught us all to conceive of being not as the objective forms of substances or phenomena, but rather under the subjective form of spiritual action, be that action, in last the resort, thought or will. I think you could find this idea in Bergson, and even in Ribot, as well as in Boutroux and myself. It may very well be the only idea that is common to all of us and that makes the unity of the philosophical movement of the last twenty years." Jules Lachelier, letter to Paul Janet, 8 December 1891, in *Lettres* (Paris: G. Girard, 1933), 139.

81. Lachelier, *Du fondement de l'induction*, in *Œuvres*, vol. 1, 80.

82. Janet, "Le spiritualisme français au XIXe siècle," 385.

83. Around the time Boutroux was his pupil (1864), Jean-Félix Nourrisson, a prolix historian of philosophy and convinced Catholic, published several works: *La nature humaine: Essai de psychologie appliquée* (Paris: Didier, 1865); the second edition of his voluminous *Saint Augustin* (Paris: Didier, 1866); and *Spinoza et le naturalisme contemporain* (Paris: Didier, 1866), which reacted against Taine and Renan: "Spinoza's maxims are, today, the soul of the most trendy and noisy of all theories" (3). In 1867, he published the third edition of his history of philosophy, *Tableau des progrès de la pensée humaine depuis Thalès jusqu'à Hegel* (Paris: Didier, 1867). In a new final chapter on German philosophy, Nourrisson appropriated Kant, Fichte, Schelling, and Hegel as "assuredly resolute spiritualists," while at the same time he rejected them for the same reasons Janet and Caro gave: "they nonetheless projected onto the nature of the soul a terrible obscurity; invalidated the ideas of the true, the beautiful, and the good by subjectivizing them; reduced God to a pure abstraction; substituted for the certainty of personal immortality the empty and desolate perspectives of a pantheistic future" (579). In both his *Tableau* and his *La philosophie de Leibniz* (Paris: Hachette, 1860), Nourrisson presented the author of the *Monadologie* as an authentic and accomplished spiritualist and, within German

philosophy, as the alternative to corrupted and regressive idealistic systems. Michel Espagne also noticed ("L'Allemagne d'Émile Boutroux," 199) that at Lycée Henry IV, Boutroux had a good German teacher, Adler-Mesnard. These historical facts indicate a possible early orientation toward German thought, a knowledge of Leibniz that would later intervene not only in Boutroux's work on Leibniz, but also in the question of ontological continuity and an awareness of the importance of history of philosophy. Boutroux mentioned Nourrisson's history, for instance, in his Inaugural Lecture at Nancy, in 1877.

84. On Lachelier's teaching and Kantianism, as Boutroux understood them, see Boutroux, "Jules Lachelier," in Nouvelles études d'histoire de la philosophie, as well as Brunschvicg, "Émile Boutroux," in Écrits philosophiques, vol. 2, 197ff. Lachelier's Neo-Kantianism was evident and much discussed within the inner circle of his students; it was also noticed by former "Normaliens" such as Paul Janet, who wrote that, for Lachelier, Ravaisson's "dynamism, even when broadened, is still one of these appearances that ought to find their truth beyond, in Kant's idealism" ("La philosophie universitaire," in La philosophie française contemporaine, 68). It was nevertheless not obvious to the vulgar. The anonymous—and hostile—report describing the defense of Lachelier's theses (La Revue Politique et Littéraire [1871]: 571) noted his antagonism to "Cousin and the Sorbonne's philosophy" (i.e., Elme Caro and Paul Janet), imagined an opposition to Ravaisson ("We thought, like many others, that M. Lachelier was a follower of M. Ravaisson. His theses prove us wrong."), but did not mention the strong and omnipresent influence of Kant.

85. See Boutroux, "Jules Lachelier," in Nouvelles études d'histoire de la philosophie, 31.

86. Ibid., in particular, 12–16.

87. See Espagne, "L'Allemagne d'Émile Boutroux," 200. The reason is clearly expressed by Renan, in praise of the German university: "What won Sadowa is the German science, it is the German virtue, it is Protestantism, it is philosophy, it is Kant, it is Fichte, it is Hegel." This "Germanization" is not perceived as a nationalistic issue, because "one could even say that the form of the German universities is not purely Germanic, as they were organized, basically, on the model of the old Parisian University" (Émile Boutroux, "La vie universitaire en Allemagne: Professeurs et étudiants," Revue Politique et Littéraire (1871): 543). If one could agree on the "form," the "spirit," especially when perceived or named as "Prussian," was often criticized. See also Boutroux's "La philosophie allemande," Revue Politique et Littéraire, 29 January 1876, 106: "German unity is the work of German universities."

88. Brunschvicg made an implicit reference to the chapters in which Taine identified the contemporary task of philosophy as a reshaping of the raw material inherited from Hegel and Goethe. Taine was indeed committed to that task; see L'idéalisme anglais, 71–86. He was in Germany at the same time as Boutroux, gathering material for a book similar to his work on England; the war killed this project.

89. In E. Zeller, La philosophie des Grecs, trans. Émile Boutroux (Paris: Hachette, 1877), xii. Zeller's lecture can be found in Vorträge und Abandlungen (Leipzig: Fuess, 1865), vol. 2, 445–466. The discussion of the "Back to Kant" motto is mainly in the Zusätze appended to his 1862 lecture in 1877.

90. Brunschvicg, "Émile Boutroux," v.

91. With the exception of a few philosophers like Friedrich W. Beneke ("Kantianism in all its purity will triumph against metaphysical method." *Kant und die philosophische Aufgabe unserer Zeit* [Berlin: Posen und Bromlery, 1832], 89); and Rudolf Haym ("The future philosophy will again be critique and transcendental. . . . To offer the general formula of future philosophy presents no difficulty. We only need to transfer to the transcendental the dogmatic metaphysic of the last system [i.e., Hegel's]." *Hegel und seine Zeit* [Berlin: Gaestner, 1857], 468–469), the first Neo-Kantian movement started with a psycho-physiological understanding of the transcendental (via Johannes Müller's "specific energy of the senses" as new ground for the transcendental aesthetic). With slight variations, it is common to Helmholtz, Zeller, and Friedrich Albert Lange. Boutroux refers to Zeller's 1862 lecture as the origin of the "Back to Kant" motto, in his 1895 article "Kant," for the *Grande encyclopédie* (reprinted in *Études d'histoire de la philosophie,* 2d ed. [Paris: Félix Alcan, 1901], 317–411). During the same period, a less empirical trend is present in Otto Liebmann's *Kant und die Epigonen* (Stuttgart: Carl Schober, 1865), which concluded every chapter with the leitmotif: "Therefore we ought to go back to Kant!" The second period was initiated by Hermann Cohen's *Kants Theorie der Erfharung* (1871). I do not believe that Boutroux ever read Cohen (whom he nonetheless mentioned), and despite his early presence on the board of *Kant-Studien* and his friendship with Alois Riehl, Boutroux's understanding of German Neo-Kantianism was rather confused.

92. At the Archives Nationales in Paris, Émile Boutroux file, F17 22028. In another letter to Duruy, dated 3 March 1869, he wrote: "I often have the opportunity to talk to the professors on particular meetings, notably at Helmholtz's home." Boutroux also told Duruy that the unity of all the sciences in the ideal of Science (including the *Geisteswissenschaften*) was less manifest in France. Mary Jo Nye, in her seminal article, "The Boutroux Circle and Poincaré's Conventionalism" (see note 5), read the passage as "dismay of the French educational ministry" (109); Rollet, "Retour aux origines: É. Boutroux et son cercle" (see also note 5), follows Nye on this point and quotes a letter from Duruy to Ravaison suggesting that Boutroux not take into account "certain opinions borrowed from foreign journalism" (109). This sentence does not refer to Boutroux's account of his own experience at the ENS, but to his summary of an article in *Unsere Zeit*. One should read his words—"I scarcely see that there has been an exchange of ideas at the École Normale between the Letters section and the Science section, and this split, which already exists at the École, becomes afterward even deeper"—in the perspective of the previous sentence: "Unfortunately the Bifurcation [literally: 'the fork' (of a road)] still exists de facto between the professors. I scarcely . . . ." The "bifurcation" was the strict separation, in high school, between the letters (humanities) major and the science major. Duruy had *suppressed* the bifurcation. Duruy and Boutroux, like Liard later, all worked in the same direction, and Boutroux's point here is that the suppression was wise, that this direction is to be reinforced by the suppression of this split in the very institution that forms professors, the ENS.

93. See Boutroux's published report, "La vie universitaire en Allemagne," 542–549.

94. Letter at the Archives Nationales in Paris, Émile Boutroux file, F17 22028. It is

very remarkable that this question still constituted the guiding thread of Boutroux's address at the Bologna Congress in 1911, "Concerning Philosophy's Relation to the Sciences," *Revue de Métaphysique et de Morale* (1911): 417–504; translated by Jonathan Nield in *The Beyond that is Within, and other addresses,* London: Duckworth, 1912, 100–138.

95. The first-mentioned was given on 28 November 1868; the second was Boutroux's inaugural lecture for the Chair of Logic and Theory of Knowledge, given on 22 October 1862. In *Vorträge und Abandlungen,* vol. 2, 445–466, 479–496. Boutroux did not finish his translation because one had already appeared in *Revue Politique et Littéraire.*

96. In Zeller, *La philosophie des Grecs,* xii.

97. See Boutroux, "La philosophie allemande," 97–106.

98. Besides his lectures on physiology, every winter Helmholtz gave public lectures on the results of the sciences and their intellectual significance.

99. His papers and lectures were summarized and translated in the *Revue des Cours Scientifiques de la France et de l'Étranger* (Paris: Germer Baillière). Examples for this period: "Les sciences naturelles et la science en général," vol. 4 (1866); "Récents progrès dans la théorie de la vision," vol. 6 (1868–1869); "Goethe naturaliste," "Revue générale du développement des sciences dans les temps modernes," "Action physiologique des courants éléctriques," and "Les axiomes de la géométrie," in vol. 7 (1870).

100. In the middle, 1869, stands "The Aim and Progress of the Natural Sciences." But Boutroux certainly did not attend this talk, which was given at the opening of the Natural Sciences Congress in Innsbruck. It is also likely that Boutroux read the rectoral speech (1862), "On the Relation of the Sciences of Nature to Science as a Whole." Later he may also have discussed this with his younger brother, Léon Boutroux, who became chemist (Ph.D. in 1880) as a student of Pasteur, and who occasionally wrote on musical theory and Helmholtz's conception of it. See, for instance, his "La génération de la gamme diatonique," *Revue Scientifique* 10 (1900): 289–299; 11 (1900): 326–331; 12 (1900): 359–365.

101. *De la contingence des lois de la nature* (Paris: Alcan, 1874), 132; trans. Fred Rothwell (Chicago and London: Open court, 1916), 151–152.

102. Ibid., 137; trans., 157.

103. Ibid., 135–136; trans., 155.

104. Ibid., 137; trans., 157.

105. Ibid., 137; trans., 157.

106. *La thèse française de M. Boutroux,* 640. See also Paul Bourget, "Discours prononcés à la séance publique tenue par l'Académie Française pour la réception de M. E Boutroux, le jeudi 22 Janv. 1914," in Institut de France, *Publications de l'année 1914,* no. 2 (Paris: Institut de France, 1915), 49.

107. Boutroux, *De la contingence,* 138; trans., 158.

108. Ibid., 138; trans., 158.

109. Ibid., 144–146; trans., 166.

110. Ibid., 139–140; trans., 160.

111. Ibid., 152; trans., 174.

112. Ibid., 157; trans., 180.

113. Ibid., 158; trans., 181.

114. Aristotle, *Metaphysics* 12.7 and *Physics* 8.

115. Boutroux, *De la contingence,* 154; trans., 177.

116. Ibid., 159; trans., 181. See also ibid., 167; trans., 191: "Because there is, for the being belonging to any degree, an ideal to follow, there should also exist, in all these beings, a degree of spontaneity, a power of changing proportionate to the nature and value of this ideal."

117. Letter from Ravaisson to Lionel Dauriac, in Papiers Lionel Dauriac, Bibliothèque Victor Cousin, ms 343, quoted in Renzo Ragghianti, "Lettres de Jules Lachelier à Guido de Ruggiero," *Revue de Métaphysique et de Morale* (2006): 406. It is worth mentioning here that Ravaisson's *De l'habitude* has finally been published in English, with a critical introduction, commentary, and original text facing the translation. See Félix Ravaisson, *Of Habit,* trans. Clare Carlisle and Mark Sinclair (London and New York: Continuum, 2008).

118. Boutroux, *De la contingence,* 167; trans., 192.

119. Ibid., 167–169; trans., 192–194.

120. The debt Boutroux contracted toward Ravaisson and Lachelier regarding this aesthetic "*Aufhebung*" of positive laws and, more generally, the aesthetic meaning of truth is well documented in Dominique Parodi, *Le mouvement idéaliste* (Paris: Alcan, 1896), 100–102.

121. Boutroux, *De la contingence,* 169; trans., 194–195. The Neo-Platonic tone was also in Ravaisson.

122. See for instance, *La philosophie de Kant* (1894–1901) (Paris: Vrin, 1926) 20–21.

123. Émile Boutroux, *La nature et l'esprit* (Paris: Vrin, 1926), 10.

124. Ibid., 27.

125. Boutroux, *Science et religion,* 234.

126. Ibid., 348.

127. Ibid., 358.

128. Ibid., 351.

129. Édouard Le Roy, "Un positivisme nouveau," *Revue de Métaphysique et de Morale* (1901): 293. Le Roy's attempt to disconnect Boutroux from Ravaisson in this quotation provides a small example of his tremendous *parti pris,* as well as a big illustration of his philosophical naïveté—or maybe his arrogance—as the last sentence is no more than a nice description of Boutroux's doctrine (though of course, Le Roy referred to his own demonstration of contingency). See Louis Couturat's witty critique, "Contre le nominalisme de M. Le Roy," *Revue de Métaphysique et de Morale* (1900): 87–93. Poincaré's last chapter in *La valeur de la science* is a critique of Le Roy. It was first published as "Sur la valeur objective de la science," *Revue de Métaphysique et de Morale* (1902): 263–293; and it was suggested in the introduction to *La science et l'hypothèse* (1902).

130. Henri Poincaré, *La science et l'hypothèse* (Paris: Flamarion, 1902), 1–2; trans. W. J. G. [*sic*] (New York: Dover, 1952), xxi–xxii.

131. Boutroux, *Science et religion,* 234; quoting Poincaré, *La science et l'hypothèse,* 237. This theme constituted the introduction to *La science et l'hypothèse.*

132. Gaston Milhaud, "La science rationnelle," *Revue de Métaphysique et de Morale* (1896): 301.

133. See Poincaré, *La Valeur de la Science,* Paris: Flammarion, 213–276; see more specifically "Sur la valeur objective de la science," *Revue de Métaphysique et de Morale* (1902): 266–276 and Boutroux, *Science et religion,* 348–349. Poincaré tended to caricature Le Roy's position; given the latter's style, it was difficult to refrain from such unfair treatment!

134. Milhaud, "La science rationnelle," 281–284.

135. Édouard Le Roy, "Science et philosophie," *Revue de Métaphysique et de Morale* (1899): 517.

136. Poincaré, "Sur la valeur objective de la science," 274–275.

137. For instance, Benrubi's precautions concerning his classification of Boutroux (*Les sources et les courants de la philosophie contemporaine en France* (Paris: Alcan, 1933) vol. 2, 695–696) result from this interpretative dilemma.

138. An interpretation is a claim made within that space of indetermination which remains once all the requisite texts are taken into account. The example I choose does not belong to interpretation, but simply to error—it can be made only by neglecting the primary sources themselves, and either neglecting or misconstruing historical context.

139. Heidelberger, "Die Kontingenz der Naturgesetze bei É. Boutroux" (see note 5), 270. The same quotation similarly de-contextualized appears in Anne Fagot-Largeault, "L'émergence," in Daniel Andler, Anne Fagot-Largeault, Bernard Saint-Sernin, eds., *Philosophie des Sciences* (Paris: Gallimard, 2002), vol. 2, 962. Indeed, Brunschvicg never made such a claim. His quotation does not concern Boutroux's doctrine in general, but *De la contingence* and, while rejecting a metaphysics of the *a priori,* it *claims* Boutroux's *spiritualism,* because it starts with the words: "Explicitly denoting a return to Aristotle's inspiration in the meaning that Ravaisson gave it . . ." M. Heidelberger's paper also reproduced a number of erroneous historical items found in the secondary literature: Renouvier is not a spiritualist (cf. Gutting, *French Philosophy in the Twentieth Century*) but the most famous French neo-criticist; Boutroux's brother Léon was not a physicist (cf. Nye, "The Boutroux Circle and Poincaré's Conventionalism") but a chemist; and so on.

140. *La philosophie de Kant,* Cours de M. Emile Boutroux (Sorbonne 1896–1897) (Paris: Vrin, 1926), 12.

141. Boutroux, *La philosophie de Kant,* 9; cf. 266.

142. Ibid., 11–12.

143. Boutroux, *La nature et l'esprit,* 31.

144. Boutroux, *De la contingence,* 146; trans., 169. *La philosophie de Kant,* 350, 354.

145. For instance: *La philosophie de Kant,* 17–18.

146. Boutroux, *La philosophie de Kant,* 4.

147. Boutroux, *De la contingence,* 133; trans., 152.

148. For us, mathematics can indeed be seen as constitutive even if both themselves and their relations to physics are contingent, "arbitrary," or "conventional." This rejection can also be found in the 1892–1893 lectures, *De l'idée de loi naturelle dans la science et la philosophie contemporaines* (Paris: Alcan 1994), 141, for instance;

trans. Fred Rothwell (New York: Macmillian, 1914), 214.

149. Boutroux, *Science et religion*, 347.

150. Ibid., 348.

151. Boutroux, *La philosophie de Kant*, 17–18, 29, 53.

152. Ibid., 55–57.

153. Boutroux, *De l'idée de loi naturelle*, 24–25; trans., 40.

154. Ibid., 26; trans., 42.

155. Ibid., 27; trans., 44.

156. In "Les géometries non euclidiennes," *Revue générale des sciences pures et appliquées* 23 (15 December 1891): 769–774. Poincaré wrote, for instance: "*Geometrical axioms are neither a priori synthetic judgments nor experimental facts. They are conventions;* our choice, made among all other possible conventions, is *guided* by experimental facts, but it remains *free*" (773, italics are Poincaré's).

157. In *La Science et l'hypothèse*, for instance: "The conventions that we find mainly in mathematics "are the product of a free activity of our spirit. . . . Here our spirit can assert because it rules. . . . These decrees govern *our* science, they do not govern nature. Are they nonetheless arbitrary? No" (3).

158. On Poincaré's Neo-Kantianism see Massimo Ferrari, "Henri Poincaré, il kantismo e l'a priori mathematico," *Discipline Filosofiche* 16.2 (2006): 137–154; on his intuitionism see Gerhard Heinzmann, "Poincaré et la racine de l'intuitionnisme," Archives Poincaré Université de Nancy 2 (http://poincare.univ-nancy2.fr/resources/?contentId=1482).

159. Regarding Kantian literature, Boutroux quoted Kuno Fischer as a foil. He mentioned relatively diverse references such as B. Erdmann, Helmholtz (for his discussion of Kantian principles), Lange's *History of Materialism*, Riehl's *Philosophischer Kriticismus*, Trendelenburg's *Logische Untersuchungen*, and Überweg and Wundt's *Philosophische Studien* (vol. 2). Hermann Cohen is mentioned for his famous claim according to which Kant is "German socialism's authentic father," but Boutroux takes no account of Cohen's monumental and innovative exegesis. Since I believe Boutroux never read Cohen, I surmise that this quotation was borrowed from Vorländer.

160. See: Ian Hacking, "Nineteenth-century cracks in the concept of determinism," *Journal of the History of Ideas* 44.3 (1983): 455–475; Pascal Engel, "Plenitude and contingency: modal concepts in nineteenth-century French philosophy," in Simo Knuuttila, ed., *Modern Modalities: Studies of the History of Modal Theories from Medieval Nominalism to Logical Positivism* (Dortrecht: Kluwer, 1988), 179–237, spec. 211–215; Anne Fagot-Largeault, "L'émergence," in Daniel Andler, Anne Fagot-Largeault, and Bernard Saint-Sernin, eds., *Philosophie des Sciences* (Paris: Gallimard, 2002), vol. 2, 962–965.

PART 4

History, Culture, and Value

Wilhelm Dilthey and the Neo-Kantians: On the Conceptual Distinctions between *Geisteswissenschaften* and *Kulturwissenschaften*

Rudolf A. Makkreel

Wilhelm Dilthey's conception of the *Geisteswissenschaften* encompasses what we would now call the humanities and the social sciences. He formulated his concept of the *Geisteswissenschaften* mainly with the theoretical problems of the historian in mind. Dilthey was himself a working historian who felt that German historicists like Ranke had made great strides in freeing history from metaphysical speculation.[1] But Dilthey also realized that unless historicism were to obtain a new philosophical grounding, it would be exposed to the dangers of relativism. Although he considered the effort to relate historical events to their national context commendable, he looked with some distaste on the narrow political concerns of the Prussian historians who felt it their main task to justify a strong constitutional Prussian monarchy. Dilthey found Burckhardt's emphasis on culture a healthy antidote, yet criticized his method for being too vague.

Dilthey was concerned about the inability of historians to utilize the results of the social sciences of their day and pointed out the need for new, more germane categories. That among these a reflective concept of experienced time should be central relates Dilthey's theory of the *Geisteswissenschaften* to the work on time by Bergson and the phenomenologists. Heidegger's hermeneutics of the historicity of human existence is openly indebted to Dilthey.

In this essay I will attempt to delineate Dilthey's theory of the *Geisteswissenschaften* by contrasting it to the theory of the *Kulturwissenschaften* (cultural sciences) which the Neo-Kantians offered as an alternative. It should become clear that the difference between the two alternatives is not just terminological but conceptual. The Neo-Kantians basically approved of the kind of history that Burckhardt wrote and were content with the current social sciences. They only wanted to arrive at a better conceptual analysis of them by means of their concept of culture. They rejected Dilthey's concept of the

Geisteswissenschaften as based on a mere distinction of subject matter, thereby ignoring the fundamental methodological innovations of Dilthey's work.

The word *Geisteswissenschaften* does not have a satisfactory English equivalent. Most translators have settled for the ambiguous expressions "human studies" or "human sciences." It is ironic that the German word probably originated as the translation of J. S. Mill's term "moral sciences." Erich Rothacker writes: "Perhaps the term *Geisteswissenschaften* first appeared in 1849 in Schiel's translation of Mill's *System of Logic.*"[2]

This claim is doubly surprising. Not only is the concept of the moral sciences inadequate to characterize *Geisteswissenschaften* as it has come to be used, but one would also have expected earlier instances of the word, given its common usage today and the long history of the words *Geist* and *Wissenschaft* in the German philosophical tradition. Rothacker does cite a few isolated cases before 1849 when contemporaries or followers of Hegel employed the related expressions *Wissenschaft des Geistes* and *Geistwissenschaft*. However, it is significant that these are in the singular: These terms can be rendered as "science of spirit" in the metaphysical sense. (Karl C. F. Krause, for example, used "science of reason" as a synonym.)[3] *Geistwissenschaft* means the philosophy of spirit, and there can thus be only one philosophical "science of spirit."

Dilthey's *Introduction to the Human Sciences* of 1883 is considered to have provided the classical formulation of the concept *Geisteswissenschaften*—a formulation which is radically pluralistic. In this work Dilthey reveals his break with the idealistic concept of science by the attention he devotes to the rigors of empiricism. Discontented with the way that metaphysical systems distort and ignore facts, Dilthey stresses that science must not sacrifice its responsibility to be empirical in its haste to create a unified order. In France, Comte had already denounced the idea of one grand science. In its stead he established a hierarchical system of the positive sciences leading up to sociology. However, Comte's system is too homogeneous according to Dilthey. Comte had refused to consider psychology a science, and claimed that all intellectual functions could be properly and exhaustively studied by biology and sociology. Dilthey considers the positivistic assumption that all of reality need be examined by external observation alone—thus dismissing introspection—to result in a narrow form of empiricism. Moreover, he condemns Comte's sociological law of historical development, according to which the largely introspective method of the theological and metaphysical stages must give way to positive science, as itself being a metaphysical remnant.[4] The *Introduction to the Human Sciences* impugns the speculative nature of idealistic philosophy of history and encyclopedic sociology alike. Neither deserves to be numbered with the *Geisteswissenschaften* because both lose sight of the human individuals active in history.

After this analysis, Dilthey commends Mill for having turned his back on Comte's hierarchical system. Mill had assigned psychology an independent status which allowed it to be the basis of a system of the moral and political sciences distinct from the system of the natural sciences. But Dilthey finds fault with the fact that his system of the moral sciences is still modeled on the natural sciences. Dilthey's primary aim is then to show that the methodology of the *Geisteswissenschaften* must be different from that of the natural sciences.

Before we examine the basis for these methodological claims which are central to Dilthey's delimitation of the *Geisteswissenschaften,* let us see what disciplines he would include in this category: It covers psychology, anthropology, political economy and history—for which Mill's expression "moral sciences" might still have served—and such "amoral" disciplines as philology and aesthetics as well.[5] The *Geisteswissenschaften* are concerned not only with the discoverable uniformities governing our attempts to realize the right conduct of life, but also with the appreciation of the ways in which individuals express their attitude toward life itself. Philosophy is very much involved with the *Geisteswissenschaften* without, however, placing them in any absolute and final perspective. Philosophy as viewed by Dilthey does not reject the ultimate questions about the meaning of life and may even help articulate possible interpretations of human existence. On the other hand, it never can claim to give *the* answer and establish *the* system of the *Geisteswissenschaften.* Far from culminating in a concept of absolute spirit, the theory of the *Geisteswissenschaften* led to an attempt to understand the variety of basic human *Weltanschauungen.*

Given the anti-metaphysical nature of Dilthey's thought, it seems better not to translate *Geist* in *Geisteswissenschaften* as "spirit." It is at this point that the alternate concept of *Kulturwissenschaft* recommends itself to the Neo-Kantians. Thus Heinrich Rickert asserts that *Geist* is an unsatisfactory idea because it tends to be either hypostatized into a supernatural reality or reduced to the psyche. The term involves the extreme dangers of noncritical idealism and psychologism. Although Dilthey comes to see a middle ground here by means of his concept of structural psychology, which I will discuss later, he obviously courted the danger of psychologism. Rickert's concept of culture was intended to be immune to such a danger. But for Rickert even the material distinction of nature and culture is inadequate and needs to be replaced by a more precise methodological distinction between generalizing and individualizing sciences. The cultural sciences are considered to be individualizing.

Rickert's case for these two kinds of sciences distinguishes two kinds of concept-formation: Obviously no science can hope to fully reproduce reality. All science must select from the empirical given to create order.

To transform reality's "indeterminable heterogeneity into *a determinable* domain of *discrete* objects,"[6] all sciences require universal concepts. This is manifestly the case for the natural sciences. Universal concepts are used to select salient features of objects which then allow them to be correlated. History deserves the rank of a science because it, too, uses some principle to select what is essential from what is inessential. What has been ignored, according to Rickert, is that universal concepts can be combined to create individual complexes. History employs complexes of universals known as values to select its material. Only those events and phenomena are reported by a historian which were either positively or negatively efficacious in realizing certain cultural values. Rickert then assures us of the scientific nature of history, although it is value-oriented and thus a cultural science. He distinguishes between evaluation and reference to values: "Valuations must always involve *praise* or *blame*. To refer to values is to do neither."[7] The science of history does not lose its objectivity by the mere reference to values.

Rickert follows his teacher Wilhelm Windelband in maintaining that the historical method deals with individuals and cannot establish laws. But he expresses doubts about the appropriateness of Windelband's distinction between the "nomothetic" and "idiographic" for the reason that the latter term does not exclude the arts.[8] Rickert, however, goes to lengths to convince us that history must be seen as more than an art which intuitively captures details. Its function is to create individualizing *concepts,* not to pursue details for their idiosyncratic charms.

Given such a theory of science that formulates either generalizing or individualizing concepts, one may ask whether the natural sciences do not also operate with complexes of universal concepts rather than just single universal concepts. The peculiarity of the historical method would then be that the complexes are more intricate so as to apply solely to one phenomenon and that its conceptual components may be less refined. It seems that Rickert's polar antithesis of method must disintegrate into a distinction of degree.

The peculiarity of the historical method manifests itself more clearly when we examine how its selective concepts are arrived at. In the case of the natural sciences trial and error is possible insofar as success in prediction can serve as a final criterion. In history predictability cannot be expected. The problem of what to select is most acute when writing universal history. Here Rickert can only suggest that there must be a universally valid system of values by which we can select phenomena.[9] Actually held values cannot serve as selective principles because these are too diverse to allow any ordering of history as a whole. No intelligible continuum of realized values exists. Values possess a superpersonal validity for Rickert which he does not expect history to actualize since they are by definition nonsensory. Nevertheless, Rickert believes that historians shall gradually become more conscious of the absolute validity of certain cultural values. In the final analysis the objectivity of the historian presupposes that the cultural values to which he refers his subject-matter be objectively valid. The metaphysical postulate that there is progress in history gives way to an epistemological postulate of progress.

Dilthey had reacted to the former postulate in the *Introduction to the Human Sciences* and was to object to the latter in his debate with the Neo-Kantians. He considered the Kantian dualism between existence and value to be the product of a narrowing formalism. Values are not to be reduced to a series of independent, *a priori* rational complexes set apart to judge reality, but are immanent to life—even though what we consider absolute values may be only partially embodied.[10] I suppose one could call these absolute values immanent tendencies. Moreover, for Dilthey values so intermesh that they can modify each other.

Perhaps the best reason for translating *Geisteswissenschaften* as "human sciences" is that the concrete human being is considered to be central to them. To render *Geisteswissenschaften* as "cultural studies" incurs the risk that culture be understood in the absolutist and impersonal manner betrayed in the Neo-Kantian sense of *Kulturwissenschaften*. Whereas psychology is excluded from the *Kulturwissenschaften*, Dilthey includes it among the human sciences and assigns it an important function.

In his *Introduction to the Human Sciences* of 1883, Dilthey regards psychology as the first and most fundamental of the human sciences. However, psychology could only be a stable foundation if its methods were revised with the goals of the human sciences in mind. In an essay published in 1894 entitled *Ideas for a Descriptive and Analytic Psychology*, Dilthey elaborates his view that psychology should not model itself on the natural sciences. Psychologists should develop a descriptive and analytic method instead of solely relying on an explanative and experimental approach.

Assuming that all knowledge seeks to relate phenomena into some kind of order, Dilthey stresses that we cannot see any immediate connection between the objects of external experience. Therefore, it is necessary to construct an artificial continuum to which every physical phenomenon is reducible by hypothesis. In classical physics, for instance, everything is explained in terms of causal laws of the motions of atoms. On the other hand, direct inner experience is such, according to Dilthey, that a continuum or nexus (*Zusammenhang*) is the first thing that we become conscious of.[11] He claims that there is no need for psychology to construct artificial systems from isolated elements: Psychical connectedness is not a product of hypothesis but a given of experience.[12]

There is thus one major advantage that the human sciences hold over the natural sciences. We possess a certain implicit understanding of psychic and social relations which does not have to be negated in the way that the natural sciences have to overcome mythical conceptions of nature. Modern scientific man can be said to preserve a basic understanding of psycho-historical life in adulthood, whereas nature no longer speaks to him. Nature is mute and alien for us.[13] It is necessary to realize that "explanation" is interpreted as hypothetical, before it becomes possible to make sense of Dilthey's succinct dictum: "Nature we explain, human or psychic life we understand."[14] This dictum does not imply that everything about the psyche is clear from the start—otherwise, description would not need to be supplemented by analysis. Moreover, Dilthey's attack on traditional explanative psychology and his proposal to make psychology descriptive and analytic does not rule out the need for explanation altogether. It is only claimed that the significance of psychic life will be lost if particular processes are abstracted from their full context, as is required by explanation. The main task of psychology is to fill in the immediate but vague sense of the wholeness of psychic life by description and analysis so that individual processes can be understood thereby.

Description, as Dilthey envisages it, does not provide contents as distinct from form, but rather concrete structures. The psychologist must work toward delineating that character-defining structure which Dilthey calls the "acquired psychic nexus" (*erworbener seelischer Zusammenhang*). This structural nexus constitutes the fund of a person's past experience, his evaluations of reality, and his dispositions to act. It is both conscious and unconscious, and establishes the context whereby individual acts can be evaluated. Because the acquired psychic nexus includes the unconscious, the task of description is interminable. Often it will still be necessary to provide an explanation for a process which is not understandable by the scheme of the whole. In such cases, traditional hypotheses about causation and the relation of mind and body are unavoidable. However, psychology can be a reliable base for the human sciences only insofar as it avoids making such hard-to-verify hypotheses central to its empirical findings. Descriptive psychology may end with hypotheses, but it should not begin with them.[15] Thus Dilthey writes that psychology can only help make the writing of history objective if it exercises restraint in speculating about what "caused" a person to perform a certain deed. For how can we isolate the specific motives that led political and military leaders in their actions? Are such men not experts in disguising their real motives? Instead of ferreting out Bismarck's motives it would be better to try to understand what meaning his actions had in relation to his values.[16] Dilthey's descriptive psychology is primarily a psychology for understanding great individuals—or rather the greatness of individuals.

Rickert claims that psychology cannot produce any concept of individuality. He thinks that psychology is a generalizing science which only differs from the other natural sciences in being nonphysical. Psychology relies on inner experience as opposed to outer experience and thus constructs a separate, but still natural, system of inner causality paralleling that of physical causality. The natural sciences, according to Rickert, cannot accommodate the two kinds of experience, "the concepts of which are mutually exclusive, in a uniform conceptual system, but can only attempt to correlate the one series of phenomena unequivocally with the other after each has been conceived in itself by way of generalization."[17] It is clear that no concept of individuality can be expected from psychology as a natural science. According to Rickert only the cultural sciences are able to derive a concept of individuality by the employment of cultural values.

Dilthey does not deny that individuals must be understood in relation to their culture. But this is then used as an argument for a comparative psychology to complement descriptive psychology and against the distinction between generalizing and individualizing sciences. Dilthey alleges that the peculiarity of the human sciences lies not in their ignoring generalizations, but in the manner in which they combine the general and the individual. Individuality can only be understood in relation to a base of generalizations. This connection of the general and the specific is especially prominent in the comparative study of psychological types.

In an essay entitled *Über vergleichende Psychologie*, printed in 1895, but not published until the next year in a curtailed and less controversial form, Dilthey carries out his plan to complement the descriptive method of psychology with a comparative method and at the same time replies to Windelband's lecture *Geschichte und Naturwissenschaft*, delivered in 1894. In this lecture, which inaugurated the controversy between Dilthey and the Neo-Kantians, Windelband argues against Dilthey that historical knowledge has no intrinsic relation to psychic experience. Dilthey's tactical move in defense of his position is to question Windelband's narrow, introspective interpretation of inner experience. He is thus aroused to go beyond the old, simple opposition of introspective and external experience by pointing to a third kind of experience which incorporates objects of external experience into the context of inner experience.[18] Dilthey, in effect, tries to use the master against the Neo-Kantians, for he claims to draw the inspiration for his concept of a third kind of experience from Kant's concept of the transcendental. By giving a psychological interpretation to the idea of providing an order to the external world by means of inner categories, Dilthey hoped to overcome the subject-object and form-content dualisms which the Neo-Kantians had so exacerbated. It was not without hesitation, however, that Dilthey labeled this third kind of experience, which is analogous to inner experience, "transcendental," for he makes no claims for any fixed innate categories which provide the external world with its order. He also calls it "reflective experience," and I will use only this term.

However, by calling it simultaneously "transcendental" and "reflective" Dilthey has perhaps unwittingly referred us to his real source of inspiration—the introduction to the *Critique of Judgment*. There, Kant related the concept of reflective judgment to his transcendental philosophy by acknowledging that the categories of the understanding derived in the *Critique of Pure Reason* provide only a schematic framework for an external world. They make possible the search for causal laws, but do not help to integrate such causal generalizations into any intelligible order. These categories do not provide any scientific principles by which to unify empirical laws. Kant admitted that such empirical principles cannot be deduced by the transcendental method. In this last *Critique*, Kant had to address himself to Hume's problem of induction again, albeit on a different plane. Any concrete, overall ordering of the phenomenal world must be a product of reflective judgment which proceeds from the particular to the universal, rather than a product of determinant judgment which subsumes the particular under a universal. This means that such an ordering cannot be legislated to hold for nature, but can only be successful to the degree that the empirical concepts created by the mind are in harmony with nature.

Insofar as Kant's concern here is the overall ordering of laws into a system, the problematic relation is not so much a particular-universal relation as a part-whole relation. It is in this context that Kant concedes that we cannot be certain that any final harmony exists between nature and our cognitive faculties, even though we may have intimations of it in aesthetic experience. Therefore, the way we integrate our experience of nature into a scientific theory is only subjectively valid according to Kant's analysis. It assumes an *a priori* principle of order which cannot be justified: "Such a transcendental principle, then, the reflective judgment can only give as a law from and to itself."[19] What Kant had done for the natural sciences Dilthey wanted to do for the human sciences. He proposed to write a "Critique of Historical Reason" but was never able to complete it. Perhaps he would have been more successful, especially in his attempt to defend himself against charges of relativism, had he been content to write a "Critique of Historical Judgment." He could then have explicitly linked his own view of the importance of the creative, artistic imagination for historical understanding to Kant's treatment of the imagination in the *Critique of Judgment*. Just as Kant had related the reflective judgment to the imagination of the aesthetic beholder in order to understand how empirical phenomena can obtain theoretical meaning by being integrated into a system of science, Dilthey could have elaborated his concept of reflective experience to claim that it provides an understanding of how historical events receive their value.[20] For as much as Kant considered any unifying system of science to possess a mere subjective validity, Dilthey claims that the validity of any interpretation of culture is subjective. However, it must be conceded that in the former case subjective validity points to an ideal, absolute end, whereas in the latter it points to an actual, initial ground. The integral vision that is merely a heuristic assumption for the natural scientist is a *condition* to be realized by the historian. This must be related to Dilthey's claim that we have a certain implicit understanding of psycho-historical reality and not of nature. Remarking on Ranke's motto that to see history objectively it is necessary to efface the self, Dilthey says that we only arrive at the goal of an objective understanding of history to the degree that we make our inner life universal.[21]

Reflective experience, as conceived by Dilthey, places cultural objects in the context of our inner experience. Only through reflective experience does anything like a universal context in which cultural objectifications can be evaluated become possible. By enlarging the sphere of the psychic to incorporate cultural values Dilthey aims to undercut Rickert's assumption that cultural values are valid apart from human experience. Rickert sees cultural values as having an *a priori* constraint on us whether we admit them or not, much like Kant's practical reason. But Dilthey does not consider Kant's categorical imperative sufficient for understanding culture, any more than Kant considered his own categories of the understanding sufficient for comprehending the systematization of scientific knowledge. For Dilthey cultural values derive their meaning from subjective human experience, and all but the most basic are subject to ever-changing enrichment. All cultural systems find their crossing point in the human being.[22]

Paradoxically, the very extension of the scope of psychology to include comparative psychology forced Dilthey to revise his initial estimate of psychology as the first of the human sciences. Once he enlarged the concept of experience to include reflective experience, Dilthey in effect stripped psychology of its autonomy. It became ever more clear to Dilthey that not all experience is self-evident to introspection. He had always been wary of introspection insofar as it was modeled on external observation. He thus searched for alternate conceptions. Introspection as internal observation (*Beobachtung*) involves taking the viewpoint of a spectator over against given data. That kind of attentiveness tends to freeze the actual flow of experience. Dilthey preferred to speak of inner perception (*Wahrnehmung*) as a direct possession of experience in his essay on descriptive psychology of 1894.[23]

Consciousness is implicitly present to itself as a kind of reflexive awareness (*Innewerden*). But the direct self-givenness of inner experience does not apply to the reflective experience introduced in the complementary essay on comparative psychology of 1895. Reflective experience encompasses knowledge of objects of the cultural world. This kind of experience is not merely intermediary in the way that in Kant's *Critique of Judgment* the imagination, as the faculty of reflective judgment, mediates the dualism of intuition and understanding. Kant's dualism of sense and reason is ultimate, and can only be reconciled subjectively. One might interpret Dilthey's concept of reflective experience to be an afterthought, much like Kant's concept of reflective judgment. However, it had the effect of forcing Dilthey to revise his concept of inner experience to the extent that in the end he ventures the view that all but very rudimentary feelings incorporate some kind of objective reference.[24] This belief, expressed in a lecture on psychic structure delivered to the Prussian Academy of Sciences in 1905, goes beyond the common conception that feelings are reactions to the objective world. A reaction is completely subjective, but a feeling that incorporates a representation, however vague, of something objective, is not purely subjective even though it remains immanent to the psyche and fundamentally understandable.

Reflective experience illustrates the true interdependence of the individual and the historical situation in which he finds himself. Dilthey reminds us that whereas cultural values would become meaningless apart from the continued human experience thereof, the experience of an individual would lack fullness without the contributions of the tradition of the cultural systems. On the one hand we can understand history only if we can relate it to our own experiences, on the other hand we cannot completely appreciate our own experiences until we understand history. The total meaning of our own experience is not just there to be described. In 1894 Dilthey was content to indicate that the meaning of our experience can only be fully grasped in relation to the overall structure of the acquired psychic nexus. By studying Dilthey's writings after 1895, it can be seen that the problem of filling in the unconscious gaps of the acquired psychic nexus comes very close to understanding how it overlaps in structure with the historical context. It is interesting to note in this regard that late in his life Dilthey preferred to call his psychology "structural" rather than "descriptive."

Dilthey always characterized human individuals as the crossing points of the cultural systems. In his early works he even referred to human beings as the carriers (*Trägern*) of these systems—as fully comprehending them and manipulating them.[25] However, in a much later essay on the nature of biography he writes more cautiously: "General movements pass through the individual as their crossing point; we must seek new foundations for the understanding of these movements which do not originate in the individual."[26] Categories which are not purely derivable from the subject of a biography must be found. Thus in his great, but unfinished intellectual biography of Schleiermacher, Dilthey developed the category of generation. It is really a psycho-historical concept which covers not only the generation of Schleiermacher's acquired psychic nexus (his personal development), but also the historical generation with which he grew up (and specifically a circle consisting of Friedrich and A. W. Schlegel, Ludwig Tieck, and other important figures). Throughout his life Dilthey continued to cherish biography and psychology as central to history and the human sciences respectively. But he recognized that psychological biography becomes a meaningless abstraction if it is not bolstered by concepts derived from other human sciences.

But it was not just writing about Schleiermacher's life that proved important for Dilthey's change in attitude toward psychology. Reading Schleiermacher's lectures on hermeneutics must have been equally momentous, for it is from there that Dilthey derived his hermeneutical tenet that an interpreter must strive to understand a work better than its author had understood it. This meant that appreciating a work of literature could no longer be given a narrow psychologistic interpretation, as it had been in Dilthey's essay on the imagination of the poet written in 1887. There the adequacy of poetic understanding was judged by how closely the reader's state of mind corresponds to that of the author while creating it. Dilthey later rejects this view as naïve, since it ignores that creation is to a large extent unconscious. Artistic expression reveals things which are unsuspected by introspection. Expression might be thought of as the counterpart to reflective experience: Whereas the latter incorporates objects into the psychic nexus, the former makes inner experience public. To be more precise, however, artistic expression is especially crucial for Dilthey because it is the expression of experience that is intrinsically related to a particular cultural context without being of a reflective nature. Artistic expression is proof that inner experience is permeated with cultural values, and that it cannot be fully understood until it is expressed.

Artistic expression really involves making explicit the connection of an individual experience with its psycho-historical context. Great works of art tend to articulate this contextual structure in a purified way. It is often easier for the critic of another time to consciously strip away the inessentials of the original historical context and thus perceive the way in which an author's work unconsciously betrays his or her times. What was an unconscious conditioning factor in the author's acquired psychic nexus may be uncovered as a cultural value of the time in which he lived. This cultural embeddedness indicates that psychology by itself can no longer serve as the basis for the other human sciences. The human sciences are perhaps best characterized by a peculiar interdependence which makes anything analogous to the hierarchy of the natural sciences impossible. Neither psychology nor any other human science can provide the overall framework which the other disciplines then fill in. Each human science endeavors to establish a concrete structural system which it cannot complete by itself because it overlaps with other such systems.

At this point it may be useful to examine Cassirer's attitude toward Dilthey's definition of the human sciences. As a Neo-Kantian he uses the expression

Kulturwissenschaften more than that of *Geisteswissenschaften*. However, as a member of the Marburg School he explicitly rejects the ideographic and absolute-value perspectives of the Baden School which were discussed earlier. Instead, Cassirer's concept of the *Kulturwissenschaften* is much closer to Dilthey's hermeneutic concept of understanding human products by studying their structural contexts. Cassirer's *Logic of the Humanities* calls for a theory of forms. Such forms are the result of approaching cultural phenomena, not causally, but in terms of meaning and function. Cassirer even prescribes an autonomous hermeneutics. Nevertheless, he differs from Dilthey by placing his theory of culture in the framework of a philosophy of symbolic forms, thus stressing the continuity of natural science and cultural science. Form or structure is conceived more abstractly than structure had been conceived by Dilthey. Cassirer finds form a purely relational concept which can also be applied to the natural sciences by means of mathematics. Thus in twentieth-century physics we witness both causal laws and mathematical structural theory. Traditional causal laws about particles need to be supplemented by probabilistic hypotheses and symbolic representations of waves.

In discussing Dilthey we saw that despite the difference which exists between explaining physical phenomena by causal law and understanding psycho-historical phenomena by placing them in a structural framework, even the natural sciences aim at an overarching theoretical framework. However, Cassirer goes beyond this by bringing to our attention that the laws used to account for the behavior of physical phenomena need not constitute causal explanations at all. The distinction between a genetic analysis and a functional or contextual analysis no longer defines a distinction between the natural sciences and the human sciences, but can be made within the natural sciences as well. Was Dilthey then a victim of his circumstances, in opposing the natural sciences and human sciences by means of the concepts of explanation and understanding? It would seem that these concepts are almost interchangeable insofar as both clarify something particular by something more general, either a causal uniformity or the concept of a framework.

It is unfortunate that Dilthey's language was shaped by the nineteenth-century belief that the natural sciences search only for causes and that explanation is therefore by definition causal. Without these assumptions it is equally justifiable to speak of structural or contextual explanation. Nonetheless, there is something about Dilthey's concept of hermeneutical understanding that makes it different even from contextual explanation. There is an emphasis on understanding the distinctive meaning of individual documents that cannot be derived from any readymade theory. If this is accepted, then it must be added that it is totally inadequate to consider hermeneutical understanding as merely pre-theoretical, as an elementary understanding of cultural achievements independent of any theoretical concepts of cultural forms. This view of hermeneutical understanding betrayed by Cassirer[27] is close to Lucien Goldmann's use of the term *comprendre*. According to the latter, to understand a text is to have analyzed what is given. To explain a work is then to place it in a sociological or, if need be, a psychoanalytical framework.[28]

Neither Cassirer nor Goldmann really answer the question of how the work of art in turn sheds light on its sociological context. Because Dilthey was concerned with this above all else, his concept of hermeneutical understanding is comprehensive enough to encompass Goldmann's concepts of understanding and of contextual explanation. Dilthey's concept of understanding involves the interplay of those two narrower concepts. It involves what Dilthey called the hermeneutic circle in which the part of a work cannot be understood except through its relation to the whole and the whole cannot be understood apart from its parts.[29] To some extent the same circle affects the formation of the uniformities of the natural sciences: Although the empiricists claim that observation of particulars leads to the formulation of a universal concept, there must have been some vague notion of a common nature which led them to consider a given group of particulars rather than another. But here the interdependence between this group of particulars and the universal ends. The universal once abstracted should apply to many more particulars. Even the empiricist's concern that generalizations be tested by the facts does not require him to continually re-consult his original set of particulars. Other particulars are to be considered to confirm the validity of his laws and theories.

In the human sciences, however, we find the need to re-consult the original data each time the structure of the total context is enlarged. Whereas in the natural sciences the refined universal allows us to enlarge the set of particulars to which it applies, in the human sciences the parts under consideration remain the same, but the general context may be widened to explicate more and more of their meaning. This expansion of the whole is never an end in itself. It only serves to illuminate individuality.

Cassirer, in his attempt to find the common bond between the natural sciences and the cultural sciences, claims that they agree in uniting the particular and the universal. The difference is that in the natural sciences the particular is *subordinated* to the universal, while in the cultural sciences the particular is merely *coordinated* with the universal.[30] By coordination Cassirer means that the cultural sciences develop what could be called ideal types which can illuminate the understanding of the given. Thus Burckhardt defined an ideal (universal) man of the Renaissance in his writings, but no empirical research can ever find such a (particular) man. This ideal type is then only a composite individual, a device to unify the epoch, and no more should be expected of it. Dilthey, however, complains that Burck-hardt's work, *Civilization of the Renaissance,* gives only background, no foreground.[31] For Dilthey the typical should not be some ideal composite of qualities but something real. Dilthey's own method of writing history was to concentrate on some actual human being as typical of his epoch. A part becomes typical of the whole. But even this part-whole relation Cassirer would want to consider as a particular-universal relation.

Whereas Kant had suggested in the *Critique of Judgment* that the study of the particular-universal relation finally leads to the problem of the part-whole relation, Cassirer seems to question the ultimacy of the latter by his treatment of the notion of the qualifying concept. In his *Philosophy of Symbolic Forms* he designates as a "qualifying concept" that product of the imaginative process whereby one central member of a series of impressions is made representative or symbolic of the surrounding members.[32] By con-sidering the qualifying concept to be the first stage in the formulation of the universal, Cassirer seems to subsume the relation of a typical part and a whole to the particular-universal relation. But surely this is a very question-able parallel, for the typical part is more like a universal than is the whole. The whole is no more than a sum of particular impressions. We thus can-not resort to the theory of a whole being greater than the sum of its parts to explain the fact that one part is more than what remains when the others are subtracted from the whole. The typical part serves a general function precisely because it is dense. It is therefore not an abstract universal con-cept. If any abstractness exists in a typical part of a complex, this is because triviality is absent from it.

Dilthey's vision of historical narrative is like that of epic literature, where the hero is a central member of his historical context much in the sense of Cassirer's qualifying concept. Dilthey attempts to do justice to the spiri-tual significance of a historical epoch without appealing to a transcendent dimension. Instead of employing some ideal type which, as a composite of universals, transcends the real components from which it was derived, Dilthey discovers the meaning of a historical epoch by tracing the concrete ways in which its parts relate to it and incorporate the sense of the whole. Dilthey is not content to sketch only the high drama of history, as a Neo-Kantian might. He insists on providing context to the plot to gain a sense of epic breadth. Rather than present a tragic ruler, poet or philosopher who is removed from the people, Dilthey would choose to study one who is active among the people. This analogy should also indicate that Cassirer's ideal type and Dilthey's intuitive type at least agree in not identifying the typical with the average or the common denominator.

Feeling that the typicality involved in the qualifying concept is too ele-mentary to be scientific, Cassirer defines the method of the cultural sciences as a mode of conceptual characterization which is ideal and therefore not intended to determine any real individuals.[33] In this way Cassirer can claim that each of the cultural sciences is autonomous. Earlier I alluded to Dilthey's belief that the human sciences have their own categories. But whereas for him these categories can only be gradually defined by interdisciplinary cooperation, Cassirer sees it as the task of each cultural science to define its own *a priori* categories independently. In the latter case we obtain formal complexes of universals defined in separate disciplines, in the former concrete structures of wholes derived from the interdependent human sciences.

Both Cassirer and Dilthey provide essentially undialectical methods for grasping human life. But Dilthey's concept of structure is intuitive enough to comprehend the dynamism of life, whereas Cassirer's forms are too general to be able to do justice to development. The Neo-Kantian is content to let the processes of life occur between two ideal poles; the dialectician may see these poles as temporarily realized but will in turn negate them and create a higher synthesis of realization. Dilthey's hermeneutic process never affirms any poles but gradually circles into what it finds central. Although Dilthey considers the aim of historical writing to be providing an intuitive understanding of what happened, he does not rely on empathetic identification as is often assumed. The hermeneutic method does not ignore the need for direct sympathy with one's subject, but it is basically a careful and *indirect* method.

Often only certain parts of a historical document may be extant, or certain terms may not be meaningful in relation to the present state of the language in which it was written. In order to arrive at an understanding of this document the historian must try to shed light on it from outside. He must seek references to it by those who wrote it or directly knew it. In order to comprehend strange terminology he must consult lexicons of that time if such are available or look for other usages which may illuminate its sense. This is then a case of the expanding hermeneutic circle we have discussed. However, it is necessary to expand one's context only to the extent that there exists incompleteness in our knowledge of the concrete material under consideration. The triumph of reliving the past is to have a sense of the continuity of one's subject-matter,[34] to be able to fill in enough of these gaps in our knowledge to intuit its essential structure.

But the ability to intuit the essential structure involves discovering the nucleus of the subject-matter. Such focusing on certain parts to the exclusion of others is made possible by that movement of the hermeneutic circle which is the inverse of expansion—namely, contraction. As we widen the context of reference, certain parts of a document may be seen to be better expressed elsewhere and thus can be subordinated in importance to other parts. Also some textual ambiguities may be eliminated so that the sphere of possible meanings contracts.

Once the significance of the document comes into focus it becomes possible to consider its contribution to our original understanding of the context. The purpose of general knowledge in history is to enrich our understanding of individuality, not just by finding a locus for it in a larger scheme, but also by capturing the typical in the individual. History becomes like literature for Dilthey in articulating typicality. It only lacks the freedom of literature to embody the typical in fictional characters and events. Whereas the novelist can freely transcend the given of experience to create the mood of a time and a sense of the whole, the historian can only, as it were, interpolate. The novelist or dramatist could create something like an ideal type; the historian may not. But Dilthey points out that the richness of fictional characters like Shakespeare's Falstaff is often such as to combine almost contradictory attributes. The tension produced serves to give the illusion of being life-like and to overcome the flatness of an ideal type. A part of reality is so enriched that it can be said to incorporate the significance of the whole. This is the typicality that Dilthey cherishes in art and wants to transfer to the writing of history. Thus Dilthey the historian strove as much as possible to focus on exceptional people, and sometimes works of art, that were representative of the *Weltanschauung* of their time and place. To discern such typicality requires much sensitivity, for it is all too easy to lose the subject's uniqueness. Nothing is simpler than to construct a hypothetical entity by filling in gaps in one's data about a person on the assumption that unless otherwise proved he has been determined by his circumstances. Only careful and sympathetic analysis of an individual can go beyond the actual data in a responsible manner. The biographer's role is then to illuminate rather than to explain. It may even be possible to illuminate what had been unconscious or relatively meaningless for the subject, by way of what we recognize to be cultural values. Though the biographer cannot create an imaginatively rich character he can suggest the implicit richness of his protagonist by his overlapping analyses of psyche and history. He can give us a multiple exposure.

Once such a richness of intuition is attained it becomes possible to discern how the individual not only reflects his environment but acts upon it. Even intellectual figures like Lessing and Schleiermacher help the historian to articulate their times. Those critics who feel that Dilthey's conception of history reduces the individual to an aspect of a *Zeitgeist* should take note that according to Dilthey, *Zeitgeist* is a unity of an age which only arises through the contribution of a genius.[35] Lessing, for example, does not passively mirror the German Enlightenment but through his life and work actively incorporates its significance and thus provides it with a unity not previously existent. Here the concept of explanation is inadequate. Any attempt to reduce Dilthey's concept of hermeneutic understanding to a mode of explanation ultimately fails to apprehend the intuitive and artistic nature of Dilthey's goals. The idea of the *Geisteswissenschaften*, as given its humanistic formulation in Dilthey's thought, demands a mode of understanding wherein the general framework does not always have the last word. It seeks to preserve the spontaneity of life wherein individuals can have their say, not just in expressing themselves but in evaluating and transforming their context.

Perhaps the difference between the concepts of *Geisteswissenschaften* and *Kulturwissenschaften* can best be indicated by seeing that the former individualize while the latter essentially individuate. The *Kulturwissenschaften* develop a sense of uniqueness instead of integral individuality. The emphasis of Rickert is on how conceptual composites known as values can account for differences, qualitative as well as quantitative. Likewise, Cassirer's ideal types measure how particular people differ from a norm which they approach. But to know whether or not a person meets a certain standard is not to understand him as a concrete individual. It is to oppose empirical facts and *a priori* cultural values. Just as reflective experience for Dilthey can incorporate traditional cultural values into inner experience and in so doing create a personal system of values, so the *Geisteswissenschaften* endeavor to overcome the dualism of an isolated ego and an *a priori* social scheme. It requires reflection to understand how a person's private attributes can be integrated into a social individual.

Dilthey's hypothesis that all normal people share the same qualities but in different quantities[36] seems at first glance to deny human beings any uniqueness and to go against the nature of the *Geisteswissenschaften* as portrayed in this paper. However, it must be realized that this quantitative theory whereby individuals differ only by degrees constitutes a mere base for Dilthey's structural theory of individuality. It is not Dilthey's intention to compare individuals directly by quantitative methods. Instead, he compares typologically, in terms of typical structures that individuals have developed in reaction to their social environment. To compare two individuals by means of charts measuring the intensity of innumerable qualities assumes that these qualities are independent variables and can be juxtaposed. Dilthey's structural psychology denies this and orders qualities hierarchically. If a particular quality is dominant this will tend to further other qualities and prevent still others from developing. Each individual is thus a configuration of certain dominant qualities in tension with a base of subordinate qualities. This tension may be unresolved for much of a person's life, until finally a functional unity is achieved. Dilthey gives the example of political ambition leading someone to gradually overcome his shyness in public.[37]

Those who criticize Dilthey's quantitative theory as inconsistent with his humanism fail to apprehend that it lies in the nature of Dilthey's concept of understanding to operate with an original continuum. Whereas for Rickert intelligibility requires discursively cutting up the irrational continuum of the given, for Dilthey it requires delineating structures implicit in this continuum. The one then constructs formal composites from isolated rational qualifies, the other traces formal relations within the concrete continuum. Individuality for one who follows Dilthey's approach is neither a qualitative construct nor a quantitative determination, but a structure articulated in the given.

It would be hard to deny that Dilthey's writings on the *Geisteswissenschaften* leave us with problems. Equally undeniable is the fact that they have been more influential on philosophers, historians, and sociologists than the more precise analyses of the *Kulturwissenschaften* by Rickert. But the debates between Dilthey and the Neo-Kantians served to clarify certain issues for both sides, and subsequently allowed Cassirer to develop some of his suggestive positions.

NOTES

This essay was originally published in the *Journal of the History of Philosophy* 7, no. 4 (1969): 423–440. It has been slightly modified and abridged. For a broader treatment of the human and cultural sciences going back to Kant, see my essay "Kant and the Development of the Human and Cultural Sciences" in *Studies in History and Philosophy of Science* 39, no. 4 (2008): 546–553.

    1. Dilthey is often labeled a historicist. Historicism as used here has nothing in common with Karl Popper's polemical use of the term. Cf. his *The Poverty of Historicism* (London: Routledge & Kegan Paul, 1960). Dilthey, for instance, does not establish any historical tendencies in a law-like fashion.

    2. Erich Rothacker, *Logik und Systematik der Geisteswissenschaften* (Bonn: H. Bouvier, 1948), 6.

    3. Ibid., 6–7.

    4. Cf. Wilhelm Dilthey, *Introduction to the Human Sciences*, in *Selected Works*, ed. Rudolf A. Makkreel and Frithjof Rodi (Princeton: Princeton University Press, 1989), vol. 1, 156–157. (Hereafter *SW* 1.)

    5. To be sure, Mill includes the study of the degree of aesthetic development of people in his scientific study of society. But it is clear that according to Mill the progress of the fine arts can be correlated with the progress of knowledge. Cf. J. S. Mill, *System of Logic* (London: Longmans, Green, Reader, & Dyer, 1868), vol. 2, 524. Two things strike us about this: (1) a lack of appeal to feeling in evaluating art sociologically; (2) an empirical (nonscientific) law of historical progress which is a refinement of Comte's natural (scientific) law of progress. Cf. ibid., 510. Dilthey's concept of intellectual history supersedes Mill on both counts. It probes the richness of the life of a historical epoch and considers the question of how progress of knowledge has been furthered as only one of many. The awareness that past peoples have had religious and aesthetic feelings which are nearly lost to modern man weighs heavily on Dilthey. This makes the ability to understand the complexity of the past such an important goal for the *Geisteswissenschaften*.

6. Heinrich Rickert, *Science and History: A Critique of Positivist Epistemology,* trans. Georg Reisman (Princeton: D. Van Nostrand, 1962), 71. (Hereafter *Science.*)

7. Ibid., 90.

8. Ibid., 72.

9. Ibid., 138.

10. Cf. Wilhelm Dilthey, *The Formation of the Historical World in the Human Sciences,* in *Selected Works,* ed. Rudolf A. Makkreel and Frithjof Rodi (Princeton: Princeton University Press, 2002), vol. 3, 310. (Hereafter *SW* 3.)

11. Cf. Wilhelm Dilthey, *Gesammelte Schriften,* 26 vols. (Göttingen: Vandenhoeck & Ruprecht, 1914–2006), vol. 5, 144–145. (Hereafter *GS* 5.)

12. Dilthey considers associationist psychology to be hypothetical, and discounts its explanation of connectedness by habit as unnecessary.

13. Cf. Dilthey, *SW* 1, 88.

14. Dilthey, *GS* 5, 144.

15. Cf. ibid., 175.

16. Cf. Dilthey, *SW* 3, 279.

17. Rickert, *Science,* 47.

18. Dilthey, *GS* 5, 246–247.

19. Cf. Immanuel Kant, *Critique of Judgment,* trans. J. H. Bernard (New York: Hafner, 1951), 16.

20. Cf. Dilthey, *GS* 5, 253.

21. Cf. ibid., 281–282.

22. Cf. Dilthey, *SW* 1, 135–137.

23. Cf. Dilthey, *GS* 5, 197–198.

24. Cf. Dilthey, *SW* 3, 40–42.

25. Cf. Dilthey, *SW* 1, 88–89, 136–137.

26. Cf. Dilthey, *SW* 3, 269.

27. Cf. Ernst Cassirer, *The Logic of the Humanities,* trans. Clarence S. Howe (New Haven: Yale University Press, 1961), 173. (Hereafter *Logic.*)

28. Cf. Lucien Goldmann, *Pour une sociologie du roman* (Paris: Gallimard, 1964), 353–354.

29. Cf. Dilthey, *GS* 5, 330.

30. Cf. Cassirer, *Logic,* 137.

31. Cf. Wilhelm Dilthey, *Hermeneutics and the Study of History,* in *Selected Works,* ed. Rudolf A. Makkreel and Frithjof Rodi (Princeton: Princeton University Press, 1996), vol. 4, 274.

32. Cf. Ernst Cassirer, *The Philosophy of Symbolic Forms,* 3 vols., trans. Ralph Manheim (New Haven: Yale University Press, 1961), vol. 1, 283–284.

33. Cf. Cassirer, *Logic,* 140.

34. Cf. Dilthey, *SW* 3, 235.

35. Cf. Wilhelm Dilthey, *Poetry and Experience,* in *Selected Works,* ed. Rudolf A. Makkreel and Frithjof Rodi (Princeton: Princeton University Press, 1985), vol. 5, 162.

36. Cf. Dilthey, *GS* 5, 229.

37. Cf. ibid., 232.

11

The Multiplicity of Virtues and the Problem of Unity in Hermann Cohen's Ethics and Philosophy of Religion

Reiner Wiehl

The following reflections on the philosophy of Hermann Cohen will attempt, based on his virtue theory, to attain insight into the unity of human self-consciousness, and moreover, to give an indication as to Cohen's formulation of the unique nature of God. Accordingly, in the first sections of the paper, the most important aspects of Cohen's virtue theory will be presented, and in the final section, we will bring into view the relationship between the unity of self-consciousness and the singularity of God.

Virtue Theories and the Grounding of Ethics

In view of his overall philosophy, Hermann Cohen's virtue theory is unique insofar as it is dated and quite contemporary at the same time. It is characterized in this way indeed as a virtue theory in general and as a narrower virtue theory in particular especially in view of the rapid change of values in our time, but also with respect to the pervasive skepticism concerning the core values of humanity. European virtue theories in the philosophical tradition since Socrates, Plato, and Aristotle aimed at the entirety of human existence—at the essence of the human being writ large, and at the particular individual human life in its entirety. In these theories, the idea of a truly good human being was brought into focus, and this idea was projected upon the whole of a possible human life. Virtues were conceived in this tradition as those ontological determinations of the human being that allow us to recognize an individual deservedly as a good human being, and to form the best possible prerequisites for the good life of success and happiness. The idea of virtue was conceived here as an original existential possibility for human life, as a timeless possibility arising out of the essence of humanity. On the other hand, one can scarcely find a definition of human

being from which one can gauge an epoch's changing values—the historical change of societal norms—so clearly as in the virtues' changing values
themselves. Thus, the virtue of courage in the literature and philosophy of
the ancient Greeks was already transformed from a military into a *spiritual* virtue, and continues to be valid as *fortitudo animi* (strength of the
soul) up to the modern European Enlightenment and into our present time.
And thus, to anticipate one aspect of his virtue theory, Hermann Cohen
has transposed this virtue of courage from the inner realm of the heart and
mind into the midst of the modern labor world, into the center of social life,
in the form of an attitude that never tires, an effort that does not cease in
attempting to achieve the good of others. The untimeliness of virtue *theories*
today is related to the present untimeliness of virtue as such: Contrary to
the eighteenth century, today a person's effort to be good appears as no less
questionable than a keeping-up of "good appearances." In the notion of the
"do-gooder" that is popular today, we find not only contempt with respect
to an effort to create and preserve the "good appearance," but also a skeptical aloofness toward the idea of an ultimate goal of someone who pursues
his or her own individual goodness for its *own sake.*

On the other hand, the idea of a true good has not yet entirely disappeared from the human community. Unmistakable signs of true human
goodness—of the truest and most *human* decency—still find sympathy. In
special cases, they even find respect and admiration. Our present problems
with being good and with virtue—problems all the more relevant for a *theory* of virtue—are problems with the idea of human integrity. Such an integrity presents a unified connection between a moral unity and an essential
unity that determines the essence of humanity. Both of these "unities" stand
before our eyes more as question marks than as exclamation points. The
work of destruction which such eminent thinkers as Nietzsche and Freud
have carried out with respect to the traditional European idea of humanity, has greatly jeopardized this idea of human integrity. Gnawing doubts
regarding the validity of the value-definitions of truth, of the true good and
wholeness, work upon this image of humanity toward which the possibility
of human integrity aims. To us, the image of a fragmentary humanity as the
idea of a manifold fragmentation of human life is in effect more concrete
and more comprehensible than the ideas of unity that vanish before it. This
concept of a fragmentary existence is not only promoted by the biological
sciences, but moreover by the very social reality of modern life. Philosophers such as Jaspers and Heidegger each struggle in their own way with
this problem of human integrity. Within this context of fragmentation, how
can one understand and judge Hermann Cohen's virtue theory, or more
precisely the way he determines the relation of virtue and the unity of the
human being? Cohen's point of departure for this question, in his *Logic of*

Pure Cognition (*Logik der reinen Erkenntnis*), is with the classical thinkers of the ancient and modern periods, primarily Plato and Kant. In the *Logic of Pure Cognition,* up until the *Ethics of Pure Willing* (*Ethik des reinen Willens*), it is the Platonic doctrine of forms—more precisely the method of purity discovered therein—that remains the guiding clue of his thinking. This method also determines its relationship to the essential paradigm of modern philosophy, namely Kant's transcendental idealism.

Hermann Cohen's virtue theory in his philosophical ethics and philosophy of religion is based on a grounding principle that one should perhaps call an *axiom,* which develops out of his understanding of the Socratic-Platonic virtue theory. According to this principle, ethics presents the true and original doctrine of humanity. It forms the origin and the grounding (*Grundlegung*) of philosophical anthropology and natural science. In a methodologically oriented formulation this means that in philosophical cognition and under its basic premises, ethics must have primacy over anthropology. In this sense, this primacy presupposes a philosophical "logic of origin" (*Ursprungslogik*) that provides the conditions for the basic prioritization of ethics with respect to and in comparison with other disciplines. The primacy of ethics postulated here, in view of anthropology and cultural science, means that it is ethics which gives the first answers to the questions of humanity. The secondary, subordinate determinations of humanity are to be derived *from* these very first answers. These primary answers are determinations which articulate the idea of the Good in view of the essence of humanity—as determinations of being, of ought, of willing the Good, and also of good conduct. One can speak here, in view of the primacy of ethics over anthropology, equally of a first as well as a *second* "Copernican turn," depending on whether one has accepted the standpoint of Socrates or of Kant, in view of their respective philosophical contemporaries and predecessors. For the virtue theory thematized here, this turn means: Virtue is an exemplary *ontological mode* of the Good in view of the human person.

This definition of virtue should not be confused with the theorem that humanity is good based upon its nature, or that humanity is essentially virtuous. Such a theorem, and a corresponding identification of humanity and virtue, is not what Cohen has in mind. Rather, the definition of virtue is to be differentiated from any comparable definition in which, misleadingly, anthropology *would* have primacy over ethics. Under these assumptions, the definition of virtue would be that it is an exemplary ontological mode of the human being in view of its conception of the Good. This definition inadvertently brings to mind the Aristotelian virtue theory. The *anthropological* assumption lies here in the idea that all humans strive for happiness (*eudaimonia*). For Cohen, Aristotle's *eudaimonism* represents a violation of the basic methodological assumptions of Aristotle's own ethics.

In contradistinction to Gadamer's philosophical hermeneutics, Cohen believes that there is an unbridgeable opposition between the Platonic and the Aristotelian doctrines of the Good, an opposition which arises precisely from within their respective doctrines of virtue. From a different vantage point, however, Cohen has returned to a more positive appreciation of the Aristotelian virtue theory, namely an appreciation of Aristotle's distinction between ethical and *dianoietic* virtues. However, this distinction which is so important for virtue theory, must allow itself to undergo a fundamental transformation which refers to the primacy of ethics over anthropology. This distinction thereby also refers to the necessity of a basic grounding of this primacy in a "logic of origin." In Aristotle, the definition of virtues is, rather, referred back to the different ways in which humans acquire virtue—to the acquisition through habituation on the one hand, and through learning on the other. Cohen, however, holds that Aristotle has thereby advanced the prejudice that what is at stake in ethics is primarily the good human *being* and not to the same extent the *being of the Good* and its manner of cognition. The flaw of the Aristotelian classification of virtues is reflected in a deficiency in the definition of the relation between theoretical and practical cognition. In Cohen's formulation of the grounding of pure will, which precedes the virtue theory itself, the categorial difference between plurality and totality has already been made. It is this distinction which underlies the classification of the virtues. Virtues express themselves in *particular* communities or prove themselves in human communities that are grounded on a certain totality of human beings and identify themselves as *legal* communities that refer to the idea of humanity. These categorial differences between particularity and generality (and between plurality and totality) already display themselves in the affective character of the will. The will is moved in two ways through two distinct affects—through *love* and *honor*. Love is active in the *particular* life-communities of human beings, whereas honor is a valid active principle that is in play insofar as human beings live together as a higher *totality* and under its conditions.

Now the transformation of Aristotelian virtue theory indicated here, with respect to Aristotle's classification of virtues, presupposes a grounding of pure willing. Here Kant is the chief authority for Cohen. Even if critical idealism and the method of purity in Socrates and Plato have found a more determinate expression, in Cohen's view, it is nevertheless with Kant's practical philosophy that the stage is set for contemporary ethics. Here Cohen has identified the necessity of a grounding, for which the perception of societal values and norms and the observations of human behavior with respect to these norms are not sufficient in order to do justice to the universal validity of the Good for the human being. Only a *grounding* of ethics makes possible the distinction between morality (*Sittlichkeit*) and tradition (*Sitte*), or between *ethics* and *ethos*. It is only here that the clear distinction of *Is* and *Ought* arises, a distinction from which one can determine the good will for moral action. Given the necessity of this grounding, however, Cohen also detected an error in Kant's groundbreaking work which was in need of correction. This error concerns precisely what Cohen has called "the Eternal" in Kant—namely Kant's discovery of the transcendental method, with its centerpiece, the "transcendental deduction." For Cohen, this method signified a grounding of the pure philosophical concepts in view of the "*factum* of science," from which the basic concepts must prove themselves in their application. For the grounding of ethics, this meant that the ethical basic concepts—such as those of the will, of action, and of agency—must prove themselves from the *factum* of the science of law, which is jurisprudence. In the application of the method it would have to be demonstrated that "the law must have its roots in ethics; so must also ethics be determined and founded in jurisprudence."[1] Cohen found that this methodological path, effectively a *double-path,* was not adequately addressed by Kant, according to the principle of the transcendental method in the relation between *The Groundwork of the Metaphysics of Morals* and *The Metaphysics of Morals.* The sought-for relation concerning origin and grounding was essentially flawed. Given our context, what is of the first concern is a particular inadequacy resulting from this flaw. In his practical philosophy, Kant has failed to include the methodological principle of the unity of self-consciousness. This concept would be *analogous* to the transcendental unity of apperception, which serves as the methodological principle of the unity of consciousness, in which the totality of representations of pure cognition are grounded. As an analogous methodological principle, it would be that in which the totality, in the sense of ethics, is grounded. Hence, there arises for Kant the particular problem of the unity of self-consciousness, in which theoretical and practical cognition are joined. This is all the more problematic insofar as this methodological principle of the unity of self-consciousness was meant to make up for the loss of that type of self-evidence in ancient ethics which accompanied the idea of the unity of human existence and life as lived.

The Definition of Virtue and the Correlation with Religion

Cohen's virtue theory presupposes this unity of self-consciousness as a *unity in the totality.* The methodological principle of the grounding of the ethical basic concepts in view of the *factum* of jurisprudence leads primarily to the definition of this unity of self-consciousness as the *legal person.* In jurisprudence, this concept of the person is authenticated in civil law, state law, and international law. But how does this legal concept of the juridical person hang together with a theory of virtue? Can the agent in such a theory be adequately construed as the legal person? This appears, at least upon first consideration, to be absurd. What is at stake here is the methodological *transition* from the concept of the legal to that of the moral person. Let us first enumerate the most important elements of Cohen's virtue theory. Virtue is (1) the *continuity* and *consistency* of the being of the Good in view of human beings, or the continuity and consistency of the Good in the human being. Moreover, virtue is (2) a special form of *plurality* of this ontological mode of the Good, in which a peculiar tendency toward unity can be discerned. Finally, virtue theory leads to (3) the problem of the basic *relationship* of ethics and religion, due to their mutual relation to the idea of *humanity*. The problem that arises here is that of the tension between the desired autonomy of ethics with respect to religion, and the indispensable distinction between ethical and religious virtues based on the different relations between humans and God entailed by these types of virtues.

The definition of virtue as consistency and continuity of the being of the Good in human beings demands a definition of this being of the Good. From the methodological viewpoint sketched above, such a definition is required according to which the ethical source is to be found in the *factum* of jurisprudence. This means that for philosophical ethics, the concept of the legal person cannot be the final word, but only a reference point and a methodological path-marker. This concept of the legal person calls for an authentication of its ethical relevance in the reality of the ontological mode of the Good. This ontological mode determines itself differently here than it does in the *Logic of Pure Cognition,* where it is the hypothetically posited being of the idea, as the being of the ideal. The difference between idea and ideal conforms to the difference between thought and theoretical cognition on the one hand, and will and practical cognition on the other. In the ideal not only do *being* and *ought* go together, but they together with *willing* as well. The question of *truth* becomes salient in determining the relation between idea and ideal. The first indicated definition of virtue as consistency and continuity of the being of the Good applies itself according to that ideal, namely the ideal of the Good. Through this relation, consistency and steadfastness are not determinants of the logic of pure cognition, nor determinants of mathematical-scientific physics, nor empirical characteristics of psychology or anthropology. These determinants are, thanks to the usage of the method of purity, purely ethical definitions. This is in keeping with the Socratic dialogues on virtue (particularly the *Meno*) in which (in view of the question of the teachability of virtue) the rigorous ethical concept is distinguished from common anthropological conceptions of power and force. The question concerning the second definition of virtue as *plurality* had already been touched upon in conjunction with the transformation of the Aristotelian distinction between ethical and *dianoietic* virtues.

The more precise explication of these definitions refers to the methodological grounding of the pure will, in whose preconditions pluralities become visible in the form of inclinations and affects. But, Cohen asserts, these pluralities belong primarily to the *mechanics* of the pure will. In this regard, they do not constitute the actual motive of acting. What holds for virtues, holds equally—because of the method of purity—for affects. Contrary to the theory of affects in Spinoza, in which the affects are natural anthropological patterns of behavior, in the grounding of pure will there is required a methodological transformation of affects into ethically relevant motives for action. Both basic affects of love and honor, of which we have already spoken, fulfill this condition of being adequate to the method of purity.

In this respect, the will in its ethical grounding takes a central categorial position between plurality and unity. With respect to motivation there is a plurality in the will, but with respect to its content—its *object*—it is rather a unity. Because of its autonomy and heautonomy[2]—here, too, Cohen alludes to Kant's grounding of the good will—the will refers to action. And the action is essentially the unity of the action, which demands the unity of the agent with respect to the act's essential unity. Self-consciousness, as the methodological principle of the *Ethics of Pure Willing*, is precisely this distinct unity of the agent—the unity of action. This unity of action is given, in view of the *factum* of jurisprudence, as a unity of a legally binding contract or as the unity of a legal transaction. Respectively, the unity of self-consciousness is, with respect to the *factum* of the unity of the juridical person, to be thought in analogy to the concept of the person. The plurality in question here—namely, the plurality of virtues and the direction and tendency of this plurality toward unity—is not sufficiently understood, however, from the particular plurality that lies within the pure will to action. Civil law, which for Cohen presents an exemplary paradigm with respect to the *factum* of jurisprudence, permits no sufficient access to virtue theory. The volitional motives of love and honor cannot be easily discerned from civil law. Civil law gives a positive clue for the ethics of pure will, but only in one respect: In civil law the primacy of the totality is asserted over that of plurality, and the founding principle of ethics as such is displayed through this primacy. But the sought-after plurality of virtues arises not from a plurality of natural persons, who sign a legally binding contract and who enter through such a signing of a contract into a juridical person, into this unity of self-consciousness. Rather, the juridical *factum* of civil law is all the more reason to point out the methodological meaning, that ethics must find its authentication in the *factum* of jurisprudence and thereby find its grounding. Thus, the totality of civility refers to other legally binding communities, particularly to the legal community of a state and to the community of states founded upon international law.

The idea of humanity lies not only *beyond* these totalities, but is in fact *prior* to all these totalities of legal communities. The idea of the one, single humanity is only to be comprehended in view of the idea of the singularity of God. For Cohen, the ethical significance of Jewish monotheism arises precisely here. God tells us not who He is; He says only what the Good is. This is the basic teaching of Jewish monotheism. The way of the juridical person does not lead organically to the moral person, but rather one can discover the ideal of the moral person in the idea of the juridical person. The moral person is the original self-consciousness that previously had been utilized only methodologically. The legal person presents only a necessary condition of the moral person. We are located here in a region of ideas and idealisms. The multiplicity of virtues and their tendency toward unity belongs to the ideal and its connection to the idea of humanity. The will in its motivation for action extends beyond the idea of singular legal communities, to the idea of humanity as a whole. The plurality that is situated in its motivation for acting, and the object or the unity of the action, belong to the plurality of virtues and their immanent unity. When we pose the question of the difference between ethical and religious virtues, we would go astray if we were to conceive the distinction as one of virtues *without* God and virtues *with* God. Such a conception would undermine the autonomy of ethics and make morality impossible even as an idea. For Cohen, ethics is bound, even prior to religion (and hence in its autonomous validity), to the idea of God's singularity: God is the truth and God is the Good. This is the content that ethics and religion share in their doctrine of God. God is, as truth and as the Good, the condition of the possibility of ethical and of religious virtues. Truthfulness and humility, courage and loyalty (to name only a few of the virtues), only exist under the condition of truth. This condition asserts truth as both illustrative and as the grounding relation between thinking and willing—between theoretical and practical cognition. Yet the virtues exist also only in view of the idea of humanity. Here is the point of convergence of Jewish monotheism and its messianism. The will extends, as determined through the love and honor of one's neighbor, beyond all particular plurality and beyond every particular totality. Its ultimately valid content is humanity *writ large,* or the humanity to come. The will is directed toward the future. To that extent it goes beyond the scope of the temporal circumstances of theoretical cognition. This futurity is, as Cohen says, the temporal eternity of futurity: It is the will, the good will of the moral person, and the will as the self-consciousness of a perpetually future humanity.

The virtues, as the continuity and consistency of the being of the Good, are ontological modes of the Good in the moral person. This state of affairs presupposes the legal person or the human legal community as a critical agency. While this community originates from the moral person, it must still be discovered within it. It will be appropriate now to introduce Cohen's central methodological concept—that of correlation. This concept asserts that, for ethics, the correlation of the juridical and the moral person obtains. The virtue theory in the *Ethics of Pure Willing* is founded upon this correlation. Given this correlation, however, the difference between ethical and religious virtues becomes quite conspicuous, and in this difference the peculiar and most important trait of Cohen's ethics becomes manifest. Here we find its essential difference in contradistinction to ancient and modern virtue theories—particularly in contradistinction to the virtue theories of Plato and Aristotle on the one hand, and Kant on the other. Therefore, the theory of the ethical virtues also cannot be separated from the theory of religious virtues. Cohen's clear assertion of the autonomy of ethics from religion seems to go against this, as does his notion of religion as a "religion of reason." In Emmanuel Levinas' ethics, it appears that the proposed connection of ethics and religion is eliminated. The difference between ethical and religious virtues is not, as mentioned, a difference between virtues without and virtues with God, or between virtues without and with theism. It is, rather, a difference of virtues in view of the multiple relationships that obtain between God and the human being. As truth and as the Good, God is the origin of the ethical virtues, insofar as God Himself belongs to the foundational concepts of ethics. In contrast, in religious virtues God is the correlate to the human being in an original correlation in which He and the human being stand. One can say that the Cohen's theory of the ethical virtues is a theory of humanity. The theory of the religious virtues is the theory of charity and peace. The autonomy of ethics authenticates itself precisely with respect to charity. This is so because, while in the *Ethics of Pure Willing* the love of *humanity* is bound to *particular* life-communities, charity is rather bound in a unique way to the messianic idea of the *whole* of humanity. The neighbor is every human being—every human, whatever his living conditions may be. Charity, then, also obtains where conditions of foreignness, alienation, and exclusion from a living community exist. Love of the enemy is not an unrealistic *phantasm,* but rather it is that which brings to expression the fact that charity itself does not depend on outer circumstances, but is possible under all conditions. In the moral person's will, love and honor are the most crucial motives for action. Charity is only possible in the light of the holiness of God. Through this light, the I *in* the Thou of the neighbor, and thus the Thou *of* the fellow human are discovered. This discovery sits beside the discovery of the moral person in the legal community, and is the chief discovery in the correlation of ethics and religion.

Self-Consciousness: Relation and the Tendency toward Unity

Given the discussion so far, a few important consequences now arise for Cohen's virtue theory. The virtues are posed simultaneously between plurality and unity on the one hand, and also particularly between ethics and religion, as modes of consistency and continuity of the Good in human beings, on the other. However, this *intermediate* position requires an important—indeed, the *most* important—amendment. This amendment fills in the intermediate position between the abstract-formal categorial definitions of plurality and unity on the one hand, and the material demands of ethics and religion on the other. Thus the virtues stand in two mutually supplemental intermediate positions. On the one hand, their systematic locus with respect to *form*, is the place between will and action. Virtue is as much an ontological mode of human willing as an ontological mode of human action. With the definition of virtue as consistency and continuity of the Good in human beings, we finally come to the most important distinction of Cohen's ethics in general, and his virtue theory in particular. For as we have stressed from the beginning, the being of the human in the philosophical ethics is determined *from* the being of the Good. Cohen identifies the ontological mode of being of the human so determined as self-consciousness. And the essential feature of this self-consciousness consists in the fact that it determines itself according to the ontological modes of the Good. From this point of view, both ancient and modern virtue theories undergo a profound modification. Virtue does not apply merely as a moral regulation to human beings, nor only to the human being as a singular individual in its concrete living-historical reality. Nor does it apply merely to humanity in general, in view of its essential determination as the rational being who is capable of moral self-determination. Self-consciousness is, in Cohen's *Ethics of Pure Willing*, a *formal* concept—more precisely, a category of ethics with diverse modes of application. Therefore, self-consciousness is not merely the formal basic determination of human individuals in their capacity of willing and action. Self-consciousness is also the human individual as a natural person under the conditions of existing legal relationships. It is also the legal person (in the sense of a corporation) as a legal contractual relation and as the *action* of a legally binding transaction. Cohen determines self-consciousness in particular as the state community qua legal community, whose systematic place is also characterized by this in-between. The legal community of a state finds itself under the conditions of a thoroughgoing idealization between the definitions of the legal and the moral person.

Beyond all of these formal definitions of self-consciousness, however, the ontological mode of the human being is bound to its own idea and ideal of humanity. These form the tension of human self-consciousness, from which arise the various basic concepts of ethics. For their part, according to Cohen's methodological conception, these must be able to be read off the *factum* of jurisprudence. Peculiar and far-reaching consequences result for virtue theory from this draft of the forms of self-consciousness. One is the fact that, due to this stipulated definition of virtue as consistency and continuity of the Good in humans, virtue stands in direct connection with every possible form of human self-consciousness. It is therefore not merely a determination of the isolated willing and acting of a respective human individual in its relation to itself and to other human individuals. It goes beyond this, and still more importantly, it is also an ontological mode of the Good with respect to the willing and acting of a *legal person* on the way to its definition as a moral person. And finally it is the ontological mode of the Good in the moral person as such, for whom it functions as a signpost toward morality. One can say with Cohen: Virtue is a signpost for human beings which points *between* the idea and the ideal of humanity *toward* the Good. The catalogue of virtues and its organization, at least according to the way that Cohen unfolds it in his *Ethics of Pure Willing* and his *Religion of Reason From Its Sources in Judaism,* is therefore not sufficiently determined through the two affective motivations of love and honor for humans, and through its original logical-categorial application in particular and universal communities. In its connection to the various formations of human self-consciousness, it spreads its sphere of influence beyond the domain of the private and beyond the mere disposition of individuals, to the whole area of public life. The virtue of truthfulness provides an example of this public character of virtue, which is particularly important for Cohen. Truthfulness is not merely, as in Kant's *Metaphysics of Morals,* the first obligation of the individual human being to his own character as a natural person. Truthfulness goes beyond this as the first obligation of the state community as a supra-individual moral person. The fulfillment of this obligation requires of this supra-individual moral person that it take responsibility for the education of its citizens and that it ensure their common and equal right to vote. These are only some of the possible obligations to which the state, as a moral community, is held.

Cohen's virtue theory requires, to that extent, a thoroughgoing determination of obligations of the public life in the culture of human communities. Here the relevance of the method of grounding as a method of purity becomes clear. The modern critique of society endeavors to work upon the inadequacies and grievances of a bad society. Contrary to this critique, in the virtue theory of the *Ethics of Pure Willing,* Cohen distinguishes himself from this modern critique through his eagerness to obtain for the first time the criteria and norms, and thereby the basic conditions, *for* such an endeavor. In this way, the hopeless breach between the publicity of the general and the privacy of the individual can be avoided. This is a breach which remains unbridgeable in the various types of existentialism—particularly in Heidegger's *Being and Time,* but also in the social criticism of the Frankfurt School, as is most clear in Adorno. Cohen's virtue theory, in contrast, provides an extremely important signpost to help effect the desired connection between the private and the public realm. In virtue as the ontological mode of the Good in the human being, theoretical and practical cognition are conjoined. It is not a conjunction of an alien standpoint, or one from a purely formal and trans-theoretical viewpoint. One of Cohen's critiques of Kant's practical philosophy is that he took just such a formal reflective standpoint. The unity of practical and theoretical rational cognition, which is asserted in the *Ethics of Pure Willing,* is a unity claimed by practical reason. The idea of God, whose function is to guarantee this unity in the sense of the basic laws of truth, is to that extent a fundamental concept of ethics. This concept contains only this transcendental determination as a condition of the possibility of truth. Truth is, as stated, a basic condition of virtue itself; it is not merely the basic condition of the *first* and *foremost* of the ethical virtues, truthfulness. Truthful*ness* can only exist where first there is truth. Without this presupposition, truthfulness is merely an impotent struggling toward honesty—and this is too little for a true ethics. The unity of theoretical and practical rational cognition, when seen from the standpoint of the practical, extends to all basic ethical concepts—thus to will, to action, and to self-consciousness in its various forms. In view of this underlying unity, the distinctions of various virtues are therefore possible. These distinctions are particularly impressive in the instance of the virtue of modesty. What Cohen has written about this virtue are the most beautiful passages within the *Ethics of Pure Willing.* When we spoke at the outset of this essay of the timeliness of Cohen's virtue theory, this holds especially for the meaning that Cohen attributes to the virtue of modesty. This virtue seems dated and yet its demand is of increasing relevance for our time, given the current society of the spectacle in which "show" is everything.

Modesty stands in contrast to vanity and pomposity. It is not dependent on a constant external recognition of outward appearances. Of the virtue of truthfulness, in which the volative motive of honor is effective in view of the dignity of the human being, Cohen has said that it must "be implemented for the entire domain of public life."[3] The virtue of modesty belongs to the virtues that arise from love of humanity and that authenticate themselves in particular areas of life. Nevertheless it would also receive a wider audience, if this virtue of restraint gained wider acceptance. Up to this point it has become clear why virtues must be construed in the *categorial* form of plurality. They are plural not because of the individual disparities of individual human being, but rather because of the dissimilarity of the public life in view of the various relations in which human self-consciousness is manifested in its manifold forms as legal and moral person. The plurality of the virtues corresponds to the polymorphy of the moral domain that exists as situated between the idea and the ideal of humanity. For the plurality of the virtues obtains that which the Socratic-Platonic virtue theories had already made clear—namely, that this plurality refers to an original unity, the unity of the idea of the Good. Each virtue is, taken for itself, one-sided, and is in this one-sidedness entangled in the conflicts of moral life. A virtue is only a determinate virtue in the *connection* and in its collaboration with the other virtues. As exemplified by the cooperation between modesty and the virtue of truthfulness, this cooperation is itself a moral task. Likewise, the virtue of modesty is to be discovered in a Socratic *docta ignorantia*—in the ideal of an ignorance that is truly knowing. As such a truthful restraining of one's own claims to knowledge, the virtue of modesty becomes a virtue of critique. It functions as a critique of erroneous claims to knowledge and cognition; it sets conscious limits to misleading claims to omniscience and omnipotence. Thus, it is equally a virtue of measure and moderation. It enables a measured attitude in the evaluation of the weaknesses observed in moral life, and moderation in the evaluation of others' behavior both in the attitude of critique and disapproval. The virtue of modesty thus proves its internal connection to a further virtue, namely the virtue of justice, insofar as this virtue finds its unique expression in *equity* (*Billigkeit*) as a virtue of legal and moral evaluation, of reconciliation and adjudication.

In the virtue of modesty, the aforementioned connection of theoretical and practical cognition now comes to the fore—especially in conjunction with the virtue of approval, and particularly in the light of primacy of praxis. For taking measure and equity in the evaluation of the action and the acting person makes use of the theoretical-practical separation of act and action. It does this in order not to be required to subject an action to juridical standards in disproportionate severity. And accordingly, an action is separated from the acting person, so that the load of the legal or moral evaluation of the action does not burden the acting subject for her whole life. In these legal and moral distinctions, carried out by the virtue of modesty, it becomes clear that the fragmentation of human beings lamented at the outset and the corresponding fragmentation of human life are by no means only the product of a socio-cultural change. Nor do they only reflect a change in the overall human constitution based on profoundly changing circumstances. Rather, fragmentation in a different sense, which the virtue of the modesty effects, lies obviously in a completely different dimension from this previous sense of fragmentation. If one takes Cohen's method of critical idealization seriously, then there is no connection between these two senses of fragmentation. The notion of fragmentation is much too formal to be able to create a material connection between the ethical and cultural-anthropological meanings of fragmentation. As said, the plurality of the virtues in Cohen's ethics and philosophy of religion are oriented to a unity. In the theory of the ethical virtues, this tendency to unity is given as a self-critical insight into the one-sidedness of the virtues. The virtue corresponding to this capacity for rational self-critique is the virtue of *humanity (Humanität)*. This virtue expresses itself as friendliness toward everyone, toward all human beings. Friendliness is, to that extent, no bare convention of social behavior, but rather a virtue firmly grounded within the idea of humanity and its ideal. Cohen argued that the feeling of *respect* for the dignity of the human being—a feeling which is effected by practical reason, and which Kant placed at the center of his practical philosophy—was unsatisfactory. In this notion of respect for human dignity, only the negative form of a demand on human behavior is implied—i.e., that human persons may not be hurt, may not be insulted, and may not be impaired in their dignity. In Cohen's view, this is too little. The definition of human being as the moral person requires more than this. Love and honor, which human beings owe to other human beings, must enter into the theory of the virtues. These are to be regarded as signposts for the human being, who will and ought to do justice to the task of the perfection of the moral ideals in ethics, law, and politics.

Divine Correlation and the Futurity of Virtue

In Cohen's philosophy, the difference between ethical and religious virtues arises out of their immanent systematics. Through these virtues, this difference refers back to the domains of the logic of origin and the logic of pure cognition. The foundations of natural science, ethics, and religion are based in thinking and in its logic of cognition. The fundamental concepts of plurality, of totality, and not least of individuality, play relevant roles in all these domains and have a functional determination that is distinct with respect to their systematic differences.

As shown, the distinction between the different ethical virtues—which are arranged into primary and secondary virtues—is oriented toward the difference between totality and plurality derived from the logic of cognition. In this logic, totality has a primacy over plurality with respect to the logic of validity, both in terms of logical cognition and of ethics. Similarly, this primacy applies to those impulses of the will which determine the primary and the secondary virtues, respectively—thus it applies to honor and love. Regardless of how one and the other impulses go together, this primacy also applies to them in their determination of the will. Honor has primacy over love because it applies to all human beings without exception, and ought not to be only effective within special communities.

For Cohen's logic a difficulty, which he explicitly acknowledges, is characteristic for the determination of the logical locus of individuality. Its logical determination in the form of the individual judgment cannot be placed so easily alongside the judgments of particularity and totality. A peculiarity of Cohen's logic of pure cognition is the fact that individuality arises *only* in the judgment of reality, and can therefore find its origin only in a structure of judgments following the logic of this judgment. Individuality is, therefore, not only subordinate to totality, as is particularity; individuality is also subordinated to particularity. This represents, for Cohen, a key issue for theoretical and practical cognition, and the category of particularity is to that extent a key problem, particularly for ethics.

The difference between ethical and religious virtues cannot be deduced simply from the difference between totality and particularity on the one hand and individuality on the other. If one follows the basics tenets of the religion of reason, this difference is to be gained from the basic definition of individuality. However, this point of origin requires a more exact definition. In the *Ethics of Pure Willing,* Cohen presents his definitive qualification of individuality: Individuality, or more so the individual, is *idea.* If at the beginning it was said that, for Cohen, ethics provides the origin and foundation for anthropology, then this is expressed most unmistakably in this definition of the individual as idea. Thus the individuality of the human being is distinctly transposed from the domain of nature and from the sphere of biological-psychological natural science into a completely different area of application—that of ethics, jurisprudence, and political science, and finally into the field of the rational science of religion. The human being is, as individual, the idea: This means that the idea of the human being is a *hypothesis* of a special uniform wholeness of *humanness,* which stands before our eyes as a question and a task for cognition. Concerning the relationship between ethics and the philosophical rational doctrine of religion, the autonomy of ethics must be protected without reservation in the unity of both. The rational doctrine of religion, on the other hand, may only bring to bear its own peculiarity. But ethics is dependent at the same time upon the completion through this peculiarity of the religion of reason. It is related to this peculiar completion. From Cohen's perspective, Kant's "doctrine of postulates" is, in view of such a necessary completion, demanded by ethics itself, but is only an insufficient appendix of the *Critique of Practical Reason.* As stated before, if ethical and religious virtues cannot be distinguished as virtues with or without God—if both have to be understood as virtues *with* God— then this realization is based on the unity of ethics and the religion of reason. Ethical and religious virtues *equally* presuppose the being of God, as well as the mutual correlation of God and the human being. What distinguishes them from each other, then, is a difference in the correlation of God and the human being: In each case there is a different *manner* of God's co-existence in the will, in action, and in the unity of the human being's being and ought.

One of the most important propositions in Cohen's *Ethics of Pure Willing* reads: God is *idea*. If the human being (as individual) is also *idea* in Cohen's ethics, then the question is thereby posed regarding the relationship between these two ideas—the idea of God and the idea of the human being. An answer to this question is to be sought in the correlation between God and human being. The grounding of the distinction between ethical and religious virtues is to be discovered in the difference of these virtues within this correlation between God and the human being. Cohen attributes this difference to the difference between two correlations: To ethics applies the correlation of *self-being* and *consciousness* of the other; to the religion of reason pertains the correlation of *Thou* and *I*. The ethical virtues arise from the former correlation, and religious virtues from the latter. The demanded autonomy of ethics and its completion through the peculiarity of the religion of reason, however, make a more exact definition necessary. Self-consciousness, according to Cohen, always presupposes consciousness *of* the other and in such a way that it discovers itself *in* the other *as self-consciousness*. This correlation between self-consciousness and the consciousness of the other can now be applied, in its pure conceptuality, to the *factum* of jurisprudence and to the particularity of corporate law. It can also be authenticated in its legality: In the contractually secured legal community of "comrades," the ego of self-consciousness discovers itself in the *Thou* of the consciousness of the other. In contrast to this, the correlation of Thou and I is different within the rational doctrine of religion. It arises directly in the correlation of God and the human being, and is characterized by the immediacy and directness of this origin. In distinction from ethics, this particular correlation is based not only upon an application to a historical *factum* and an authentication of its validity in such a *factum*. In a methodological regard, the correlation between the human Thou and I in the doctrines of the religion of reason belongs, rather, to the domain of the grounding of pure concepts. The religiously determined correlation between a human Thou and I is substantially different from the comparable ethical correlation and its characteristics. It does not form the singularity of an inter-human correlation within a specific legal and life-community under their specific conditions. It is, rather, a singularity of a singular co-human correlation of Thou and I independent of the characteristics of these peculiarities and specific communal totalities. This independence constitutes the religious characteristic of co-human correlations of Thou and I. In contrast to ethical love, religious love is marked by this characteristic of independence from specific communal totalities. It is the love of the neighbor, a love present in the correlation between Thou and I, which occurs under *all* conditions, independently of the peculiarity of specific legal and life-communities. This love of the neighbor is a love which is capable of discovering the fellow human being *in* the neighbor. It does so in view of common human suffering, and is capable of finding in this neighbor the common human Thou. It is upon this discovery that the human being finds its own I *as I.*

In Cohen's philosophy, the difference between ethical and religious virtues arises from the differences in the correlations of I and Thou in view of the original correlation of God and the human being. For his ethics of pure willing and his religion of reason, Cohen appeals equally to the teachings of the Jewish prophets and the religion of Judaism. But, according to his methodological self-understanding, these sources had to have different validities in keeping with the difference between rational cognition in ethics and in religion. To ethics applies the correlation of truth and morality, arising from the correlation of God and the human being. To the religion of reason applies the correlation of morality and holiness. Holiness is not the characteristic of a transcendent God, but a definition of the correlation of God and human being according to the peculiarity of the rational definition of religion. From this holiness—Cohen speaks of the holiness of the spirit—arises human knowledge of guilt and redemption, and of the sanctification of the human self in such a redemption. Ethics circumscribes the area of application of the truly good, and also describes the certainty of its victory over human weakness, over inadequacies, and over evil. Under the banner of this victory, evil loses its power and its reality. And the rational teachings of religion indicate the holiness of the spirit in its power to overcome human suffering and human guilt. Humankind owes the idea of the uniqueness of God to the Jewish religion, and with this, the idea of humankind's own unmistakable singularity. And with the idea of messianism, humankind owes to Judaism the category and the judgment of a reality in which the *future* has clear primacy over the past. In this reality the future is always anticipated in the present. This anticipatory trait obtains both in theoretical and in practical rational cognition. In practical rational cognition—that is, in ethics *and* the religion of reason—*every* correlation between self-consciousness and consciousness of the other, as much as the original correlation of Thou and I, is unique to a reality aligned toward the future. Cohen's philosophy is a philosophy of the future. For him, the idea of a primacy of the past over the future is a myth. This philosophy of the future understands itself as critical idealism, as the rational cognition of philosophical scientificity. Its great antipode, Nietzsche's philosophy of the future, grows from a different cultural-historical source. The utopian streak in Cohen's philosophy of the future has its source in Jewish messianism.

Nihilism, which Nietzsche made the outrageous cornerstone of his thinking, has its source in European Platonism and its Christian adaptations. But the Plato of Cohen is not the Plato of Nietzsche.

The timeliness of Cohen's doctrine of virtue in his *Ethics of Pure Willing* and *Religion of Reason* is not limited to the fact that it updates the received human virtues and applies them to the modern labor world and its value conceptions. Neither is it limited to its freeing of the horizon beyond these value conceptions, for the super-temporal idea of peace in its validity for ethics, politics, and a reason of religion. (Peace designates the virtue with which Cohen concludes his religio-philosophical work, *Religion of Reason from its Sources in Judaism.*) The timeliness of Cohen's rational doctrine of ethical and religious virtues extends, at the same time, to their methodological definition. This doctrine owes its method of purity, in the form of a grounding of pure concepts of ethics and religion, to critical idealism in the context of a philosophical rational science. For this idealism there are no immediate givennesses, no natural data. Rather, each givenness is bound to the presupposition of its cultural mediation and imparted through philosophical rational science. Modern critical idealism unfolds itself in the consciousness of an historical differentiation of science, in which empirical positive science and purely philosophical rational science diverge. For critical idealism, reality is a *task*. Philosophical rational cognition must authenticate itself in the facts of the empirical positive sciences, in such a way that this authentication shows itself in the *historicity* of these facts. The term "task" is taken from Kant's *Critique of Pure Reason*, but it is spelled out by Cohen through the arrangement of his entire system of philosophy. The task of cognition applies to the sciences of nature, law, and politics, just as it does for philosophical rational cognition. The reality of the task of cognition is immanent to an orientation toward the future. Cohen's critical idealism is noticeably marked by an extreme formalism which, in its methodological purity, exceeds the formalism of the Kantian rational critique in its transcendental methodology. Labeling this idealism as "epistemology" is neither more nor less appropriate than it is for Kant's own philosophy of reason. Heidegger's definition of Marburg Neo-Kantianism as epistemology aims at a reduction of the content of this philosophy, by robbing it of its depth, only to claim such a depth for his own thinking of Being exclusively.

The methodologically grounded formalism of Cohen's idealism should not be misunderstood as a theory of the justification of the factual sciences or, more precisely, the *factum* of the sciences. His virtue theory, which has been presented here in outline, is suitable to counter such a misinterpretation. The authentication of truth in Cohen's grounding science (*Grundlegungswissenschaft*) of pure rational cognition is anything but a theory of the justification of a *factum*. The authentication of truth takes place, rather, in the opposite direction: It concerns the *authentication* of the pure concepts of the philosophical grounding science in a concrete historical *factum*. Authentication, however, means applicability; and applicability means that the pure concepts of rational philosophical cognition are no fictions, and that their content agrees with reality as such, not with the reality of an *as-if*. In the exhibited applicability of the pure philosophical basic concepts lies, at the same time, the function of their critique—that is, their capacity for being critiqued. That these concepts are applicable to the *factum* of an historically inherited science does not mean that one science is in complete agreement with the other. It means only that there is something in the historically factual science that meets rational cognition halfway. Cohen's idealism understands itself as a critical idealism. As such, he draws the possibility of criticism from the respective *factum* of science—a *factum* in which pure concepts authenticate themselves. The philosophy of critical idealism provides the conceptual tools for a methodological critique as such in its applicability. At the same time it provides, by its difference vis-à-vis the *factum* of a science, a space for the critique of this *factum*.

The systematic *locus* of the ethical and the religious virtues in Cohen's system of philosophical rational cognition cannot be determined with exactitude. It lies between the grounding of the pure concepts and their authentication in the *factum* of science. In addition, their systematic *locus* within this grounding and within their authentication allows no unambiguous assignment of place. Thus, the systematic locus of the ethical virtues lies between will, action, and the correlation of self-consciousness and the consciousness of others. The systematic locus of religious virtues resides between these loci and the locus of the correlation of *Thou* and *I*. Regarding the authentication of the pure concepts of virtue, this cannot be limited to a determinate *factum*. In their validity, the ethical virtue of humanity and the religious virtue of peace reach beyond every *factum* of science toward a future humanity and toward the *factum* of a future science of human culture. Cohen's doctrine of virtue is one more indication that his critical idealism does not represent a closed system of concepts with fixed meanings. It forms, rather, an open system in which the modification of meanings is secured through the systematic nexus of these meanings, and which intends to secure the validity of rational cognition vis-à-vis relativism, through the conservation of continuity in these modifications.

TRANSLATED BY MICHAEL J. YSTAD

NOTES

1. Hermann Cohen, *Ethik des reinen Willens*, 5th ed. = *Werke*, vol. 7 (Hildesheim: Olms, 1981), 227.

2. [Editors' note: "Heautonomy" is a technical term in Cohen's philosophy of religion. The Greek *autos* means "self," whereas *heautos* means "oneself." It is thus comparable to the German reflexive, *sich selbst*. Cohen presumably means that autonomy, literally being the self-giving of one's own moral law, implies a reflexive relation to oneself. This is a reference to a distinction Kant makes in the third *Critique*. In his introduction to the work, Kant identifies autonomy as "a principle by which judgment prescribes . . . to nature," whereas heautonomy is a principle which "holds only for the subject," by which "judgment prescribes . . . to itself." Cf. Immanuel Kant, *Critique of Judgment*, trans. Werner S. Pluhar (Indianapolis and Cambridge: Hackett, 1987), 25.]

3. Hermann Cohen, *Ethik des reinen Willens*, 509.

WORKS RESEARCHED

Casper, Bernhard: "Korrelation oder Ereignetes Ereignis? Zur Deutung des Spätwerkes Hermann Cohens Durch Franz Rosenzweig." In Stéphane Moses and Hartwig Wiedebach, eds. *Hermann Cohen's Philosophy of Religion*. International Conference in Jerusalem 1996. Hildesheim: Olms, 1997. 51–69.

Edel, Geert. *Von der Vernunftkritik zur Erkenntnislogik. Die Entwicklung der Theoretischen Philosophie Hermann Cohens*. Freiburg and Munich: Alber, 1988.

———. "Zum Problem der Rechtsgeltung. Kelsens Lehre von der Grundnorm und das Hypothesis-Theorem Cohens." In Peter A. Schmid and Simone Zurbuchen, eds. *Grenzen der kritischen Vernunft. Helmut Holzhey zum 60. Geburtstag*. Basel, 1997. 178–194.

Fiorato, Pierfrancesco. "Cohen—Denker in dürftiger Zeit? Über Sprache und Stil der Cohenschen Hermeneutik." In Peter A. Schmid and Simone Zurbuchen, eds. *Grenzen der kritischen Vernunft. Helmut Holzhey zum 60. Geburtstag*. Basel, 1997. 77–94.

Gibbs, Robert. "Hermann Cohen's Messianism: The History of the Future." In Helmut Holzhey et al., eds. *"Religion der Vernunft aus den Quellen des Judentums." Tradition und Ursprungsdenken in Hermann Cohens Spätwerk*. International Conference in Zürich 1998. Hildesheim: Olms, 2000. 331–349.

Hake, Ann-Kathrin. *Vernunftreligion und historische Glaubenslehre. Immanuel Kant und Hermann Cohen*. Würzburg: Königshausen & Neumann, 2003.

Holzhey, Helmut. "Gott und Seele. Zum Verhältnis von Metaphysikkritik und Religionsphilosophie bei Hermann Cohen." In Stéphane Moses and Hartwig Wiedebach, eds. *Hermann Cohen's Philosophy of Religion*. International Conference in Jerusalem 1996. Hildesheim: Olms, 1997. 85–104.

Launay, Marc de. "Die Versöhnung als Abwandlung des Ursprungsprinzips in der Korrelation zwischen Gott und Mensch." In Helmut Holzhey et al., eds. *"Religion der Vernunft aus den Quellen des Judentums." Tradition und Ursprungsdenken in Hermann Cohens Spätwerk*. International Conference in Zürich 1998. Hildesheim: Olms, 2000. 77–87.

Levy, Ze'ev. "Hermann Cohen and Emmanuel Lévinas." In Stéphane Moses and Hartwig Wiedebach, eds. Hermann Cohen's *Philosophy of Religion*. International Conference in Jerusalem 1996. Hildesheim: Olms, 1997. 133–143.

Motzkin, Gabriel. "The Problem of Knowledge in Hermann Cohen's Philosophy of Religion." In Stéphane Moses and Hartwig Wiedebach, eds. *Hermann Cohen's Philosophy of Religion*. International Conference in Jerusalem 1996. Hildesheim: Olms, 1997. 145–159.

———. "Love and Knowledge in Cohen's 'Religion of Reason.'" In Helmut Holzhey et al., eds. *"Religion der Vernunft aus den Quellen des Judentums." Tradition und Ursprungsdenken in Hermann Cohens Spätwerk*. International Conference in Zürich 1998. Hildesheim: Olms, 2000. 89–104.

Munk, Reinier. "The Self and the Other in Cohen's Ethics and Works on Religion." In Stéphane Moses and Hartwig Wiedebach, eds. *Hermann Cohen's Philosophy of Religion*. International Conference in Jerusalem 1996. Hildesheim: Olms, 1997. 161–181.

Ollig, Hans Ludwig. "Die Aktualität des Neukantianismus. Bemerkungen zu einem unumgänglichen Thema der Neukantianismusforschung." In Peter A. Schmid and Simone Zurbuchen, eds. *Grenzen der kritischen Vernunft. Helmut Holzhey zum 60. Geburtstag*. Basel, 1997. 61–76.

Schmid, Peter A. "Die Tugendlehre in der ‚Religion der Vernunft.'" In Helmut Holzhey et al., eds. *"Religion der Vernunft aus den Quellen des Judentums." Tradition und Ursprungsdenken in Hermann Cohens Spätwerk*. International Conference in Zürich 1998. Hildesheim: Olms, 2000. 287–302.

Wiehl, Reiner. "Das Prinzip Treue in Hermann Cohens Ethik und Religionsphilosophie." In Stéphane Moses and Hartwig Wiedebach, eds. *Hermann Cohen's Philosophy of Religion*. International Conference in Jerusalem 1996. Hildesheim: Olms, 1997. 245–261.

———. Das Prinzip des Ursprungs in Hermann Cohens "Religion der Vernunft aus den Quellen des Judentums." In Helmut Holzhey et al., eds. *"Religion der Vernunft aus den Quellen des Judentums." Tradition und Ursprungsdenken in Hermann Cohens Spätwerk*. International Conference in Zürich 1998. Hildesheim: Olms, 2000. 63–75.

———. "Identität und Korrelation in Hermann Cohens System der Philosophie." In *Trumah. Zeitschrift der Hochschule für Jüdische Studien Heidelberg* 11 (2001): 29–49.

12

Is Cassirer a Neo-Kantian Methodologically Speaking?

Massimo Ferrari

"How does Heidegger understand Neo-Kantianism?" This is the question posed by Ernst Cassirer at the outset of his debate with Martin Heidegger in Davos.[1] While Heidegger considers Neo-Kantianism to be the "scapegoat of contemporary philosophy," he seems unable to name a single "existing Neo-Kantian." Cassirer, for his part, thinks there is but one response possible to such a question: "One must take 'Neo-Kantianism' as a definition not of substance but of function." This admonition serves as the historical and systematic principle by which to evaluate Neo-Kantian philosophy—of course not as a "dogmatic system, but as a line of questioning."[2] And this "line of questioning"—so Cassirer claims in Davos, April 1929—is captured in Hermann Cohen's transcendental method:

> I abide by Cohen's formulation of Kant's transcendental inquiry. For him, the essence of the transcendental method lies in its beginning with a fact; only, he narrowed this general principle, i.e., to begin with a fact, in order to ask about its possibility, by repeatedly proposing that it is mathematical natural science which is really worth scrutiny. This narrowed frame of reference is not Kant's own. Still, I inquire into the possibility of the fact of language. How can it be and how is it conceivable that we communicate, *Dasein* to *Dasein*, via this medium? How is it at all possible that we can see an artwork as an objective determination, as an objectively existing entity, as a meaningful whole?[3]

One can of course object that the purported "narrowing" of the transcendental method is foreign to Cohen's systematic approach, for that main figure of Marburg Neo-Kantianism also holds that every cultural "fact" must be investigated from the standpoint of transcendental justification. So, for instance, the justification of ethics in turn refers to the fact of jurisprudence and thus substantially co-determines the issue of the unity of culture—i.e., of the natural sciences and the humanities—which rests on the unity of reason.[4] And as Paul Natorp most clearly shows, it is "primary" for the Marburg School that transcendental justification refer back to "the existing, historically documented facts of science, of custom, of art, of religion" and "the entire creative work of culture."[5] Cassirer defends and further develops this perspective, and while he examines other 'facts' (such as language and myth), he in no way disassociates himself from this original approach of Marburg Neo-Kantianism. It must be emphasized that the mature Cassirer remained bound in principle to the methodology of the Marburg School. This surfaces not only in the Davos debate with Heidegger, but also in a series of similarly meaningful statements he made in the 1930s. For instance, in the preface to his study of quantum mechanics, which was published in Sweden, Cassirer writes that the question of whether he should be viewed as a "Neo-Kantian" is best dealt with by adopting Paul Natorp's view, as stated in his well-known lecture on Kant and the Marburg School: "Talk of an orthodox Kantianism has never been justified," and it has nothing to do with the intellectual development of the Marburg School, since Kant himself understood philosophy to be a method, i.e. "philosophizing," and not a philosophy. Hence it would be absurd to want to "absolutely hold fast to Kant's doctrines" and ignore "corrections that are necessary."[6] It is precisely in this vein that Cassirer wishes to identify himself as a "Neo-Kantian," so that this open stance toward Kant should also apply to the Marburg School without thereby eliminating Cassirer's "connection" to its main figures. Cassirer comments:

> As one sees, Natorp here relates to Kant much as a modern physicist relates to Galileo or Newton, to Maxwell or Helmholtz. He rejects every dogma by invoking Kant himself, who continually emphasizes that there should be "no classic author" in philosophy. In the same vein, my relation to the founders of the "Marburg School" is not weakened and my debt to them is not lessened should the following inquiries show that I draw markedly different conclusions concerning the epistemological interpretation of the foundational concepts of modern natural science than does Cohen in *Logik der reinen Erkenntnis* (1902) or Natorp in *Die logischen Grundlagen der exakten Wissenschaften* (1910).[7]

Can this "debt" be interpreted functionally, such that Cassirer's "philosophizing"—despite its distance from Cohen's and Natorp's solutions to certain epistemological problems—can and possibly must still be placed within the tradition of Neo-Kantianism and in particular Marburg Neo-

Kantianism? In other words, does Cassirer's philosophical *method* show him to be continuing that tradition, or does a transformation occur in the course of his intellectual development which would justify our speaking of a break with Neo-Kantianism? Cassirer should be allowed to speak for himself via a late, yet enlightening and somewhat retrospective text which he wrote while exiled in Sweden, in 1939. In the attempt he makes there to describe and define "subjectivism," Cassirer initially notes that he himself has often been billed as a Neo-Kantian. To this he remarks: "I accept the label in the sense that all my work in theoretical philosophy presupposes the methodological foundation set out by Kant in the *Critique of Pure Reason*. Yet many of the theories ascribed to Neo-Kantianism in the contemporary philosophical literature are not only foreign, but are diametrically opposed to my own views."[8]

It can unfortunately not be derived from the context which Neo-Kantian theories Cassirer takes to be foreign and opposed to his own. The more important point here, though, is that Cassirer once more identifies himself as a Neo-Kantian in terms of the methodological foundation of his theoretical work. Such a stance toward method does trace back to Kant's first *Critique*, but it is obviously meant in terms of the transcendental-methodological insight of the Marburg School. Cassirer is in fact continually concerned to present his "functional" interpretation of Neo-Kantianism as the further development of a method. Thus, in order to know the actual role the transcendental approach consistently played in Cassirer's thought, including his mature thought, we must better understand this methodological attitude and examine the relatively "weak" link between Cassirer and the Marburg Neo-Kantian tradition. Of course, this has to do not merely with the biographical or purely historical issue of Cassirer's membership in the Marburg *Arbeitsgemeinschaft*—a membership that in fact all Marburgers understood to be based on a shared methodological-systematic procedure, and not at all as inclusion in a school in the narrow sense, or a "sect" even.[9] Not coincidentally, Cassirer himself writes to Natorp in 1917, a time when the golden age of the Marburg School had already passed: "The superficial cohesiveness of the School continues to lessen; but the more each one of us tries to head his own way, the more we again approach one another in our concerns and aims. And that in the end is the best and surest confirmation of our connection that we could hope for."[10]

In respect to these systematic "concerns and aims," the methodological connection can be divided into four main topics: First, the development and function of the transcendental method. Second, the problem of the *a priori* and its dynamic interpretation. Third, the theory of categories, i.e., cognitive functions that underlie scientific experience and cultural forms. And fourth, the status of subjectivity and the relation of subject and object. These four systematic areas characterize some of the fundamental doctrines of Marburg Neo-Kantianism, as well as its characteristic transformation in Cassirer's more "liberal" conception—where 'transformation' implies neither a sudden break nor an overcoming.

The Transcendental Method

Cassirer repeatedly praised Cohen's concept of the "transcendental method" both as being "at the core of scientific philosophy" and as being a methodological principle in respect to Kant-interpretation, calling it "fertile, productive, and helpful."[11] Cassirer thought that Kant's theory of experience should be interpreted as beginning with the premise that Kant treated scientific experience and solved the question of synthetic *a priori* judgments within the framework of the transcendental conditions of the possibility of the "fact" of mathematical natural science. "The essential content of the Kantian doctrine is neither the I nor its relation to external objects, but rather what it primarily refers to is the lawfulness and the logical structure of experience."[12] It is for this reason that Cassirer dedicated one of the most original sections of his main work *The Problem of Knowledge* to a historical-systematic presentation of the long way "from Newton to Kant."[13] He also characterized transcendental philosophy as capable of demonstrating the "different forms of objectivity" only through the "mediation of a specific form of cognition." "The matter to which it refers is hence always already in some way formed"; 'reality' is accessible to it not *per se,* but only through the "medium of geometry and mathematical physics."[14]

This interpretation of Kant, still conducted in the spirit of Cohen, does not at all mean that Cassirer wishes to conceal his divergence from Cohen's view.[15] This divergence primarily concerns the radically *dynamic* way in which Cassirer transforms Cohen's motto, to "begin with a fact, in order to ask about its possibility." To be sure, Cohen based his *Logik der reinen Erkenntnis* on the "developing fact (*Werdefaktum*) of mathematical natural science."[16] Yet it was Cassirer who first took the historical and mutable dimensions of this "developing fact" seriously; with this, he linked the fate of critical philosophy to its relation to the development of the exact sciences. Cassirer thus locates the sole enduring task of a critical inquiry based on the transcendental method in the "continually renewed examination of the fundamental concepts of science, . . . which simultaneously effects a thorough subjective self-examination of critique itself."[17] But if the fact of science is "in its nature a historically developing fact,"[18] reflection about the forms of knowledge that underlie this fact and make it possible must also be characterized by a fundamental dynamism—a dynamism, which indeed co-determines the formation of the transcendental method and also enables its extension to all areas of mental objectifications.

These two points are not accidentally broached in Cassirer's marvelous text on the general theory of relativity. His concern there initially rests with the necessity of understanding relativity theory as a new scientific fact for "the domain of epistemological inquiry," in the face of which "critical philosophy too must examine itself anew."[19] Though Cohen, as Cassirer notes, took Kant's epistemology to be a systematic reflection on Newtonian natural science, the *Critique of Pure Reason* is clearly not to be seen as a finished and completely determined system, whose fate is exclusively linked to that of Newtonian physics. In other words, the transcendental method is not bound to a circumscribed form of the mathematical natural sciences. It rather demands going beyond Cohen's 'Newtonianism' to epistemological reflection on the problems that respectively emerge from the development of science.[20] This also has the effect that the transcendental method deals not only with a plurality of scientific forms or modes of object-constitution, but that it also treats "different formal principles," since reality can be characterized as a process of successive determinations. And such determinations are to be taken precisely as mental forms or as the sum-total of the forms of world-knowledge, as the totality of "the symbolic forms" (myth, art, religion, science, etc.).[21]

The latter point is crucial because it is precisely here, in the extension of the transcendental method beyond the privileged paradigm of Newtonian mathematical natural science, that the possibility of a "critique of culture" emerges for Cassirer. This critique is, on the one hand, still bound to the transcendental approach, while on the other it puts into question the triadic model of logic, ethics, and aesthetics which is standard for the Marburg School's philosophy of culture. The domain of linguistic expression or linguistic form, for instance, can be explored in Wilhelm von Humboldt's sense; as a fact or an objectification of mind, it must be considered from the perspective of the transcendental approach.[22] The same goes for myth, whose treatment in terms of a "critique of culture" only becomes possible when mythical thought is considered together with the "method of critical analysis." This is accomplished by adopting the principle that one must always start "with the given, with the empirically established and secured facts of cultural consciousness" in order to derive the "conditions of possibility" of the fact from its "reality."[23] The philosophy of symbolic forms, as a systematic examination of the different cognitive functions that underlie cultural forms and make them possible, thus represents an extension of the transcendental method—just as Cassirer emphasizes in his discussion with Heidegger, especially in reference to language. ("How can it be . . . that we communicate, *Dasein* to *Dasein*, via this medium?") "The concept of the transcendental," Cassirer explains already in the early 1920s, "is applicable everywhere the concern is with forms of mental lawfulness from which emerge an objective conception and an objective construction of 'reality.'"[24]

Later as well, Cassirer continually points out that the actual task of a philosophy of culture as a philosophy of symbolic forms consists in asking about the conditions for the possibility of cultural facts. This new formulation of transcendental philosophy as philosophy of culture,[25] which after all seems to have originated with Cohen himself,[26] is still in the foreground in Cassirer's notes on the problem of the "basis phenomena" (*Basisphänomene*) and in his Göteborg lectures on the problems of cultural philosophy (1939/1940),[27] as well as in his 1939 study of Axel Hägerström.[28] As Cassirer states in an earlier Göteborg lecture (1935), philosophy must take a step back from the various products of culture in order to grasp the mental "functions" and "energies" they generate.[29] It is not without reason then that Cassirer, in a lecture delivered a year later in London (1936), at the newly transplanted Warburg Institute, noted that philosophical inquiry into human culture aims at unearthing its conditions and examining them critically.[30] Even here, the "correlation of the principle and the principled" in the grounding of a cultural philosophy is what is at issue, its indispensability being taken for granted by Neo-Kantian cultural theory.[31] Cassirer's later clarifications can thus serve as the best evidence for his more 'liberal' version of Marburg cultural philosophy—without thereby assuming a turn away from Neo-Kantianism toward a hermeneutics of the cultural generation of sense or symbolic meaning, and without corroborating the picture of Cassirer as a purported 'Hegelian.'[32]

The Problem of the *A Priori*

From the perspective of seeing Cassirer's thought as representing a certain deviation but not a total divorce from Cohen and Natorp, we can now investigate the second question, concerning the status of the *a priori* and the *a priori* forms of knowledge. Even in this case, one can speak of Cassirer's *continuity* with Cohen's interpretation of Kant, which was so influential throughout the history of the Marburg School. Already in his epoch-making interpretation of Kant's theory of experience of 1871, Cohen located the real meaning of the *a priori* in the "indivisible unity" formed between the transcendental and the *a priori*.[33] Accordingly, the function of *a priori* forms lies in making experience, specifically scientific experience, possible: "The *a priori* is only the formal condition of experience that makes the latter possible at all."[34] For Cohen, along with the Marburg School as a whole, the task is thus not to ascertain the *a priori* determination of material contents, but rather to anticipate *a priori* the general *form* of experience according to the "plan of reason."[35] Starting from the present, historically determined fact of natural science, the critique of knowledge therefore aims to uncover the *a priori* presuppositions of and foundations for scientific facts. "For the *transcendental*," Cohen states, "refers to the *possibility* of a concept whose *a priori* or *scientific* justification supports its validity."[36]

So it is that the *a priori*, for Cassirer too, becomes identified as the "arch concept" (*Oberbegriff*) of the possibility of experience.[37] In his *Studien zur deutschen Geistesgeschichte* (1916), which are still strongly influenced by Goethe's morphological studies, Cassirer views the main task of the Kantian critique as locating the "stable structure of empirical objects" by means of transcendental analysis. In other words, such analysis "does not question directly what the object is, but asks what the claim to objectivity means in all cases; it does not determine any universal properties of the object, but rather drives at the sense of the term 'object' itself."[38] Cassirer summarizes this logical-structural determination of the *a priori* in *Substanzbegriff und Funktionsbegriff* (1910), by reinterpreting the *a priori* conditions of scientific experience for a "universal invariant theory of experience."

> The procedure of the "transcendental philosophy" can be directly compared . . . with that of geometry. Just as the geometrician selects for investigation those relations of a definite figure, which remain unchanged by certain transformations, so here the attempt is made to discover those universal elements of form, that persist through all change in the particular material content of experience. . . . From this point of view, the strictly limited meaning of the "*a priori*" is clearly evident. Only those ultimate logical invariants can be called *a priori*, which lie at the basis of any determination of a connection according to natural law. A cognition is called *a priori* not in any sense as if it were *prior* to experience, but because and in so far as it is contained as a necessary premise in every valid judgment concerning facts.[39]

This central passage gives the clearest overview of Cassirer's theory of the *a priori* and also forms the essential core of his theory of scientific experience as a universal invariant theory of experience.[40] For on the one hand, such a theory represents an original extension of Marburg Neo-Kantianism. On the other hand, a persistent presupposition of Cassirer's investigation remains to epistemologically justify the transformations of the physical world on the basis of a more 'liberal' view of the *a priori* conditions of mathematical natural scientific experience.

In fact, it is precisely because of this functional interpretation of the problem of the *a priori* that Cassirer examines the general theory of relativity at the start of the 1920s (and in particular the decisive issue of the role of Riemann's geometry within Einstein's physical theory), and that he inquires into quantum mechanics in the mid-1930s. In contrast to other Neo-Kantian 'immunization strategies,' Cassirer concentrates on the attempt to 'liberalize' Kant's apriorism so that it can be compatible both with the new physical worldview and with the loss of the "universal meaning" of the forms of intuition, space and time.[41] The same goes for the concept of causality in quantum mechanics, however, which is simply to be understood as "the general requirement of lawfulness."[42] Thus, it is necessary for Cassirer to epistemologically justify the theory of relativity and quantum mechanics based on a methodological view of the *a priori* as "process." This, however, also means that the essential contribution of modern physics is to uncover a purely functional or relational concept of objectivity that is not in the least anthropomorphic, to echo Max Planck. "There is 'objectivity' or objective 'reality,' because and in so far as there is lawfulness—and not vice versa."[43]

Cassirer especially emphasized the role of co-variance in the general theory of relativity, noting that it "summarizes the requirement not of the constancy of things, but of the invariance of certain magnitudes and laws as set against all transformations of the relevant systems."[44] If the theory of relativity is also to be classified within a universal invariant theory of experience or within the purely relational structures of scientific thought, then one must assume that in this case space and time, or better, spatiality and temporality, serve as conceptual tools or simple "schemas of connection" (*Schema der Verknüpfung*).[45] Here Cassirer is in accord with the Marburg treatment of Kant's transcendental aesthetic, which must be "corrected,"[46] and its tension with the spontaneity of thought as resolved by counting space and time as productions of pure thought and its *categorical* apparatus.[47] Accordingly, Cassirer has no trouble acknowledging the 'crisis of intuition' in modern physics and the necessary overcoming of the Newtonian 'paradigm.' In his opinion, it suffices to prove the "objective meaning" of space and time in the construction of physical theory and to view both concepts "not as rigid," but "as active and flexible forms."[48] This, however, entails that the *a priori* of space and of time be taken as pure forms of alignment (*Reihenform*) of following-alongside or following-after; as such they are "final ideal determinacies" that owe more, it seems, to the Leibnizian idea of an 'order of phenomena' than to the Kantian notion of intuition.[49] Such forms of "functional thinking" are only graspable as *a priori forms*—hence the *a priori* of space contains "no assertion regarding a single determinate structure of space in itself," rather it concerns "only the function of 'spatiality' in general," which is "wholly distinct from its more specific determination."[50] The question of the 'real,' Euclidean or non-Euclidean structure of space therefore loses "all relevance," as the new task at hand is to ascertain the *a priori* validity of spatiality as a general relation, and not to define its empirical measurement. The constitutive power of this more liberal, Leibnizian, relational *a priori* is herewith not put into question, and Cassirer—as he remarks in his polemical correspondence with Moritz Schlick regarding the epistemological interpretation of relativity theory—is convinced that Kant is in need of a "revision," since he bound the *a priori* forms of space and time to determinate contents in a one-sided and absolutely fixed manner.[51]

From this 'revisionist' perspective, Cassirer went on to further show that a *plurality* of dimensions or directions can be ascribed to the forms of space and time, *a priori* and freed from all particular content. So, for instance, it seems very reasonable to distinguish physical from psychological space, mythic from aesthetic space, as well as physical from psychological time, mythic from aesthetic time. The possibility then arises to define different *modalities* within a common *a priori,* i.e., form-giving ordering function, or—to use the terminology of Cassirer's mature cultural theory—to anchor the different "symbolic forms" in their symbolizing function.[52] In this way, Cassirer's more dynamic and liberal theory of the *a priori* is extended to include the whole world of mental forms and human culture: "The *a priori* now does not speak only *one* language, rather many idioms; but these idioms . . . still share a common grammar, namely that of symbolic forms."[53] Cassirer first adopted this perspective at the point in his philosophical career when he was considering the Marburg School's conception of the *a priori* together with the problem of freedom and autonomy. As stated in *Freiheit und Form* (1916), "the problem of the *a priori* and the problem of freedom [should be defined as] merely different expressions of one and the same foundational requirement. The autonomy of the will and the autonomy of thought entail one another and reciprocally point to one another."[54] If the *a priori* of knowledge and the freedom of the will are understood as "expressions" of a single lawfulness of reason, the next foundational step toward a philosophy of culture has already been made. For Kant's apriorism develops the tendency towards a "strict particularity" of its application in the various "cultural realms" via the *Critique of Judgment.*[55] And it is precisely because of this "enlargement of the realm of validity,"[56] which Cassirer emphasizes in his novel reading of Kant's third *Critique,* that the theory of the *a priori* and of the forms can be viewed as being in mutually productive harmony with one another, in reference to "the *whole* of natural and spiritual life."[57]

The Theory of Categories

The problem of the categories is intimately linked with the determination of *a priori* forms of knowledge and mental formation of symbols—in fact it essentially characterizes Neo-Kantianism and underlies its systematic contours.[58] And yet it is precisely here that the question concerning Cassirer's supposed Neo-Kantianism, albeit understood in a strictly methodological sense, either becomes more complicated or, following numerous Cassirer interpreters, becomes easy to solve by simply judging him no longer to be a Neo-Kantian. Now it is of course undeniable that Cassirer did not develop his own theory of categories; nor, which is even more striking, did he undertake any attempt to carefully distinguish his views from the relevant systematic reflections of his teachers Cohen and Natorp. This does not mean, however, that Cassirer renounced an *operative* use of the Marburg categorical apparatus; nor does it mean that he misunderstood or neglected the import of a categorical apparatus in setting up systematic philosophy.

To be sure, Cassirer viewed the problem of the categories from a special perspective. He attached epistemological primacy to a particular category, namely that of *relation,* which he took as the paradigm of all functional concept-building and every anti-substantializing interpretation of the problem of knowledge. In spite of Cohen's objections to Cassirer's concept of function, due to its supposed detachment from the systematic structure of the "logic of origin" (*Ursprungslogik*),[59] Cassirer was convinced that "we can only arrive at the category of thing through the category of relation."[60] Because of this foundational role of the concept of relation, Cassirer builds neither a complete system of categories nor one which rests on the four main groupings in the Kantian table of categories (such as we find in Cohen's *Logik der reinen Erkenntnis* or Natorp's *Logische Grundlagen der exakten Wissenschaften*). Rather, Cassirer develops a comprehensive historical-systematic interpretation of the modern natural sciences, which in essence represent a story of self-liberation—the liberation from every concept of substance. This story reaches its climax mainly thanks to relativity theory, which represents the "triumph of the critical function-concept over naïve thing and substance representation."[61] Within this hermeneutic scheme Cassirer is chiefly concerned to show how the *dynamism* of the categorical apparatus in science can supplant and to a certain extent dismiss the requirement for a *system* of categorical functions in science. Cassirer programmatically expressed himself on this matter at an important juncture in his masterful work on *The Problem of Knowledge:*

> The "fact" of science is and will of course remain in its nature a historically developing fact. If in Kant this insight does not yet appear explicitly, if his categories can still appear as *finished* "core concepts of reason" in number and content, so the modern development of critical and idealistic logic [here Cohen's *Logik der reinen Erkenntnis* is meant] has made this point perfectly clear. The *forms of judgment* mean for it the unified and active *motivations* (Motive) of thought, which course through the manifold of its particular formations and are continually put to use in the generation and formulation of new categories.[62]

In this presentation of the "idealistic logic" of the Marburg School, Cassirer has, to be sure, left the question concerning the "new categories" entirely open, and has also not further treated their principle of deduction (neither in the sense of Cohen's "origin" [*Ursprung*] nor in the sense of Natorp's "synthetic unity"). More specifically, Cassirer allows the "active motivations" of pure thought within modern mathematical natural science to emerge from the assumption that the categorical apparatus of scientific knowledge organizes those "elements of form" or "invariants" that "cannot be lacking in any empirical judgment or system of judgments" (e.g., the *relational* 'pure concepts of the understanding': space, time, magnitude, causality, functional dependence, etc.).[63] But these forms—and this is Cassirer's most important point—reveal themselves to be fertile and of foundational significance, also in respect to a theory of symbolic forms, i.e., a theory of the forms of world-understanding.

In the preface to the first volume of his *Philosophy of Symbolic Forms*, Cassirer famously speaks of an "enlargement in principle" of the "methodological grounding of the humanities" in line with the epistemological standpoint represented in his *Substanzbegriff und Funktionsbegriff*. This enlargement is to occur within the framework of the "'morphology' of the mind" that the "critique of culture" strives to be.[64] The basic idea is that every cultural form inherently possesses its own categories and forms of thought. So, for example, myth is characterized as a seemingly 'irrational' life and cultural form, yet one that also makes use of categories such as space, time, and causality which serve an explanatory function in so far as they can be defined as conditions of the possibility of myth as cultural 'fact.' Cassirer emphasizes that "mythological thought transforms sensuous impressions according to its own structural form, and in this transformation it makes use of certain characteristic 'categories' through which it assigns the various objects to various basic classes."[65] Such immanent 'structural forms' are hence as involved in myth as in language, in art as in science: It is the task of the "critique of culture" to point out these forms and to isolate them, according to a procedure that, in Kantian parlance, could be defined as a metaphysical deduction, i.e., an *expositio metaphysica*. Cassirer's problem in this situation lies not in supplying a 'deduction' in the sense of Kant's transcendental deduction, but rather to formulate a core reflection concerning the necessity of differentiating the main categories within the unified world of 'symbolic forms.'

This categorial differentiation comes about with the help of the distinction between the quality and modality of the cognitive and cultural forms: Whereas quality characterizes the determinate relation through which a category or mental form generates and grounds a series of elements, modality points to the context that determines the nature of that relation within a specific cultural form. So, for instance, time as a general relation is characterized by the determinate quality or lawfulness of "simultaneity" (*Beisammen*) in contrast to "succession" (*Nacheinander*); its modality however depends upon whether we are focused on the time of scientific knowledge, mythical time, or the intuited time of art.[66] To summarize: The quality of the categories expresses the stable structures or the invariants of human reason, while their modality depends on the respective context, i.e., the respective cultural forms (myth, language, science, art, etc.).

The categories, for Cassirer, are thus "the various expressions" of the *lawfulness* of reason in general.[67] However, he views this lawfulness mainly in its 'phenomenological,' i.e. in its historical-cultural manifestations: There seems to be no place within the framework of Cassirer's cultural critique for a logic of philosophy as theory of categories, in Emil Lask's sense.[68] Naturally one can interpret the *Philosophy of Symbolic Forms* as a variation of Natorp's late striving for an "infinitely open system of categories."[69] But from Cassirer's perspective, such a system chiefly aims to found a "critique of culture" that is an extension of the Kantian "critique of reason" and to trade in the "proud name" of ontology for the more modest "analytic of judgment."[70] The function which the "general theory of categories" plays in the founding of a philosophy of culture is therefore totally different from the one that the late Natorp ascribes to it, for in the meantime Natorp views the task, or more precisely the chief question, of philosophy in a completely different light than Cassirer does. Thus we read in Natorp's *Lectures on Practical Philosophy*: "The question of philosophy, in contrast to any other inquiries into being and meaning, concerns the whole, the all-encompassing unity of being and meaning."[71] And this divergence becomes even more evident in recalling that the late Natorp far-reachingly transformed the fact, that is to say, the Marburg School's fact of science, by identifying that basic fact, to which the transcendental question refers, with life itself—with that "primal factor" (*Urfaktor*) that is always becoming.[72] The task of a philosophical systematization hence consists in categorically grounding the *categorical system of the primal categories* (*Urkategorien*); the concern for Natorp, initially, is not to determine the categories of the natural sciences or humanities or of cultural creation in general, but rather to ascertain the limited number of basic categories (*Grundkategorien*) that reveal the meaning of being itself.[73] For Natorp, the chief question of philosophy must in the end be simply directed at the fact that there is anything at all: "the being not of science alone or of consciousness, but *being* as such."[74] Against this background of an 'ontological' interpretation of transcendental philosophy, as suggested in the late Natorp, we can suggest that Cassirer did in fact remain more loyal to the original approach of the Marburg School by repeatedly attempting to link the problem of the categories to the various 'facts' of culture.

The Status of Subjectivity

The last point that demonstrates Cassirer's 'functional' connection to Marburg Neo-Kantianism concerns the question of the relationship of subject and object. Here is most evident the extent to which Cassirer is grounded in the 'objective turn' of Neo-Kantian transcendental philosophy, which Cohen inaugurated with his interpretations of Kant on the unity of consciousness as the core principle of scientific knowledge.[75] In particular, it is Natorp's conception of the objective foundation of knowledge that enabled and encouraged this turn, in respect to the elaboration of a purely "reconstructive psychology" into a theory of subjectivity or a subjectification of the objective "world" of knowledge (and later the "worlds" of objectifications in general).[76] Natorp specially noted that "objective" and "subjective" refer to two correlative directions, i.e., to the opposed, unending tasks of objectifying and subjectifying,[77] in which the traditional subject-object relation, seen as poles of a relation whose *relata* are already assumed, must be transcended in favor of a method of reconstruction of the immediate contents of consciousness.[78] Cassirer for his part is in total agreement with this premise, though in the third volume of his *Philosophy of Symbolic Forms*, he criticizes Natorp's interpretation of objectification as still being too intimately linked with the scientific concept of law, and he laments the misguided understanding of its "morphological" plurality.[79]

In general, one can say that Cassirer, beginning from the standpoint of Marburg Neo-Kantianism, took a critical look at the Kantian problem of transcendental subjectivity. According to his interpretation, subjectivity refers only to the "lawfulness of cognition": It always "expresses a foundation in a necessary procedure and a universal law of reason."[80] All of this has of course nothing to do with the traditional concept of the subject of 'classical' empiricism.[81] Instead, Cassirer states, the actual meaning of subjectivity as justification for lawful reason is revealed in the procedure and methods of scientific knowledge, which in no way grasps 'reality' in itself, but rather grasps it "through the medium of geometry or mathematical physics."[82] The task of the transcendental method simply consists in going from an already formed material back to its conditions of possibility: Hence this "reconstructive analysis"[83] never assumes subjectivity, but rather reconstructs or can reconstruct it from its immanent and procedural relation to objectivity. Cassirer actually formulated these theses on subjectivity most clearly in *Substanzbegriff und Funktionsbegriff*, when he remarks that the concept of subjectivity can initially be defined "in a new sense" only from the standpoint of the concept of objectivity. For "the 'spontaneity' of thought is thus not the opposite but the necessary correlate of 'objectivity,' which can only be reached by means of it."[84]

Cassirer therewith lays the ground to sketch the plan for a "psychology of relations" that must validate "the inseparable correlation of sensations with the pure relations" or of perception with the act of judgment that always accompanies it.[85] Equally apparent is the fact that Cassirer is still working within the framework of Natorp's reflections, in respect to the "correlation" of objectification and subjectification as grounding the method of "reconstruction." Late in the 1920s, Cassirer characteristically discusses Natorp's *Allgemeine Psychologie*, especially emphasizing that the world of the "immediate" or of subjective experience must never be given through a "metaphysical intuition" or an "empirical observation." Quite the opposite: It becomes "indirectly accessible through a kind of systematic 'reconstruction' [that] provides us in general with the method by means of which we are able to expose the unique character of 'subjectivity.'"[86] What is however even more interesting in this context is the fact that in *Was ist Subjektivismus?*—an essay that is too often judged as proof of his final break with Neo-Kantianism— Cassirer cites the central propositions of Natorp's theory of subjectivity, in order to focus on the claim concerning the correlation of "subjective" and "objective." Cassirer is there mainly interested in grasping the process of knowing (and of formation in general) as one of "continuous progression," such that the poles of subject and object only gradually permit themselves to be defined within this unending movement. On this he remarks: "Yet the border between both determinations does not present itself once and for all, to be treated as an absolutely *stable* border."[87] If one supposes for a moment that "so-called 'subjectivity'" can be grounded or, if one likes, reconstructed based on objective assessments,[88] then for Cassirer it is clear that subject and object are not self-subsisting substances, but are "members in a functional relationship." They "are the expression of the process of separation and reunification" wherein consists the progressive determination of knowledge.[89] However, this *functional* interpretation of the subject-object relation, an equally important problem for other strains of 'physiological' Neo-Kantianism, does not only demonstrate the uniqueness of Cassirer's way of thinking: This interpretation also demonstrates the extent to which he remained indebted to Marburg Neo-Kantianism and in particular to Natorp, and why he took himself to be a Neo-Kantian in 1939, despite the fact that—to again cite the relevant passage—"many of the theories" that had been "ascribed to Neo-Kantianism in the contemporary philosophical literature," were "not only foreign, but diametrically opposed" to Cassirer's views.[90]

Conclusion

With this last point we return to the questions posed at the start of the essay. One can say, in summary, that to speak of Cassirer's 'Neo-Kantianism' is not reducible to any one sweeping statement. This obvious and uncontroversial triviality signifies that the systematic idea of Neo-Kantianism, and in particular of the Marburg School, involves a plurality of meanings—such that it is barely possible, without prior clarification of these meanings, to answer the question regarding Cassirer's place within Neo-Kantianism. Nevertheless, it seems plausible that Cassirer's systematic philosophy rests on several basic propositions of the Marburg School and that it can be viewed as an attempt to develop this systematic basis—more precisely, to take these propositions as the *operative* basis in regards to a more dynamic interpretation of Marburg Neo-Kantianism. The foundational role of "operative concepts" for Cassirer has long been recognized and widely accepted in Cassirer scholarship.[91] In this context it also makes sense to assume that Cassirer, methodologically speaking, always remained a 'Neo-Kantian,' that is to say, he continuously applied the critical apparatus of Cohen and Natorp to his own 'philosophizing' and 'operationalized' it.[92] But such a transformation is not of dramatic significance—it should not be viewed as a break from, but as a variation within the original philosophical project of the Marburg Neo-Kantians. One could even claim that Cassirer remained the true Neo-Kantian by rejecting the attempt at ultimate grounding (as the late Natorp attempted to work out) and instead trying to bring Cohen's early proposal (namely, that *a priori* forms of knowledge and culture are to be understood as *processes*[93]) to fruition.[94] To be sure, Cassirer's novel attempt at a "philosophy of symbolic forms" represents the greatest challenge ever to arise within the Marburg School; nevertheless, this challenge is not "to be located outside of (Marburg) Neo-Kantianism,"[95] rather it is best seen through the lens of the Neo-Kantian tradition. For Cassirer, too, there was "no classic author" in philosophy—as Natorp had proclaimed in his lecture on "Kant and the Marburg School," with reference to Kant's well-known conclusion against Eberhard. For Cassirer, too, it was entirely senseless to want to philosophize independently of all tradition—since the activity of philosophical thought is intrinsically linked to the existing 'facts' of culture, and occurs only within a tradition of thought. And it is also the case that, for Cassirer, Marburg Neo-Kantianism constituted such a tradition—the tradition in which he matured, with which he continuously had to grapple, and which in the end he indeed transformed, but certainly did not destroy.

TRANSLATED BY FRANCES BOTTENBERG

NOTES

1. We are quoting from the texts of the Davos debate found in the appendix to Martin Heidegger, *Kant und das Problem der Metaphysik,* 5th ed.
2. Ibid., 274.

3. Ibid., 294–295.

4. Cf. Cohen, *Ethik des reinen Willens*, 66ff., 83ff., 224ff.

5. Natorp, "Kant und die Marburger Schule," 196–197.

6. Cf. ibid., 193–194, 196.

7. Cassirer, *Zur modernen Physik*, 132–133.

8. Cassirer, *Erkenntnis, Begriff, Kultur*, 201–202.

9. On this topic, with reference also to unpublished sources, I refer the reader to Ferrari, *Il giovane Cassirer e la scuola di Marburgo*, 144–145.

10. Cassirer's letter, dated 1 January 1917, is preserved in Natorp's *Nachlass* (Marburg University Library: Hs 831/658) and was already partially cited in my work on the young Cassirer; cf. Ferrari, *Il giovane Cassirer e la scuola di Marburgo*, 145.

11. Cassirer, *Kant's Life and Thought*, 3; cf. also Cassirer, "Hermann Cohen und die Erneuerung der Kantischen Philosophie," 252–282.

12. Cassirer, *Das Erkenntnisproblem*, vol. 2, 662; cf. also Ihmig, *Cassirers Invariantentheorie*, 158ff.

13. Cf. Cassirer, *Das Erkenntnisproblem*, vol. 2, 396ff.

14. Cassirer, *Kant's Life and Thought*, 154.

15. Ibid., 3.

16. Cohen, *Logik der reinen Erkenntnis*, 76.

17. Cassirer, "Kant und die moderne Mathematik," 1.

18. Cassirer, *Das Erkenntnisproblem*, vol. 1, 18.

19. Cassirer, *Zur modernen Physik*, 7.

20. Cf. ibid., 8.

21. Cf. ibid., 107–110.

22. Humboldt's major contribution was to validate the "basic principle of the transcendental method" in respect to the fact of language: "The basic idea of the transcendental method: the thoroughgoing connection of philosophy to science, which Kant demonstrated for mathematics and mathematical physics, now seemed supported in a totally new field"—i.e., language; Cassirer, *Philosophy of Symbolic Forms*, vol. 1, 162.

23. Cassirer, *Philosophy of Symbolic Forms*, vol. 2, 11.

24. Cassirer, *Idee und Gestalt*, 68.

25. Cf. Graeser, *Ernst Cassirer*, 47; Geyer, *Einführung in die Philosophie der Kultur*, 34–52.

26. Cohen, for instance, spoke of the "cultural fact of religion," which in his view could be analyzed transcendentally; cf. Cohen, *Der Begriff der Religion*, 9.

27. Cf. Cassirer, *Philosophy of Symbolic Forms*, vol. 4, 165–166, 188–189; Cassirer, "Probleme der Kulturphilosophie," in *Nachgelassene Manuskripte und Texte*, vol. 5, 88.

28. Cf. Cassirer, "Axel Hägerström," 108.

29. Cf. Cassirer, *Symbols, Myth, and Culture*, 55–56.

30. "We are no longer studying the works of art, the products of mythical or religious thought, but the working powers, the mental activities that are required in order to produce these works. If we succeed in gaining an insight into the character of the powers, if we understand them, not in their historical origin, but in their structure, if we conceive in what way they are different from each other, we have

reached a new knowledge about the character of human culture. We can understand the work of human civilization not only in its historical but also in its *systematic conditions;* we have entered, so to speak, into a new dimension of thought"; Cassirer, *Symbols, Myth, and Culture,* 81.

31. Krijnen, "Philosophieren im Schatten des Nihilismus," 21.

32. In this sense we cannot agree with Michael Friedman's thesis, that "the philosophy of symbolic forms represents a decisive break with Marburg Neo-Kantianism," in that Cassirer there "deploys an historical dialectic self-consciously derived from Hegel," that is "quite incompatible with both Marburg Neo-Kantianism and Kant's original conception." Cf. Friedman, *A Parting of the Ways,* 99–101. Cassirer stands in deep contrast to Hegel, for Hegel cancelled out the difference between the facts of science and culture and the principles of reason, such that the necessity "in experience"—which for Cassirer forms the core of the transcendental question—becomes the "necessity of experience itself"; cf. Cassirer, *Das Erkenntnisproblem,* vol. 3, 371. In contrast to Hegel, Kant and the (Neo-)Kantian method wished to bring the "interminable work of intellectual culture" to the tribunal of reason, according to Cassirer, in order to discover its rules of constitution. "Critical philosophy," Cassirer adds, "recognizes these rules, without creating them as such: its task here as well is not to derive the manifold cultural forms and holdings, down to their details, from reason; rather, it is to evince the unity of reason as such in its various core directions, in the construction and in the structuring of the scientific, artistic, moral, and religious world"; ibid., 373. Cassirer—and this is important for our inquiry—agrees wholly with Natorp's critique of Hegel, who precisely summarized the central points of the Marburg treatment of Hegel; cf. Natorp, "Kant und die Marburger Schule," 212–213. On Cassirer and Hegelianism, see also Ferrari, "Preface," xiii–xvi; and Ferrari, "Natur- und Kulturwissenschaften. Cassirer, Hegel und der Neukantianismus," 67–78.

33. Cassirer, *Zur modernen Physik,* 41.

34. Cohen, *Kants Theorie der Erfahrung,* 1st ed., 100.

35. Cassirer, *Kant's Life and Thought,* 167.

36. Cohen, *Das Prinzip,* 7.

37. Cf. Cassirer, "Hermann Cohen und die Erneuerung der Kantischen Philosophie," 259.

38. Cassirer, *Freiheit und Form,* 158.

39. Cassirer, *Substance and Function,* 268–269.

40. Karl-Norbert Ihmig's work must be credited for revealing the role of the universal invariant theory of experience within Cassirer's scientific-philosophical *oeuvre;* cf. Ihmig, *Cassirers Invariantentheorie der Erfahrung,* and Ihmig, *Grundzüge einer Philosophie der Wissenschaften bei Ernst Cassirer,* 200ff.

41. Cassirer, *Zur modernen Physik,* 319; cf. Ferrari, "Il neocriticismo tedesco e la teoria della relatività," 239–281, and Ferrari, *Ernst Cassirer. Dalla scuola di Marburgo alla filosofia della cultura,* 111ff., which is also available in German translation: Ferrari, *Ernst Cassirer. Stationen einer philosophischen Biographie,* 99ff.

42. Cassirer, *Zur modernen Physik,* 268.

43. Ibid., 212, 279. On Cassirer's interpretation of quantum mechanics, cf. Schmitz-Rigal, *Die Kunst offenen Wissens,* 256–302.

44. Cassirer, *Zur modernen Physik*, 62. On Cassirer's interpretation of co-variance, cf. the penetrating analysis of Ryckman, *The Reign of Relativity*, 39–46.

45. Cassirer, *Zur modernen Physik*, 71.

46. Natorp, "Kant und die Marburger Schule," 196.

47. Cf. Cohen, *Logik der reinen Erkenntnis*, xii, 12, 26–27, 150–152, 188–192.

48. Cassirer, *Zur modernen Physik*, 70, 81.

49. Ibid., 78–79; cf. Rudolph, "Raum, Zeit und Bewegung," 58.

50. Cassirer, *Zur modernen Physik*, 93.

51. Cf. Ferrari, *Ernst Cassirer*, 140–141.

52. Cf. Cassirer, *Zur modernen Physik*, 107ff.

53. Orth, *Von der Erkenntnistheorie zur Kulturphilosophie*, 188.

54. Cassirer, *Freiheit und Form*, 157.

55. Cassirer, *Kant's Life and Thought*, 322–323.

56. Cf. ibid., 318.

57. Cf. ibid., 360.

58. A brief presentation of the major Neo-Kantian category theories can be found in my book *Categorie e a priori*, 151–164.

59. Cf. Gawronsky, "Ernst Cassirer: His Life and his Work," 21.

60. Cassirer, *Substance and Function*, 306.

61. Cassirer, *Zur modernen Physik*, 64.

62. Cassirer, *Das Erkenntnisproblem*, vol. 1, 18.

63. Cf. Cassirer, *Substance and Function*, 269.

64. Cf. Cassirer, *The Philosophy of Symbolic Forms*, vol. 1, 69.

65. Cassirer, *Wesen und Wirkung des Symbolbegriffs*, 22.

66. Cf. Cassirer, *The Philosophy of Symbolic Forms*, vol. 1, 95–96.

67. Cassirer, *Erkenntnis, Begriff, Kultur*, 57.

68. Interestingly, Cassirer critiqued Lask's theory of the categories elsewhere; cf. ibid., 10ff., 36ff.

69. Cf. Natorp, *Vorlesungen über praktische Philosophie*, 22; Cassirer, "Paul Natorp," 291–292.

70. Cf. Cassirer, *The Philosophy of Symbolic Forms*, vol. 1, 80, 316. Heidegger insists on Cassirer's "concurrence" with "Natorp's efforts"; cf. Heidegger, *Kant und das Problem der Metaphysik*, 310. It is in any event interesting to recall that Cassirer was well-informed about Natorp's project of a "general logic" as categorical doctrine; this perspective encouraged him in his own systematic work. This claim is supported by an unpublished letter written by Cassirer to Natorp, dated 8 September 1919, which is preserved in the Natorp-*Nachlass* in the University of Marburg library (UB 831/662).

71. Natorp, *Vorlesungen*, 72.

72. Cf. Natorp, *Philosophische Systematik*, 12.

73. Cf. ibid., 16–17.

74. Natorp, *Vorlesungen*, 5.

75. Cf. Cohen, *Kants Theorie der Erfahrung*, 3d ed., 752.

76. Cf. Natorp, "Über objective und subjective Begründung der Erkenntnis," 257–286; Natorp, *Einleitung*.

77. Cf. Natorp, *Allgemeine Psychologie*, 189–213.
78. Cf. ibid., 62, 71.
79. Cf. Cassirer, *Philosophy of Symbolic Forms*, vol. 3, 51–57.
80. Cf. Cassirer, *Kant's Life and Thought*, 151.
81. Cf. Cassirer, "Hermann Cohen und die Erneuerung der Kantischen Philosophie," 255–257.
82. Cf. ibid., 163–165.
83. Cassirer, *Philosophy of Symbolic Forms*, vol. 3, 57.
84. Cassirer, *Substance and Function*, 317.
85. Ibid., 342.
86. Cassirer, *Philosophy of Symbolic Forms*, vol. 4, 53.
87. Cassirer, *Erkenntnis, Begriff, Kultur*, 209.
88. Ibid., 210.
89. Ibid., 214–215.
90. Ibid., 202.
91. Cf. Orth, "Operative Begriffe," 45–74.
92. Cf. Marx, "Cassirers Philosophie," 82.
93. Cf. Cohen, *Kants Theorie der Erfahrung*, 1st ed., 38.
94. We cannot here discuss the possibility that even Cohen's "logic of origin"(*Ursprungslogik*) might not be a paradigmatic example of Neo-Kantian thinking in terms of ultimate grounding. The fact is that Cassirer did read Cohen's *Logik der reinen Erkenntnis* as such, and that he used it as a basis for comparison for his own program of functionalization. This thesis is supported, among other things, by Cassirer's reaction to Cohen during his fight with Leonard Nelson; cf. Cassirer, *Der kritische Idealismus und die Philosophie des "gesunden Menschenverstandes,"* 32 n. 1.
95. Paetzold, "Die Frage nach Ernst Cassirers Neukantianismus mit Blick auf Cohen und Natorp," 233.

BIBLIOGRAPHY

Cassirer, Ernst. "Axel Hägerström: Eine Studie zur schwedischen Philosophie der Gegenwart." *Göteborgs Högskolas Arksskrift* 45 (1939): 1–119.

———. *Erkenntnis, Begriff, Kultur.* Ed. R. A. Bast. Hamburg: Felix Meiner Verlag, 1993.

———. *Das Erkenntnisproblem in der Philosophie und Wissenschaft der neueren Zeit,* 2 vols. Darmstadt: Wissenschaftliche Buchgesellschaft, 1995.

———. *Das Erkenntnisproblem in der Philosophie und Wissenschaft der neueren Zeit,* vol. 3: *Die nachkantischen Systeme.* Darmstadt: Wissenschaftliche Buchgesellschaft, 1991.

———. *Das Erkenntnisproblem in der Philosophie und Wissenschaft der neueren Zeit,* vol. 4: *Die nachkantischen Systeme.* Darmstadt: Wissenschaftliche Buchgesellschaft, 1991.

———. *Freiheit und Form. Studien zur deutschen Geistesgeschichte.* Darmstadt: Wissenschaftliche Buchgesellschaft, 1975.

———. "Hermann Cohen und die Erneuerung der Kantischen Philosophie." *Kant-Studien* 17 (1912): 252–282.

————. *Idee und Gestalt. Goethe-Schiller-Hölderlin-Kleist*. Darmstadt: Wissenschaftliche Buchgesellschaft, 1971.

————. *Kant's Life and Thought*. Trans. James Haden. New Haven: Yale University Press, 1981. Originally published as *Kants Leben und Lehre* (Darmstadt: Wissenschaftliche Buchgesellschaft, 1994).

————. "Kant und die moderne Mathematik." *Kant-Studien* 12 (1907): 1–49.

————. *Der kritische Idealismus und die Philosophie des "gesunden Menschenverstandes."* Gießen: Töpelmann, 1906.

————. *Nachgelassene Manuskripte und Texte, vol. 5: Kulturphilosophie. Vorlesungen und Vorträge 1929–1941*. Ed. R. Kramme and J. Fingerhut. Hamburg: Meiner, 2004.

————. "Paul Natorp." *Kant-Studien* 30 (1925): 273–298.

————. *Philosophy of Symbolic Forms*, vol. 1: *Language*. Trans. Ralph Manheim. New Haven: Yale University Press, 1957. Originally published as *Philosophie der symbolischen Formen*, vol. 1: *Die Sprache* (Darmstadt: Wissenschaftliche Buchgesellschaft, 1988).

————. *Philosophy of Symbolic Forms*, vol. 2: *Mythical Thought*. Trans. Ralph Manheim. New Haven: Yale University Press, 1955. Originally published as *Philosophie der symbolischen Formen*, vol. 2: Das mythische Denken (Darmstadt: Wissenschaftliche Buchgesellschaft, 1987).

————. *Philosophy of Symbolic Forms*, vol. 3: *The Phenomenology of Knowledge*. Trans. Ralph Manheim. New Haven: Yale University Press, 1957. Originally published as *Philosophie der symbolischen Formen*, vol. 3: *Phänomenologie der Erkenntnis* (Darmstadt: Wissenschaftliche Buchgesellschaft, 1990).

————. *Philosophy of Symbolic Forms*, vol. 4: *The Metaphysics of Symbolic Forms*. Trans. John Michael Krois. New Haven: Yale University Press, 1996. Originally published as *Nachgelassene Manuskripte und Texte*, vol. 1: Zur *Metaphysik der symbolischen Formen*, ed. J. M. Krois (Hamburg: Meiner, 1995).

————. *Substance and Function and Einstein's Theory of Relativity*. Trans. William Curtis Swabey and Marie Collins Swabey. Chicago: Dover Publications, 1953. Originally published as *Substanzbegriff und Funktionsbegriff. Untersuchungen über die Grundfragen der Erkenntniskritik* (Darmstadt: Wissenschaftliche Buchgesellschaft, 1994).

————. *Symbols, Myth, and Culture: Essays and Lectures of Ernst Cassirer 1935–1945*. Ed. Donald Phillip Verene. New Haven and London: Yale University Press, 1979.

————. *Wesen und Wirkung des Symbolbegriffs*. Darmstadt: Wissenschaftliche Buchgesellschaft, 1983.

————. *Zur modernen Physik*. Darmstadt: Wissenschaftliche Buchgesellschaft, 1987.

Cohen, Hermann. *Der Begriff der Religion im System der Philosophie*. Gießen: Töpelmann, 1915.

————. *Ethik des reinen Willens* = *Werke*, vol. 7. Ed. Hermann-Cohen-Archiv. Hildesheim and New York: Olms, 1981.

————. *Kants Theorie der Erfahrung*, 1st ed. = *Werke*, vol. 1.3. Ed. Hermann-Cohen-Archiv. Hildesheim, Zürich, and New York: Olms, 1987.

——. *Kants Theorie der Erfahrung,* 3d ed. = *Werke,* vol. 1.1. Ed. Hermann-Cohen-Archiv. Hildesheim, Zürich, and New York: Olms, 1987.

——. *Logik der reinen Erkenntnis* = *Werke,* vol. 6. Ed. Hermann-Cohen-Archiv. Hildesheim and New York: Olms, 1977.

——. *Das Prinzip der Infinitesimal-Methode und seine Geschichte* = *Werke,* vol. 5. Ed. Hermann-Cohen-Archiv. Hildesheim, Zürich, and New York: Olms, 1984.

Ferrari, Massimo. *Categorie e a priori.* Bologna: Il Mulino, 2000.

——. *Ernst Cassirer. Stationen einer philosophischen Biographie.* Trans. Marion Lauschke. Hamburg: Felix Meiner Verlag, 2003. Originally published as *Ernst Cassirer. Dalla scuola di Marburgo alla filosofia della cultura* (Florence: Olschki, 1996).

——. *Il giovane Cassirer e la scuola di Marburgo.* Milan: Franco Angeli, 1988.

——. "Il neocriticismo tedesco e la teoria della relativitá." *Rivista di filosofia* 86 (1995): 239–281.

——. "Natur- und Kulturwissenschaften. Cassirer, Hegel und der Neukantianismus." *Internationale Zeitschrift für Philosophie* 16.2 (2007): 67–78.

——. Preface to Ernst Cassirer, *Le problème de la connaissance dans la philosophie et la science des temps modernes,* vol. 3: *Les systems postkantiens.* Paris: Cerf, 1999. i–xx.

Friedman, Michael. *A Parting of the Ways: Carnap, Cassirer, and Heidegger.* Chicago and La Salle: Open Court, 2000.

Gawronsky, Dimitry. "Ernst Cassirer: His Life and his Work." In *The Philosophy of Ernst Cassirer,* 2d ed., ed. Paul Arthur Schilpp (New York: Tudor Publishing, 1958), 1–37.

Geyer, Carl-Friedrich. *Einführung in die Philosophie der Kultur.* Darmstadt: Wissenschaftliche Buchgesellschaft, 1994.

Graeser, Andreas. *Ernst Cassirer.* Munich: Beck, 1994.

Heidegger, Martin. *Kant und das Problem der Metaphysik.* 5th ed. Frankfurt: Klostermann, 1991.

Ihmig, Karl-Norbert. *Cassirers Invariantentheorie der Erfahrung und seine Rezeption des "Erlanger Programms."* Hamburg: Meiner, 1997.

——. *Grundzüge einer Philosophie der Wissenschaften bei Ernst Cassirer.* Darmstadt: Wissenschaftliche Buchgesellschaft, 2001.

Krijnen, Christian. "Philosophieren im Schatten des Nihilismus. Eine Hinführung zum neukantianischen Beitrag." In *Sinn, Geltung, Wert. Neukantianische Motive in der modernen Kulturphilosophie,* ed. Christian Krijnen and Ernst Wolfgang Orth (Würzburg: Königshausen & Neumann, 1998), 11–24.

Marx, Wolfgang. "Cassirers Philosophie—ein Abschied von kantianisierender Letztbegründung?" In *Über Ernst Cassirers Philosophie der symbolischen Formen,* ed. Hans-Jürg Braun, Helmut Holzhey, and Ernst Wolfgang Orth (Frankfurt: Suhrkamp, 1988), 75–88.

Natorp, Paul. *Allgemeine Psychologie nach kritischer Methode,* vol. 1: *Objekt und Methode der Psychologie.* Tübingen: Mohr, 1912. (Note: No other volumes of this work ever appeared.)

——. *Einleitung in die Psychologie nach kritischer Methode.* Tübingen: Mohr, 1888.

———. "Kant und die Marburger Schule." *Kant-Studien* 17 (1912): 193–221.

———. *Philosophische Systematik*. Ed. H. Knittermeyer. Hamburg: Meiner, 1958. Reprinted in 2000.

———. "Ueber objective und subjective Begründung der Erkenntnis." *Philosophische Monatshefte* 23 (1887): 257–286.

———. *Vorlesungen über praktische Philosophie*. Erlangen: Verlag der philosophischen Akademie, 1925.

Orth, Ernst Wolfgang. "Operative Begriffe in Ernst Cassirers Philosophie der symbolischen Formen." In *Über Ernst Cassirers Philosophie der symbolischen Formen*, ed. Hans-Jürg Braun, Helmut Holzhey, and Ernst Wolfgang Orth (Frankfurt: Suhrkamp, 1988), 45–74.

———. *Von der Erkenntnistheorie zur Kulturphilosophie. Studien zu Ernst Cassirers Philosophie der symbolischen Formen*. Würzburg: Königshausen & Neumann, 1996.

Paetzold, Heinz. "Die Frage nach Ernst Cassirers Neukantianismus mit Blick auf Cohen und Natorp." In *Sinn, Geltung, Wert. Neukantianische Motive in der modernen Kulturphilosophie*, ed. Christian Krijnen and Ernst Wolfgang Orth (Würzburg: Königshausen & Neumann, 1998), 219–235.

Rudolph, Enno. "Raum, Zeit und Bewegung. Cassirer und Reichenbach über die philosophischen Anfänge des physikalischen Relativismus." In *Von der Philosophie zur Wissenschaft. Cassirers Dialog mit der Naturwissenschaft*, ed. Enno Rudolph and Ion-Olimpiu Stamatescu (Hamburg: Meiner, 1997), 45–61.

Ryckman, Thomas. *The Reign of Relativity: Philosophy in Physics 1915–1925*. Oxford: Oxford University Press, 2005.

Schmitz-Rigal, Christiane. *Die Kunst offenen Wissens. Ernst Cassirers Epistemologie und Deutung der modernen Physik*. Hamburg: Meiner, 2002.

Contributors

RUDOLF BERNET is Professor of Philosophy at the Catholic University of Leuven (Louvain), Belgium. He is author of *La vie du sujet: Recherches sur l'interprétation de Husserl dans la phénoménologie; Conscience et existence: Perspectives phénoménologiques;* and, with Eduard Marbach and Iso Kern, of *Edmund Husserl: Darstellung seines Denkens.* He is editor, with Dieter Lohmar, of *Husserliana XXXIII, Die 'Bernauer Manuskripte' über das Zeitbewußtsein (1917/1918).*

FABIEN CAPEILLÈRES is Maître de Conférences H.d.R. at the University of Caen, France. He is author of *Kant Philosophe Newtonien* and editor of Ernst Cassirer's complete works in French. The last of four volumes he has edited on Neo-Kantianism is *Kant et les kantismes dans la philosophie contemporaine: 1804–2004* (in collaboration with Christian Berner).

STEVEN G. CROWELL is Mullen Professor of Philosophy at Rice University. He is author of *Husserl, Heidegger, and the Space of Meaning: Paths toward Transcendental Phenomenology,* and the editor, with Jeff Malpas, of *Transcendental Heidegger.*

MASSIMO FERRARI is Professor of History of Philosophy at the University of Turin, Italy. He is author of *Retours à Kant* and *Ernst Cassirer: Stationen einer philosophischen Biographie.*

MICHAEL FRIEDMAN is Frederick P. Rehmus Family Professor of Humanities at Stanford University. He is author of *Foundations of Space-Time Theories: Relativistic Physics and Philosophy of Science; Kant and the Exact*

Sciences; Reconsidering Logical Positivism; A Parting of the Ways: Carnap, Cassirer, and Heidegger; and *Dynamics of Reason.*

JEAN GRONDIN is Professor of Philosophy at the University of Montreal, Canada. He is author of *Kant et le problème de la philosophie: l'a priori; Introduction to Philosophical Hermeneutics; Immanuel Kant zur Einführung; Sources of Hermeneutics; Hans-Georg Gadamer: A Biography; Le tournant herméneutique de la phénoménologie;* and *Introduction à la métaphysique.*

HELMUT HOLZHEY is Professor Emeritus of Philosophy at the University of Zurich, Switzerland. He is author of *Kants Erfahrungsbegriff* (translated into Italian); *Cohen und Natorp* (2 vols.); and *Neukantianismus.* He is the main editor of the critical edition of Hermann Cohen's works and co-author of the *Historical Dictionary of Kant and Kantianism.*

MANFRED KÜHN is Professor of Philosophy at Boston University. He is author of *Immanuel Kant: A Biography* and *Scottish Common Sense in Germany,* and has written many articles on Thomas Reid, David Hume, and Immanuel Kant.

SEBASTIAN LUFT is Associate Professor of Philosophy at Marquette University. He is author of *"Phänomenologie der Phänomenologie": Systematik und Methodologie der Phänomenologie in der Auseinandersetzung zwischen Husserl und Fink;* the editor of *Husserliana XXXIV, Zur phänomenologischen Reduktion: Texte aus dem Nachlass (1926–1935);* and has written articles on figures from the phenomenological movement and Neo-Kantianism.

RUDOLF A. MAKKREEL is Charles Howard Candler Professor of Philosophy at Emory University. He is author of *Dilthey, Philosopher of the Human Studies* (translated into German, Japanese, and Chinese) and *Imagination and Interpretation in Kant: The Hermeneutical Import of the Critique of Judgment* (translated into German); is co-editor of Wilhelm Dilthey's *Selected Works; Dilthey and Phenomenology;* and *The Ethics of History;* and has authored essays on aesthetics, hermeneutics, and the philosophy of history.

JÜRGEN STOLZENBERG is Professor of Philosophy at the University of Halle-Wittenberg, Germany. He is author of *Fichtes Begriff der intellektuellen Anschauung: Die Entwicklung in den Wissenschaftslehren von 1793/94* *bis 1801/02* and *Ursprung und System: Probleme der Begründung systematischer Philosophie im Werk Hermann Cohens, Paul Natorps und beim frühen Martin Heidegger;* and is editor, with Karl Ameriks, of *Internationales Jahrbuch des Deutschen Idealismus / International Yearbook of German Idealism.*

REINER WIEHL is Professor Emeritus of Philosophy at the University of Heidelberg, Germany. He is author of *Metaphysik und Erfahrung: Philosophische Essays; Zeitwelten: Philosophisches Denken an den Rändern von Natur und Geschichte;* and *Subjektivität und System;* as well as numerous articles on Plato, Spinoza, Kant, Hegel, Nietzsche, Cohen, Rosenzweig, Heidegger, Jaspers, and Whitehead.

Index

a posteriori, 78, 220–221, 223, 235
a priori, 28–29, 44, 47, 63–64, 70, 72–73,
    77, 81, 105, 114, 121, 123, 126, 133–135,
    138, 142, 146nn2,6, 152, 178, 181, 183,
    186–187, 194–195, 201, 205, 211, 216–
    217, 220–221, 223–224, 230–235,
    248n139, 249nn156,158, 257, 260–261,
    267, 269, 295–296, 298–301, 307,
    310n58; formal, 9; material, 76; syn-
    thetic, 133, 178, 296
absolute spirit, 114, 151, 255
acquired psychic nexus (*erworbener see-
    lischer Zusammenhang*), 258, 262–263
Adorno, Theodor Wiesengrund, 5, 283
aesthetic, 37, 77–78, 219, 223–224,
    247n120, 255, 260, 270n5, 297, 300;
    Aesthetics (Cohen), 119; intuition, 37;
    judgment, 31; space, 301. *See also*
    transcendental: aesthetic
Ampère, André-Marie, 204, 206
analogy, 46, 223, 266, 278
anthropology, 13, 255, 274–275, 277, 286
Aristotle, 30, 84n1, 147n20, 187n1, 208,
    222, 241nn47,65, 247n114, 248n139,
    272, 274–275, 280
art, 18, 37, 43, 51, 77, 202, 205, 207, 215,
    240n24, 256, 263, 265, 268–269,
    270n5, 293–294, 297, 303–304,
    308n30, 309n32

articulate/articulation, 31, 43–45, 50, 54,
    124, 164, 173n36, 180, 215–216, 263,
    268, 270, 274; differential, 44; discur-
    sive, 167
artistic expression, 263
As-if, 125, 290
autonomy, 48, 101, 104, 120–121, 217, 261,
    277–280, 286–287, 291, 301

Baden School, 3, 18, 115, 121, 123, 264. *See
    also* Southwest School
Baillaud, Benjamin, 193
Bamberger, Fritz, 131n59
Bauch, Bruno, 3, 20n11, 21n19, 89n39,
    90n52
Being (*Sein*), 51, 54, 57n20, 97–98, 100–
    101, 104–107, 110n39, 289; *Being and
    Time*, 21, 32, 95, 104, 283
Beneke, Friedrich Eduard, 245n91
Bergson, Henri, 1, 5, 17, 19n3, 194–195,
    225–228, 234, 236, 240n37, 243n80,
    253
Berkeley, George, 116, 231
Berlin Academy, 199, 240n27
Bernet, Rudolf, 15
biography, 262–263
biology, 65, 125, 254
Bismarck, Otto von, 2, 215, 258
Bolzano, Bernhard, 4

Bosanquet, Bernard, 125
Boutroux, Émile, 3, 17, 192–249
Boutroux, Pierre, 193–194; *On the Contingency of Nature's Laws,* 192, 219, 224
Brandom, Robert, 19n3, 150–151, 164, 170n3, 171n14
Brentano, Franz, 4, 19n3, 59, 61, 69, 85nn4,6
Breslau School, 92
British Empiricists, 61
Brunschvicg, Léon, 3, 180–181, 188nn7,8, 192–249
Buber, Martin, 18
Burckhardt, Carl Jacob, 253, 265–266
Burtt, Edwin, 180, 188n6

Calignon de Peyrins, Alexandre, 234
Capeillères, Fabien, 17
Carnap, Rudolf, 5, 12, 20n8, 190n16
Carnot, Sadi, 181
Cassirer, Ernst, 3–7, 10–15, 17–19, 20nn8,11,12, 21n16, 36–37, 41–58, 61, 63, 75, 77–78, 85n4, 86n8, 88n36, 89n39, 90n47, 91n68, 95, 97–98, 100, 102, 105, 109n23, 115–117, 122, 129nn9,11,16,17, 130nn25,31, 131n60, 151, 171–191, 263–271, 293–314
categorical imperative, 261
category/categorial, 13, 26, 34, 36, 43, 46–47, 62, 105, 117, 121, 140–141, 147n10, 152–156, 160–170, 173nn36,39, 174nn40,41, 188n8, 206–207, 232–233, 253, 255, 259–262, 267, 275, 278, 281–283, 286, 288, 295, 300–304, 310nn58,70
causal/causality, 31, 66, 74, 79, 87n20, 102, 117, 122, 150, 153, 156–157, 159, 161–164, 167, 169, 172n26, 174n39, 211, 219, 224, 232, 257, 259–260, 264, 300, 303
Christianity, 18
cognition (*Erkenntnis*), 4, 25–38, 43–44, 62–63, 70, 74, 76–78, 80, 82, 90n55, 129n21, 132–149, 152, 154–155, 161,

164–168, 170, 171n13, 174n40, 178, 210–211, 230, 274–276, 277, 279, 283–286, 288–290, 296, 299, 305; *Logic of Pure Cognition,* 16, 38n6, 134, 140, 273–274, 277. *See also* knowledge (*Erkenntnis*)
Cohen, Hermann, 3, 7–8, 10–13, 16, 18–19, 34–35, 37, 38n6, 59–60, 63–64, 70–71, 82, 84n3, 86nn8,13, 102, 115–120, 122–124, 127–128, 130nn33,34, 132–149, 151, 178, 188n2, 245n91, 249n159, 272–292, 293–294, 296–299, 302–303, 205, 307, 308n26, 310nn47,75, 311nn81,94; *Ethics of Pure Willing,* 18, 272–292
coherentism, 153, 157, 162, 171n14
common sense, 99
Comte, Auguste, 192, 197, 217, 240n22, 243n78, 254–255, 270n5
concept of function (*Funktionsbegriff*), 178, 299, 303, 305. *See also* concept of substance (*Substanzbegriff*)
concept of substance (*Substanzbegriff*), 178, 299, 303, 305. *See also* concept of function (*Funktionsbegriff*)
concept-formation, 255
conceptual content, 152
concretion/concrete, 6, 8–9, 11, 32–33, 36–37, 46, 48, 59–62, 65–66, 76, 79, 81–82, 200, 205, 257–258, 260, 263, 266–267, 269–270, 273, 281, 290
Condillac, Étienne Bonnot de, 200
configuration, 269
consciousness, 4, 13, 29, 34, 43, 48, 49, 51, 57nn19,21, 60, 65–69, 75–76, 79–80, 86n13, 87n23, 90n52, 98, 100–101, 114, 119–120, 124, 133, 136, 150–151, 154, 243n78, 261, 276, 287, 305; cultural, 297; historical, 101; immediate, 206; individual, 151; intentional, 27, 29, 68, 163; methodological, 116; natural, 71, 76, 88n34; perceptual, 150; time-, 90n59; transcendental, 29, 81
constellation-analysis, 17, 194

constitution, 21, 53, 70–71, 73–74, 77, 79, 88nn31,33, 90n55, 192, 195, 211, 214, 219, 221, 227, 232–233, 235, 253, 284, 297, 309n32; doctrinal, 34; transcendental, 45, 72
construction, 22–26, 31–33, 43, 64–66, 68–71, 73, 76–77, 89n37, 120–121, 128, 168, 201 206, 210, 229, 298, 300, 309n32. *See also* reconstruction
contextual explanation, 264–265
contextual structure, 263
contingency, 53, 179, 207–208, 210, 213–214, 216, 220–222, 224, 227, 247n129
continuum, 256–257, 269–270
coordination, 181, 183, 189n11, 265
Copernican revolution, 155
Count Yorck von Wartenburg, Paul, 94
Cournot, Antoine, 192, 194, 237n1
Cousin, Victor, 196, 198–200, 202, 204–205, 210, 239n10, 243n75, 244n84, 247n117
Cramer, Konrad, 68, 86n16
Cramer, Wolfgang, 20n13
crisis, 7–8, 12, 16, 125, 194–198, 201–204, 210, 212–213, 215, 217–219, 226, 236, 239n11, 300
critical philosophy, 6, 12, 61, 113, 178, 197, 228, 296–297, 309
Croce, Benedetto, 37
crossing points, 262
Crowell, Steven Galt, 16, 170n7, 171n10, 172nn25,27
cultural sciences (*Kulturwissenschaften*), 5, 18, 95, 253, 255, 259, 265–267, 270. *See also* human sciences (*Geisteswissenschaften*)
cultural values, 100, 256–257, 259, 261–263, 268–269

Darwin, Charles, 114, 197
Dasein, 10, 41, 44–46, 51, 53–54, 56n10, 57nn20,24, 101, 293, 297
Davos debates, 5, 15, 20n8, 21n16, 42, 45, 51, 56n6, 57n21, 85n4, 131n60, 293–294, 307n1

deconstruction, 5, 109n32
Descartes, René, 4, 13, 61, 119, 155, 180, 231–232, 241n47
descriptive phenomenology, 28
descriptive psychology, 28, 61–70, 258–259, 261
desiring, 66
destruction, 94, 95, 100–101, 103, 273
Dicker, Ernst B., 238n5
Dijksterhuis, Eduard Jan, 180, 189n8
Dilthey, Wilhelm, 2, 5, 11, 13–14, 18, 32, 94, 253–271
doctrine of v., 289, 290
Droysen, Johann Gustav, 94
Duhem, Pierre, 193, 229, 237
Dummett, Michael, 19n3
dynamic structures, 65

Eberhard, Johann August, 307
École Normale Supérieure (ENS), 193, 202, 205, 208, 210, 214, 218, 239n10, 240n29, 245n92
education/edification (*Bildung*), 60, 99, 193, 214–215, 225, 236, 245n92, 282
effective history (*Wirkungsgeschichte*), 101, 104, 128
eidetic intuition/eidetic reduction, 29, 33, 90n55
Einstein, Albert, 12, 182–187, 188n1, 190n22, 233, 299
empathetic identification, 267
empiricism, 16, 35, 75, 117, 121, 123, 150–174, 182, 184, 210, 231, 234, 254, 305
Enlightenment, 268, 273
epistemology, 5, 21n14, 33–34, 42, 63, 75–77, 82, 89n38, 95, 120, 123, 128, 133, 155, 172n23, 192, 194, 201, 208, 229–230, 233, 236, 237n4, 238n5, 289, 297
epoché, 67, 69
equity (*Billigkeit*), 284
Erkenntnis. See cognition (*Erkenntnis*); knowledge (*Erkenntnis*)
ethics, 13–14, 18, 34, 42, 121, 135, 272–292, 294, 297
Euclid/Euclidian, 178–179, 183–187,

189n14, 194, 233, 249n156, 300. *See also* geometry: Euclidian

existence, 8, 43, 51, 53–54, 62, 72–73, 95, 99, 114, 122, 124, 164, 183, 196, 203, 211, 213, 217, 219, 221, 224, 243n78, 253, 255, 257, 272–273, 276, 287

existentialism, 5, 8, 95, 283

experience, 10, 29, 32–33, 35, 37n2, 42, 46–48, 50, 53–54, 62, 67, 70–71, 74–76, 87n25, 98, 101, 103, 104–107, 114, 121–122, 126, 132–139, 146nn2,6, 147nn9,10, 150–158, 160, 163–168, 170, 174n39, 183, 185, 188nn4,5, 189n14, 190n18, 205, 211, 216, 220, 222, 231–232, 235, 253, 257–263, 268, 295–296, 298–300, 306, 309nn32,40; inner, 28, 257, 259, 261–263, 269; lived (*Erlebnis*), 5, 18, 32, 67–70, 88n36; perceptual, 16, 162, 165–168, 170, 183; reflective, 259–263, 269

explanation, 27, 28, 31, 51, 74, 80, 136–137, 146n2, 147n7, 148n25, 189n11, 197, 203, 213, 222–224, 226, 229, 258, 264, 268, 271n12; contextual, 264–265

explanation-understanding, 18

expression, 31–32, 38n6, 43, 47, 50, 51, 56n12, 118, 123, 138–139, 142, 162, 169, 183, 192–193, 211–212, 224, 232, 263, 275, 280, 297, 301, 304, 306

expressive formations, 32

fact/*factum*, 18, 27, 29, 31, 34, 47n7, 63, 65–67, 74, 87n23, 92, 98, 114, 133, 138–139, 147n7, 152, 188n5, 192, 200, 203, 206–207, 210–211, 219, 222, 227, 229–231, 235, 237n1, 249n156, 254, 265, 269, 276–278, 282, 287, 289–290, 293–294, 296–299, 302–304, 307, 308nn22,26; 309n32; of science, 35, 63, 136–137, 139, 141, 276, 289, 290

facticity, 15, 47, 51, 53, 137–138

feeling, 66, 119, 130n34, 201, 262, 270n5, 285

Ferrari, Massimo, 18–19, 89n39, 249n158, 308nn9,10, 309n32

Feyerabend, Paul Karl, 12

Fichte, Johann Gottlieb, 2, 13–14, 126, 151, 243n83, 244n87. *See also* Neo-Fichteanism

Ficino, Marsilio, 119

finitude, 10, 38n6, 41–42, 44–45, 53–55

formalism, 257, 289

formative activity, 44, 51

Fouillée, Alfred, 204

foundation (*Grundlage*), 139, 140–143, 148n25. *See also* grounding/ground-laying (*Grundlegung*)

Frank, Manfred, 10

Frankfurt School, 5, 6, 14, 283

freedom, 8, 102, 124, 155, 207–208, 212, 219, 231, 268, 301

Frege, Gottlob, 19n3

Freiburg, 3, 8, 41, 84n3, 97. *See also* Baden School; Southwest School

French School of Neo-Kantianism, 2, 17, 194–195, 237n2

Freud, Sigmund, 273

Friedman, Michael, 17, 20n8, 188n2, 189nn9,15, 190nn16,19,20,22,24, 232, 238n5, 309n32

Fries, Jakob Friedrich, 114

function/functional, 12, 25, 30, 43–50, 69, 76, 78, 88n31, 105, 109n19, 135, 138, 140–141, 143, 150, 153–154, 162–164, 181–183, 189n11, 194n5, 203, 205, 212, 219, 228–230, 232, 254, 264, 266, 285, 293–295, 297–306, 311n94. *See also* concept of function (*Funktionsbegriff*)

functional unity, 269

Gadamer, Hans-Georg, 8, 13–15, 28, 41, 89nn39,40, 92–110, 275

Galilei, Galileo, 12, 180, 188n7, 294

Garnier, Adolphe, 196

Gassendi, Pierre, 180

Geiger, Moritz, 36

generation, 8, 35, 42, 95, 193, 233, 246n100, 262, 298, 302

genetic, 17, 54, 59–62, 64–65, 72, 75,

77–82, 86n15, 91n60, 178–180, 188n8, 192, 235, 264
genetic analysis, 80–81, 264
geometry, 185–186, 207, 219, 230, 296, 299, 305; Euclidian, 178–179, 183–186, 189n14
German Idealism/German Idealists, 1, 5, 10–11, 82, 151
German *Kaiserreich*, 2, 7
German Romanticism, 10
Gestalt psychology, 44, 48
Gifford lectures, 225
givenness/given, 25–27, 29–30, 34–36, 44–49, 52, 63–66, 69, 72, 74, 77, 88n34, 116–117, 120–121, 123, 133–134, 138, 144, 146n6, 147nn7,10, 148n25, 150, 152–153, 158, 163–168, 170, 174n39, 180, 183, 186, 188n4, 192–193, 198, 201, 203, 207, 211, 220, 223–224, 227, 232–234, 240n35, 242n63, 255, 257, 261, 265, 268, 270, 289, 297; myth of, 162, 165, 173n36
God, 18, 124, 187, 196–197, 200, 203, 206, 209, 219, 222, 224, 243n83, 272, 277, 279–280, 283, 286–288
Goethe, Johann Wolfgang von, 51, 244n88, 246n99, 299
Goldmann, Lucien, 265
good/goodness, 123–124, 143, 233, 240n35, 243n83, 272–288
Göttingen Circle, 27
gravity, 184, 186
Green, Thomas Hill, 125
Grondin, Jean, 15, 109n19
grounding/ground-laying (*Grundle-gung*), 16, 33, 88n36, 106, 123, 139–145, 148n25, 274, 289. *See also* foundation (*Grundlage*); ultimate grounding (*Letztbegründung*)
Guattari, Félix, 37n1
Guéroult, Martial, 194, 237n2

Habermas, Jürgen, 14, 109n22
Hägerström, Axel, 298
Haldane, Richard Burdon, 125

Hartmann, Nicolai, 35–36, 86n8, 93–94, 96, 101–102, 108n9, 109n28
heautonomy, 278, 291n2
Hegel, Georg Wilhelm Friedrich, 1–2, 55, 86n16, 102, 109n20, 114, 117–118, 150–152, 171n14, 196–201, 215–217, 233, 239n18, 240nn24,27, 243n83, 244n8, 245n91, 254, 309n32
Hegel Society, 97
Hegelian/Hegelianism, 12, 41, 102–103, 117, 119, 124, 150, 181, 198–199, 216, 239n18, 298, 309n32
Heidegger, Martin, 1, 5, 8, 10–11, 13–16, 20n8, 21nn15,16, 30–32, 35, 37n3, 38n6, 41–58, 84n2, 85nn4,8, 89n37, 92–109, 115, 127–128, 131n60, 167, 171n10, 172nn23,27, 194, 239n8, 253, 273, 283, 289, 293–294, 297, 307n1, 310n70
Heidelberg, 3, 8, 87n16, 96–97, 121, 215–219. *See also* Baden School; Southwest School
Heidelberger, Michael, 230, 238n5, 248n139
Heimsoeth, Heinz, 36
Held, Klaus, 28
Henrich, Dieter, 10
Herbart, Johann Friedrich, 114
hermeneutics, 5, 8, 14, 18, 41–58, 92–93, 95, 99, 106, 107n1, 194, 208, 234, 253, 263–264, 275, 298; of facticity, 15
Herzl, Theodor, 84n3
historical context, 41, 186, 248n138, 262–263, 266
historicism, 201, 253, 270n1
historicity, 95, 253, 289
history of concepts (*Begriffsgeschichte*), 13–15, 98, 102–103
history of effects (*Wirkungsgeschichte*). *See* effective history (*Wirkungsgeschichte*)
history of philosophy. *See* philosophy, history of
history of problems (*Problemge-schichte*), 13, 15, 98, 101–102

Hitler, Adolf, 7, 20n11
Hobbes, Thomas, 180
Holzhey, Helmut, 15, 20n7, 21n15, 75, 85n3, 86nn10,12, 89n39, 141, 145, 148n29
Hönigswald, Richard, 3, 7–8, 92–94, 96, 98, 100, 102, 104–105, 109n23
horizon, 31–32, 46, 48, 77–78, 99, 167, 289
Horkheimer, Max, 5, 120
human sciences (*Geisteswissenschaften*). *See* sciences, human
humanism, 5, 99–100, 269
Humboldt, Wilhelm von, 218, 297, 308n22
Hume, David, 113, 129n21, 210, 233, 260
Husserlian/Husserl, Edmund, 1, 4, 6, 8, 10–15, 21nn17,18, 25–40, 41–58, 59–91, 93–94, 97, 108n12, 117, 119, 131n36, 154, 166; *Crisis of European Sciences and Transcendental Phenomenology*, 61, 71, 86n8; *Ideas I* and *II*, 37n4, 52, 60, 67, 72, 78, 80, 84n1, 85n4, 88n31, 90nn50,56
hypothesis, 140–141, 143–146, 147n16, 148nn20,25, 210, 257, 269, 286
hypothetical, 133, 188n5, 220, 226, 258, 268, 271n12, 277

idea, 5–7, 12–14, 16, 18, 20n11, 27, 29, 35–36, 41, 62, 67, 69, 71, 75, 79, 82, 85n6, 95–96, 98, 100–101, 103–104, 114, 116–117, 119–121, 123–124, 126, 128, 136–140, 142–145, 147n16, 151–155, 157, 159–160, 165, 173n36, 179, 182, 186, 188n8, 196, 198, 199, 201–202, 206, 208–211, 213, 215, 219, 223–224, 227–228, 231, 234, 243nn80,83, 245n92, 254–255, 257, 259, 269, 272–277, 279–289, 300, 303, 307, 308n22; Platonic, 45, 143, 179
ideal limit, 179
ideal object, 46–47, 53
idealism, 6, 20n7, 34, 60, 71, 85n6, 117–118, 180n10, 199, 215–216, 231, 244n84, 255, 279, 289–290;

critical, 275, 288–290; Kantian, 116; methodological, 118; modern philosophical, 180, 182; psychological, 116; transcendental, 61, 71, 117, 119, 122, 274
idiographic, 18, 256. *See also* nomothetic
imagination, 24, 44, 52, 55, 260–261, 263
individual/individuality, 7, 18, 25–26, 30, 46–47, 51, 53, 78, 118, 124–125, 135, 150–151, 161, 167, 201–202, 205, 223, 240n35, 254–256, 258–259, 262–265, 267–270, 272–273, 281–283, 285–287
inference/inferential, 151, 153, 156, 162–164
inferentialism, 151
intentional consciousness, 27, 29, 68, 163
internalism, 151
interpretation, 9–10, 12–13, 16–17, 19n4, 21n15, 25, 27–28, 30–31, 38n6, 44–45, 57n20, 63–64, 69, 76, 80n81, 94, 100, 115–116, 119–120, 122, 126–128, 132–134, 137, 140, 143–145, 147nn10,16, 148nn25,29, 151, 167, 180, 182, 194, 199, 206–207, 222–223, 228–231, 233–234, 236, 238n5, 239n8, 248n138, 255, 259–260, 263, 294–296, 298–299, 301–302, 304–307, 309n43, 310n44; misinterpretation, 289; reinterpretation, 30; self-interpretation, 38n6, 61, 90n59
introspection, 28, 62, 69, 254, 261, 263
intuition, 15, 25–40, 43, 45, 47, 50, 56n12, 62, 69, 80, 87n16, 94, 105, 114, 117, 121, 129, 133, 135, 151–153, 155, 173n36, 183, 206, 210, 219, 234–236, 249n158, 261, 268, 300, 306; eidetic, 33; of essences, 30, 32; originarily giving, 26, 27, 31–32, 35, 37n2
intuitive fulfillment, 26, 30

James, William, 125
Janet, Paul, 193, 196, 198–199, 202–204, 209–210, 213–215, 218, 221, 230, 239n17, 240n27, 242nn59,60,63, 243nn80,83, 244n84
Jaspers, Karl, 273

Jouffroy, Théodore Simon, 199–200, 202, 210
Judaism, 18, 84n3, 148n25, 282, 288–289
judgment, 16, 31, 64, 72, 76–77, 99, 123–124, 135, 140, 142, 144, 151–154, 156, 159–161, 166–170, 173n35, 205, 209, 230, 232, 234–235, 249n15, 286, 288, 291n2, 296, 299, 302–304, 306; reflective, 260–261; determinant, 260
jurisprudence, 276, 286, 294; *factum* of, 276–278, 282, 287
justification (*Rechtsgrund/Rechtfertigung*), 64, 76, 98, 136–137, 139, 151, 154–158, 165, 169, 171nn13,15, 173n35, 202, 219, 289, 293–294, 299, 305

Kern, Iso, 60, 80, 84n2, 85n5, 90n59, 91n65
Kierkegaard, Søren, 5, 95, 122
knowledge (*Erkenntnis*), 13, 41–43, 55, 63–64, 71, 78, 87n16, 92–93, 98–100, 102, 106, 109n24, 113, 117, 120, 127, 129n21, 133–134, 151–155, 157–158, 171n10, 172n23, 178–180, 182–183, 188n4, 195, 200, 202–203, 205–208, 210, 215–219, 222, 227, 229–233, 244n83, 246n95, 257, 259, 261, 267–268, 270n5, 284, 288, 296–299, 301–307, 309n30; genetic conception of, 17, 178–180. *See also* cognition (*Erkenntnis*)
Köhnke, Klaus-Christian, 2, 20nn7,13, 114, 119, 129nn3,4, 130n33, 147n10, 170n7
Koyré, Alexandre, 180–181, 188n7, 189nn8,9,12, 194, 236, 237n4
Kroner, Richard, 35
Kühn, Manfred, 16
Kühneman, Eugen, 92
Kuhnian/Kuhn, Thomas Samuel, 2, 12, 17, 177–191

Lacan, Jacques, 97
Lachelas, G., 234
Lachelier, Jules, 3, 17, 193–194, 196, 200,

202–206, 209–216, 218, 225, 227, 230–232, 236, 241n55, 242nn60,75, 243nn78,80, 244n84, 247nn117,120
Landgrebe, Ludwig, 28, 85n4
Lange, Friedrich Albert, 3, 135, 147n10, 188n8, 245n91
language, 6, 42–44, 49–52, 54–55, 70, 78, 97–98, 103–107, 110n39, 159, 169, 200, 208, 224, 264, 267, 293–294, 297, 301, 303–304, 308n22
Laplace, Pierre-Simon, 200
Lask, Emil, 3, 5–6, 16, 150–174, 304
Lavoisier, Antoine Laurent de, 181
law/lawfulness, 16, 18, 31, 49, 63–66, 76, 80, 89n44, 102, 117, 133–134, 136–139, 142, 144–146, 147n7, 148n25, 157, 159, 181, 186, 189nn11,14, 192, 197, 201, 203, 205, 207, 210–213, 215–217, 219, 220, 222–225, 227, 229, 233, 235, 247n120, 254, 256–257, 260, 264–265, 270nn1,5, 276, 278, 283, 285, 287, 289, 291n2, 296–297, 299–301, 304–305
Lazarus, Moritz, 28
Le Roy, Edouard, 226–229, 235, 247n129, 248n133
Lebensphilosophie (philosophy of life, life-philosophy), 14
legal community, 278–281, 287
legal person, 276–277, 279, 281–282
Leibniz, Gottfried Wilhelm, 13, 180, 205–206, 241n47, 244n83
Leibnizian/Leibnizianism, 36, 118, 200, 206, 234, 300
Lembeck, Karl-Heinz, 119, 147n16
Lessing, Gottfried Ephraim, 268
Levinas, Emmanuel, 19, 280
Liebmann, Otto, 3, 114–115, 129nn3,4, 245n91
life-world, 8–9, 11
limit/limitation, 26, 63, 80, 87n20, 109n24, 121, 124, 145, 172n26, 179, 192, 201, 203, 211–213, 215–216, 228, 230, 234, 284; delimitation/delimited, 37n4, 212, 219, 222, 229, 235, 255; unlimited, 165

limitlessness, 16, 152, 155, 159–161, 170
Littré, Émile, 197, 199, 217, 240n22
lived present, 79, 80
Locke, John, 155, 231
logic: formal, 154, 180; of origin (*Ursprungslogik*), 140, 143–144, 274–275, 285, 302, 311n94; transcendental, 16, 117, 121, 127, 150–174
logical positivism, 14, 249n159
Lotze, Rudolf Hermann, 4, 13, 16, 115, 117, 119, 124–125, 156, 172n26
Löwith, Karl, 96
Luft, Sebastian, 15, 37
Luhmann, Niklas, 14

Mach, Ernst, 185
Mahnke, Dietrich, 13
Maier, Anneliese, 180, 188n7, 189n8
Maine de Biran, François-Pierre-Gonthier, 17, 200, 204, 214
Makkreel, Rudolf A., 18
Marburg School, 3–6, 8, 15–19, 20n11, 32, 34–36, 41, 60, 62–63, 82, 84nn1,3, 86n13, 88n36, 89n40, 91n68, 92–93, 96, 115–116, 118–124, 127–128, 151, 155, 163, 171n14, 178–180, 183, 185–187, 188n2, 189n10, 190n18, 216, 264, 289, 293–307, 309n32
Marx, Karl, 101
Marx, Wolfgang, 120
mathematical-natural science, 18, 120, 133, 136–139, 141, 178, 293, 296–297, 199, 303
mathematics/mathematical, 25–26, 85n6, 117, 119–120, 133–135, 146n2, 163, 178–187, 189nn10,11, 190n18, 197, 200, 207, 219, 223, 226, 230, 232, 234–235, 148n148, 249n157, 254, 277, 293, 296, 305, 308n22
matter/material, 35, 49, 75, 116–117, 119–122, 153, 155, 161–170, 173n39, 174n40, 181, 205, 209–210, 219, 220, 233–234, 244n88, 255–256, 267, 281, 285, 296, 298–299, 305
Maxwell, Grover, 294

McDowell, John Henry, 9, 16, 150–174
meaning/meaningful, 12, 14, 26, 31–32, 34, 37, 44–54, 63, 68, 77–78, 102–103, 106–107, 118, 130n34, 131n51, 132–133, 140, 144, 152, 154, 158–163, 165–170, 172n27, 174n39, 177, 185–186, 190n22, 195, 197, 200–201, 205–207, 219, 223–225, 229–230, 232, 234, 236, 247n120, 248nn120,139, 255, 258, 260–268, 278, 283, 285, 290, 293, 294, 298–300, 304–305, 307; intention, 26; structures, 181, 161; objective, 45, 116, 300; word, 26
meaning-giving, 43
meaning-intention, 26
Merleau-Ponty, Maurice, 44, 55n3
metaphor/metaphorical, 46, 206–207
metaphysics, 17, 67, 72, 93, 96–97, 105–107, 113, 128, 133, 144, 142–249, 172n27; of science, 17, 192–249; *Metaphysics of Morals* (Kant), 276, 282
method: phenomenological, 28, 30, 32, 25, 60, 86n10, 87n16, 90n55, 91n60; reconstructive (of reconstruction), 61–62, 65–67, 72–74, 78, 81–82, 86n16, 89n39, 133, 305; transcendental, 6, 15–16, 19n4, 34–35, 60, 63–64, 69–70, 73, 76–77, 79, 82, 90n55, 116–117, 126, 133–136, 138, 147n8, 216, 260, 276, 289, 293, 295–297, 305, 308n22
Metzger, Hélène, 180–181, 188n7, 189n8
Meyerson, Émile, 180–181, 188nn7,8, 189nn9,10,12 193–194, 229, 236–237
Mill, John Stuart, 201, 210, 234, 242n75, 254–255, 270n5
moral sciences. *See* sciences: moral
Moran, Dermot, 87n22
Müller, Johann, 245n91
myth, 36, 43, 45, 47, 50–51, 54, 55n3, 57n20, 78, 91n68, 258, 288, 294, 297, 301, 303–304, 308n30

Nagel, Thomas, 10, 87n20
National Socialism, 96
Natorp, Paul, 2–6, 8, 10–11, 13, 15, 18,

32–35, 37nn4,5, 51–52, 57n22, 59–91,
92–94, 96–98, 102, 106–107, 108n14,
115–119, 122–123, 127–128, 130nn25,34,
151, 178, 188n2, 189n10, 294–295, 298,
302–307, 308n10, 309n32, 310n70
natural attitude, 29, 71–72, 74–75,
88nn34,35
natural sciences. *See* sciences: natural
naturalism, 116, 118–119, 122–123, 126,
130n25, 159, 201, 203, 225
Neo-Fichteanism, 2, 19n6
Newtonian/Newton, Isaac, 177–178,
182–187, 188n1, 189n13, 294, 296–297,
300
nexus (*Zusammenhang*), 18, 32, 142,
257–258, 290; acquired psychic
(*erworbener seelischer Zusammenhang*), 258, 262–263; psychic, 263
Nietzschean/Nietzsche, Friedrich Wilhelm, 5, 11, 16, 115, 122, 125, 130n34,
273, 288–289
nihilism, 289
nomothetic, 18, 256. *See also* idiographic
norm/normative, 64, 125, 152–154, 156–
161, 165, 167–168, 170, 174nn39,40,
269, 275, 282
normativity, 117, 126, 152, 156, 160
noumena, 44, 155, 157, 231
Nourrisson, Jean-Félix, 214, 218, 243n83

objective presence, 32
objectivity, 53, 65–66, 68, 70–71, 73, 77,
79, 87n20, 89n37, 90n55, 134, 139, 142,
164, 179, 182, 256–257, 296, 299–300,
305
Odebrecht, Rudolf, 56n6
Ollig, Hans-Ludwig, 84n3, 170n7
ontic, 156, 161, 168, 172nn26,27
ontological difference, 46, 66, 70, 73
ontology, 5, 42, 51–52, 57n20, 77, 106–
107, 122–123, 128, 171n10, 172n27, 181,
187n1, 190n18, 209, 304
origin (*Ursprung*), 16, 27, 32, 34, 43, 52,
79, 90n55, 120, 132–149, 197–198, 204,
208, 213, 216, 219, 223–224, 229, 232,

235, 274–276, 280, 285–287, 302–303,
308n30, 311n94
originary-intuitive givenness, 30
Orth, Ernst Wolfgang, 36

panlogism, 153, 171n14
paradigm, 8, 82, 86n13, 87n16, 169, 177–
178, 187, 207, 217, 274, 278, 297, 300,
302
Pasteur, Louis, 193, 246n100
perception, 15, 30–32, 41–58, 122, 150,
152–154, 156–157, 159, 161, 163, 165–
168, 182, 194, 206, 261, 275, 306
Pfänder, Alexander, 36
phenomenological description, 36, 60,
69, 94
phenomenology/phenomenological,
4–6, 8–11, 13–15, 19n3, 21nn15,17,
25–40, 41–42, 44–45, 51–53, 55nn2,3,
56n12, 59–91, 94–95, 127, 129n8, 154,
170n7, 253, 304; descriptive, 28; genetic, 60, 75, 78, 80–82, 91n60; static,
91n60; transcendental, 29, 53, 59–61,
75, 79, 90n55
phenomenon/phenomena, 2, 7, 27, 29,
31–32, 44–50, 65–68, 126, 155, 157,
174n41, 177, 181, 189n14, 197, 204–205,
207, 210–211, 216, 220–222, 224–225,
231, 233–235, 243n80, 256–257, 259–
260, 264, 298, 300
philology/philological, 12–13, 97, 108n12,
116, 120, 128, 255
philosophical psychology, 10, 33, 59–60,
62–63, 65, 75, 83, 84n1, 87n20
philosophy: analytic/continental, 3, 10,
19n3; history of, 9, 12, 13, 15, 98, 102–
104, 126, 128, 155, 179, 215, 237n2,
243n83; of history, 3, 215, 224, 254; of
religion, 18–19, 224, 272–292; of science, 11–12, 17–19, 177–191, 192–249;
transcendental, 6, 10, 13–16, 18, 28,
59, 61, 63, 114, 138, 155, 186–187,
190n22, 260, 296, 298–299, 304–305
philosophy of culture, 13, 19, 57n21, 297–
298, 301, 304

Piché, Claude, 131n62
Pieper, Josef, 37n2
Planck, Max, 180, 300
Plato, 13, 16, 46, 85n6, 93–94, 107, 115, 118–121, 123–124, 128, 130nn25,33, 147n16, 148n20, 155, 217, 272, 274–275, 280, 289
Platonism/Platonic, 16, 45, 78–79, 117–119, 123–124, 126, 130n34, 140, 143, 147nn16,17, 179–180, 247n121, 274–275, 284, 289
Pöggeler, Otto, 97, 105–106, 108nn12,13,14
Poincaré, Henri, 17, 185–187, 190n22, 193–195, 208–209, 226–229, 235–237, 237nn1,5, 247n129, 248n133, 249nn156,158
Popper, Karl, 270n1
Pos, Hendrik Josephus, 83
positivism, 14, 197, 201, 217, 241n47, 243n78, 247n129
prejudice, 27, 35, 99, 104, 114, 120, 275
presentation, 48, 105, 146
presupposition, 12, 27, 34, 60, 79, 92, 102, 106, 120–121, 124–139, 141, 143, 186, 190n22, 283, 289, 299
principle, 15, 26–27, 30, 33, 35–36, 37n2, 52–54, 62, 76–77, 80, 90nn48,55, 116–117, 121–122, 124, 126, 132–149, 153–155, 172n27, 177, 181, 185–187, 188n5, 189n14, 197, 203, 205–208, 210–212, 220–226, 231–233, 237n5, 239n18, 243nn75,78, 249n159, 256, 260, 274–276, 278, 291n2, 293–294, 296–298, 303, 305, 308n22, 309n32; highest, 16, 132–149, 188n5, 189n14, 224
Proust, Marcel, 49
Pryor, James, 173n35
psychologism, 10, 28–29, 32–33, 118–119, 126–127, 130n25, 255
psychology, 18, 28, 32–33, 44, 48, 51–52, 59, 61–65, 72–73, 75–77, 81, 85n6, 87n23, 88n36, 89nn37,38, 133, 197, 201, 209–210, 223, 232, 237, 254–255, 257–259, 261–263, 271n12, 277, 306;

descriptive, 28, 58–61, 70, 258–259, 261; empirical, 28; experiential, 88n36; philosophical, 10, 33, 59, 62–63, 65, 75, 83, 84n1, 87n20; reconstructive, 305; structural, 255, 269; transcendental, 65, 83, 147n8
purity/pure, 25–40, 45, 48, 62, 66–69, 75–76, 79, 87n25, 88n31, 114, 117–118, 120–122, 133–135, 142, 144, 146, 146nn2,7, 152, 183, 206, 219, 232–235, 243n83, 245n9, 274–278, 282, 285–290, 300, 303, 306

qualifying concept, 266

Ranke, Leopold von, 94, 253, 261
Ravaisson, Félix, 3, 17, 192–249
realism, 27, 95, 122, 182, 211–213, 243n78
reason (Vernunft), 25, 30, 51–52, 57nn19,25, 99, 114, 118, 121, 123–124, 132–134, 142, 147n7, 148nn20,25, 150, 153–159, 163, 165, 172n25, 173nn32,35, 181, 192, 194, 203, 206–207, 225, 232, 234, 242n63, 254, 261–262, 280, 283, 285–289, 294, 298, 301–302, 304–305, 309n32
receptivity, 54, 152, 162. See also spontaneity
reconstruction, 8, 12, 15, 34, 59–91, 102, 128, 132–133, 140–141, 180, 209, 305–306. See also construction; method, reconstructive (of reconstruction)
reduction: phenomenological, 4, 29, 60, 69, 71, 73–74, 88n30; transcendental, 59, 71–72, 81, 88n35, 90n55
reflection/reflective, 5, 9–15, 26, 31, 36, 50, 54, 62, 68–69, 71, 73–75, 86n15, 88n35, 91nn60,63,68, 92, 101, 106, 115, 165, 167–168, 174n41, 193, 202, 206, 209–213, 215–216, 222, 225–226, 253, 259–263, 269, 283, 296–297, 302–303, 306
reflective judgment, 260–262
reflexive awareness (Innewerden), 261
regressive analysis, 74, 79, 80

Reichenbach, Hans, 183, 186, 189n16, 232
Reinach, Adolf, 88n36
relativism, 10, 55, 253, 260, 290
relativity, theory of, 12, 182–184, 186,
    189n14, 297, 299–300
religion, 13, 18–19, 42–43, 51, 55, 78, 123,
    193, 195, 197, 212, 214–216, 218–219,
    224–226, 229, 236, 272–292, 294, 297,
    308n26
Renaissance, 13, 119, 265–266
Renan, Joseph Ernest, 196–199, 215–216,
    243n83, 244n87, 248n139
Renouvier, Charles, 192, 194, 214, 230,
    234
re-presentation (*Vergegenwärtigung*),
    29, 48
representation (*Vorstellung*), 25–27,
    43–50, 65–66, 116–117, 150, 153, 158–
    159, 168, 181, 206, 262, 264, 276, 302
responsibility, 11, 197, 204, 254, 282
Rickert, Heinrich, 3, 5, 8, 11, 13, 18, 38n7,
    84n3, 86n8, 91n68, 95–96, 100,
    109n24, 115, 121–126, 131nn43,46,51,
    151–152, 255–256, 258–259, 261,
    269–270
Ricœur, Paul, 41, 52, 92, 107n1
Riehl, Alois, 2, 3, 115, 129n8, 245n91,
    249n159
Riemann, Bernhard, 184–186, 299
Ritschl, Albrecht, 125
Ritter, Joachim, 103, 109n34
Rorty, Richard, 20n9, 21n14, 113, 173n32
Rosenzweig, Franz, 19
Rothacker, Erich, 254
Rothwell, Fred, 225
Royce, Josiah, 125

Santayana, George, 125
Scheler, Max, 5, 8, 13, 76, 85n8
Schelling, Friedrich Wilhelm Joseph, 2,
    86n15, 114, 199, 205, 207, 209, 241n47,
    243nn78,83
schema/schematic/schematism, 44, 105,
    194, 235, 260, 300
Schlegel, August Wilhelm, 262

Schlegel, Friedrich, 262
Schleiermacher, Friedrich, 14, 94, 262–
    263, 268
Schlick, Moritz, 5, 301
Schopenhauer, Arthur, 5, 114
sciences: cultural, 5, 18, 95, 253, 255, 259,
    264–267, 270n1, 274; grounding/
    foundational, 63; historical, 203, 221;
    human, 5, 14, 18, 41, 98–100, 109n24,
    254, 257–261, 263–265, 267; moral,
    213, 254–255; natural, 17–18, 27, 31,
    41–42, 54, 99, 109n24, 117, 133–134,
    193, 197–198, 207, 230, 246n100, 255–
    260, 261–265, 274, 285–286, 293–294,
    297, 299, 302–304; normal, 177; poli-
    tical, 255, 268; positive, 8, 11–12, 63,
    72, 74, 76, 192, 198, 201–203, 208,
    212–213, 217, 221–222, 239n17, 254,
    289
Searle, John, 10
self-consciousness, 82, 86n15, 87n16,
    212, 272, 276, 278–279, 281–284, 287–
    288, 290
self-givenness, 27, 28, 261
selfness (*Selbsteigenheit*), 130n34
Sellars, Wilfrid, 9, 150–153
sensibility, 44, 121, 127, 151–153, 157, 162–
    163, 183, 187, 203, 233, 235
Shakespeare, William, 240n35, 268
skepticism, 10, 228, 272
sociology, 178, 223, 254
Socrates, 272, 274–275
Sorbonne, 196, 198, 210, 217, 244n84
Southwest School, 13, 16, 20n11, 84n3,
    91n68. *See also* Baden School; Frei-
    burg; Heidelberg
speculation/speculative, 11, 21n15, 60,
    69, 106, 114, 193, 240n27, 253–254
Spinoza, Baruch de, 180, 200–201,
    243n83, 278
spirit (*Geist*), 20n11, 21n18, 43, 45, 50,
    53–54, 57n19, 65, 84n3, 95, 100, 114,
    124, 151, 172n25, 192–249, 254–255,
    288; objective, 41, 42, 43, 45, 47,
    51–52, 55, 124

spiritualism, 192–249
spontaneity, 45, 152–153, 162, 166, 168,
    213, 223–224, 247n116, 269, 300, 305.
    See also receptivity
Stolzenberg, Jürgen, 16, 89n39, 106
Strawson, Sir Peter Frederick, 9, 19n4,
    147n8
Ströker, Elizabeth, 30
subjectivity, 6, 9, 10, 15, 28, 33, 34, 52,
    59–91, 106, 154, 163, 165, 168, 187, 295,
    305–306; concrete, 59
substance, 124, 181, 214, 231, 243n80, 293,
    302, 306. *See also* concept of sub-
    stance (*Substanzbegriff*)
supersensible being, 155
symbolism, 10, 14, 31, 41; symbolic form,
    7, 11, 13, 36, 42–55, 58n27, 63, 75, 77,
    88n36, 91n68, 105, 264, 266, 297–298,
    301, 303–305, 307, 309n32, 310n70;
    symbolic formation, 45; symbolic
    function, 43–50, 54; symbolic preg-
    nance, 46–47; symbolic understan-
    ding, 26; symbolic vision, 45
sympathy, 6, 190n16, 267, 273
synthesis/synthetic, 13, 30, 35, 44, 120,
    132–133, 135, 141, 146n2, 147nn7,10,
    153, 178, 180, 183, 200, 204–206, 208,
    213, 218, 230, 232, 234–235, 240n29,
    249n156, 267, 296, 303

Taine, Hippolyte Adolphe, 192–249
Tannery, Jules, 193, 214, 218–219, 236
teleology, 12, 66, 213, 223
thing-in-itself (*Ding-an-sich*), 114, 165
things themselves, 8, 9, 21n15, 26, 27–28,
    30–31, 60, 69, 106, 161, 165
thinking (*das Denken*), 25, 30, 34–35,
    37n4, 38nn6,7, 76, 117–123, 130n34,
    137, 141–146, 148n24, 150–151, 153–154,
    156–157, 159–160, 163–164, 170,
    171n13, 174n41, 219–220, 224, 279,
    285, 289, 300
Tieck, Ludwig, 262
transcendental: aesthetic, 117, 121, 123,
    127, 151, 245n91; consciousness, 29, 81;

deduction, 121, 133, 276, 303; idealism,
    61, 71, 117, 119, 122, 274; logic, 16, 117,
    121, 127, 150–174; method, 6, 15–16,
    19n4, 34–35, 60, 63–64, 69–70, 73,
    76–77, 79, 82, 90n55, 116–117, 126, 133–
    136, 138, 147n8, 216, 260, 276, 289,
    293, 295–297, 305, 308n22; phenome-
    nology, 29, 53, 59–61, 75, 79, 90n55;
    philosophy, 6, 10, 13–16, 18, 28, 59, 61,
    63, 114, 138, 155, 186–187, 190n22, 260,
    296, 298–299, 304–305; psychology,
    65, 83, 147n8; reduction, 59, 71–72, 81,
    88n35, 90n55; turn, 6, 59, 69–71, 85n4
transcendentals, 105
Travis, Charles, 159–161, 165, 173nn36,38,
    174n41
truth/truthfulness, 16, 30–31, 34, 81,
    85n3, 95, 98–99, 105–106, 117, 119, 122,
    134–135, 139–140, 146, 152, 154–156,
    159, 161, 165–170, 172n23, 177–179,
    182, 202, 215, 217, 224, 228, 233–234,
    241n39, 244n84, 247n120, 273, 277,
    279–280, 282–284, 288–289; truth
    claims, 64, 98, 154, 170
Tugendhat, Ernst, 26, 30
typical/typicality, 216, 234, 266, 268–269

ultimate foundation (*Letztbegründung*),
    8. *See also* ultimate grounding
    (*Letztbegründung*)
ultimate grounding (*Letztbegründung*),
    8, 133, 307, 311n94. *See also* groun-
    ding/ground-laying (*Grundlegung*)
understand/understanding, 2, 12, 15,
    17–18, 25–26, 28, 31–32, 35–36, 44–47,
    50–51, 54, 57n19, 58n27, 60, 63, 70,
    94, 97–101, 104–107, 113–131, 132–135,
    137, 140–143, 151–153, 155, 157–159,
    165–167, 183, 185, 187, 189nn8,14, 194,
    196–198, 201, 206, 208–209, 215, 218,
    223, 226–227, 229–230, 232–236,
    238n5, 241n55, 245n91, 255, 257–258,
    260–265, 267–270, 273–274, 288, 290,
    293, 295, 297, 303, 305, 308n30; her-
    meneutic, 268; intuitive, 267

unified science, 135
unity, 13, 18, 44, 47, 49–50, 52–53, 69,
    90nn48,52, 118, 123–124, 127, 135, 138,
    140, 142, 146, 153, 162–163, 173n36,
    174n41, 183, 189n14, 193, 205–206, 211,
    216–218, 227, 234, 243n80, 244n87,
    254n92, 268–269, 272–292, 294, 298,
    303–305, 309n32
universal validity, 26, 275
universality, 109n20, 133–134, 138,
    146n6, 205, 210
Ursprungslogik (logic of origin), 140,
    143–144, 274–275, 285, 302, 311n94

Vacherot, Étienne, 194, 196–197, 199,
    201, 214, 230, 239n10, 240n29
Vaihinger, Hans, 3, 125
validity (*Geltung*), 26, 29, 34, 47, 54–55,
    99, 121, 133, 136, 138–140, 142, 144–
    146, 156, 162–163, 174n39, 186–187,
    220, 235, 256–257, 260–261, 265, 273,
    275, 279, 285, 287, 289–290, 299–301;
    claim, 98, 100
value, 2, 3, 8–9, 13, 16, 18, 49, 54–55, 94,
    100, 115, 117–118, 121–126, 131n51,
    146n6, 152, 156, 166, 168, 174n40, 202,
    208, 225, 228, 247n116, 256–264, 268–
    269, 272–273, 275, 289
value theory, 5, 8

Vermeer, Johannes, 49
Vienna Circle, 5
Vorländer, Karl, 249n159

Wagner, Hans, 20n13, 145, 148nn27,29
Warburg Institute, 298
Weber, Max, 95
Weltanschauung. See worldview
    (*Weltanschauung*)
Welton, Donn, 60, 83, 88n31, 90nn48,59
Weyl, Hermann, 12
Whitehead, Alfred North, 125, 317
Wiehl, Reiner, 18
willing, 18, 29, 66, 125, 130n34, 274–275,
    277–283, 286–289
Windelband, Wilhelm, 3, 5, 13, 18, 86n8,
    91n68, 95, 100, 109n24, 115, 151, 256,
    259
Witt, Cornelius de, 201
Wittgenstein, Ludwig, 5
world-constitution, 69, 77–79
worldview (*Weltanschauung*), 8, 11, 18,
    27, 34, 105, 300

Zeitgeist, 8, 268
Zeller, Eduard, 3, 193, 199, 214–215, 216–
    218, 244n89, 245n91
Zusammenhang. See continuum; nexus
    (*Zusammenhang*)